Bonus Material!

Thank you for purchasing a new copy of *Engineering Computation with MATLAB*®. Your textbook includes six months of prepaid access to the book's Companion Website. This prepaid subscription provides you with full access to online student resources, including:

- **Six bonus chapters covering Data Structures topics**
  - Searching Graphs
  - Object-Oriented Programming
  - Linked Lists
  - Binary Trees
  - N-ary Trees and Graphs
  - Cost of Computing
- **Two additional appendices**
  - Web References
  - Solutions to selected problems from the book
- **Source code**

To access the *Engineering Computation with MATLAB* Companion Website for the first time:

You will need to register online using a computer with an Internet connection and a Web browser. The process takes just a couple of minutes and only needs to be completed once.

1. Go to **http://www.aw-bc.com/smith_mat** to begin.
2. Click on **Student Resources**.
3. Click the **Register** button.
4. Use a coin to scratch off the gray coating below and reveal your student access code.* *Do not use a knife or other sharp object, which can damage the code.*

5. On the registration page, enter your student access code. Do not type the dashes. You can use lowercase or uppercase.
6. Follow the on-screen instructions. If you need help at any time during the online registration process, simply click the **Need Help?** icon.
7. Once your personal Login Name and Password are confirmed, you can begin using the *Engineering Computation with MATLAB* Companion Website!

To log in after you have registered:

You only need to register for this Companion Website once. After that, you can log in any time at **http://www.aw-bc.com/smith_mat** by providing your Login Name and Password when prompted.

*IMPORTANT: The Access Code on this page can only be used once. This subscription is valid for six months upon activation and is not transferable. If this access code has already been scratched off, it may no longer be valid. If this is the case, you can purchase a subscription by going to **http://www.aw-bc.com/smith_mat** and following the on-screen instructions.

Engineering Computation
with MATLAB®

DAVID M. SMITH
Georgia Institute of Technology

PEARSON

Addison
Wesley

Boston San Francisco New York
London Toronto Sydney Tokyo Singapore Madrid
Mexico City Munich Paris Cape Town Hong Kong Montreal

Publisher	Greg Tobin
Executive Editor	Michael Hirsch
Assistant Editor	Lindsey Triebel
Associate Managing Editor	Jeffrey Holcomb
Composition	Laura Wiegleb
Electronic Publishing Specialist	Dawn Stratchko
Cover Design	Joyce Cosentino Wells
Photo Researcher	Beth Anderson
Digital Assets Manager	Marianne Groth
Media Producer	Bethany Tidd
Senior Marketing Manager	Michelle Brown
Marketing Assistant	Sarah Milmore
Senior Manufacturing Buyer	Carol Melville
Production Coordination, Copyediting, and Illustrations	Kathleen Cantwell, C4 Technologies
Proofreading	Genevieve d'Entremont
Indexing	Joseph Wizda
Text Design	Susan Carsten Raymond

Cover Image: The cover demonstrates three significant capabilities in MATLAB: manipulating images, specifying the surface texture on models of solid objects, and viewing those objects from various angles. The pictures on the cover were generated by adding polar caps to a globe image, "pasting" that image onto a solid sphere, and then viewing the sphere from different angles.

Photo Credits: Figure 1.2 *The Colossus computer* on page 4 is provided courtesy of the United Kingdom Government. Figure 2.10 *Space Ship One* on page 41 is © AP Wideworld Photos. Figure 3.5 *Conveyer moving dirt* on page 76 is provided courtesy of Hartsfield-Jackson International Airport. The photograph of a nautilus shell in Figure 9.3 *Fibonacci in nature* on page 220 is © PhotoDisc. Figure 14.13 *Oil platform* on page 382 is provided courtesy of NASA, U.S. Federal Government. Figure 14.14 *Model diagram* and Figure 14.15 *Analysis results* on page 383 are provided courtesy of Aerospace Report ATR-82(2830)-IND written in 1981 for the U.S. Department of the Interior, Conservation Division, Geological Survey, Reston, VA 22086. Figure 17.4 *Map of the London Underground* on page 453 is provided courtesy of Transport for London (http://www.tfl.gov.uk/tube/).

This interior of this book was composed in QuarkXpress 6.5.

Library of Congress Cataloging-in-Publication Data

Smith, David M., 1942-
  Engineering computation with MATLAB / David M. Smith. -- 1st ed.
      p. cm.
  Includes index.
  1. Engineering mathematics--Data processing. 2. MATLAB. I. Title.

TA345.S585 2007
620.001'51--dc22

2007001172

ISBN-13: 978-0-321-48108-5
ISBN-10: 0-321-48108-9

1 2 3 4 5 6 7 8 9 10—CRS—11 10 09 08 07

This book is dedicated to the
glory of Almighty God

~David M. Smith

Contents

Chapter 1 **Introduction to Computers and Programming** 1
  1.1 Background 2
  1.2 History of Computer Architectures 3
  1.3 Computing Systems Today 5
  1.4 Executing a MATLAB Program 15
  1.5 Problem Solving 15

Chapter 2 **Getting Started with MATLAB** 19
  2.1 Programming Language Background 21
  2.2 Basic Data Manipulation 23
  2.3 The MATLAB User Interface 27
  2.4 Scripts 37
  2.5 Engineering Example—Spacecraft Launch 41

Chapter 3 **Arrays** 49
  3.1 Concept: Using Built-in Functions 50
  3.2 Concept: Data Collections 50
  3.3 MATLAB Vectors 50
  3.4 Engineering Example—Forces and Moments 63
  3.5 MATLAB Arrays 64
  3.6 Engineering Example—Computing Soil Volume 76

Chapter 4 **Execution Control** 89
  4.1 Concept: Code Blocks 90
  4.2 Conditional Execution in General 90
  4.3 if Statements 91
  4.4 switch Statements 96
  4.5 Iteration in General 98
  4.6 for Loops 99
  4.7 while Loops 102
  4.8 Engineering Example—Computing Liquid Levels 105

Chapter 5 **Functions** 117
  5.1 Concepts: Abstraction and Encapsulation 118
  5.2 Black Box View of a Function 118
  5.3 MATLAB Implementation 119
  5.4 Engineering Example—Measuring a Solid Object 125

Chapter 6 **Character Strings** 135
  6.1 Character String Concepts: Mapping and Casting 136
  6.2 MATLAB Implementation 137

6.3   Format Conversion Functions 139
6.4   Character String Operations 142
6.5   Arrays of Strings 145
6.6   Engineering Example—Encryption 146

Chapter 7   Cell Arrays and Structures 157
7.1   Concept: Collecting Dissimilar Objects 158
7.2   Cell Arrays 158
7.3   MATLAB Structures 163
7.4   Structure Arrays 166
7.5   Engineering Example—Assembling a Structure 172

Chapter 8   File Input and Output 185
8.1   Concept: Serial Input and Output (I/O) 186
8.2   MATLAB Workspace I/O 186
8.3   High-Level I/O Functions 187
8.4   Lower-Level File I/O 192
8.5   Engineering Example—Spreadsheet Data 196

Chapter 9   Recursion 203
9.1   Concept: The Activation Stack 204
9.2   Recursion Defined 205
9.3   Implementing a Recursive Function in MATLAB 206
9.4   Exceptions 208
9.5   Wrapper Functions 212
9.6   Tail Recursion 215
9.7   Mutual Recursion 217
9.8   Generative Recursion 217
9.9   Examples of Recursion 217
9.10   Engineering Example—Robot Arm Motion 223

Chapter 10   Principles of Problem Solving 231
10.1   Solving Simple Problems 232
10.2   Assembling Solution Steps 232
10.3   Summary of Operations 232
10.4   Solving Larger Problems 248
10.5   Engineering Example—Processing Geopolitical Data 250

Chapter 11   Plotting 259
11.1   Plotting in General 260
11.2   2-D Plotting 264
11.3   3-D Plotting 270
11.4   Surface Plots 273
11.5   Engineering Example—Visualizing Geographic Data 291

Chapter 12   Matrices 303
12.1   Concept: Behavioral Abstraction 304
12.2   Matrix Operations 304
12.3   MATLAB Implementation 307
12.4   Rotating Coordinates 310
12.5   Solving Simultaneous Linear Equations 317
12.6   Engineering Examples 321

Chapter 13   **Images**   **329**
13.1   Nature of an Image   330
13.2   Image Types   331
13.3   Reading, Displaying, and Writing Images   333
13.4   Operating on Images   333
13.5   Engineering Example—Detecting Edges   349

Chapter 14   **Processing Sound**   **357**
14.1   The Physics of Sound   358
14.2   Recording and Playback   358
14.3   MATLAB Implementation   359
14.4   Time Domain Operations   360
14.5   The Fast Fourier Transform   369
14.6   Frequency Domain Operations   374
14.7   Engineering Example—Oil Rig Structural Integrity   381

Chapter 15   **Numerical Methods**   **389**
15.1   Interpolation   390
15.2   Curve Fitting   394
15.3   Numerical Integration   400
15.4   Numerical Differentiation   404
15.5   Engineering Example—Analyzing Rocket Data   407

Chapter 16   **Sorting**   **421**
16.1   Measuring Algorithm Cost   422
16.2   Algorithms for Sorting Data   425
16.3   Performance Analysis   435
16.4   Applications of Sorting Algorithms   436
16.5   Engineering Example—A Selection of Countries   440

Chapter 17   **Searching Graphs**   (online)

Chapter 18   **Object-Oriented Programming**   (online)

Chapter 19   **Linked Lists**   (online)

Chapter 20   **Binary Trees**   (online)

Chapter 21   **N-ary Trees and Graphs**   (online)

Chapter 22   **The Cost of Computing**   (online)

Appendices
Appendix A   MATLAB Special Characters, Reserved Words, and Symbols   A–1
Appendix B   The ASCII Character Set   B–1
Appendix C   Internal Number Representation   C–1
Appendix D   Web Reference Materials   (online)
Appendix E   Answers to True or False and Fill in the Blanks   (online)

Index   **I–1**

About the Author

David Smith has been teaching introductory computer science classes for engineers at the Georgia Institute of Technology since 1997 when he retired from industry. Previously, he worked 31 years for Lockheed-Martin at their Marietta, Georgia facility as a systems and software specialist with a focus on intelligent systems. He was active in designing and developing software for the C-130J, C-27J, F-22, and C-5 aircraft, and was the technical leader of the Pilot's Associate program, a $42 million research project sponsored by the Defense Advanced Research Projects Agency.

Mr. Smith has a bachelor's degree in aeronautical engineering from Southampton University, and a master's degree in control systems from Imperial College, London.

Preface

This book introduces the power, satisfaction, and joy of computing to beginning engineering students who have little or no previous computing experience. It began as a snapshot of the content of a Georgia Tech course that introduces engineers to computing. However, it has been extensively enhanced to meet the needs of a wider audience of students and educators who want to understand programming for other reasons. In this book, to understand computing, we use MATLAB, a user-friendly language that is emerging as one of the most popular computing languages in engineering.

Pedagogical Style

Computing is not a spectator sport. Students learn computing by computing. This text not only presents computing concepts and their MATLAB implementation, but also offers students extensive hands-on exercises. The text illustrates the ideas with examples from the world of engineering, provides style points, and presents sample problems that students might encounter.

Each chapter includes topics that go a step beyond the basic content of an introductory class. This gives professors the choice to progress slowly, and more thoroughly, through the material in two semesters. It also offers advanced students enrichment materials for their personal study.

The overall philosophy of this text approaches programming tools in the following manner:

1. Explain a computing concept in general

2. Discuss its implementation in MATLAB

3. Provide exercises to master the concept

To help facilitate students' understanding of the concept and its implementation, the text uses two features: general templates and MATLAB listings. The general templates provide a foundation for students to understand concepts in general, and can be applied to any language. The MATLAB listings show students how to implement concepts in MATLAB, and are followed by detailed explanations of the code.

Features of the Text

- **Exercises:**   Allow students a "Do It Yourself" approach to master concepts by trying what they just learned. Exercises follow each new topic.

- **Style Points:**   Advise students about writing quality code that is easy to understand, debug, and reuse.

- **Hints:**   Enrich students' understanding of a topic. Hints are interspersed through the book at points where students may benefit from a little extra "aside."

- **Engineering Examples:**   Provide robust models and apply to real-world issues that will motivate students. Examples from different engineering disciplines are presented at the end of each chapter.

- **Special Characters, Reserved Words, and Functions:**   Provides a quick reference for the key MATLAB principles discussed in each chapter.

- **Self Test:**   Helps students to check their understanding of the material in each chapter.

- **Programming Projects:**   Offer a variety of large-scale projects that students can work on to solidify their skills.

Chapter Overview

Chapter 1: *Introduction to Computers and Programming* discusses the history of computer architectures as they apply to computing systems today. The chapter provides an overview of computer hardware and software, and how programs execute.

Chapter 2: *Getting Started with MATLAB* discusses some basic concepts of computing and then introduces the basic operation of the MATLAB user interface. The chapter also describes how to capture simple MATLAB programs in the form of a script.

Chapter 3: *Arrays* introduces the fundamental machinery that sets MATLAB apart from other languages—its ability to perform mathematical and logical operations on homogeneous collections of numbers.

Chapter 4: *Execution Control* describes the common techniques used to control the execution of code blocks—conditional operation and iteration.

Chapter 5: *Functions* describes how to implement procedural abstraction by defining reusable code blocks.

Chapter 6: *Character Strings* discusses how MATLAB operates on variables containing text.

Chapter 7: *Cell Arrays and Structures* discusses two kinds of heterogeneous data collections accessed by index and by name.

Chapter 8: *File Input and Output* describes three levels of ability provided in MATLAB for transferring data to and from data files—saving workspaces, specific tools that read and write specific data files, and general-purpose tools for processing any kind of file.

Chapter 9: *Recursion* discusses and illustrates a widely used alternative approach to repetitive code block execution.

Chapter 10: *Principles of Problem Solving* introduces ideas that help students design solutions to new problems and avoid the "blank sheet of paper" problem—how to start.

Chapter 11: *Plotting* takes the student from basic plotting in two dimensions to the advanced tools that draw representations of three-dimensional objects with smooth shading and even multiple light effects.

Chapter 12: *Matrices* describes specific MATLAB capabilities that implement matrix algebra.

Chapter 13: *Images* discusses how to use vector and array algebra to manipulate color pictures.

Chapter 14: *Processing Sound* shows how to analyze, synthesize, and operate on sound files.

Chapter 15: *Numerical Methods* introduces numerical techniques that commonly occur in engineering: interpolation, curve fitting, integration, and differentiation.

Chapter 16: *Sorting* presents five algorithms for ordering data, each of which has applicability under certain circumstances—Insertion Sort, Bubble Sort, Quick Sort, Merge Sort, and Bucket Sort—and then compares their performance on large quantities of data.

Appendices provide a summary of the MATLAB special characters, reserved words, and functions used throughout the text, the ASCII character set, the internal number representation inside the computer, Web reference materials, and answers to the True or False and Fill in the Blanks questions.

Paths through the Book

Not all courses that cover programming and MATLAB follow the same syllabus. *Engineering Computation with MATLAB* is designed to facilitate teaching the material with different styles and at different speeds. For example, Chapters 3, 4, and 5 cover MATLAB array manipulation, iteration, and writing your own functions. There are three schools of thought about the appropriate way to introduce these concepts. One would introduce array constructs first and follow up with the more "traditional" concept of iteration; another would teach iteration first and deal with the MATLAB-specific array operations later; and the third would treat functions first. I chose to order the book according to the arrays-first approach, to suit a particular teaching style. However, should you prefer iteration or functions first, Chapters 3, 4, and 5 can be used in any order you wish.

I have attempted numerous approaches to the sequence of lessons covering Chapters 1–9. The order in which these chapters appear has been the most intuitive for me as an instructor, and, by and large, for the students. Chapters 10–16 are virtually independent, and can be taught in any order.

Supplements

Various supplemental materials for this text are available at the book's Companion Website: www.aw-bc.com/smith_mat. The following are accessible to all readers (register using the code in the front of this book):

- Solutions to selected Programming Projects
- Source code for all MATLAB listings
- Bonus chapters including: Searching Graphs, Object-Oriented Programming, Linked Lists, Binary Trees, N-ary Trees and Graphs, and the Cost of Computing.

In addition, the following supplements are available to qualified instructors at Addison-Wesley's Instructor Resource Center. Please visit www.aw.com/irc, or send email to computing@aw.com.

- Web reference materials
- Solutions to all of the Programming Projects
- PowerPoint lecture slides

Acknowledgments

The underlying philosophy of this book and the material that forms its skeleton originated in the work of Professor Russell Shackelford around 1996.

Dr. Melody Moore, currently an assistant professor in the Computer Information Systems department of the College of Business Administration at Georgia State University, was instrumental in creating many of the teaching materials (then as overhead transparencies) from which this class was first taught.

I am deeply indebted to Professor James Craig from the Aerospace Engineering department at Georgia Tech, who joined me in co-teaching the first engineering version of CS1, taught me much about MATLAB, and pioneered this class from the original 35 students to its current size of over 1,000 engineering students per semester. This engineering class became a vessel for introducing the students to the MATLAB language.

I would like to thank the following reviewers for their insight and wisdom during the process of manuscript development:

> Kenneth Rouse, *Auburn University*
> Suparna Datta, *Northeastern University*
> Gerardine G. Botte, *Ohio University*
> Mica Grujicic, *Clemson University*
> Kuldip S. Rattan, *Wright State University*
> Y.J. Lin, *The University of Akron*
> Mark Nagurka, *Marquette University*
> Michael Peshkin, *Northwestern University*
> Howard Silver, *Fairleigh Dickinson University*
> Steve Swinnea, *The University of Texas at Austin*

The material has benefited from the efforts of every Georgia Tech teaching assistant (TA), graduate student, instructor, and professor who has taught CS1, a list too long to enumerate. In particular, those wonderfully creative TAs who developed the ideas for examples used in this text have enriched it immeasurably. I wish to credit Professor Aaron Bobick with an important contribution, made in the course of one short conversation. That conversation was responsible for pulling the class back from the brink of being merely a MATLAB programming class to one with roots in CS concepts. Professor Bobick taught CS1 with me in the fall of 2004. Early in the semester he made a very simple request: he said it would be easier for him to teach the class if we explicitly expressed the computing concepts inherent in each lesson, rather than leaving him—and the students—to tease the concepts out of the teaching materials.

I cannot adequately express my appreciation for the team at Addison-Wesley who helped bring this book to fruition. Many of them have done, and I am sure continue to do, their work "behind the scenes": Michael Hirsch, Lindsey Triebel, Michelle Brown, Jeff Holcomb, and Laura Wiegleb. I would like to thank Greg Cantwell for creating the illustrations. I have developed a personal appreciation for three people on this team: Kathy Cantwell, my copyeditor, who has been so talented, patient, and ready to work with material that must seem to her to be in a foreign language; Joyce Wells, who did an incredible job transforming my vague idea into a stunning cover design; and Marika Sharpe, Addison-Wesley's representative at Georgia Tech, who finally convinced me to write this book, and continues to support and encourage me.

Most importantly, I would like to acknowledge the personal contributions of those people without whom this book would not exist. My wife and best friend, Julie, has been an unwavering source of strength and encouragement during the process of writing this text. Bill Leahy was a student in the first CS1 class I taught in the spring of 1998. In spite of this beginning, he continued to a master's in computer science from Tech, and is now an instructor in the College of Computing. Beyond his uncountable technical contributions to the material in this book, I want to acknowledge his friendship, encouragement, and wise judgment, which have been an inspiration to me during the process of developing this text. Most of all, if there is any enduring wisdom in this book, I give all the credit to Almighty God and His Son, Jesus.

CHAPTER 1

Introduction to Computers and Programming

1.1 Background
1.2 History of Computer Architectures
1.2.1 Babbage's Difference Engine
1.2.2 Colossus
1.2.3 The von Neumann Architecture
1.3 Computing Systems Today
1.3.1 Computer Hardware
1.3.2 Computer Memory
1.3.3 Computer Configurations
1.3.4 Computer Software
1.3.5 Executing a Computer Program
1.4 Executing a MATLAB Program
1.5 Problem Solving

Chapter Objectives

This chapter presents an overview of the historical background of computing and the computer hardware and software concepts that build the foundation for the rest of this book:

- Hardware architectures

- Software categories

- Programming languages

- Problem solving

1.1 Background

Advances in technology are achieved in two steps as follows:

- A visionary conceives an idea that has never been tried before
- Engineers find or invent tools that will bring that vision to reality

The search for new software tools is therefore an inescapable part of an engineer's life. The process of creating these tools frequently spawns sub-problems, which themselves require creative solutions.

The pace of change in our world is increasing, and nowhere is this phenomenon more dramatically obvious than computer science. In the span of just a few generations, computers have invaded every conceivable aspect of our lives, and there is no indication that this trend is slowing.

This book will help you become familiar with one specific programming tool: MATLAB. It is intended to bring you to a basic proficiency level so that you can confidently proceed on your own to learn the features of other programming languages that are useful to your interests.

A word of caution: Learning a programming language is very much like learning to speak a foreign language. In order to find something to eat in Munich, you must be able to express yourself in terms a German can understand. This involves knowing not only some vocabulary words, but also the grammatical rules that make those words comprehensible—in German, for example, this means putting the verbs at the ends of phrases.

If languages were a strictly theoretical exercise, you could make up your own vocabulary and grammar, and it would undoubtedly be an improvement over existing languages—especially English, with its incredibly complex spelling and pronunciation rules. However, language is not a theoretical exercise; it is a practical tool for communication, so we can't make up our own rules, but are constrained to the vocabulary and grammar expected by the people with whom we want to converse.

Similarly, this book is not an abstract text about the nature of computer languages. It is a practical guide to creating solutions to problems. Accomplishing this involves expressing your solutions in such a form that the computer can "understand" your solutions; therefore, it requires that you use the vocabulary (that is, the appropriate key words) and grammar (the syntax) of the language.

To become proficient in this, as in any other language, it is not enough to merely know the grammar and vocabulary. You have to practice your language skills by communicating. For foreign languages, this means traveling to the country, immersing yourself in the culture, and talking with people. For computer languages, this means actually writing programs, seeing what they do, and determining how to use their capabilities to solve your engineering problems.

 ## 1.2 History of Computer Architectures

Computing concepts developed as tools to solve previously intractable problems. This section will trace the growth of computing architectures, review the basic organization of computer hardware components, and emphasize the implementation of the data storage and processing capabilities by highlighting three milestones on the road to today's computers: Babbage's difference engine, Colossus, and the von Neumann architecture.

1.2.1 Babbage's Difference Engine

Charles Babbage (1791–1871) is generally recognized as the earliest pioneer of the modern computer. Babbage's **difference engine**—a relatively simple device that can subtract adjacent values in a column of numbers—is a good example of a computing device designed to improve the speed and repeatability of mathematical operations. Babbage was concerned about the process engineers used to develop the tables of logarithms and trigonometric functions. In his day, the only way to develop these tables was for mathematicians to calculate the values in the tables by hand. While the algorithms were simple—combining tables of the differences between adjacent values—the opportunity for human error was unacceptably high. In 1854 Babbage designed a difference engine that could automate the process of generating tables of mathematical functions. Since the objective was to create numerical tables, the output device was to be a set of copper plates ready for a printing press. The memory devices for storing numerical values were wheels arranged in vertical columns. The arithmetic operations were accomplished by ratchet devices cranked by hand.

Sadly, the manufacturing tools and materials available then prevented him from actually building his machine. However, in 1991 the Science Museum in London built a machine to his specifications, as shown in Figure 1.1. With only minor changes to the design, they were able to make the machine work. Although limited in its flexibility, the machine was able to compute difference equations up to the seventh order with up to 13 significant digits.

1.2.2 Colossus

Colossus was a computing machine developed to solve large, complex problems quickly. Early in the Second World War, Britain was losing the Battle of the Atlantic—German U-boats were sinking an enormous number of cargo ships that were resupplying the Allied war effort. The Government Code and Cypher School was established at Bletchley Hall in Britain with the goal of

Figure 1.1 *The Babbage difference engine*

breaking the German codes used to communicate with their U-boats in the North Atlantic. They were using Enigma machines, relatively simple devices that encrypted messages by shifting characters in the alphabet. However, to crack the code they needed to exhaustively evaluate text shifted by arbitrary amounts. Although the algorithm was known, the manual solution took too long, and it was often too late to make use of the information. A computer later named Colossus (see Figure 1.2) was designed by Max Newman and was custom built for this purpose. While not a general-purpose processor, Colossus was fast enough to crack all but the most sophisticated Enigma codes. Sadly, due to security concerns, the machine was destroyed when the war ended. However, the dawn of ubiquitous computing was breaking, and general-purpose computers were soon to be available.

1.2.3 The von Neumann Architecture

These and other contemporary achievements demonstrated the ability of special-purpose machines to solve specific problems. However, the creativity of John von Neumann ushered in the current era of general-purpose computing in which computers are flexible enough to solve an astonishing array of different problems. Dr. von Neumann proposed a computer architecture that separated the Central Processing Unit (CPU) from the computer memory and the Input/Output (I/O) devices (see Figure 1.3).

Figure 1.2 *The Colossus computer*

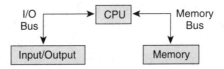

Figure 1.3 *The von Neumann architecture*

Together with binary encoding for storing numerical values, this was the genesis of general-purpose computing as we know it today. Although the implementation of each component has improved beyond recognition, the fundamental processing architecture remains unchanged today.

1.3 Computing Systems Today

Today's computing systems—the combination of hardware and software that collectively solve problems—retain many of the key characteristics of these inventions: they process more data than is humanly possible, quickly enough for the results to be useful, and they basically follow the von Neumann architecture. Computer **hardware** refers to the physical equipment: the keyboard, mouse, monitor, hard disk, and printer. The **software** refers to the programs that describe the steps we want the computer to perform.

1.3.1 Computer Hardware

All computers have a similar internal organization, as shown in Figure 1.4, that is closely related to the von Neumann architecture. The CPU is usually separated into two parts: the Control Unit, which manages the flow of data between the other modules, and the Arithmetic and Logic Unit (ALU). The ALU performs all the arithmetic and logical operations required by the software.

The individual logic devices that comprise the electronic components of the computer operate in binary mode, which is represented electrically by the presence or absence of voltage at a connection. These states, called **bits**, have

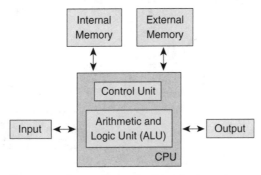

Figure 1.4 *Internal organization of a computer*

the value of 1 (present) or 0 (absent). Most computer operations assemble these bits into larger collections—a **byte** being 8 bits, and **words** consisting of 16, 32, 64, or more bits. We refer to the data items coming into the computer as the **input**, and the results coming from the computations as the **output.**

Input and output (I/O) is accomplished by moving data between the memory (CPU) and external equipment designed to communicate with users or other computers. In the early days all devices had to be individually installed in the computer with dedicated wiring—a process called **hard-wiring**. In contrast, today this is usually accomplished merely by plugging devices into one of many **data buses** (see Figure 1.5). A data bus is an electronic "pathway" for transporting data between devices. Since most devices expect to be able to send data on the bus as well as receive data from it, data bus design always involves a protocol that ensures only one device is writing to the bus at any given time.

1.3.2 Computer Memory

Memory comes in many forms. Not long ago it could be nicely divided into two categories—solid state and mechanical. Solid-state memory modules were directly connected to the processor and used digital addresses to save and restore data. Mechanical memory relied upon devices that moved rewriteable storage media past sensors that converted the impressions on the storage media to digital form. Tape drives, floppy disks, hard drives, and optical disks (CDs and DVDs) share this architecture, and they are usually externally connected to the input/output system. Recently, however, these

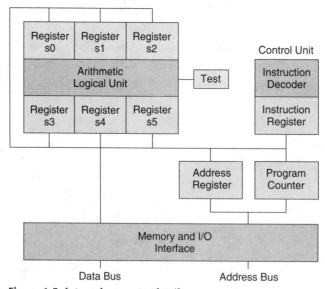

Figure 1.5 *Internal computer details*

distinctions have been blurred by the arrival of devices like **flash cards**, which are solid-state memory devices but attach to the computer's I/O ports and behave as if they were mechanical memory.

Today CPUs use many forms of solid-state memory. The first instructions executed when power is turned on are usually stored in **Read-Only Memory (ROM)**, sometimes referred to as the **Basic Input/Output System (BIOS)**. These instructions are just enough to wake up the keyboard and screen in basic mode and look around for a memory device containing the real programs. These real programs are transferred from the memory device, frequently referred to as "mass memory," to **Random-Access Memory (RAM)**—large amounts of high-speed, solid-state memory used to hold all of the programs and data users need immediately.

Most processors achieve significant performance improvement by using smaller amounts of even higher speed memory as **cache**. Cache memory processors are smart devices that "guess" what instructions and data the computer needs next, and preload those guesses into cache memory where the CPU can reach them quickly. These guesses are based on the likelihood that the program will continue linearly through the program as opposed to branching to go somewhere else for the next instruction. A significant amount of today's computer architecture design effort focuses on the effective use of cache memory to improve performance.

As programs become larger and process more data, and the systems allow more than one program to run simultaneously, RAM occasionally fills up. Most operating systems today use **virtual memory**—a data file usually on the hard drive that contains an image of everything you would like to have in RAM divided into **pages**. When the CPU requires access to a page that is not actually in RAM, it has to take the time to find a special area in RAM referred to as a "page buffer" that it can safely use, write its contents back to virtual memory, and read in the page needed. No matter how smart this process might be about looking ahead and predicting required pages, there is always a huge performance loss when a computer begins using virtual memory.

Figure 1.6 illustrates some aspects of how computer memory is managed. The operating system (UNIX, Windows, Mac OS X, or whatever) consumes some memory and determines from the I/O devices available what internal

Heap		
Stack A	Stack B	Stack C
Program A	Program B	Program C
Operating System		
Driver	Driver	Driver	Driver	Driver

Figure 1.6 *Typical memory layout*

software (**drivers**) must be present to enable the application programs to communicate with the outside world. As mentioned earlier, many programs are loaded automatically when the operating system starts, and others are loaded upon user request. In addition to the memory needed to store the instructions, each program is allocated some **stack** space for storing local static data. The remaining memory, the **heap**, is accessible to all programs upon request to the operating system. The heap is typically used to store most of the data being manipulated by the programs. When a program finishes with a block from the heap, it is usually released by that program for other programs to use as necessary.

1.3.3 Computer Configurations

Depending on the application, there is a broad range of computer configurations, the most common of which are discussed in this section. As these components become cheaper to produce and as they operate at comparable reliabilities, computers are used more and more frequently to replace mechanical and electrical devices. These are called **embedded computers**—computers that are built into other equipment rather than standing alone. Because they usually run a fixed set of programs, embedded computers are known as **special-purpose processors**. The programs are usually in ROM, start running as soon as power is applied, and continually read data from multiple sensors and send out signals to control the equipment for which they are responsible. Modern automobiles use embedded computers to implement the complex algorithms that improve the efficiency of the engines and reduce emissions, and many of the I/O devices connected to computers are controlled by embedded processors. **Personal computers (PCs)** are small, inexpensive, **general-purpose computers** that can run a wide variety of programs; they are commonly used in offices, homes, and laboratories. **Mainframes** are even more powerful computers that are often used in businesses and research laboratories. **Supercomputers**, the fastest of all computers, can process billions of instructions per second. Because of their speed, supercomputers are capable of solving very complex problems that cannot feasibly be solved on other computers. Mainframes and supercomputers require special facilities and a specialized staff to maintain them.

1.3.4 Computer Software

Computer software contains the instructions that the CPU uses to run programs. There are several important categories of software, including operating systems, software applications, and language compilers. Not all processors need all these facilities. Figure 1.7 illustrates the interactions among these categories of software and the computer hardware, and the following sections describe each in more detail.

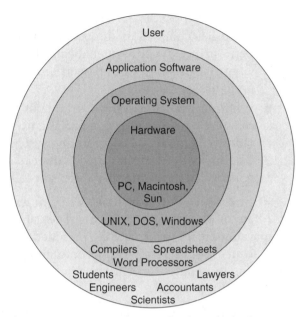

Figure 1.7 *Interactions between hardware and software*

Operating Systems The **operating system (OS)** serves as the manager of the computer system as a whole. It controls access to the processor by users and networked devices, and it organizes the hardware and software according to the users' specifications. The OS is the first major software component fetched by the BIOS from mass storage, and it automatically loads and starts the myriad programs that make computers "user friendly." It also provides the tools for making the computer's peripheral devices—such as printers, scanners, and DVD drives—available to other software. Common modern operating systems are Microsoft Windows, Linux, UNIX, and Apple Mac OS.

Operating systems also contain a group of programs called **utilities** that allow you to perform functions such as printing files, copying files from one disk to another, and listing the files that you have saved on a disk. Although these utilities are common to most operating systems, the commands themselves vary from operating system to operating system. While computer systems give the appearance of stability, like automobiles, they require periodic maintenance to maintain peak performance.

- You should protect your computer by installing and configuring utilities that protect it from viruses, intrusive advertising, and external influences that make illegal use of the processor or its data. Refer to the documentation for your specific operating system.

- Over time most disk drives become fragmented—the available space gets chopped up into smaller and smaller pieces—and performance of your system begins to suffer. Defragmentation of a large disk drive may be an overnight effort, but should be done periodically.

- While very reliable, computers are not indestructible. You should establish a regular policy of backing up your personal files onto removable media. Most operating systems provide such utilities. You do not need to back up commercial software that can be reloaded from the manufacturer's installation disks.

Software Tools Software tools are commercial programs that have been written to solve specific problems. They are highly sophisticated, complex applications that use the facilities provided by the operating system to enable you to create, save, recall, manipulate, and present ideas in the form of data files on your computer. The specific nature of those files depends on the nature of the problem.

If you need a well-formatted document or report, **word processors**, such as Microsoft Word, are programs that enable you to enter and format text and graphics. They allow you to develop documents in outline form; move words, sentences, and paragraphs; and check your spelling and grammar. **Desktop publishing** combines a very powerful word processor with a high-quality printer to produce professional-grade documents.

If you need relatively unsophisticated results from tabular data, **spreadsheets** let you work easily with data that can be displayed in a grid of rows and columns. Most spreadsheet packages include plotting capabilities to create charts and graphs, so they can be especially useful in analyzing and displaying information. Microsoft Excel and Lotus 1-2-3 are popular spreadsheet programs.

If you need to store, quickly retrieve, and format large amounts of data, **database management** programs such as Microsoft Access, MySQL, and Oracle are useful tools. They are used by large organizations, such as banks, hospitals, universities, hotels, and airlines, to store and organize crucial information; they are also used to analyze large amounts of scientific data. Meteorology and oceanography are examples of scientific fields that commonly require large databases for storage and analysis of data.

Computer-aided design (CAD) packages such as AutoCAD let you define computer models of real-world objects, assemble groups of such models, and then manipulate them graphically. CAD packages are frequently used in engineering applications, and the designs of most automobiles and aircraft (e.g., the Lockheed Martin F-22 and F-35) are now "paperless"—the essential information is in a CAD database rather than on paper.

MATLAB, Mathematica, Mathcad, and Maple are very powerful **mathematical computation** programs that combine mathematical functions and commands with extensive capabilities for presenting results in graphical form. The programs usually include the ability to express logic in a particular manner, and to save and reuse the logic in the form of programs customized by the user. This combination of computation and visualization power makes them particularly useful tools for engineers.

Programming Languages A computer programming language is the tool a programmer uses to express the logic for a computer to implement. Like any language, a computer language is defined by its grammar (**syntax**) and its vocabulary. Computer languages are described in terms of levels that reflect the layers of abstraction separating the programmer from the CPU that actually implements the logic. Low-level languages, or **machine languages**, are the most primitive languages. Machine language is tied closely to the design of the computer hardware. Since the basic logic of the CPU is binary, the syntax of machine language is expressed as sequences of 0s and 1s, called **binary strings**.

An **assembly language** is a means of programming symbolically in machine language. Each line of code usually produces a single machine instruction. Assembly language is also closely tied to the architecture of a specific processor, such as the Intel Corporation 80×86 series or the Sun Microsystems SPARC series. Programming in assembly language is certainly easier than programming in binary language, but it is still a tedious process.

The assembly code shown in Listing 1.1 demonstrates typical assembly language syntax. Each instruction is listed on a separate line and consists of an operation, or **op code**, followed by the **operands** that specify the data to be used.

High-level languages, such as C, FORTRAN, Ada, Pascal, COBOL, and BASIC, have commands and instructions that are more similar to spoken languages. Writing programs in high-level languages is certainly easier than writing programs in a machine or assembly language. However, a high-level language has many commands and an extensive set of syntax rules for using the commands. To illustrate the syntax and punctuation required by both

Listing 1.1 Typical assembly language code

```
mov        cx,bx
shl        cx,8
shl        bx,6
add        bx,cx
add        ax,bx
mov        cx,es: [ax]
```

software tools and high-level languages, Listing 1.2 shows how to compute the area of a circle with a specified diameter in several different languages. Notice both the similarities and the differences in this simple computation.

Languages are also defined in terms of **generations**. The first generation of computer languages is machine language, the second generation is assembly language, and the third generation is high-level language. Early implementations of fourth-generation languages, referred to as **4GLs**, include IBM's *RPG* (1960), which could be described as the first 4GL; the *Informatics MARK-IV* (1967) product; and Sperry's *MAPPER* (1979). The current trend is to let the programmer express the desired logic in graphical form, and have the 4GL tools automatically convert the diagrams to working programs. Programmers involved with these implementations still need expertise in the underlying high-level language to complete the implementation of the algorithms. The fifth generation of languages is intended to be **natural languages**. Programming in a fifth-generation language would use the syntax of natural speech. Clearly the implementation of a natural language would require the achievement of one of the grand challenges: computerized speech understanding.

Programming languages continue to evolve and proliferate. The following is a brief, partial discussion of the most common languages. **FORTRAN** (FORmula TRANslation) was developed in the mid-1950s for solving engineering and scientific problems. New standards have updated the language over the years, and the current standard, FORTRAN 90, contains powerful numerical computation capabilities. **COBOL** (COmmon Business-Oriented Language) was developed in the late 1950s to solve business problems. Many legacy COBOL programs exist today and were a common source of the Year 2000 (Y2K) "programming bug" (which could probably be described in hindsight as the worst disaster in history that never happened). **BASIC** (Beginner's All-purpose Symbolic Instruction Code) was developed in the mid-1960s and was often used as an educational programming tool; in the 1980s a BASIC interpreter was often included with the system software for a PC.

Listing 1.2 Comparing high-level languages

```
Software      Example Statement
MATLAB        area = pi*((diam/2)^2);
C             area = 3.141593*(diam/2)*(diam/2);
FORTRAN       area = 3.141593*(diam/2)**2
Ada           area := 3.141593*(diam/2)**2;
Pascal        area := 3.141593*(diam/2)*(diam/2);
BASIC         let a = 3.141593*(d/2)*(d/2);
COBOL         compute a = 3.141593*(diam/2)*(diam/2);
Python        a = pi*(diam/2)**2
```

Lisp (**Lis**t **P**rocessor) is a language originally developed for artificial intelligence (AI) applications. It emphasizes three aspects of programming important to that community: manipulating symbols, recursive programming, and the dynamic creation of programs. **Forth**, a Lisp-like programming language, was developed by Charles H. Moore at the U.S. National Radio Astronomy Observatory in the early 1970s. Its name predated the notion of fourth-generation languages, but its language capability lacks the sophistication to be included in that category today. **Pascal** was developed in the early 1970s, and during the 1980s it was widely used in computer science programs to introduce students to computing. **Ada** was developed at the initiative of the U.S. Department of Defense as a high-level language appropriate to embedded computer systems, which are typically implemented using microprocessors. The final design of the language was accepted in 1979. The language was named in honor of Ada Lovelace (1815–1852), who developed instructions for doing computations on an analytical machine in the early 1800s.

Bell Laboratories developed **C**, a general-purpose language, in the early 1970s to write the UNIX operating system. A committee of the American National Standards Institute (ANSI) was created in 1983 to provide a machine-independent and unambiguous definition of C, and in 1989 the C ANSI standard was approved. **C++** is an object-oriented programming language that is a superset of the C language. Much of the early development of C++ was made in the mid-1980s by Bjarne Stroustrup at Bell Laboratories. During the 1990s, C++ became the dominant programming language for applications in such diverse fields as engineering, finance, telecommunications, embedded systems, and computer-aided design. Although C and C++ are included here as high-level languages, many people like to describe them as mid-level languages because they allow access to the internal components of the computer and its operating system.

Two emerging languages are worthy of special note. The developers of Java and Python broke with tradition and made these languages available at no cost to the user. As a consequence, large user communities have contributed to the language definitions and available libraries. **Java** was developed in the early 1990s by James Gosling at Sun Microsystems. Its primary design goal was to enable programs to be shared across the World Wide Web, and this led to a number of innovative implementation decisions. Java programs are stored in machine-independent form, which can be executed on processors of different types, and the language provides significant protection for computers using other peoples' code from the World Wide Web. **Python** is rapidly emerging in universities as the language of choice for teaching introductory programming classes. It was developed in the early 1990s in Amsterdam at the National Research Institute for Mathematics and Computer Science as a scripting language to support a new operating system. It was named for the popular comedy troupe *Monty Python*, and like Java it is available and supported by developers at no cost to users.

1.3.5 Executing a Computer Program

Programs written in most high-level languages, such as C, need to be compiled (that is, translated into machine language) before the instructions can be executed by the computer. A special program called a **compiler** performs this translation. Thus, in order to write and execute C programs on a computer, the computer's software must include a C compiler.

If any errors (often called **bugs**, a reference to an unidentified insect that caused a short in one of the early digital computers) are detected by the compiler during compilation, the compiler generates corresponding error messages. Programmers must correct the program statements and then perform the compilation step again. The errors identified during this stage are called **compile errors** or **compile-time errors**. For example, if you want to divide the value stored in a variable called sum by 3, the correct expression in C is sum/3. If you incorrectly write the expression using the backslash, as in sum\3, you will get a compiler error. The process of compiling, correcting statements (or **debugging**), and recompiling often must be repeated several times before the program compiles without compiler errors. When there are no compiler errors the compiler generates a program in machine language that performs the steps specified by the original C program. The original C program is referred to as the **source code**, and the machine-language version is called the **object code**. Thus the source code and the object code specify the same steps, but the source code is specified in a high-level language and the object code is specified in machine language.

Once the program has compiled correctly, additional steps are necessary to prepare the object code for **execution**. A **linker** will search libraries of built-in capabilities required by this program and collect them in a single executable file stored on the hard drive. A **loader** is then used to copy the executable program into memory where its instructions can be executed by the computer. New errors, synonymously called **execution errors**, **runtime errors**, **logic errors**, or **program bugs**, may be identified in this stage. Execution errors often cause the termination of a program. For example, the program statements may attempt to perform a division by zero, which generates an execution error.

Some execution errors do not stop the program from executing, but they cause incorrect results to be computed. These types of errors can be caused by programmer errors in determining the correct steps in the solutions and by errors in the data processed by the program. When execution errors occur because of errors in the program statements, you must correct the errors in the source program and then begin again with the compilation step. Even

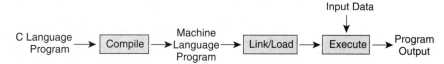

Figure 1.8 *Program compilation, linking/loading, and execution*

when a program appears to execute properly, you must check the results carefully to be sure that they are correct. The computer will perform the steps precisely as you specify them. If you specify the wrong steps, the computer will execute these wrong (but syntactically legal) steps and present you with an answer that is incorrect.

The process of converting an assembly language program to binary language is performed by an **assembler**, and the corresponding processes are called assembly, linking/loading, and execution. These processes are outlined in Figure 1.8.

1.4 Executing a MATLAB Program

MATLAB is officially classed as an interpreted language—one that does not require compilation. It does have a compilation step, but it is hidden from users. In the MATLAB environment you can develop and execute programs (**scripts**) that contain MATLAB commands. You can also execute a MATLAB command, observe the results, and then execute another MATLAB command that interacts with the information in memory, observe its results, and so on. This **interactive environment** does not require the formal compilation, linking/loading, and execution process described earlier for high-level computer languages. However, errors in the syntax of a MATLAB command are detected when the MATLAB environment attempts to translate the command, and logic errors can cause execution errors when the MATLAB environment attempts to execute the command.

1.5 Problem Solving

If we think about a computer program as a logical component that consumes data in one form and produces data in another, we can think about problem solving as the process of designing a collection of solutions to subproblems. The term **state** refers to the collection of data handed off from one subproblem solution to another.

In general terms, solutions to nontrivial problems are found by the two-pronged approach shown in Figure 1.9. We can consider the original information and ask ourselves what could be done with that information

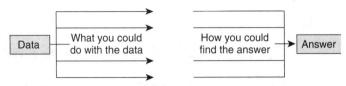

Figure 1.9 *Generalized problem solving*

using existing tools, and we can also consider the objective and the different ways in which that objective might be achieved. The process of creative problem solving then becomes a search for a match between states that can be achieved from the given data and states from which the answer can be achieved.

For example, say you have a big collection of baseball cards and you want to find the names of the 10 "qualified" players with the highest lifetime batting averages. To qualify, the players must have been in the league at least 5 years, had at least 100 plate appearances per year, and made fewer than 10 errors per year.

The cards contain all the relevant information for each player. You just have to organize the cards to solve the problem. Clearly there are a number of steps between the stack of cards and the solution. In no particular order these are:

    a.   Write down the names of the players from some cards

    b.   Sort the stack of cards by the lifetime batting average

    c.   Select all players from the stack with 5 years or more in the league

    d.   Select all players from the stack with fewer than 10 errors per year

    e.   Select all players from the stack with over 100 plate appearances per year

    f.   Keep the first 10 players from the stack

When you think about it from right to left as shown in Figure 1.9, step a is probably the last step and step f is probably the step before that. The hard work starts when you think about it from left to right. Intuitively when you think about sorting the stack of cards, this seems like a lengthy process. Since the sorting should probably be done on a small number of cards, you should do all the selecting before the sorting. Continuing that line of reasoning, you would reduce the total effort if the first selection pass was the criterion that eliminated most cards. You might even consider combining all three selection steps into one.

One logical way to find the players' names that you need would be to perform the steps in this order: c, d, and e in any order, followed by b, f, and then a.

Chapter Summary

This chapter presented an overview of the historical background of computing and the computer hardware and software concepts that build the foundation for the rest of this book:

- How the basic von Neumann architecture has been adopted for the full range of computers, from small, embedded processors to massive mainframes
- The spectrum of software products, ranging from operating systems to the many flavors of specific programming tools
- The rich variety of programming languages currently in use, and the place of MATLAB in that spectrum as a legitimate fourth-generation language
- The basics of problem solving as a search for a path from the data provided to the answers required

 Self Test

Use the following questions to check your understanding of the material in this chapter:

True or False

1. Computers were originally conceived as tools for solving specific problems.

2. Bill Gates designed the first working computer.

3. Programs cannot interact with the world outside the computer without an operating system.

4. Programs cannot interact with the world outside the computer without drivers.

5. Programs cannot interact with the world outside the computer without hardware interfaces.

6. Application programs have access to shared memory.

7. An algorithm bridges the gap between the available data and the result to be achieved.

Fill in the Blanks

1. A computer language is not a _____ exercise; it is a
   _____ tool for communication and problem solving.

2. Together with the use of binary encoding for storing numerical
   values, _____ was the genesis of general-purpose
   computing as we know it today.

3. Most operating systems today use _____, which is
   actually a data file containing an image of everything you would
   like to have in RAM.

4. Operating systems contain a group of programs called
   _____ that allow you to perform functions such as
   printing, copying files, and listing the file names.

5. Many _____ are loaded automatically when the
   operating system starts, and others are loaded upon user request.

6. Even when a program appears to execute properly, you must check
   the results carefully to find _____ errors.

7. Problem solving is the process of designing a collection of
   _____.

8. The process of problem solving is a search for a match between
   _____ one can achieve from the given data and
   _____ from which the answer can be achieved.

CHAPTER 2

Getting Started with MATLAB

2.1 Programming Language
  Background
  2.1.1 Abstraction
  2.1.2 Algorithms
  2.1.3 Programming
    Paradigms
2.2 Basic Data Manipulation
  2.2.1 Starting and
    Stopping MATLAB
  2.2.2 Assigning Values to
    Variables
  2.2.3 Data Typing
  2.2.4 Classes and Objects
2.3 The MATLAB User
  Interface
  2.3.1 Command Window
  2.3.2 Command History
  2.3.3 Workspace Window
  2.3.4 Current Directory
    Window
  2.3.5 Document Window
  2.3.6 Graphics Window
  2.3.7 Editor Window
  2.3.8 Start Button
2.4 Scripts
  2.4.1 Text Files
  2.4.2 Creating Scripts
  2.4.3 The Current
    Directory
  2.4.4 Running Scripts
  2.4.5 Punctuating Scripts
  2.4.6 Debugging Scripts
2.5 Engineering Example—
  Spacecraft Launch

Chapter Objectives

This chapter introduces you to some of the fundamentals of computing that apply to all programming languages, and specifically to the programming environment used for MATLAB program development.

The fundamentals of programming include:

- How to use abstraction to think in a general way about a collection of data and procedural steps

- How to describe the solution of a problem as an algorithm

- The three paradigms of computing and the position of MATLAB in that spectrum

- Three aspects of the apparently simple task of assigning a value to a variable

As you study the MATLAB user interface, you will understand:

- How to use the Command window to explore single commands interactively and how to recall earlier commands to be repeated or changed

- Where to examine the variables and files created in MATLAB

- How to view and edit data tables created in MATLAB

- How MATLAB presents graphical data in separate windows

- How to create scripts to solve simple arithmetic problems

Introduction

The name MATLAB is a contraction of **Ma**trix **Lab**oratory. It was developed for engineers to create, manipulate, and visualize matrices—rectangular arrays of numerical values. As you will see, at its most basic level MATLAB can perform the same functions as your scientific calculator, but MATLAB has expanded far beyond its original capabilities and now provides an interactive system and programming language for many applications, including financial analysis as well as general scientific and technical computation.

The following are the fundamental components of MATLAB:

- A computing system that accepts one instruction at a time in text form and implements the logic of that instruction. Instructions must conform to a specific syntax and vocabulary, which will be the topic of Chapters 3–9.
- A large library of modules that provide high-level capabilities for processing data. These modules will be the major topic of Chapters 10–17.
- A large collection of toolboxes, which are separate application programs that provide graphical capabilities for computing in a number of engineering and scientific disciplines.
- A graphical user interface (GUI) that lets users assemble and implement programs that solve specific problems. The rest of this chapter will describe the basic behavior of these windows.

MATLAB offers a number of advantages to users over conventional, compiled languages like C++, Java, or FORTRAN:

- Because MATLAB programs are interpreted rather than compiled, the process of producing a working solution can be much quicker than with compiled languages.
- MATLAB excels at numerical calculations, especially matrix calculations.
- MATLAB includes a wide spectrum of toolboxes that implement fourth-generation language concepts for graphical problem solving.
- One of the MATLAB tools, the Graphical User Interface Development Environment (GUIDE), enables you to build your own GUIs.
- MATLAB has built-in graphics capabilities that produce professional-looking images for reports.

However, because MATLAB is not a compiled language, there are problems you should not attempt to solve using MATLAB. For example:

- MATLAB does not work well for large computing projects where a number of developers share coding responsibilities.
- Professional GUIs and windowing applications (like MATLAB itself) are best written in a compiled language.

2.1 Programming Language Background

Before learning about concepts in computing, you need to understand the background of programming languages. This section discusses the following aspects of programming languages: abstraction, algorithms, programming paradigms, and three fundamental concepts of programming—assigning values to variables, data typing, and the difference between classes and objects.

2.1.1 Abstraction

For the purpose of this text, we will define **abstraction** as "expressing a quality apart from a particular implementation." We use the concept of abstraction in everyday conversation without thinking about it:

> "To convert from degrees Celsius to Kelvin, you add 273 to *the temperature*."

> "He *drove home* from the office."

The first is an example of **data abstraction**. "The temperature" could mean a single reading from the thermometer hanging outside the window or a table of temperature readings for the month of August. The specifics are unimportant; the phrase captures all you need to know.

The second example is actually much more complex—an example of multiple levels of **procedural abstraction**. To a businessperson taking the same route home every night, "drive home" is all that is required to understand the idea. To a competent driver unfamiliar with the route, the next level of abstraction might be necessary—turn right out of the parking lot, left onto Main Street, and so on. For instructions to guide a future robotic commuter vehicle, an incredibly fine-grained level of abstraction will be required. Everything taken for granted in these abstractions will need to be meticulously spelled out for the robotic vehicle—start the engine, accelerate the vehicle, look out for traffic, keep in the lane, find the turn, steer the vehicle, control the speed, observe and obey all signs, and so on.

2.1.2 Algorithms

Chapter 1 defined problem solving as the ability to isolate subproblems that seem simple and appropriate to solve, and then assemble the solutions to these subproblems. The solutions to each of these subproblems would be expressed as an **algorithm**, which is a sequence of instructions for solving a problem. The process of solving each subproblem and assembling the solutions to form the solution to the whole problem would also be expressed as an algorithm at a higher level of abstraction.

The level of abstraction needed to describe an algorithm varies greatly with the mechanism available. For example, describing the algorithm (recipe) for baking cookies might take the following forms:

- To your grandmother, who has been baking cookies for the last 50 years, it might be "Bake some cookies."
- To others it might be "Buy a cookie mix and follow the directions."
- To a young person learning to cook from scratch, the algorithm might include an intricate series of instructions for measuring, sifting, and combining ingredients; setting the oven temperature and preheating the oven; forming the cookies and putting them on the cookie sheet; and so on.

In programming terms, algorithms are frequently expressed first conceptually at a high level of abstraction, as demonstrated in Section 1.5. The solutions to each subproblem would then be expressed at lower and lower levels of abstraction until the description is sufficient to write programs that solve each subproblem, thereby contributing the pieces that, when assembled, solve the whole problem.

2.1.3 Programming Paradigms

From the Greek word *paradeigma*—"to show alongside"—the *American Heritage Dictionary* defines a paradigm as "a set of assumptions, concepts, values, and practices that constitutes a way of viewing reality for the community that shares them, especially in an intellectual discipline." So a programming paradigm becomes a codified set of practices allowing the community of computing professionals to frame their ideas. This section considers three radically different paradigms: functional programming, procedural programming, and object-oriented programming.

Functional programming is typically associated with languages like Lisp and Forth, in which every programming operation is actually implemented as a function call with no side effects (changes of state of the program surroundings) permitted or implemented in the language. Without side effects, a programming solution can be mathematically proven to be correct—an enormous advantage. Except for the discussion of recursion, this paradigm will not be mentioned again.

Procedural programming is typical of languages like FORTRAN, C, and MATLAB, where the basic programs or subprograms are sequences of operations on data items that are generally accessible to all programs. Although side effects from subprograms—such as changing the values of variables outside that subprogram—are considered poor practice, they are not prohibited by the language.

Object-oriented programming (OOP), typical of languages like C++, Ada, and Java, is a relatively new addition to the world of programming paradigms. It is characterized by the concept of encapsulating, or packaging, data items together with the methods or functions that manipulate those data items. In this paradigm, side effects are explicitly managed by controlling access to the data and methods in a particular grouping. The major theme in true OOP is that "everything is an object." You will see MATLAB exhibit many traits of OOP as you work through this book, but you will not need to use this programming paradigm.

 ## 2.2 Basic Data Manipulation

In order to use MATLAB to demonstrate basic data manipulation, we begin with an exercise in starting and stopping the MATLAB system.

2.2.1 Starting and Stopping MATLAB

MATLAB is available in both a professional version and a student version. Student versions for the Windows, Macintosh, and Linux operating systems include the most commonly used components of the professional version. See the documentation for your particular installation for details.

The only obvious difference between the student and the professional versions is that the command prompt in the professional version is >>, whereas the student version's prompt is EDU>>. Exercise 2.1 shows you how to start and stop the MATLAB user interface.

We will soon see the details of all the program's windows. For the moment, however, we will interact with MATLAB by typing instructions in the large Command window that occupies the right side of your screen.

 Exercise 2.1 Starting and stopping MATLAB

Do It Yourself

If you have not installed MATLAB on your computer yet, follow the manufacturer's directions for performing the installation.

To start MATLAB on a PC or Macintosh, double-click on the MATLAB icon (which should be located on the desktop) or use the Start menu. If you are using a UNIX operating system, type MATLAB at the shell prompt. In the Command window you should see the MATLAB prompt (>> or EDU>>), which tells you that MATLAB is waiting for you to enter a command.

To exit MATLAB, type quit or exit at the MATLAB prompt, choose the menu option File > Exit MATLAB, or click the close icon (x) in the upper-right corner of the screen.

2.2.2 Assigning Values to Variables

The concept of assigning values to variables is the first challenge facing novice programmers. The difficulty arises because many programming languages (including MATLAB) present this simple concept in a syntax that is very similar to conventional algebra, but with significantly different meaning. Consider, for example, the following algebraic expression:

```
z = x + y
```

In normal algebra, this is a two-way relationship that is an identity for the duration of the problem. If you knew the values of z and x, you could derive the value of y with no further analysis. To a programmer, however, this statement has a different meaning. It means that you want to sum the values given to the variables x and y, and store the result in a variable called z. If either x or y are unknown at the time of executing this statement, an error ensues. In particular, this relationship is true *only for this statement*. The relationship can be revoked in the next instruction, which might be:

```
z = 4*x - y
```

In algebra, this pair of statements collectively constrains the values of x, y, and z. In programming, the only significance is that the programmer decided to calculate the current value of z differently. A few languages are sensitive to this dilemma and use a different symbol for assigning values to a variable. For example, in Pascal or Ada z = x + y would be written as follows:

```
z := x + y
```

This clearly indicates that this is an assignment statement, not an algebraic identity.

Style Points

1. Some early versions of the FORTRAN and Basic languages severely restricted the number of characters you could use for variable names. It is no longer necessary to program as if you were still in the "bad old days." Choose names for variables that describe their content. For example, a variable used to store the velocity of an object should be named `velocity_in_feet_per_second` rather than `v`.

2. Since the space character is not permitted in variable names, there are two conventions for joining multiple words together to make a single variable name. One uses the underscore character to separate the words (`file_size`), and the other capitalizes the first letter of additional words (`fileSize`). You should choose one convention and be consistent with it. You cannot use a hyphen to concatenate words—MATLAB treats the name `file-size` as the arithmetic operation subtracting the value of the variable `size` from the value of the variable `file`.

In general, variable names may contain any combination of uppercase and lowercase alphabetic letters, numbers, and the special characters _ (underscore) and $ (dollar sign). The underscore character is frequently used to represent a space in a variable name because spaces are not allowed. However, variable names may not begin with a numeric character, and even though the names may be hundreds of characters long, the first 64 characters must be unique.

Exercise 2.2 demonstrates the assignment of values to variables.

Exercise 2.2 Assigning variables

Do It Yourself

Start MATLAB according to the directions.

When MATLAB finishes initialization, you will see three windows on the screen (see Figure 2.1). For now just focus on the Command window, the large panel to the right in the default screen configuration.

You should see a prompt in the Command window—it will be >> or EDU>> depending on your MATLAB license. This is your invitation to type something. Text that you should type will be shown like this throughout this book:

```
>> radius = 49
```

Note that all entries in the MATLAB Command window terminate with the [Enter] key. The MATLAB system response will be shown like this:

```
radius =
    49
>>
```

This response indicates that MATLAB has stored the value 49 in a variable named radius. To retrieve the value of radius, you just type its name and press [Enter]:

```
>> radius
ans =
    49
```

This response shows that MATLAB retrieved the value 49. Since you didn't specify where to put this result, MATLAB stored the result in a default variable named ans.

2.2.3 Data Typing

It is important to understand how MATLAB treats the data stored in a variable. Different languages take varying approaches to this, and languages in general fall into two broad categories: untyped and typed. In general, interpreted languages like Lisp, Forth, Python, and MATLAB determine the type of data contained by a variable based on the type of data being stored there. Such languages are referred to as **untyped languages**. Each assignment statement is presumed correct. If the variable already exists, both its type and value are reassigned; if it did not exist before, a new variable is created. Exercise 2.3 illustrates the effect of performing simple mathematical operations in MATLAB.

By putting 49 into the variable radius in Exercise 2.3, you established its type as numeric and enabled it to be used in normal arithmetic operations. Character strings are specified by including arbitrary characters between single quote marks. These have the type char, and must be handled differently, as discussed fully in Chapter 6. When you stored a character string in the variable radius, adding 1 to it did not cause an error in MATLAB as it would in some other languages, because addition is actually defined

Exercise 2.3 Performing basic mathematical operations

Do It Yourself

Make the following entries in the MATLAB Command window. You should see
the responses as shown here:

```
>> radius = 49
radius =
    49
>> radius + 1
ans =
    50
>> radius = 'radius of a circle'
radius =
    radius of a circle
>> radius + 1
 ans =
    115 98 101 106 118 116 33 112 103 ...
```

for character strings It just did something radically different—it actually
converted the individual characters to numbers and then added 1.

While this ability to assign data types dynamically is good for interpreted
languages, it has two undesirable consequences that are really hard to unravel
as the program runs:

- Typographical errors that misspell variable names in assignment
  statements cause new variables to be declared unintentionally and
  without the user noticing the error
- Logical errors that assign incompatible data to the same variable
  can cause obscure runtime errors

Typed languages require that programmers specify both the name and type
of a variable before a value can be assigned to it. With this information a
compiler can then do a better job of ensuring that the programmer is not
using a variable in an unintended way. Typed languages fall into two
categories: weak typing and strong typing.

If programmers decide to use only the normal data types, such as `double`
and `char` as we saw above, this is known as **weak typing**, and is the usual
approach to typing.

In some extreme circumstances programmers may choose to be more
restrictive and define specific data types with a limited set of permitted
interactions. This is called **strong typing**. For example, programmers might
define the following data types, all of which are actually of type `double`:
`Meters`, `Seconds`, and `MetersPerSecond`. The compiler would then be provided
with a set of rules specifying the legal relationships between these types. For

example, assignments can only be made to a variable of type `MetersPerSecond` from another variable of the same type, or by dividing a variable of type `Meters` by a variable of type `Seconds`.

Before rushing to judge on the pickiness of this approach, note that this would have avoided the loss in 1999 of the Mars Climate Orbiter, which crashed into Mars because one group of programmers used English units while another used metric.

2.2.4 Classes and Objects

This section discusses two different attributes of a variable: its type and its value. In Section 2.2.2 you saw that a variable is a container for data, whose **value** is determined by what is assigned to the variable. In Section 2.2.3 you saw that by making that assignment to a variable, MATLAB also infers the **type** of data stored in that variable. You will see that while MATLAB is an untyped language, the programs you write will behave differently if applied to data of different types. For example, the type `double` specifies the form and expected behavior of number. Adding 1 to a variable of class `double` containing 4 will, as expected, produce the result 5. Similarly, the type `char` is intended to hold a single character. Adding 1 to a `char` variable containing the value `'d'` will produce the numerical equivalent of the character `'e'`.

MATLAB refers to the type of data in a variable as its **class**, and the value contained in the variable at any time as an **object**, an instance of that class. So in the following operation:

```
thisNumber = 42.0
```

the variable `thisNumber` would be defined (if it didn't already exist); its class would be set to `double`, the inherent type of a floating point number; and its value to `42.0`. So the word `double` corresponds to a type definition or `class`, while the variable `thisNumber` is a variable of that type, which is an instance of that class or, in programming terms, an `object`.

2.3 The MATLAB User Interface

MATLAB uses several display windows (see Figure 2.1). The default view includes a large Command window on the right, and stacked on the left are the Current Directory, Workspace, and Command History windows.

The tabs near the middle of the windows on the left indicate which views are layered in that particular window. Selecting a tab will bring that view to the top. Older versions of MATLAB included a Launch Pad window, which has been replaced by the Start button in

Hint

You can customize how your initial MATLAB window will display. If you make a mistake and close an essential window, you can always restore the default configuration by choosing Desktop > Desktop Layout > Default.

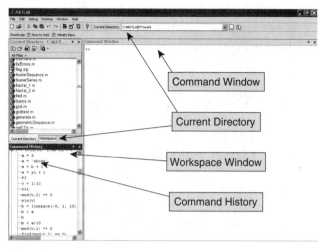

Figure 2.1 *The MATLAB default window configuration*

the lower left corner. Other windows, such as the Document window, Graphics window, and Editor window, will automatically open when needed.

2.3.1 Command Window

You can use MATLAB in two modes: Command mode, which is useful if you need instant responses to specific MATLAB commands, and Edit mode, in which practical solutions are developed. When working in Command mode, we use the Command window, which offers an environment similar to a scientific calculator. This window lets you save any values you calculate, but you cannot permanently save the commands used to generate those values. You will see in the next section how to use the Editor window to create and execute a text file of commands as the first step to unleashing the full programming capability of the language.

The Command window is very useful for performing quick experiments to discover the effects of different commands in MATLAB before embedding them in a larger program. You can perform calculations in the Command window much like doing calculations on a scientific calculator. Most of the syntax is even the same. Exercise 2.4 shows how you might use the Command window to test two simple calculations.

Hint

When you make a mistake, you cannot easily correct it as you would in a word processor. The Command window really is functioning like a calculator, performing one instruction at a time exactly as you specify them. When you enter the command, it is immediately executed, regardless of whether that is what you intended. MATLAB offers several ways to correct erroneous commands. One way is to use the arrow keys, usually located on the right side of your keyboard. The up and down arrows let you move through the list of commands you have executed. Once you find the appropriate command, you can edit it and then press Enter to execute your new version.

Exercise 2.4 Using the Command window

Do It Yourself

To compute the value of 5^2, type this command:

```
>> 5^2
```

The following output will be displayed:

```
ans =
     25
```

To find the cosine of π, type:

```
>> cos(pi)
```

which results in the following output:

```
ans =
-1
```

Notice that in both of the examples in Exercise 2.4, MATLAB echoes the result as if it was saved in a variable called `ans`. This is the default variable used to save the result of any calculation you perform in the Command window that is not specifically assigned to another variable.

Notice also the use of one of MATLAB's many built-in functions, `cos(...)`, that computes the cosine of an angle in radians, and of the built-in constant `pi`.

2.3.2 Command History

The Command History window records the commands you issued in the Command window in chronological sequence. When you exit MATLAB or when you issue the `clc` (Clear Commands) instruction, the commands listed in the Command window are cleared. However, the Command History window retains a list of all the commands you issued. You can clear the Command History using the Edit menu if you need to by selecting Edit and then Clear Command History.

Hint

As a security precaution, when you use MATLAB on a public computer, you can set MATLAB's defaults to clear the Command History window when you exit MATLAB or when you log off the computer.

If you entered the sample commands in Exercise 2.4, notice that they are repeated in the Command History window. This window lets you review previous MATLAB sessions, and you can transfer the commands to the Command window.

Exercise 2.5 demonstrates the use of the Command History window. You will find the Command History window useful as you perform more and more complicated calculations in the Command window.

Exercise 2.5 Using the Command History window

Do It Yourself

In the Command window, type:

```
>> clc
```

This should clear the Command window but leave the data in the Command History window intact. You can transfer any command from the Command History window to the Command window by double-clicking it (which also executes the command) or by clicking and dragging the line of code into the Command window. Try double-clicking:

```
cos(pi)
```

This should result in the following display in the Command window:

```
ans =
    -1
```

Now click and drag 5^2 from the Command History window into the Command window. The command won't execute until you press ⌷Enter⌷, and then you'll get the following result:

```
ans =
    25
```

2.3.3 Workspace Window

The Workspace window keeps track of the variables you have defined as you execute commands in the Command window. As you have seen in the exercises so far, because you have not created other variables yet, the Workspace window should just show one variable, ans. The columns in the window display the name of the variable, its current value, and two indications of its data type—an icon to the left and an entry in the class column (see Figure 2.2). In this case the variable ans has a value of 25 and is a double array. Actually, even a single number you would usually consider a scalar is a 1 × 1 array to MATLAB. Exercise 2.6 shows how to obtain more information about a particular variable. Figure 2.2 shows the normal workspace display for the variable ans.

Figure 2.3 shows that the variable ans is a 1 × 1 array, uses 8 bytes of memory, and is an object of class double.

 Exercise 2.6 Showing more details in the Workspace window

Do It Yourself

Set the Workspace window to show more about the variable ans by right-clicking on the bar with the column labels. On the drop-down menu, check the boxes next to Size and Bytes, so that these will display in addition to Name, Value, and Class. Your Workspace window should now look like Figure 2.3.

Figure 2.2 *The Workspace window*

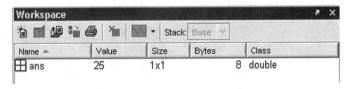

Figure 2.3 *Additional information in the Workspace window*

In Exercise 2.7, variable A has been added to the Workspace window, which lists variables in alphabetical order. Variables beginning with capital letters are listed first, followed by variables starting with lowercase letters, as shown in Figure 2.4.

Exercise 2.8 added the variable B to the Workspace window, and in Figure 2.5 you can see that its size is a 1 × 4 array.

 Exercise 2.7 Defining other variables

Do It Yourself

You can define additional variables in the Command window and they will be listed in the Workspace window. For example, type:

```
>> A = 5
```
This returns:
```
A =
      5
```

 Exercise 2.8 Creating a vector

Do It Yourself

Entering matrices into MATLAB is not discussed in detail in this section. However, you can enter a simple one-dimensional matrix by typing:

```
>> B = [1, 2, 3, 4]
```
This returns:
```
B =
   1    2    3    4
```
The commas are optional. You would see the same result from:
```
>> B = [1 2 3 4]
```

Workspace

Name ▲	Value	Size	Bytes	Class
A	5	1x1	8	double
ans	25	1x1	8	double

Figure 2.4 *Additional variables*

Workspace

Name ▲	Value	Size	Bytes	Class
A	5	1x1	8	double
B	[1 2 3 4]	1x4	32	double
ans	25	1x1	8	double

Figure 2.5 *Vector added in the Workspace window*

You define two-dimensional arrays in a similar fashion. Semicolons are used to separate rows, as illustrated in Exercise 2.9. As you can see in Figure 2.6, variable c appears in the Workspace window as a 3 × 4 array. Vectors and arrays are discussed fully in Chapter 3.

Style Points

MATLAB presents numerical results in the following default format: If the value is an integer, there are no decimal places presented, but if there is a fractional part, four decimal places appear. You can change this by using the `format` command. See MATLAB help for details.

You can recall the values for any variable by just typing in the variable name, as shown in Exercise 2.10.

If you prefer to have a less cluttered desktop, you can close any of the windows (except the Command window) by clicking the x in the upper-right corner of each window. You can also personalize which windows you prefer to keep open by selecting View from the menu bar and checking the appropriate windows. If you suppress the Workspace window, you can still find out what variables have been defined by using the

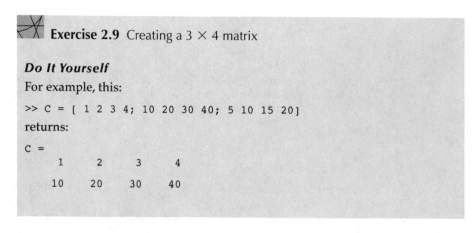

Exercise 2.9 Creating a 3 × 4 matrix

Do It Yourself

For example, this:

```
>> C = [ 1 2 3 4; 10 20 30 40; 5 10 15 20]
```

returns:

```
C =
         1      2      3      4
        10     20     30     40
```

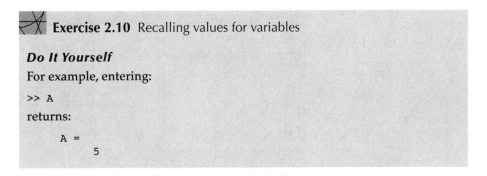

Exercise 2.10 Recalling values for variables

Do It Yourself

For example, entering:

>> A

returns:

    A =
        5

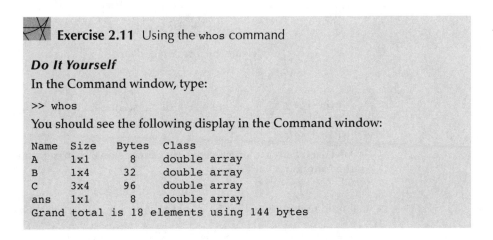

Figure 2.6 *Array added in the Workspace window*

commands who or whos. The command who lists the variable names and whos lists the variable names together with their size and class. Exercise 2.11 illustrates this capability.

2.3.4 Current Directory Window

When MATLAB accesses files from and saves information to your hard drive, it uses the current directory. The default for the current directory depends on your version of the software and how it was installed. The current directory is listed at the top of the main window (see Figure 2.7).

Exercise 2.11 Using the whos command

Do It Yourself

In the Command window, type:

>> whos

You should see the following display in the Command window:

```
Name  Size    Bytes   Class
A     1x1         8    double array
B     1x4        32    double array
C     3x4        96    double array
ans   1x1         8    double array
Grand total is 18 elements using 144 bytes
```

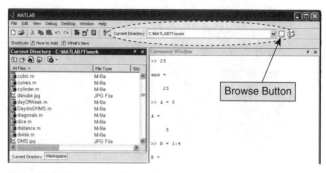

Figure 2.7 *The current directory*

This can be changed by selecting another directory from the drop-down list to the right of the current directory name, or by browsing through your computer files using the browse button located to the right of the drop-down list (circled in Figure 2.7).

2.3.5 Document Window

Double-clicking on any variable listed in the Workspace window automatically launches a Document window containing the Array editor (see Figure 2.8). Values stored in the variable are displayed in a spreadsheet-like format. You can change values in the Array editor, or you can add new values (try Exercise 2.12).

Notice that placing a semicolon at the end of the command (see Exercise 2.12) suppresses the display of that assignment so that the variable value is

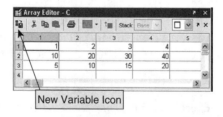

New Variable Icon

Figure 2.8 *The Array editor*

  Exercise 2.12 Creating a two-dimensional matrix

Do It Yourself

If you haven't already entered the two-dimensional matrix C, enter the following in the Command window:

```
>> C = [ 1 2 3 4; 10 20 30 40; 5 10 15 20];
```

C should now be listed in the Workspace window. Double-click it.

not repeated in the Command window. A Document window will open above the Command window, as shown in Figure 2.8. You can now add additional values to the array c, or change existing values by clicking the appropriate cell in the array.

The Document window that displays the Array editor can also be used in conjunction with the Workspace window to create entirely new arrays. Run your mouse slowly over the icons in the shortcut bar at the top of the Workspace window (see Figure 2.2). The function of each icon should appear if you are patient. The icon to create new variables looks like a page with a large asterisk behind it. Click this icon and a new variable called unnamed should appear in the variable list. You can change its name by right-clicking the variable and selecting Rename from the pop-up menu. To add values to this new variable, double-click it and add your data from the Command window.

2.3.6 Graphics Window

The Graphics window is created automatically when a MATLAB command requests a graph. Exercise 2.13 guides you through creating a graph.

The Graphics window opens automatically (see Figure 2.9). Any additional graphs you create will overwrite the plot in the current Graphics window unless you specifically command MATLAB to open a new Graphics window.

MATLAB makes it easy to modify graphs by adding titles, x and y labels, multiple lines, and more with MATLAB built-in commands. Details of these commands will be presented in Chapter 11.

2.3.7 Editor Window

MATLAB provides a text editor, enabling you to create or modify text files that run in the Editor Window. The Editor Window is opened by choosing File > New > M-File. This window lets you type and save a series of

---

 Exercise 2.13 Creating a graph

Do It Yourself

To create a simple graph, first create an array of x values:

```
>> x = [ 1 2 3 4 5];
```

A new variable, x, appears in the Workspace window. Now create a list of y values:

```
>> y = [10 20 30 40 50];
```

To create a graph, use the plot command:

```
>> plot(x,y)
```

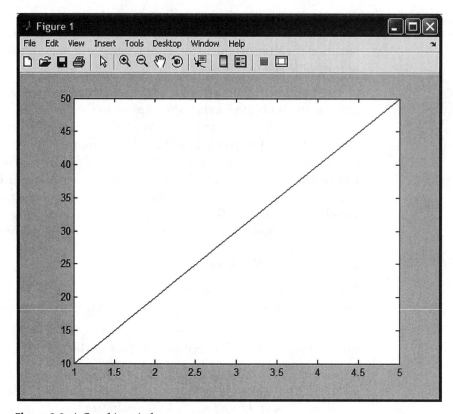

Figure 2.9 *A Graphics window*

commands without executing them. You can also open the Editor window by double-clicking a file name in the Current Directory window or by typing:

```
>> edit <file_name>
```

in the Command window, where `<file_name>` is the name of the file you want to open. You can open multiple files at the same time, using the tabbed overlays to identify the files. An asterisk appears on the tab with the file name to indicate that the file has been modified since it was saved. Options under the Window menu let you organize the multiple files in various ways that make more than one file visible at once. When closing the Editor window, MATLAB displays a dialog asking if you need to save any changed files.

2.3.8 Start Button

The Start button is located in the lower-left corner of the MATLAB window. It offers access to the many features of MATLAB that are beyond the scope of this book. The Start button is new to MATLAB 7 and replaces the Launch Pad window used in MATLAB 6.

2.4 Scripts

This section describes the basic mechanism for creating, saving, and executing scripts as m-files. Building script files lets you save and reuse program statements without retyping them in the Command window.

2.4.1 Text Files

MATLAB uses text files as a permanent means of saving scripts (sets of instructions) rather than just entering commands in the Command window. As you will see in Chapter 8, text files are streams of characters stored sequentially with "markers" that indicate the end of each line of text. For now, think of a script much like writing an e-mail message—a number of lines of text written in a "smart" editor. The MATLAB Editor uses various techniques to help you format commands in these files.

2.4.2 Creating Scripts

A MATLAB script consists of a combination of executable instructions that MATLAB interprets and comment statements that help readers understand the script. You create **comments** by putting a percent sign (%) in the text file. MATLAB will ignore all text from that mark to the end of the current line. The MATLAB editor colors all such comments green to distinguish them from the executable instructions.

Most application programs that use text files specify a particular file name extension (the characters after the period in the file name) to identify how the text files will be used. MATLAB uses the extension .m, and its script files are often referred to as **m-files**.

In MATLAB you create a new script file either by choosing File > New > M-File or by clicking the new file icon on the far left of the tool bar. The MATLAB Editor will then open a blank file in which you can enter the commands and comments of your script. Try creating the script described in Exercise 2.14 and shown in Listing 2.1.

 Exercise 2.14 Creating a script

Do It Yourself

Create a script derived from the Pythagorean theorem to compute the hypotenuse of a right triangle:

$$H^2 = A^2 + B^2$$

where A and B are the sides adjacent to the right angle, and H is the hypotenuse opposite.

Open a new script file and type the commands shown in Listing 2.1 (don't type the accompanying line numbers—MATLAB automatically displays these).

Listing 2.1 Script to solve for the hypotenuse

```
1. clear
2. clc
3.
4. A = 3;    % the first side of a triangle
5. B = 4;    % the second side of a triangle
6. hypSq = A^2 + B^2;    % the square of the
7.                       % hypotenuse
8. H = sqrt(hypSq)    % the answer
```

In Listing 2.1:

> Line 1: Instructs MATLAB to delete all variables in your working directory.
>
> Line 2: Instructs MATLAB to clear the Command window. Any text that now appears in the Command window will be the result of running this script, not the result of previous activities.
>
> Line 3: Blank lines help improve the readability of a script.
>
> Lines 4 and 5: Assign values to A and B. The semicolon prevents MATLAB from displaying the result in the Command window; the percent sign begins the legible comment.
>
> Line 6: Intermediate results with suitable names sometimes improve the legibility of the algorithm.
>
> Line 7: Lines may contain nothing but a comment.
>
> Line 8: Invokes the built-in library function `sqrt(...)` to compute the final result.

2.4.3 The Current Directory

After you have entered a script, you must name it and save it in a directory. MATLAB will need to find that directory—its working directory—in order to run the script. By default, MATLAB expects scripts to be stored in the work directory, with a path like `c:\MATLABxxx\work`. The specific path will vary with your version of MATLAB. However, the Current Directory window circled in Figure 2.7 always shows the default location when MATLAB starts. If you decide to store your scripts elsewhere, you will need to redirect MATLAB to that directory by typing it into the Current Directory window or using the browse feature.

Once script files are saved in your working directory, you can edit them again by selecting and opening them with the MATLAB editor. To open them, either use the File > Open menu command or double-click the file name in the current directory window. Do Exercise 2.15 to understand how to save your script.

Exercise 2.15 Saving a script

Do It Yourself
Save the file you just created with the name *hypotenuse.m*.

2.4.4 Running Scripts

After you have built and saved a script, you can run it using any of the following methods:

- Type the name of the script in the Command window.
- Choose the Debug > Run menu item in the MATLAB Editor window.
- Press the F5 key when the script is visible in the editor. Doing this saves the script automatically before executing it.

After you execute the script, the trace output is written to the Command window as if you had typed the script instructions there one at a time. Do Exercise 2.16 to run your script.

2.4.5 Punctuating Scripts

Many programming languages put a semicolon (;) at the end of a line—whether in the Command window or a text file—to indicate the end of a command. Since MATLAB uses the end of a line to indicate the end of a command, it does not require an end-of-command character. If a long command needs to be extended to the next line for convenience in viewing the program, three periods, frequently referred to as **ellipses**, must be placed at the end of the line to continue the script.

MATLAB uses the semicolon for a different purpose. By default, all assignment commands display their results in the Command window in text form. For more complex programs, the volume of this output can become large. Whenever you really don't want to see all that output, putting a semicolon character at the end of a command line will prevent the results of that assignment from displaying in the Command window.

 Exercise 2.16 Running a script

Do It Yourself
Run the hypotenuse script by one of the methods just discussed in Section 2.4.4. You should see the following in the Command window:

```
H =
     5
```

Now run the script using the other two methods.

2.4.6 Debugging Scripts

MATLAB provides extensive debugging capabilities based on the use of **break points**, which are places in your program where you want to verify that the code is doing what you expect. You insert break points as you edit a code segment by clicking the small dash between the line number and the start of the text. If the program is ready to run, a red dot appears in place of the dash where you clicked. If the file has been changed and hasn't been saved, the dot will be gray, in which case you should save the file and then enter the break point. You can set any number of break points throughout your code.

After you start running a program, when MATLAB reaches a break point, execution stops, an arrow overwrites the break point symbol, and you can examine the contents of the variables either in the Workspace window or by passing the mouse slowly over the variable in the Editor window. A Debugging tool bar is then available with icons that let you:

- Continue executing the logic from this point (other break points may come into effect)

- Step over the logic in this line to the next line in this code block
- Step into any modules referenced by this line of code
- Step out of this current code block

Do Exercise 2.17 to practice inserting break points.

Style Points

1. When writing scripts, you should invest some time to add comments. Comments make the scripts easier to understand as you are developing them, and make it more likely that you will be able to reuse the script later.

2. Scripts should be written incrementally—build a little, test a little—rather than writing a whole script and then trying to find out where in that pile of code you made the mistake(s).

Common Pitfalls

You will quickly become accustomed to understanding the general flow of your script by observing the assignment statements reported in the Command window. However, especially if you have programmed in a language that requires semicolons at the end of a command, you may inadvertently put semicolons in your script. These will suppress the presentation of results and could mislead you into believing that a specific set of instructions haven't been executed.

 Exercise 2.17 Debugging a script

Do It Yourself

Put a break point at Line 5 of the script in Listing 2.1 and run the script again. Observe that the code does not complete; it stops with a yellow arrow at the break point. Examine the Workspace window for the values of the variables and step through the rest of the script one line at a time, noting the display of new variables in the Workspace window and their updated values.

2.5 Engineering Example—Spacecraft Launch

In 1996 the Ansari X Prize was offered for the first time for a private venture: a reusable spacecraft. The requirements were for the same vehicle to carry three people into outer space twice in a two-week time period. The competition was won in 2004 by Tier 1, a company led by Burt Rutan. Their concept was to have a mother ship take off and land on a conventional runway carrying Space Ship One (see Figure 2.10). The spacecraft would be launched at 25,000 feet altitude and would reach outer space (an altitude of 100 km), then glide back and land on the same runway. They repeated this within a week, and they won the prize.

Figure 2.10 *Space Ship One*

Problem:

Assuming that the spacecraft uses all its fuel to achieve a vertical velocity u at 25,000 feet, what is the value of u for the spacecraft to reach outer space?

Solution:

There are two parts to this problem: Converting units to the metric system, and choosing and solving an equation for motion under constant acceleration (the rocket motor is no longer burning).

1. ***Convert the launch altitude from feet to meters.*** I like to remember as few numbers as possible. I do remember that 1 inch = 2.54 cm., so we will use this in a MATLAB script to find the conversion from feet to meters. The appropriate chain of calculations is this:

$$\frac{meters}{foot} \times \frac{meters}{cm} \times \frac{cm}{inch} \times \frac{inch}{foot}$$

Listing 2.2 shows the beginning of the script to solve this problem.

In Listing 2.2:
Lines 1 and 2: Should be at the beginning of any script.

Style Points

Notice that when presented in this manner, the "inner values" like *cm* and *inch* cancel to ensure that the conversions are consistent.

Listing 2.2 Script to compute the spacecraft's velocity (Part 1)

```
1. clear
2. clc

3. cmPerInch = 2.54;      % general knowledge
4. inchesPerFt = 12;      % general knowledge
5. metersPerCm = 1/100;   % general knowledge
6. MetersPerFt = metersPerCm * cmPerInch * inchesPerFt;

7. startFt = 25000;   % ft - given
8. startM = startFt * MetersPerFt;
```

Lines 3–5: Define general knowledge with meaningful variable names to enable subsequent use of these values without ambiguity.

Line 6: The conversion factor needed. Notice that because the variable names are consistent with the logic, they help to avoid errors.

2. ***Find and solve the equation.*** Given the following:

- Initial and final altitudes from which you can compute the distance traveled: s
- The motion is under constant acceleration, the force of gravity: g
- To just reach outer space, the final velocity, v, is 0
- The initial velocity, u, is needed

So after some diligent head scratching, we remember the equation of motion under constant acceleration connecting u, v, s, and a is:

$$v^2 = u^2 + 2as$$

However, this is not yet in a useful form. For computers to be able to solve an equation, you need the unknown quantity on the left of the equation and everything known on the right. Since u is the unknown, we move this to the left side of the assignment, and organize the known quantities to the right. These are the final velocity, v (that is, 0) the given distance, s, and the acceleration, a. Since the positive direction for u and s is upwards, but gravity is downwards, we must use $a = -g$, and the equation can be transformed to:

$$u = \sqrt{2gs}$$

With this information you can now solve this problem. Listing 2.3 shows the rest of Listing 2.2 to complete this calculation.

Listing 2.3 Script to complete the computation of the spacecraft's velocity

```
 9. g = 9.81;  % m/sec^2
10. top = 100; % km - given

11. s = (top*1000) - startM;  % m

12. initial_v = (2*g*s)^0.5 % the final answer
```

In Listing 2.3:

Line 9: The standard value for the acceleration due to gravity.

Line 10: The altitude of outer space is given in the problem statement.

Line 11: Compute the distance traveled, including the unit conversion from kilometers to meters. Note the optional, and in this case unnecessary, use of parentheses to define the order of operations.

Line 12: The final computation. The operator ^ is the MATLAB expression for exponentiation; x^y in MATLAB results in computing x^y. Notice that the parentheses are required here to force the multiplication to happen before the exponentiation.

Although most modern computing environments, including MATLAB, have tools that actually solve symbolic equations, these tools are not appropriate for an introduction to programming and will not be discussed in this book.

 Chapter Summary

This chapter presented some fundamental notions of computing and introduced you to the nature of MATLAB, its user interface, and the fundamental tools for making programs work.

- Abstraction lets you refer to collections of data or instructions as a whole.
- An algorithm is a set of instructions at an appropriate level of abstraction for solving a specific problem.
- A data class describes the type of data and the nature of operations that can be performed on that data.
- An object is a specific instance of a class with specific values that can be assigned to a variable.
- The Command window lets you experiment with ideas by entering commands line-by-line and seeing immediate results.
- The Command History window lets you review and recall previous commands.

- The Workspace window lists the names, values, and class of your local variables.
- The Current Directory window lists the current files in the directory to which MATLAB is currently pointed.
- A Document window opens when a variable in the Workspace window is selected, to let you view and edit data items.
- The Graphics window presents data and/or images when invoked by programs.
- The Editor window lets you view and modify text files.
- Scripts provide the basic mechanism for implementing solutions to problems.

 Special Characters, Reserved Words, and Functions

Special Characters, Reserved Words, and Functions	Description	Discussed in This Section
`'abc'`	Single quotes enclose a literal character string	2.2.3
`%`	A percent sign indicates a comment in an M-file	2.4.2
`;`	A semicolon suppresses output from assignment statements	2.4.5
`...`	Ellipses continue a MATLAB command to the next line	2.4.5
`=`	The assignment operator assigns a value to a memory location; this isn't the same as an equality test	2.2.2
`ans`	The default variable name for results of MATLAB calculations	2.3.1
`clc`	Clears the Command window	2.3.2
`clear`	Clears the Workspace window	2.4.2
`sqrt(x)`	Calculates the square root of `x`	2.4.2

 Self Test

Use the following questions to check your understanding of the material in this chapter:

True or False

1. A bag of groceries is an example of abstraction.

2. An algorithm is a series of logical steps that solves one specific problem.

3. It is impossible to write a complete, practical program in any paradigm other than procedural.

4. To be useful to an algorithm, the result of every computation must be assigned to a variable.

5. In programming, if you know the values of z and x in the expression z = x + y, you can derive the value of y.

6. Untyped languages are free to ignore the nature of the data in variables.

7. Anything assigned to be the value of a variable is an object.

8. Class is a concept restricted to object-oriented programming.

9. You can permanently save the commands entered in the Command window.

10. Double-clicking an entry in the Command History window lets you rerun that command.

11. You can manually change the values of variables displayed in the Workspace window.

12. You double-click a file name in the Current Directory window to run that script.

13. A Document window lets you view and edit data items.

14. MATLAB permits multiple Graphics windows to be open simultaneously.

15. An asterisk on the File Name tab in the Editor window indicates that this is a script that can be executed.

16. MATLAB echoes comments entered in a script in the Command window.

17. When the name of script is typed in the Command window, it will be saved if necessary before it is executed.

Fill in the Blanks

1. _____ means expressing a quality apart from a particular implementation.

2. _____ is a sequence of instructions for solving a problem.

3. Without _____, a programming solution can be mathematically proven to be correct.

4. Variable names must not begin with _____.

5. Armed with both the _____ and _____ of a variable, a compiler can do a better job of ensuring that the programmer isn't misinterpreting data.

6. An instance of a _____ is _____ that is usually stored in a variable of that _____.

7. You can _____ in the Command window in a manner similar to the way you _____ on a scientific calculator.

8. You _____ an entry in the Command History window to _____ that command.

9. The columns in the Workspace window show the _____ of the variable, its _____, and two indications of its _____.

10. You _____ the name of a file in the Current Directory window to edit that file.

11. A Document window opens automatically when you _____ a _____ in the Workspace window.

12. Graphics windows are created _____ when a _____ requests a graph.

13. You create comments by putting a _____ in the text file.

14. MATLAB will _____ all text from the comment mark to _____.

Programming Projects

1. In the Command window, write the commands that will solve the following problems:
    a. You throw a ball straight up in the air with an initial speed of 25 m/s. [g 5 9.8 m/sec^2]. Compute tp, the time it takes to reach the highest point, and hp, the highest distance the ball rises from the release point.
    b. You are constructing a hemispherical dome with an outer radius of 50 feet. The walls will be solid concrete, 9 inches thick. Calculate the volume, v, of the number of cubic yards of concrete that will be needed.
    c. A jet aircraft is flying 100 feet above a level plain at 600 mph. Suddenly the ground begins to rise at a 4 degree slope. Calculate t_x, the amount of time the pilot has to raise the nose before the aircraft strikes the ground.

2. You are given a circle with radius 5 centered at $x = 1, y = 2$. You want to calculate the intersection of some lines with that circle. Write a script to find the x and y coordinates of each point of intersection (if they exist) for the following three lines:

    $$y = 2x - 1$$
    $$y = -2x - 10$$
    $$y = x + 5.9054$$

    The equation of a circle is:

    $$(x - a)^2 + (y - b)^2 = r^2$$

    where (a, b) is the center of the circle, and r is the radius.

    The equation of a line is:

    $$y = mx + c$$

    where m is the slope of the line, and c is the intercept on the y-axis.

    Recall that you can extract the roots of the equation $A^2 + Bx + C = 0$ with the formula:

    $$x = \frac{-B \pm \sqrt{B^2 - 4AC}}{2A}$$

Hint

You will need to solve this twice for the two roots: once with the $+$ and once with the $-$.

3. After a very hard week at work, Kirk is driving to Helen, Georgia for a tubing trip (to cool off). He drives 200 miles north from his home to Timbuktu. He then turns right and travels 400 miles east to Helen. Write a script to compute the linear distance, d, from his home to Helen.

4. Write a script to compute the sum of the cubes of:
    a. The first 10 numbers
    b. The first 65 numbers
    c. The sum of cubes from 100 through 150

Hint

The sum of the cubes of the first n numbers is $n^2 * (n + 1)^2 / 4$.

CHAPTER 3

Arrays

3.1 Concept: Using Built-in Functions

3.2 Concept: Data Collections
3.2.1 Data Abstraction
3.2.2 Homogeneous Collection

3.3 MATLAB Vectors
3.3.1 Creating a Vector
3.3.2 Size of a Vector
3.3.3 Indexing a Vector
3.3.4 Shortening a Vector
3.3.5 Operating on Vectors

3.4 Engineering Example— Forces and Moments

3.5 MATLAB Arrays
3.5.1 Properties of an Array
3.5.2 Creating an Array
3.5.3 Accessing Elements of an Array
3.5.4 Removing Elements of an Array
3.5.5 Operating on Arrays

3.6 Engineering Example— Computing Soil Volume

Chapter Objectives

This chapter discusses the basic calculations involving rectangular collections of numbers in the form of vectors and arrays. For each of these collections, you will learn how to:

■ Create them

■ Manipulate them

■ Access their elements

■ Perform mathematical and logical operations on them

This study of arrays will introduce the first of many language characteristics that sets MATLAB apart from other languages: its ability to perform arithmetic and logical operations on collections of numbers as a whole. You need to understand how to create these collections, access the data in them, and manipulate the values in the collections with mathematical and logical operators. First, however, we need to understand the idea of functions built into the language.

3.1 Concept: Using Built-in Functions

We are familiar with the use of a trigonometric function like cos(θ) that consumes an angle in radians and produces the cosine of that angle. In general, a function is a named collection of instructions that operates on the data provided to produce a result according to the specifications of that function. In Chapter 5 we will see how to write our own functions. In this chapter we will see the use of some of the functions built into MATLAB. At the end of each chapter that uses built-in functions, you will find a summary table listing the function specifications. For help on a specific function, you can type the following in the Command window:

```
>> help <function name>
```

where <function name> is the name of a MATLAB function. This will produce a detailed discussion of the capabilities of that function.

 ## 3.2 Concept: Data Collections

Chapter 2 showed how to perform mathematical operations on single data items. This section considers the concept of grouping data items in general, and then specifically considers two very common ways to group data: in arrays and in vectors, which are a powerful subset of arrays.

3.2.1 Data Abstraction

It is frequently convenient to refer to groups of data collectively, for example, "all the temperature readings for May" or "all the purchases from Wal-Mart." This allows us not only to move these items around as a group, but also to consider mathematical or logical operations on these groups.

For example, we could discuss the average, maximum, or minimum temperatures for a month, or that the cost of the Wal-Mart purchases had gone up 3 percent.

3.2.2 Homogeneous Collection

In Chapter 7 we will encounter more general collection implementations that allow items in a collection to be of different data types. These first collection types, however, will be constrained to accept only items of the same data type. The collections with this constraint are called **homogeneous collections**.

 ## 3.3 MATLAB Vectors

A vector is the simplest means of grouping a collection of like data items. Initially we will consider vectors of numbers or logical values. Some languages refer to vectors as *linear arrays* or *linear matrices*. As these names suggest, a vector is a one-dimensional grouping of data, as shown in Figure 3.1.

Individual items in a vector are usually referred to as its **elements**. Vector elements have two separate and distinct attributes that make them unique in a specific vector: their *numerical value* and their *position* in that vector. For example, the individual number 66 is in the third position in the vector in Figure 3.1. Its value is 66 and its index is 3. There may be other items in the vector with the value of 66, but no other item will be located in this vector at position 3.

3.3.1 Creating a Vector

There are two ways to create vectors that are directly analogous to the techniques for creating individual data items:

- Creating vectors as a series of constant values
- Producing new vectors by operating on existing vectors

The following shows how you can create vectors from constant values:

- Entering the values directly, for example, A = [2, 5, 7, 1, 3] (the commas are optional and are frequently omitted)
- Entering the values as a range of numbers using the colon operator, for example, B = 1:3:20, where the first number is the starting value, the second number is the increment, and the third number is the ending value (you may omit the increment if the increment you need is 1)
- Using the linspace(...) function to create a fixed number of values between two limits, for example, C = linspace (0, 20, 11), where the first parameter is the lower limit, the second parameter is the upper limit, and the third parameter is the number of values in the vector
- Using the functions zeros(1,n), ones(1,n), rand(1,n) (uniformly distributed random numbers), and randn(1,n) (random numbers with normal distribution) to create vectors filled with 0, 1, or random values between 0 and 1

Try working with vectors in Exercise 3.1.

Value:	45	57	66	48	39	• • • •	71	68
Index:	1	2	3	4	5		n-1	n

Figure 3.1 *A vector*

 Exercise 3.1 Working with vectors

Do It Yourself

In the Command window, enter the following:

```
>> A = [2 5 7 1 3]
A =
```
continued on next page

```
        2   5   7   1   3
>> B = 1:3:20
B =
        1   4   7  10  13  16  19
>> C = linspace(0, 20, 11)
C =
        0   2   4   6   8  10  12  14  16  18  20
>> D = [4]
D =
        4
>> E = zeros(1,4)
E =
        0   0   0   0
```

Now, open the Workspace tab in the upper-left MATLAB window and study the contents.

The Workspace window gives you three pieces of information about each of the variables you created: the name, the value, and the "class," which for now you can equate to "data type."

Notice that if the size of the vector is small enough, the value field shows its actual contents; otherwise, you see a description of its attributes, like <1 x 11 double>.

Exercise 3.1 deliberately created the vector D with only one element, and perhaps the result surprised you. D was presented in both the Command window and the Workspace window as if it were a scalar quantity. This is generally true in MATLAB—all scalar quantities are considered vectors of unit length.

3.3.2 Size of a Vector

A vector also has a specific attribute: its length (n in Figure 3.1). In most implementations this length is fixed when the vector is created. However, as you will see shortly, MATLAB provides the ability to increase or decrease the size of a vector by inserting or deleting elements. MATLAB provides two functions to determine the size of arrays in general, and of vectors in particular. The function size(V) when applied to the vector v returns another vector containing two quantities: the number of rows in the vector (always 1) and the number of columns (the length of the vector). The function length(V) returns the maximum value in the size of an array—for a vector, this is a number indicating its length.

3.3.3 Indexing a Vector

As mentioned earlier, each element in a vector has two attributes: its value and its position in the vector. You can access the elements in a vector in either of two ways: by indexing with a numerical vector or indexing with a logical vector.

Numerical Indexing The elements of a vector can be accessed individually or in groups by enclosing the index of the one or more required elements in parentheses. Continuing Exercise 3.1, A(3) would return the third element, 7. If you attempt to read beyond the length of the vector or below index 1, an error will result.

You can also change the values of a vector element by using an assignment statement where the left-hand side indexes that specific element (try Exercise 3.2).

A feature unique to MATLAB is its behavior when attempting to write beyond the bounds of a vector. While it is still illegal to write below the index 1, MATLAB will automatically extend the vector if you write beyond its current end. If there are missing elements between the current vector elements and the index at which you attempt to store a new value, MATLAB will zero-fill the missing elements. Try Exercise 3.3 to see how this works.

In Exercise 3.3 we asked to store a value in the eighth element of a vector with length 5. Rather than complaining, MATLAB was able to complete the instruction by doing two things automatically: it extended the length to 8 and stored the value 0 in the as yet unassigned elements.

This process is referred to as **indexing a vector**. In these simple examples, we used a single number as the index. However, in general, we can use a vector of index values to index another vector. Furthermore, the size of the index vector does not need to match the size of the vector being indexed—it can be either shorter or longer. However, all values in an index vector must

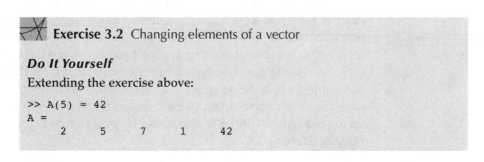

Exercise 3.2 Changing elements of a vector

Do It Yourself
Extending the exercise above:

```
>> A(5) = 42
A =
     2     5     7     1    42
```

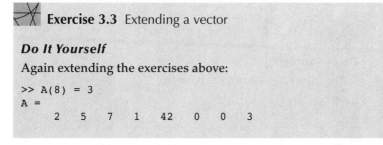

Exercise 3.3 Extending a vector

Do It Yourself
Again extending the exercises above:

```
>> A(8) = 3
A =
     2     5     7     1    42     0     0     3
```

be positive, and if they are being used to extract values from a vector, the index values must not exceed the length of that vector.

Logical Indexing So far, the only type of data we have used has been numerical values of type `double`. The result of a logical operation, however, is data of a different type, with values either `true` or `false`. Such data are called **Boolean** or **logical** values. Like numbers, logical values can be assembled into arrays by specifying true or false values. For example, we might specify the variable `mask` as follows:

```
>> mask = [true false false true]
mask =
     1    0    0    1
```

Notice that the Command window echoes the values of logical variables as if 1 represented true and 0 represented false.

We can index any vector with a logical vector as follows:

```
>> A = [2 4 6 8 10];
>> A(mask)
ans =
     2 8
```

When indexing with a logical vector, the result will contain the elements of the original vector corresponding in position to the `true` values in the logical index vector. The logical index vector can be shorter than the source vector, but it cannot be longer.

3.3.4 Shortening a Vector

There are times when we need to remove elements from a vector. For example, if we had a vector of measurements from an instrument, and it was known that the setup for the third reading was incorrect, we would want to remove that erroneous reading before processing the data. To accomplish this we make a rather strange use of the empty vector, [ ]. The empty vector, as its name and symbol suggest, is a vector with no elements in it. When you assign the empty vector to an element in another vector—say, A—that element is removed from A, and A is shortened by one element. Try shortening the vector in Exercise 3.4.

Exercise 3.4 Shortening a vector

Do It Yourself

Using the vector A from Exercise 3.3:

```
>> A(4) = []
A =
     2    5    7    42    0    0    3
```

Common Pitfalls

Shortening a vector is very rarely the right solution to a problem, and can lead to logical difficulties. Wherever possible, use indexing to copy the elements you want to keep.

As you can see, we asked for the fourth element to be removed from a vector initially with eight elements. The resulting vector has only seven elements, and the fourth element, originally with value 1, has been removed.

3.3.5 Operating on Vectors

The essential core of the MATLAB language is a rich collection of tools for manipulating vectors and arrays. This section first shows how these tools operate on vectors, and then generalizes to how they apply to arrays (multi-dimensional vectors) and, later, matrices.

Three techniques extend directly from operations on scalar values:

- Arithmetic operations
- Logical operations
- Applying library functions

Two techniques are unique to arrays in general, and to vectors in particular:

- Concatenation
- Slicing (generalized indexing)

Arithmetic Operations Arithmetic operations can be performed collectively on the individual components of two vectors as long as both vectors are the same length, or one of the vectors is a scalar (i.e., a vector of length 1). Addition and subtraction have exactly the syntax you would expect, as illustrated in Exercise 3.5. Multiplication, division, and exponentiation, however, have a small syntactic idiosyncrasy related to the fact that these are element-by-element, not matrix operations. We will discuss matrix operations in Chapter 12. When the MATLAB language was designed, the ordinary symbols were allocated to the matrix operations. However, since element-by-element multiplicative operations are fundamentally different from matrix operations, a new set of symbols is required for them. The symbols .*, ./, and .^ (the dots are part of the symbols, but the commas are not) are used respectively for element-by-element multiplication, division, and exponentiation. Because matrix and element-by-element addition and subtraction are identical, no special operation symbols are required for + and –.

 Exercise 3.5 Using vector mathematics

Do It Yourself

In the Command window, enter the following:

```
>> A = [2 5 7 1 3];
>> A + 5
```

Continued on next page

```
ans =
       7      10     12     6      8
>> A .* 2
ans =
       4      10     14     2      6
>> B = -1:1:3
B =
      -1       0      1     2      3
>> A .* B % element-by-element multiplication
ans =
      -2       0      7     2      9
>> A * B % matrix multiplication!!
??? Error using ==> mtimes
Inner matrix dimensions must agree.
>> C = [1 2 3]
C =
       1       2      3
>> A .* C % A and C must have the same length
??? Error using ==> times
Matrix dimensions must agree.
```

Here, we first see the addition and multiplication of a vector by a scalar quantity, and then element-by-element multiplication of A and B. The first error is generated because we omitted the '.' on the multiply symbol, thereby invoking matrix multiplication, which is improper with the vector A and B. The second error occurs because two vectors involved in arithmetic operations must have the same size. Notice, incidentally, the use of the % sign indicating that the rest of the line is a comment.

You can change the signs of all the values of a vector with the unary minus (-) operator.

Logical Operations In the earlier discussion about logical indexing, you might have wondered why you would ever use that. In this section, we will see that logical operations on vectors produce vectors of logical results. We can then use these logical result vectors to index vectors in a style that makes the logic of complex expressions very clear.

As with arithmetic operations, logical operations can be performed element-by-element on two vectors as long as both vectors are the same length, or if one of the vectors is a scalar (i.e., a vector of length 1). The result will be a vector of logical values with the same length as the original vector(s). Try Exercise 3.6 to see how vector logical expressions work.

First we built the vectors A and B, and then we performed two legal logical operations: finding where A is not less than 5, and where each element of A is not less than the corresponding element of B. As with arithmetic operations, an error occurs if you attempt a logical operation with vectors of different sizes (neither size being 1).

Exercise 3.6 Working with vector logical expressions

Do It Yourself

In the Command window, enter the following:

```
>> A = [2 5 7 1 3];
>> B = [0 6 5 3 2];
>> A >= 5
ans =
     0    1    1    0    0
>> A >= B
ans =
     1    0    1    0    1
>> C = [1 2 3]
>> A > C
??? Error using ==> gt
Matrix dimensions must agree.
```

Logical operators can be assembled into more complex operations using logical and (`&`) and or (`|`) operators. These operators actually come in two flavors: `&`/`|` and `&&` / `||`. The single operators `&` and `|` operate on logical arrays of matching size to perform element-wise matches of the individual logical values. The doubled operators `&&` and `||` combine individual logical results, and are usually associated with conditional statements (see Chapter 4). Try Exercise 3.7 to see how logical operators work.

In Exercise 3.7 we combine two logical vectors of the same length successfully, but fail, as with arithmetic operations, to combine vectors of different lengths.

If you need the indices in a vector where the elements of a logical vector are true, the function `find(...)` accomplishes this by consuming an array of logical values and producing a vector of the positions of the true elements. Try Exercise 3.8 to see how this function works.

 Exercise 3.7 Working with logical vectors

Do It Yourself

In the Command window, enter the following:

```
>> A = [true true  false false];
>> B = [true false true  false];
>> A & B
ans =
     1    0    0    0
>> A | B
ans =
     1    1    1    0
>> C = [1 0 0]
>> A & C
??? Error using ==> and
Matrix dimensions must agree.
```

Exercise 3.8 Using the `find(...)` function

Do It Yourself

In the Command window, enter the following:

```
>> A = [2 5 7 1 3];
>> A > 4
ans =
     0 1 1 0 0
>> find(A > 4)
ans =
     2 3
```

You can negate the values of all elements of a logical vector (changing `true` to `false` and `false` to `true`) using the unary not operator, ~. For example:

```
>> na = ~[true true false true]
na = 0 0 1 0
```

As you can see, each element of `na` is the logical inverse of the corresponding original element. As is usual with arithmetic and logical operations, the precedence of operators governs the order in which operations are performed. Table 3.1 shows the operator precedence in MATLAB. Operations listed on the same row of the table are performed from left to right. The normal precedence of operators can be overruled by enclosing preferred operations in parentheses: `(...)`.

Table 3.1 Operator precedence

Operators	Description
`.'`, `.^`	Scalar transpose and power
`'`, `^`	Matrix transpose and power
`+`, `-`, `~`	Unary operators
`.*`,`./`,`.\`,`*`,`/`,`\`	Multiplication, division, left division
`+`, `-`	Addition and subtraction
`:`	Colon operator
`<`, `<=`, `>=`, `>`, `==`, `~=`	Comparison
`&`	Element-wise AND
`|`	Element-wise OR
`&&`	Logical AND
`||`	Logical OR

Applying Library Functions MATLAB supplies the usual rich collection of mathematical functions that cover mathematical, trigonometric, and statistics capabilities. A partial list is provided in Appendix A. For a complete list, refer to the Help menu option in the MATLAB tool bar. All MATLAB functions accept vectors of numbers rather than single values and return a vector of the same length. The following functions deserve special mention because they provide specific capabilities that are frequently useful:

- `sum(v)` and `mean(v)` consume a vector and return the sum and mean of all the elements of the vector respectively.
- `min(v)` and `max(v)` return two quantities: the minimum or maximum value in a vector, as well as the position in that vector where that value occurred. For example:

  ```
  >> [value where] = max([2 7 42 9 -4])
  value = 42
  where = 3
  ```

indicates that the largest value is 42, and it occurs in the third element of the vector. You will see in Chapter 5 how to implement returning multiple results from a function.

- `round(v)`, `ceil(v)`, `floor(v)`, and `fix(v)` remove the fractional part of the numbers in a vector by conventional rounding, rounding up, rounding down, and rounding toward zero, respectively.

Concatenation In Section 3.3.1 we saw the technique for creating a vector by assembling numbers between square brackets:

```
A = [2 5 7 1 3]
```

This is in fact a special case of concatenation. MATLAB lets you construct a new vector by concatenating other vectors:

```
A = [B C D ... X Y Z]
```

where the individual items in the brackets may be any vector defined as a constant or variable, and the length of A will be the sum of the lengths of the individual vectors. The simple vector constructor in Section 3.3.1 is a special case of this rule because each number is implicitly a 1×1 vector. The result is therefore a $1 \times N$ vector, where N is the number of values in the brackets. Try concatenating the vectors in Exercise 3.9.

 Exercise 3.9 Concatenating vectors

Do It Yourself

In the Command window, enter the following:

```
>> A = [2 5 7];
>> B = [1 3];
>> [A B]
ans =
2 5 7 1 3
```

Notice that the resulting vector is not nested like `[[2 5 7], [1 3]]`, but is completely flat.

Slicing As mentioned earlier, the basic operation of extracting and replacing the elements of a vector is called indexing. However, indexing is not confined to single elements in a vector; you can also use **vectors of indices**. These index vectors either can be the values of previously named variables, or they can be created anonymously as they are needed. When you index a single element in a vector—for example, `A(4)`—you are actually creating an anonymous 1 × 1 index vector, `4`, and then using it to extract the specified element(s) from the array `A`.

Creating anonymous index vectors as needed makes some additional features of the colon operator available. The general form for generating a vector of numbers is:

```
<start> : <increment> : <end>
```

We already know that by omitting the `<increment>` portion, the default increment is 1. When used anonymously while indexing a vector, the following features are also available:

- The key word `end` is defined as the length of the vector
- The operator `:` by itself is short for `1:end`

Finally, as you saw earlier, it is legal in MATLAB to index with a vector of logical values of the same length as, or shorter than, the vector being indexed. For example, if `A` is defined as:

```
A = [2 5 7 1 3];
```

then `A([false true false true])` returns:

```
ans =
        5       1
```

yielding a new vector containing only those values of the original vector where the corresponding logical index is `true`. This is extremely useful, as you will see later in this chapter, for indexing items in a vector that match a specific test.

The general form of statements for slicing vectors (moving sections of one vector into sections of another) is:

```
B(<rangeB>) = A(<rangeA>)
```

where `<rangeA>` and `<rangeB>` are both index vectors, `A` is an existing array, and `B` can be an existing array, a new array, or absent altogether (giving `B` the name ans). The values in `B` at the indices in `rangeB` are assigned the values of `A` from `rangeA`. The rules for use of this template are as follows:

- Either the size of rangeB must be equal to the size of rangeA or rangeA must be of size 1
- If B did not exist before this statement was implemented, it is zero filled where assignments were not explicitly made
- If B did exist before this statement, the values not directly assigned in rangeB remain unchanged

Study the comments in Listing 3.1 and do Exercise 3.10.

Listing 3.1 Vector indexing script

```
1. clear
2. clc
3. A = [2 5 7 1 3 4];
4. odds = 1:2:length(A);
5.
6. disp('odd values of A using predefined indices')
7. A(odds)
8. disp('odd values of A using anonymous indices')
9. A(1:2:end)
10. disp('put evens into odd values in a new array')
11. B(odds) = A(2:2:end)
12. disp('set the even values in B to 99')
13. B(2:2:end) = 99
14. disp('find the small values in A')
15. small = A < 4
16. disp('add 10 to the small values')
17. A(small) = A(small) + 10
18. disp('this can be done in one ugly operation')
19. A(A < 4) = A(A < 4) + 10
```

 Exercise 3.10 Running the vector indexing script

Do It Yourself

Execute the script in Listing 3.1. You should see the following output in the Command window:

```
odd values of A using predefined indices
ans =
     2     7     3
odd values of A using anonymous indices
ans =
     2     7     3
put even values into odd values in a new array
B =
     5     0     1     0     4
set the even values in B to 99
B =
     5    99     1    99     4
```

continued on next page

```
find the small values in A
small =
      1      0      0      1      1      0
add 10 to the small values
A =
     12      5      7     11     13      4
this can be done in one ugly operation
A =
     12      5      7     11     13      4
>>
```

In Listing 3.1:

Lines 1 and 2: `clear` and `clc` should be the first two commands in a script.

Line 3: Creates a vector `A` with five elements.

Line 4: When predefining an index vector, if you want to refer to the size of a vector, you must use either the `length(...)` function or the `size` function.

Line 5: Blank to improve readability.

Line 6: The `disp(...)` function shows the contents of its parameter in the Command window, in this case: `'odd values of A using predefined indices'`. We use `disp(...)` rather than comments because comments are visible only in the script itself, not in the program output, which we need here.

Line 7: Using a predefined index vector to access elements in vector `A`. Since no assignment is made, the variable `ans` takes on the value of a three-element vector containing the odd-numbered elements of `A`. Notice that these are the odd-numbered elements, not the elements with odd values.

Line 8: Again, the `disp(...)` function shows the contents of its parameter in the Command window. In this case, `'odd values of A using anonymous indices'`.

Line 9: The anonymous version of the command given in Line 7. Notice that you can use the word `end` within the vector.

Line 10: Displays `'put evens into odd values in a new array'`.

Line 11: Since `B` did not previously exist (a good reason to run the `clear` command at the beginning of a script is to be sure this is true), a new vector is created with five elements (the largest index assigned in `B`). Elements in `B` with fewer than five indices that were not assigned are zero filled.

Line 12: Displays `'set the even values in B to 99'`.

Line 13: If you assign a scalar quantity to a range of indices in a vector, all values at those indices are assigned the scalar value.

Line 14: Displays 'find the small values in A'.

Line 15: Logical operations on a vector produce a vector of Boolean results. This is not the same as the line small = [1 0 0 1 1 0]. If you want to create a logical vector you must use true and false, for example:

```
small = [true false false true true false]
```

Line 16: Displays 'add 10 to the small values'.

Line 17: This is actually performing the scalar arithmetic operation + 10 on an anonymous vector of three elements, and then assigning those values to the range of elements in A.

Line 18: Displays 'this can be done in one ugly operation'.

Line 19: Not only is this unnecessarily complex, but it is also less efficient because it is applying the logical operator to A twice. It is better to use the form in Line 17.

3.4 Engineering Example—Forces and Moments

MATLAB vectors are ideal representations of the concept of a vector used in physics. Consider two forces acting on an object at a point P, as shown in Figure 3.2. Calculate the resultant force at P, the unit vector in the direction of that resultant, and the moment of that force about the point M. We can represent each of the vectors in this problem as a MATLAB vector with three components: the x, y, and z values of the vector. The solution to this problem for specific vectors is shown in Listing 3.2.

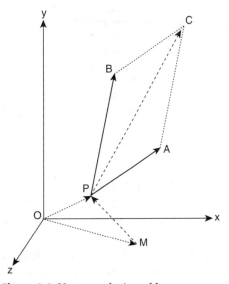

Figure 3.2 *Vector analysis problem*

Listing 3.2 Script to solve vector problems

```
1. clear
2. clc

3. PA = [0 1 1]
4. PB = [1 1 0]
5. P = [2 1 1]
6. M = [4 0 1]
7. % find the resultant of PA and PB
8. PC = PA + PB
9. % find the unit vector in the direction of PC
10. mag = sqrt(sum(PC.^2))
11. unit_vector = PC/mag
12. % find the moment of the force PC about M
13. %  this is the cross product of MP and PC
14. MP = P - M
15. moment = cross( MP, PC )
```

In Listing 3.2:

Lines 1 and 2: The usual script beginning, followed by a blank line to improve readability.

Lines 3–6: Typical initial values for the problem.

Line 8: PC is the sum of the vectors PA and PB.

Lines 10 and 11: The unit vector along PC is PC divided by its magnitude. The magnitude is the square root of the sum of the squares of the individual components.

Line 14: The vector PM is the vector difference between P and M.

Line 15: MATLAB has a built-in function, cross, to compute the cross product of two vectors.

Common Pitfalls

After any nontrivial computation, a good engineer will always perform a sanity check on the answers. When you run the code for this problem, the answers returned are:

```
PC = [ 1   2   1]
unit_vector =   [0.4082    0.8165    0.4082]
moment = [ 1     2    -5]
```

To check the moment result, visualize the rotation of PC about M and apply the right-hand rule to find the axis of rotation of the moment. Roughly speaking, the right-hand rule states that the direction of the moment is the direction in which a normal, right-handed screw at point M would turn under the influence of this force. Without being too accurate, we can conclude that the axis of the moment is approximately along the negative z-axis, an estimate confirmed by the result shown.

 ## 3.5 MATLAB Arrays

In Section 3.2 we saw that a vector is the simplest way to group a collection of similar data items. We will now extend these ideas to include arrays of multiple dimensions, initially confined to two dimensions. Each row will have the same number of columns, and each column will have the same number of rows.

At this point, we will refer to these collections as *arrays* to distinguish them from the *matrices* discussed in Chapter 12. While arrays and matrices are stored in the same way, they differ in their multiplication, division, and exponentiation operations. Figure 3.3 illustrates a typical two-dimensional array A with m rows and n columns, commonly referred to as an m $\times$ n array.

3.5.1 Properties of an Array

As with vectors, individual items in an array are referred to as its *elements*. These elements also have the unique attributes combining their value and their position. In a two-dimensional array, the position will be the row and column (in that order) of the element. In general, in an n-dimensional array, the element position will be a vector of *n* index values.

When applied to an array A with n dimensions, the function size will return the information in one of two forms.

- If called with a single return value like sz = size(A), it will return a vector of length n containing the size of each dimension of the array.
- If called with multiple return values like [rows, cols] = size(A), it returns the individual array dimension up to the number of values requested. To avoid erroneous results, you should always provide as many variables as there are dimensions of the array.

The length(...) function returns the maximum dimension of the array. So if we created an array A dimensioned 2 $\times$ 8 $\times$ 3, size(A) would return [2 8 3] and length(A) would return 8.

The transpose of an m $\times$ n array, indicated by the apostrophe character (') placed after the array identifier, returns an n $\times$ m array with the values in the rows and columns interchanged. Figure 3.4 shows a transposed array.

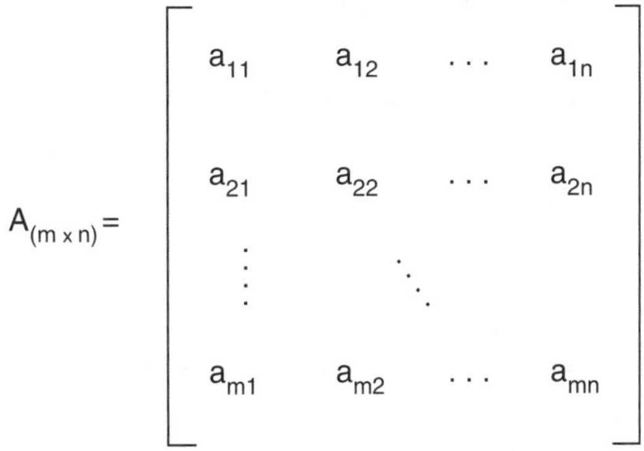

$$A_{(m \times n)} = \begin{bmatrix} a_{11} & a_{12} & \cdots & a_{1n} \\ a_{21} & a_{22} & \cdots & a_{2n} \\ \vdots & & \ddots & \\ a_{m1} & a_{m2} & \cdots & a_{mn} \end{bmatrix}$$

Figure 3.3 *An array*

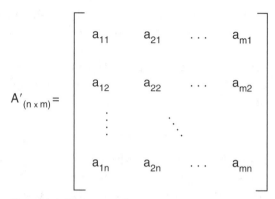

$$A'_{(n \times m)} = \begin{bmatrix} a_{11} & a_{21} & \cdots & a_{m1} \\ a_{12} & a_{22} & \cdots & a_{m2} \\ \vdots & & \ddots & \\ a_{1n} & a_{2n} & \cdots & a_{mn} \end{bmatrix}$$

Figure 3.4 *Transpose of an array*

A number of special cases arise that are worthy of note:

- When a 2-D matrix has the same number of rows and columns, it is called **square**.
- When the only nonzero values in an array occur when the row and column indices are the same, the array is called **diagonal**.
- When there is only one row, the array is a **row vector**, or just a *vector* as you saw earlier.
- When there is only one column, the array is a **column vector**, the transpose of a row vector.

3.5.2 Creating an Array

Arrays can be created either by entering values directly, or by using one of a number of built-in MATLAB functions that create arrays with specific characteristics.

- As with vectors, you can directly enter the values in an array using either a semicolon (;) or a new line to indicate the end of a row, for example: A = [2, 5, 7; 1, 3, 42].
- The functions zeros(m, n) and ones(m, n) create arrays with m rows and n columns filled with zeros and ones respectively.
- The functions rand(m, n) and randn(m, n) fill an array with random numbers in the range 0 .. 1.
- The function diag(...) takes several forms, the most useful of which are diag(A), where A is an array, that returns its diagonal as a vector, and diag(V), where V is a vector, that returns a square matrix with that diagonal.
- MATLAB also provides the function magic(m), which fills a square matrix with the numbers 1 to m^2 organized in such a way that its rows, columns, and diagonals all add up to the same value. Try Exercise 3.11 to practice working with arrays.

Exercise 3.11 Creating arrays

Do It Yourself

Enter the following in the Command window and observe the results:

```
>> A = [2, 5, 7; 1, 3, 42]
A =
       2       5       7
       1       3      42
>> z = zeros(3,2)
z =
       0       0
       0       0
       0       0
>> [z ones(3, 4)]   % concatenating arrays
ans =
       0       0       1       1       1       1
       0       0       1       1       1       1
       0       0       1       1       1       1
>> rand(3,4)
ans =
     0.9501    0.4860    0.4565    0.4447
     0.2311    0.8913    0.0185    0.6154
     0.6068    0.7621    0.8214    0.7919
>> rand(size(A))
ans =
     0.9218    0.1763    0.9355
     0.7382    0.4057    0.9169
>> diag(A)
ans =
       2
       3
>> diag(diag(A))
ans =
       2       0
       0       3
>> magic(4)
ans =
      16       2       3      13
       5      11      10       8
       9       7       6      12
       4      14      15       1
>>
```

3.5.3 Accessing Elements of an Array

The elements of an array may be addressed by enclosing the indices of the required element in parentheses, with the first index being the row index and the second index the column index. Considering the values produced by Example 3.11, A(2, 3) would return the element in the second row, third column: 42. If you were to attempt to read outside the length of the rows or columns, an error would result.

We can also store values that are elements of an array. For example, continuing Example 3.11, A(2, 3) = 0 would result in this answer:

```
A =
        2       5       7
        1       3       0
```

As with vectors, MATLAB will automatically extend the array if you write beyond its boundaries. If there are missing elements between the current array elements and the index at which you attempt to store a new value, MATLAB will zero fill the missing elements. For example, again continuing Example 3.11, A(4, 1) = 3 would result in this answer:

```
A =
        2       5       7
        1       3       0
        0       0       0
        3       0       0
```

3.5.4 Removing Elements of an Array

You can remove elements from arrays in the same way that you remove elements from a vector. However, since the arrays must remain rectangular, elements have to be removed as complete rows or columns. For example, for the array A in the previous section, entering A(3, :) = [] would remove all elements from the third row, and the result would be:

```
A =
        2       5       7
        1       3       0
        3       0       0
```

Similarly, if A(:, 3) = [] was then entered, the result would be:

```
A =
        2       5
        1       3
        3       0
```

Common Pitfalls

Removing rows or columns from an array is very rarely the right solution to a problem and can lead to logical difficulties. Wherever possible, use indexing to copy the rows and columns you want to keep.

3.5.5 Operating on Arrays

This section discusses how array operations extend directly from vector operations: arithmetic and logical operations, the application of functions, concatenation, and slicing. This section will also discuss two topics peculiar to arrays: reshaping and linearizing arrays.

Array Arithmetic Operations Arithmetic operations can be performed collectively on the individual components of two arrays as long as both arrays have the same dimensions or one of them is a scalar (i.e., has a vector of

Common Pitfalls

Performing array multiplication, division, or exponentiation without appending a dot operator requests one of the specialized matrix operations that will be covered in Chapter 12. The error message that displays when this occurs is quite obscure if you are not expecting it:

```
??? Error using ==> mtimes
Inner matrix dimensions must
agree.
```

Even more obscure is the case where the dimensions of the arrays happen to be consistent (when multiplying square arrays), but the results are not scalar multiples.

length 1). Addition and subtraction have exactly the syntax you would expect, as shown in Exercise 3.12. Multiplication, division, and exponentiation, however, *must* use the "dot operator" symbols: .*, ./, and .^ (the dot is part of the symbol, but the commas are not) for scalar multiplication, division, and exponentiation.

Array Logical Operations As with vectors, logical array operations can be performed collectively on the individual components of two arrays as long as both arrays have the same dimensions or one of the arrays is a scalar (i.e., has a vector of length 1). The result will be an array of Boolean values with the same size as the original array(s). Do Exercise 3.13 to see how array logical operations work.

Here, we successfully compare the array A to a scalar value, and to the array B that has the same dimensions as A. However, comparing to the array C that has the same number of elements but the wrong shape produces an error.

 Exercise 3.12 Working with array mathematics

Do It Yourself

Enter the following in the Command window and observe the results.

```
>> A = [2 5 7
   1 3 2]
A =
     2     5     7
     1     3     2
>> A + 5
ans =
     7    10    12
     6     8     7
B = ones(2, 3)
B =
     1     1     1
     1     1     1
>> B = B * 2
B =
     2     2     2
     2     2     2
>> A.*B % scalar multiplication
ans =
     4    10    14
     2     6     4
>> A*B % matrix multiplication does not work here
??? Error using ==> mtimes
Inner matrix dimensions must agree.
```

Exercise 3.13 Working with array logical operations

Do It Yourself

In the Command window, enter the following:

```
>> A = [2 5; 1 3]
A =
      2     5
      1     3
>> B = [0 6; 3 2];
>> A >= 4
ans =
      0     1
      0     0
>> A >= B
ans =
      1     0
      0     1
>> C = [1 2 3 4]
>> A > C
??? Error using ==> gt
Matrix dimensions must agree.
```

Applying Library Functions In addition to being able to consume vectors, most MATLAB mathematical functions can consume an array of numbers and return an array of the same shape. The following functions deserve special mention because they are exceptions to this rule and provide specific capabilities that are frequently useful:

- sum(v) and mean(v) when applied to a 2-D array return a row vector containing the sum and mean of each column of the array, respectively. If you want the sum of the whole array, use sum(sum(v)).

- min(v) and max(v) return two row vectors: the minimum or maximum value in each column and also the row in that column where that value occurred. For example:

```
>> [values rows] = max([2   7 42;
                        9  14  8;
                        10 12 -6])
values = [10 14 42]
rows = [3 2 1]
```

This indicates that the maximum values in each column are 10, 14, and 42 respectively, and they occur in rows 3, 2, and 1. If you really need the row and column containing, say, the maximum value of the whole array, continue the preceding example with the following lines:

```
>> [value col] = max(values)
value = 42
col = 3
```

This finds the maximum value in the whole array and determines that it occurs in column 3. So to determine the row in which that maximum occurred, we index the vector of row maximum locations, rows, with the column in which the maximum occurred.

```
>> row = rows(col)
row = 1
```

Therefore we correctly conclude that the maximum number in this array is 42, and it occurs at row 1, column 3.

Array Concatenation MATLAB permits programmers to construct a new array by concatenating other arrays in the following ways:

- Horizontally, as long as each component has the same number of rows:
  ```
  A = [B C D ... X Y Z]
  ```
- Vertically, as long as each has the same number of columns:
  ```
  A = [B; C; D; ... X; Y; Z]
  ```

The result will be an array with that number of rows and a number of columns equaling the sum of the number of columns in each individual item. Exercise 3.14 gives you the opportunity to concatenate an array.

Slicing Arrays The general form of statements for moving sections of one array into sections of another is as follows:

```
B(<rangeBR>, <rangeBC>) = A(<rangeAR>,<rangeAC>)
```

where each <range..> is an index vector, A is an existing array, and B can be an existing array, a new array, or absent altogether (giving B the name ans). The values in B at the specified indices are all assigned the corresponding values copied from A. The rules for using this template are as follows:

- Either each dimension of each sliced array must be equal, or the size of the slice from A must be 1 × 1.
- If B did not exist before this statement was implemented, it is zero filled where assignments were not explicitly made.
- If B did exist before this statement, the values not directly assigned remain unchanged.

 Exercise 3.14 Concatenating an array

Do It Yourself

In the Command window, enter the following:

```
>> A = [2 5; 1 7];
>> B = [1 3]';     % makes a column vector
>> [A B]
ans =
2 5 1
1 7 3
```

Reshaping Arrays Occasionally it is useful to take an array with one set of dimensions and reshape it to another set. The function `reshape( ... )` accomplishes this. The command:

```
reshape(A, rows, cols, ...)
```

will take the array A, whatever its dimensions, and reform it into an array sized:

```
(rows × cols × ...)
```

out to as many dimensions as desired. However, `reshape(...)` does not pad the data to fill any empty space. The product of all the original dimensions of A must equal the product of the new dimensions. Try Exercise 3.15 to see how to reshape an array.

Here, we first take a 1 × 10 array, A, and attempt to reshape it to 4 × 3. Since the element count does not match, an error results. When we concatenate two zeros to the array A, it has the right element count and the reshape succeeds.

Linearized Arrays A discussion of arrays would not be complete without revealing an infamous MATLAB secret: multi-dimensional arrays are not stored in some nice, rectangular chunk of memory. Like all other blocks of memory, the block allocated for an array is sequential, and the array is stored in that space in column order. Normally, if MATLAB behaved as we "have a right to expect," we would not care how an array is stored. However, there are circumstances under which the authors of MATLAB needed to expose this secret.

The primary situation in which array linearization becomes evident is the mechanization of the `find(...)` function. If we perform a logical operation

---

Exercise 3.15 Reshaping an array

Do It Yourself

In the Command window, enter the following:

```
>> A = 1:10
A =
     1    2    3    4    5    6    7    8    9   10
>> reshape(A, 4, 3)
??? Error using ==> reshape
To RESHAPE the number of elements must not change.
>> reshape([A 0 0], 4, 3)
ans =
     1    5    9
     2    6   10
     3    7    0
     4    8    0
```

on an array, the result is an array of logical values of the same size as the original array. In general, the true values would be scattered randomly about that result array. If we wanted to convert this to a collection of indices, what would we expect to see? An array of [row column] index pairs would be really awkward to process. Consequently, the developers of MATLAB decided to return a vector of the linear positions of the true values. Indexing with this result exposes the linearized nature of MATLAB arrays. The way this facet manifests itself is shown in Exercise 3.16.

Here, we build a 4 × 3 array A and calculate the logical array where A is greater than 5. When we save the result of finding these locations in the variable ix, we see that this is a vector of values. If we count down the columns from the top left, we see that the second, seventh, eighth, and eleventh values in the linearized version of A are indeed true. We also see that it is legal to use this linearized index vector to access the values in the original array—in this case, to add 3 to each one. Finally, we would expect a loud complaint from

Style Points

1. It is best not to expose the detailed steps of finding logical results in arrays, but to use an integrated approach:

        5) = A(A>5) + 3

This produces the expected answers without exposing the nasty secrets underneath.

2. Never use an array linearization as part of your program logic. It makes the code hideous to look at and/or understand, and it is never the "only way to do" anything.

Exercise 3.16 Linearizing an array

Do It Yourself

In the Command window, enter the following:

```
>> A = [2  5  7  3
        8  0  9  42
        1  3  4  2]
A =
        2       5       7       3
        8       0       9      42
        1       3       4       2
>> A > 5
ans =
        0       0       1       0
        1       0       1       1
        0       0       0       0
>> ix = find(A > 5)
ix =
        2    7    8    11
>> A(ix) = A(ix) + 3
A =
        2       5      10       3
       11       0      12      45
        1       3       4       2
>> A(11)
ans =
       42           % (sigh!)
```

MATLAB when trying to reference the eleventh element of an array with only three rows. In fact MATLAB "unwinds" the storage of the array, counts down to the eleventh entry—3 for column 1, 3 for column 2, and 3 for column 3—and then extracts the second element of column 4.

To understand all these array manipulation ideas fully, you should work carefully through the script in Listing 3.3, study the explanatory notes that follow, and do Exercise 3.17.

Listing 3.3 Array manipulation script

```
 1. A = [2 5 7 3
 2.      1 3 4 2];
 3. [rows, cols] = size(A);
 4. odds = 1:2:cols;
 5. disp('odd columns of A using predefined indices')
 6. A(:, odds)
 7. disp('odd columns of A using anonymous indices')
 8. A(end, 1:2:end)
 9. disp('put evens into odd values in a new array')
10. B(:, odds) = A(:, 2:2:end)
11. disp('set the even values in B to 99')
12. B(1, 2:2:end) = 99
13. disp('find the small values in A')
14. small = A < 4
15. disp('add 10 to the small values')
16. A(small) = A(small) + 10
17. disp('this can be done in one ugly operation')
18. A(A < 4) = A(A < 4) + 10
19. small_index = find(small)
20. A(small_index) = A(small_index) + 100
```

 Exercise 3.17 Running the array manipulation script

Do It Yourself

Execute the script in Listing 3.3 and observe the results:

```
odds =
     1     3
odd columns of A using predefined indices
ans =
     2     7
     1     4
odd columns of A using anonymous indices
ans =
     1     4
put evens into odd values in a new array
B =
     5     0     3
     3     0     2
set the even values in B to 99
```

continued on next page

```
B =
       5      99       3
       3       0       2
find the small values in A
small =
       1       0       0       1
       1       1       0       1
add 10 to the small values
A =
      12       5       7      13
      11      13       4      12
this can be done in one ugly operation
A =
      12       5       7      13
      11      13       4      12
do the same thing with indices
small_index =
       1
       2
       4
       7
       8
A =
     112       5       7     113
     111     113       4     112
```

In Listing 3.3:

> Lines 1 and 2: Create a 2 × 4 array A.
>
> Line 3: Determines the number of rows and columns.
>
> Line 4: Builds a vector odds containing the indices of the odd-numbered columns.
>
> Line 6: Uses odds to access the columns in A. The : specifies that this is using all the rows.
>
> Line 8: The anonymous version of the command in Line 7. Notice that you can use the word end in any dimension of the array to mean the end of that dimension.
>
> Line 10: Because B did not previously exist (a good reason to have clear at the beginning of the script to be sure this is true), a new array is created. Elements in B that were not assigned are zero filled.
>
> Line 12: Puts only 99 into selected locations in B.

Style Points

1. Do not forget to begin all scripts with the two commands clear and clc.

   a. clear empties the current Workspace window of all variables and prevents the values of old variables from causing strange behavior in this script.

   b. clc clears the Command window to prevent confusion about whether an output line was caused by this script or some earlier activity.

2. It is better to enter a few lines at a time and run each version of the script incrementally, rather than editing one huge script and running the whole thing for the first time. When you have added only a few lines to a previously working script, it is easy to locate the source of logic problems that arise.

3. It is very tempting to build large, complex vector operation expressions that solve messy problems "in one line of code." While this might be an interesting mental exercise, the code is much more maintainable if the solution is expressed one step at a time using intermediate variables.

Line 14: Logical operations on arrays produce an array of logical results.

Line 16: Adds 10 to the values in A that are small.

Line 18: Not only is this unnecessarily complex, but it is also less efficient because it is applying the logical operator to A twice.

Line 19: The function find(...) actually returns a column vector of the index values in the linearized version of the original array, as shown in Exercise 3.16

Line 20: As illustrated above, it is not necessary to use find(...) before indexing an array. However, this does still work.

Notice that all the results are consistent with our expectations.

 ## 3.6 Engineering Example—Computing Soil Volume

Building a highway across rugged terrain requires careful planning to minimize the amount of dirt to be moved for cutting through hills and filling valleys. Significant amounts of money can be saved if the quantity of soil removed when cutting into a hillside can be used to fill in a nearby valley without transporting the soil too far.

However, this is not always possible. The City of Atlanta recently paid almost $300 million for fill dirt in the construction of the fifth runway at Hartsfield-Jackson Airport because they had to make the level of the runway match the terrain. In other words, the runway had to be at the same ground level as the other runways and terminal areas so airplanes could taxi to and from the new runway. Figure 3.5 shows part of the conveyor that moved 27 million cubic yards of fill dirt over five miles from a quarry to the site of the new runway. At 2,600 cubic yards an hour, 7,000 tons a day, if the conveyor had run continuously night and day, it would have taken nearly a year and a half to move the dirt.

Figure 3.5 *Conveyer moving dirt*

Here is a slightly simpler problem: estimating the amount of soil that must be removed to prepare the foundations of a building. The first step is to survey the land on which the building is to be built, which results in a rectangular grid defining the altitude of each grid point as shown in Figure 3.6.

The next step is to consider an architectural drawing of the basement of the building as shown in Figure 3.7. The shaded areas indicate those places where the soil really must be removed to make the building foundation. We can estimate from this figure the fraction of each surveyed square (for our purposes, a number between 0 and 1) where the soil must actually be removed.

The total amount of soil to move is then the sum of the individual square depths multiplied by the area in each square to be removed. The code in Listing 3.4 solves this problem.

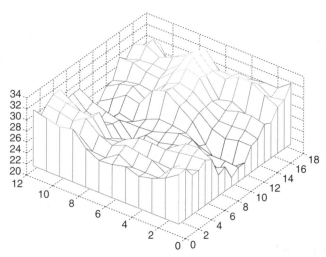

Figure 3.6 *Landscape survey*

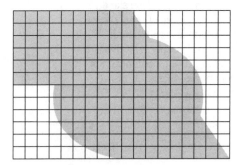

Figure 3.7 *Calculating soil volume*

Listing 3.4 Script to compute total soil

```
clear
clc
% soil depth data for each square produced by the survey
dpth = [8  8  9  8  8  8  8  8  7  8  7  7  7  7  8  8  8  7
        8  8  8  8  8  8  8  7  7  7  7  7  8  7  8  8  8  7
        8  8  8  8  7  7  8  7  8  8  8  8  8  7  8  8  8  8
        7  7  7  8  7  8  8  8  8  8  8  8  7  6  7  7  7  7
        8  8  8  8  8  8  8  7  7  7  7  7  7  6  6  7  7  8
        8  7  7  8  7  7  8  7  7  7  7  7  7  7  7  7  7  8
        9  8  8  9  8  7  8  7  7  7  7  7  7  6  7  6  7  7  8
        8  8  8  9  9  8  8  8  7  6  6  6  6  7  7  8  7  8
        9  8  8  7  7  7  7  7  7  6  6  7  7  7  8  8  7  8
        9  8  8  7  7  7  6  7  7  6  6  8  8  8  9  9  7  8
        9  9  8  8  8  8  7  7  7  7  7  8  8  9  9  9  8  8
        9  8  8  7  7  8  7  7  7  7  8  8  9  9  9  8  7  8];

% estimated proportion of each square that should be excavated
area = [1  1  1  1  1  1  1  1  1  1 .3  0  0  0  0  0  0  0
        1  1  1  1  1  1  1  1  1  1 .7  0  0  0  0  0  0  0
        1  1  1  1  1  1  1  1  1  1  1 .8 .4  0  0  0  0  0
        1  1  1  1  1  1  1  1  1  1  1  1  1 .8 .3  0  0  0
        1  1  1  1  1  1  1  1  1  1  1  1  1  1 .7 .2  0  0
        1  1  1  1  1  1  1  1  1  1  1  1  1  1  1 .6  0  0
        0  0  0 .7  1  1  1  1  1  1  1  1  1  1  1 .8  0  0
        0  0  0 .7  1  1  1  1  1  1  1  1  1  1  1 .7  0  0
        0  0  0 .4  1  1  1  1  1  1  1  1  1  1  1 .6  0  0
        0  0  0 .1 .8  1  1  1  1  1  1  1  1  1  1  1 .4  0
        0  0  0  0 .2 .7  1  1  1  1  1  1  1  1  1  1 .9 .1
        0  0  0  0  0  0 .4 .8 .9  1  1  1  1  1  1  1  1 .6];

square_volume = dpth .* area;
total_soil = sum(sum(square_volume))
```

When you run this script, it produces the answer: 1,117.5 cubic units.

Common Pitfalls

The code in Listing 3.4 produces an answer around 1,120, and we should ask whether this is reasonable. There are 12 $\times$ 18 squares, each with area 1 unit, about 80 percent of which are to be excavated, giving a surface area of about 180 square units. The average depth of soil is about 7 units, so the answer ought to be about 180 $\times$ 7 $\cong$ 1,300 cubic units. This is reasonably close to the computed result.

Chapter Summary

This chapter introduced you to vectors and arrays. For each collection, you saw how to:

- Create them by concatenation and a variety of special-purpose functions
- Access and remove elements, rows, or columns
- Perform mathematical and logical operations on them
- Apply library functions, including those that summarize whole columns or rows
- Move arbitrary selected rows and columns from one array to another
- Reshape and linearize arrays

 ## Special Characters, Reserved Words, and Functions

Special Characters, Reserved Words, and Functions	Description	Discussed in This Section
[ ]	The empty vector	3.3.4
[...]	Concatenates data, vectors, and arrays	3.2.1
:	Specifies a vector as `from:incr:to`	3.2.1
:	Used in slicing vectors and arrays	3.3.5
( )	Used with an array name to identify specific elements	3.3.3
'	Transposes an array	3.5.1
;	Separates rows in an array definition	3.5.2
+	Scalar and array addition	3.3.5
-	Scalar and array subtraction	3.3.5
-	Unary negation	3.3.5
.*	Array multiplication	3.3.5
./	Array division	3.3.5
.^	Array exponentiation	3.3.5
<	Less than	3.3.5
<=	Less than or equal to	3.3.5
>	Greater than	3.3.5
>=	Greater than or equal to	3.3.5
==	Equal to	3.3.5
~=	Not equal to	3.3.5

Special Characters, Reserved Words, and Functions	Description	Discussed in This Section
&	Element-wise logical AND (vectors)	3.3.5
&&	Short-circuit logical AND (scalar)	3.3.5
|	Element-wise logical OR (vectors)	3.3.5
||	Short-circuit logical OR (scalar)	3.3.5
~	Unary not	3.3.5
false	Logical false	3.2.3
help	Invokes help utility	3.3.5
true	Logical true	3.2.3
sum(a)	Totals the values in a	3.3.5
cross(a, b)	Vector cross product	3.3
disp(value)	Displays an array or text	3.3.5
find()	Computes a vector of the locations of the true values in a logical array	3.3.5, 3.5.5
linspace(fr,to,n)	Defines a linearly spaced vector	3.2.1
rand(r, c)	Calculates an $r \_ c$ array of evenly distributed random numbers in the range 0...1	3.2.1
randn(r, c)	Calculates an $r \_ c$ array of normally distributed random numbers in the range 0...1	3.2.1
[v,in] = max(a)	Finds the maximum value and its position in a	3.3.5
mean(a)	Computes the average of the elements in a	3.3.5
[v,in] = min(a)	Finds the minimum value and its position in a	3.3.5
diag(a)	Extracts the diagonal from an array or, if provided with a vector, constructs an array with the given diagonal	3.5.2
length(a)	Determines the largest dimension of an array	3.2.2, 3.5.1
magic(n)	Generates a magic square	3.5.2
ones(r, c)	Generates an array filled with the value 1	3.2.1
size(a)	Determines the dimensions of an array	3.2.2, 3.5.1
zeros(r, c)	Builds an array filled with the value 0	3.2.1
ceil(x)	Rounds x to the nearest integer toward positive infinity	3.3.5
fix(x)	Rounds x to the nearest integer toward zero	3.3.5
floor(x)	Rounds x to the nearest integer toward minus infinity	3.3.5
round(x)	Rounds x to the nearest integer	3.3.5
end	Last element in a vector	3.3.5

Self Test

Use the following questions to check your understanding of the material in this chapter:

True or False

1. A homogeneous collection must consist entirely of numbers.

2. The function `linspace(...)` can create only vectors, whereas the functions `zeros(...)`, `ones(...)`, and `rand(...)` produce either vectors or arrays of any dimension.

3. The `length(...)` function applied to a column vector gives you the number of rows.

4. You can access any element(s) of an array of any dimension using a single index vector.

5. Mathematical or logical operators are allowed only between two arrays of the same shape (rows and columns).

6. You can access data in a vector A with an index vector that is longer than A.

7. You can access data in a vector A with a logical vector that is longer than A.

8. When moving a block of data in the form of specified rows and columns from array A to array B, the shape of the block in A must match the shape of the block in B.

Fill in the Blanks

1. Vector elements have two attributes that make them unique: their _____ and their _____.

2. Vectors can be created using the colon operator, for example, B = `1:3:20`, where the first number is the _____, the second number is the _____, and the third number is the _____.

3. When indexing a source vector with a logical vector, the result will contain the _____ of the source vector corresponding in position to the _____ in the logical vector.

4. The normal precedence of operators can be overruled by the use of
    _____.

5. Arithmetic operations can be performed collectively on the
    individual components of two arrays as long as both arrays
    _____ or one of them is _____.

6. To remove elements from arrays, you write _____ in
    _____.

7. Removing rows or columns from an array is _____,
    and can lead to _____. Wherever possible, use
    _____ to _____.

Programming Projects

1. Vector manipulation is an integral part of MATLAB. Do the following
    exercises using the vector shown below to practice your skills.

    Notes:

    Do not hard code any of the answers for this problem.

    You cannot use iteration for any of the parts of this problem.
    ```
    vec = [4 5 2 8 4 7 2 64 2 57 2 45 7 43 2 5 7 3 3 6523 3 ...
       4 3 0 -65 -343];
    ```
    a. Create a new vector, vecA, that is the same as the vector vec
        except that all of the 2s have been deleted.
    b. Create a new vector, vecR, that is the reverse of vec.
    c. Create a new vector, vecB, that swaps the first and second
        halves of vec, so vecB will contain the second half of vec
        followed by the first half of vec.
    d. Create a new vector, vecS, that contains all of the elements in
        vec that are smaller than 45. The numbers should be in the same
        order as they were in vec.
    e. Create a new vector, vecT, that contains true wherever vec is
        greater than 10 and false everywhere else.
    f. Create a new vector, vec2, that contains every other element of
        vec starting with the second element.
    g. Create a new vector, vec3R, that contains every third element of
        vec starting from the last element and going toward the first
        element in vec.
    h. Create a new vector, vecF, that contains the indices of every
        element in vec that is equal to 2.

    i.   Create a new vector, vecN, that contains the indices of every element in vec that is equal to 2 or 4.

    j.   Create a new vector, vecG, that is the same as vec but with every 2 or 4 at odd indices deleted.

2.   The following two lines are entered at the command prompt:

```
>> x = [ 9 3 0 6 3]
>> y = mod((sqrt(length(((x+5).*[1 2 3 4 5]))*5)),3)
```

What is the value of y?

3.   Consider the following vector in MATLAB:

```
vec = [1 0 0 0 0];
```

Which of the following will produce an error?

    a.   `vec(6) = 1;`

    b.   `vec(4) = [];`

    c.   `vec(0) = 1;`

    d.   `vec([4 5]) = 1;`

    e.   `vec = [[6 [5] vec]];`

4.   The following commands are executed in MATLAB:

```
a = [3, 7, 2, 7, 9, 3, 4, 1, 6];
b = [7];
a(4) = [];
vec1 = a==b;
vec2 = mod(a,2)==0;
c = sum(vec1);
vec3 = vec1+vec2;
d = vec3.*a;
vec4 = find(a > 5);
e = a(vec4) + 5;
vec5 = find(a < 5);
f = vec5.^2;
```

Find the values of c, d, e, and f.

5.   Which of the following statements are false?

    a.   `[a, b] = max([1 2 3;7 8 9])` will return:

        `a = [7 8 9]` and `b = [2 2 2]`.

    b.   `max([1 2 3 4 5])` will return 5.

    c.   Typing `max(1)` at the command prompt will produce an error.

6. You are given the following three vectors:

    ```
    nums1 = [7 1 3 5 32 12 1 99 10 24];
    nums2 = [54 1 456 9 20 45 48 72 61 32 10 94 11];
    nums3 = [44 11 25 41 84 77 998 85 2 3 15];
    ```

    Write a script to create the corresponding vectors newNums1, newNums2, and newNums3 containing every other element of the original vectors, starting with the first element.

    Example:

    ```
    numsEx = [6 3 56 7 8 9 445 6 7 437 357 5 4 3]
    newNumsEx => [6 56 8 445 7 357 4]
    ```

Hint
The solution should look identical for each of the three vectors, with only the names of the vectors changed.

    Note: You cannot type the numbers directly into your answer; that is, if you typed

    ```
    >> newNumsEx = [6 56 8 445 7 357 4]
    ```

    at the command prompt, you will not receive any credit.

7. Write a *single* MATLAB statement that does each of the following:
    a. Creates a plot of the square root of all the odd numbers from 1 to 99. The values on the *y*-axis should line up with the appropriate places on the *x*-axis.
    b. Multiplies all the even columns of all the odd rows of a 10 × 10 array called A by 2.
    c. Given a vector X, returns the number of positive elements in X.

8. Write the commands that take a vector of numbers, *a*, and return a new vector *b*, containing the cubes of the positive numbers in *a*. If a particular number is negative, then 0 is put in its place.

Hint
It might be helpful as an intermediate step to create another vector consisting of only 1s and 0s, corresponding to the positive and negative values of *a*, respectively.

    Example:

    ```
    [1 2 -1 5 6 7 -4 3 -2 0]
    ```

    will produce

    ```
    [1 8 0 125 216 343 0 27 0 0]
    ```

9. You have just been selected to appear on the show *Jeopardy!* this spring. You decide that it might be to your advantage to use MATLAB to generate a matrix representing the values of the questions on the board.

a. Generate the matrix *jeopardy* that consists of 6 columns and 5 rows. The columns are all identical, but the values of the rows range from 200 to 1,000 in equal increments.

b. Next, generate the matrix *doubleJeopardy*, that has the same dimensions as *jeopardy* but whose values range from 400 to 2,000.

c. You've decided to go even one step further and practice for a round that does not even exist yet. Generate the matrix *squaredJeopardy* that contains each entry of the original *jeopardy* matrix squared.

Hint

You can use the array *jeopardy* to help arrive at your answer.

10. The Taylor polynomial is a powerful mathematical tool that helps approximate the value of various functions within a reasonable range of approximation. For example, it helps in the calculation of an irrational number like *e*.

The Taylor polynomial of degree *n* for e^x for any *x* is given by:

$$e^x = 1 + \frac{x}{1!} + \frac{x^2}{2!} + \frac{x^3}{3!} + \frac{x^4}{4!} + \ldots + \frac{x^n}{n!}$$

Using n = 10, write the MATLAB commands to calculate the value of e^2 (x = 2, in the formula). Your final answer should be stored in the variable *e2approx*. You cannot use iteration.

11. You are given a vector `excalibur` of undeterminable length. However, you do know that it has an odd number of elements. `excalibur` is said to be magical if its middle element is a prime number. Write a MATLAB script that will create the variable `sword` that holds either the value `magical` if `excalibur` is magical or the phrase `just a plain sword` if it isn't magical.

You may use the following functions:

a. `isprime(...)`, (e.g., `isprime(3)=1`)

b. `floor(...)`, (e.g., `floor(3.999999)=3`)

12. Given the array A defined as:

```
A = [1 3 2; 2 1 1; 3 2 3];
```

which of the following commands will produce this array?

$$B = \begin{bmatrix} 3 & 2 \\ 2 & 1 \end{bmatrix}$$

a. `B = [A(3,2:3) ; A(2,1:2)];`

b. `B = [A(3,1:2) ; A(2,1:2)];`

c. `B = [A(1,2:3) ; A(1:2,3)'];`

d. `B = [A(3,3:-1:2) ; A(2,2:-1:1)];`

13. Write a script that uses a two-dimensional array A and doubles the size of the array by replicating each item horizontally, vertically, and diagonally.

    You should not use iteration to solve this problem.

    Example:

    ```
    >> A = [1 4 7; 8 9 3]
       < your script here >
    ans =
            1 1 4 4 7 7
            1 1 4 4 7 7
            8 8 5 5 3 3
            8 8 5 5 3 3
    ```

14. Write a script that changes one array a into another array b of the same size. The first number in each row of b is the "macho" number; it cannot stand to have any larger numbers following it on the row. Any number larger than it on the row is set to zero.

    Example:

    ```
    >> a = [1 2 3; 5 4 3; 9 10 8]
       < your script here>
    ans =
         1   0   0
         5   4   3
         9 0   8
    ```

15. Write a script to process a two-dimensional array named A. This script will calculate the product of the even values in each row and store that product in a vector. If a row has one even value, the product will be simply that value. If there aren't any even values, the product is one.

    Example:

    ```
    A = [1 2 4; 3 6 9; 0 6 8; 5 7 9]
       < your script here>
    ans = [8 6 0 1]
    ```

16. Write a script called *createArray* that does the following:
    a. Considers a positive integer N that is divisible by *either* two or three.
    b. Creates an array filled with all the numbers from one to N.

c.   If N is divisible by two, the script should produce a two-column array; otherwise, it should produce a three-column array.

d.   Returns the filled array.

   Note: You can use the MATLAB function `rem(x,y)` to check whether the remainder of dividing x by y is equal to zero. Also, it does not matter if your result is in ascending or descending order.

   Examples:

```
>> N = 8
      < your script here>
   ans =
         8      7
         6      5
         4      3
         2      1
>> N = 9
      <your script here>
   ans =
         9      8      7
         6      5      4
         3      2      1
```

17.   Write a script called *multiples* that processes an array (of any dimensionality) called `numbers` and a number called `divisor`, and creates a vector called `multiplesVec` that contains only those elements of `numbers` that are multiples of `divisor`. If there aren't any elements in the array `numbers` or the resulting vector, your script should produce an empty vector.

Hint

You shouldn't need iteration to solve this problem.

Note: You can use the MATLAB function `rem(x,y)` to check whether the remainder of dividing x by y is equal to zero.

18.   Write a script to create a multiplication table. This should be a 10 by 10 array where the product of `1*1` is in the upper-left square and the product of `10*10` is in the bottom right. The beginning should look like this:

1	2	3	4	...
2	4	6	8	...
3	6	9	12	...
4	8	12	16	...
...	...	...	...	...

19. Write a script called *getMMM* that will process a matrix of any size, iterate through the entire matrix, and compute the minimum, maximum, and mean of all the elements of the matrix.

    Note: Do not use the `min`, `max`, or `mean` built-in functions.

20. Write a script called *pyramid* that processes a positive, odd integer `N` and produces an `N` by `(2* N - 1)` array containing a pyramid of numbers.

    Example:

    ```
    N = 5:
    ans =
    [0 0 0 0 1 0 0 0 0
     0 0 0 2 1 2 0 0 0
     0 0 3 2 1 2 3 0 0
     0 4 3 2 1 2 3 4 0
     5 4 3 2 1 2 3 4 5]
    ```

CHAPTER 4

Execution Control

Chapter Objectives

This chapter discusses techniques for changing the flow of control of a program, which may be necessary for two reasons:

- You may want to execute some parts of the code under certain circumstances only

- You may want to repeat a section of code a certain number of times

In Chapter 3 we used the array notation to gather numbers into a form where they could be processed collectively rather than individually. This chapter deals with collections of lines of code (**code blocks**) that solve a particular segment of a problem in the same way. We will see how to define a code block, how to decide to execute a code block under certain conditions only, and how to repeat execution of a code block.

4.1 Concept: Code Blocks

4.2 Conditional Execution in General

4.3 `if` Statements
   4.3.1 General Template
   4.3.2 MATLAB Implementation
   4.3.3 Important Ideas

4.4 `switch` Statements
   4.4.1 General Template
   4.4.2 MATLAB Implementation

4.5 Iteration in General

4.6 `for` Loops
   4.6.1 General `for` Loop Template
   4.6.2 MATLAB Implementation
   4.6.3 Indexing Implementation
   4.6.4 Breaking a `for` Loop

4.7 `while` Loops
   4.7.1 General `while` Template
   4.7.2 MATLAB `while` Loop Implementation
   4.7.3 MATLAB Loop-and-a-Half Implementation
   4.7.4 Breaking a `while` Loop

4.8 Engineering Example—Computing Liquid Levels

4.1 Concept: Code Blocks

Some languages identify code blocks by enclosing them in braces (`{. . .}`); others identify them by the level of indentation of the text. MATLAB uses the occurrence of key command words in the text to define the extent of code blocks. Keywords like `if`, `switch`, `while`, `for`, `case`, `otherwise`, `else`, `elseif`, and `end` are identified with blue coloring by the MATLAB text editor. They are not part of the code block, but they serve as instructions on what to do with the code block and as delimiters that define the extent of the code block.

 ## 4.2 Conditional Execution in General

To this point, the statements written in our scripts have been executed in sequence from the instruction at the top to the instruction at the bottom. However, it is frequently necessary to make choices about how to process a set of data based on some characteristic of that data. We have seen logical expressions that result in a Boolean result—`true` or `false`. This section discusses the code that implements the idea shown in Figure 4.1.

In the flowchart shown in Figure 4.1 a set of statements (the code block to be executed) is shown as a rectangle, a decision point is shown as a diamond, and the flow of program control is indicated by arrows. When decision points are drawn, there will be at least two arrows leaving that symbol, each labeled with the reason one would take that path.

This concept makes the execution of a code block conditional upon some test. If the result of the test is `true`, the code block is executed. Otherwise, the code block is omitted and the instruction(s) after the end of that code block are executed next.

An important generalization of this concept is shown in Figure 4.2. Here the solution is generalized to permit the first code block to be implemented under the first condition as before. Now, however, if that first logical test

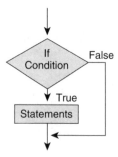

Figure 4.1 *A simple conditional statement*

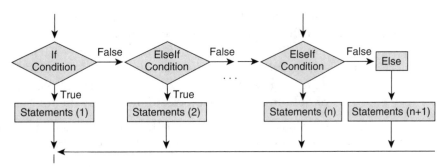

Figure 4.2 *A compound conditional statement*

returns `false`, a second test is performed to determine whether the second code block should be executed. If that test returns `false`, as many further tests as necessary may be performed, each with the appropriate code block to be implemented when the result is `true`. Finally, if none of these tests returns true, the last code block, usually identified by the `else` keyword—(n + 1) in the figure—is executed. As the flowchart shows, as soon as one of the code blocks is executed, the next instruction to execute is the one that follows the conditional code after the `end` statement.

In particular, if there is no `else` clause, it is possible that no code at all is executed in this conditional statement.

There are two common styles in which to implement this conditional behavior. First we will discuss the most general form, the `if` statement, and then we will discuss the more restrictive, but tidier, `switch` statement. Both implementations are found in most modern languages, albeit with slightly different syntax. In each case, the code block to be implemented is all the statements between the introductory test statement and the next test statement or the end of the conditional.

4.3 `if` Statements

Here we introduce the concept of a programming template. Many programming texts still use the idea of **flowcharts**, such as those illustrated in Figures 4.1 and 4.2, to describe the design of a solution in a manner independent of the code implementation. However, since this graphical form cannot be maintained with a text editor, if the design of the solution changes during coding, it is difficult to maintain any design description that is separate from the code itself.

Throughout the remainder of this text, we will describe the overall design of a code module using a **design template**. Design templates are a textual form of flowchart consisting of the key words that control program flow and placeholders that identify the code blocks and expressions that are necessary to implement the solution logic. Design templates are powerful tools for the novice programmer to overcome the "blank sheet of paper" problem—"how do I start solving this problem?" All programmers need to do is recognize the nature of the solution and write down the appropriate template. Then solving a particular problem becomes the relatively simple task of defining the code blocks identified by the template.

To discuss the `if` statement, first we consider its general, language-independent template and then its MATLAB implementation.

4.3.1 General Template

Template 4.1 shows the general template for the `if` statement.

Note the following:

- The only essential ingredients are the first `if` statement, one code block, and the `end` statement. All other features may be added as the logic requires.
- The code blocks may contain any sequence of legal MATLAB statements, including other `if` statements (nested `if`s), `switch` statements, or iterations (see Section 4.5).
- Nested `if` statements with a code block are an alternative implementation of a logical AND statement.
- Recall that logical operations can be applied to a vector, resulting in a vector of Boolean values. This vector may be used as a logical expression. The `if` statement will accept this expression as `true` if all of the elements are `true`.

4.3.2 MATLAB Implementation

Listing 4.1 shows the MATLAB solution to a typical logical problem: determining whether a day is a weekday or a weekend day. It is assumed that the variable `day` is a number containing integer values from 1 to 7.

Template 4.1 General template for the `if` statement

```
if <logical expression 1>
    <code block 1>
elseif <logical expression 2>
    <code block  2>
      .
      .
      .
elseif <logical expression n>
    <code block  n>
else
    <default code block>
end
```

Listing 4.1 if statement example

```
1. if day == 7        % Saturday
2.   state = 'weekend'
3. elseif day == 1    % Sunday
4.   state = 'weekend'
5. else
6.   state = 'weekday'
7. end
```

In Listing 4.1:

Line 1: The first logical expression determines whether day is 7.

Line 2: The corresponding code block sets the value of the variable state to the string 'weekend'. In general, there can be as many statements within a code block as necessary.

Line 3: The second logical expression determines whether day is 6.

Line 4: The corresponding code block also sets the value of the variable state to the string 'weekend'.

Line 5: The key word else introduces the default code block executed when none of the previous tests pass.

Line 6: The default code block sets the value of the variable state to the string 'weekday'.

Exercise 4.1 gives you the opportunity to practice using if statements, and Listing 4.2 shows a script that will satisfy Exercise 4.1.

 Exercise 4.1 Using if statements

Do It Yourself

Write a script that uses input(...) to request a numerical grade in percentage and uses if statements to convert that grade to a letter grade according to the following table:

90% and better: A

80%–90%: B

70%–80%: C

60%–70%: D

Below 60%: F

Test your script by running it repeatedly for legal and illegal values of the grade percentage.

Check your work against the script shown in Listing 4.2.

Listing 4.2 Script with `if` statements

```
1. grade = input('what grade? ');
2. if grade >= 90
3.      letter = 'A'
4. elseif grade >= 80
5.      letter = 'B'
6. elseif grade >= 70
7.      letter = 'C'
8. elseif grade >= 60
9.      letter = 'D'
10. else
11.      letter = 'F'
12. end
```

In Listing 4.2:

Line 1: Requests a grade value from the user with the `input(...)` function. The prompt appears in the Command window, and the system waits for a line of text from the user and converts that line as it would any other Command window line, returning the result to the variable `grade`.

Line 2: The first logical expression looks for the grade that earns an A.

Line 3: The corresponding code block sets the value of the variable `letter` to `'A'`.

Lines 4–9: The corresponding logic for letter grades B, C, and D.

Lines 10–12: The default logic setting the variable `letter` to `'F'`.

4.3.3 Important Ideas

There are two important ideas that are necessary for the successful implementation of `if` statements: the general form of the logical expressions and short-circuit analysis.

Logical Expressions The `if` statement requires a logical expression for its condition. A logical expression is any collection of constants, variables, and operators whose result is a Boolean `true` or `false` value. Unfortunately, the MATLAB Command window echoes Boolean results as 1 (`true`) or 0 (`false`). In fact, in many (but not all) cases MATLAB will treat an array of logical results as if they were numerical values.

Logical expressions can be created in the following ways:

- The value of a Boolean constant (e.g., `true` or `false`)
- The value of a variable containing a Boolean result (e.g., `found`)
- The result of a logical operation on two scalar quantities (e.g., `A > 5`)

- The result of logically negating a Boolean quantity using the unary negation operator (e.g., ~found)
- The result of combining multiple scalar logical expressions with the operators && or || (e.g., A && B or A || B)
- The results of the MATLAB functions that are the logical equivalent of the &&, ||, and ~ operators: and(A, B) or(A, B) and not(A)
- The results of other MATLAB functions that operate on Boolean vectors: any(...) and all(...)

The result from any(...) will be true if any logical value in the vector is true. The result from all(...) will be true only if all logical values in the vector are true. The function ll(...) is implicitly called by MATLAB if you supply a vector of logical values to the if statement, as shown in Listing 4.3.

In Listing 4.3:

Line 1: Makes the variable A a logical vector.

Line 2: Using this as a logical expression internally converts this expression to all(A).

Line 3: All the values of A are not true; therefore, this code body does not execute.

Line 4: The end of the first code body and of the first ID statement.

Line 5: Now, all the elements of A are true.

Lines 6–8: If we repeat the test, the code body will now execute.

Short-Circuit Evaluation When evaluating a sequence of logical && or ||, MATLAB will stop processing when it finds the first result that makes all subsequent processing irrelevant. This concept is best illustrated by an example. Assume that A and B are logical results and you want to evaluate A && B. Since the result of this is true only if both A and B are true, if you evaluate A and the result is false, no value of B can change the outcome A && B. Therefore there is no reason to evaluate any more components of a logical and expression once a false result has been found. Similarly, if you want A || B, if A is found to be true, you do not need to evaluate B.

Listing 4.3 The if statement with a logical vector

```
1. A = [true true false]
2. if A
3.    % will not execute
4. end
5. A(3) = true;
6. if A
7.    % will execute
8. end
```

For example, suppose you want to test the *n*th element of a vector v using a variable n, and you are concerned that n might not be a legal index value. The following code could be used:

```
if (n <= length(v)) && (v(n) > 0)
    % success!
end
```

If n were not a legal index, the indexed accessor v(n) would cause an error for attempting to reach beyond the end of the vector. However, by putting the test of n first, the short-circuit logic would not process the second part of the expression if the test of n failed.

 ## 4.4 `switch` Statements

`switch` statements implement the logic shown in Figure 4.2 in a different programming style by allowing the programmer to consider a number of different cases for the value of one variable. First we consider the general, language-independent template for `switch` statements, and then its MATLAB implementation.

4.4.1 General Template

Template 4.2 shows the general template for the `switch` statement.

Note the following:

- All tests refer to the value of the same parameter
- `case` specifications may be either a single value or a set of parameters enclosed in braces { ... }
- `otherwise` specifies the code block to be executed when none of the case values apply
- The code blocks may contain any sequence of legal MATLAB statements, including other `if` statements (nested `if`s), `switch` statements, or iterations

Template 4.2 General template for the `switch` statement

```
switch <parameter>
   case <case specification 1>
      <code block 1>
   case <case specification 2>
      <code block 2>
   .
   .
   case <case specification n>
      <code block n>
   otherwise
      <default code block>
end
```

4.4.2 MATLAB Implementation

Listing 4.4 shows the MATLAB implementation of a typical logical problem: determining the number of days in a month. It assumes the value of `month` is 1 … 12, and `leapYear` is a Boolean variable identifying the current year as a leap year.

Hint

The second parameter to the `input(...)` statement prevents MAT-LAB from attempting to parse the data provided, returning a string instead. Without that activity suppressed, if you enter the string `'yes'`, MATLAB will rush off looking for a variable by that name.

Style Points

1. The use of indentation is not required in MATLAB, and it has no significance with regard to syntax. However, the appropriate use of indentation greatly improves the legibility of code and you should use it. You have probably already noted that in addition to colorizing control statements, the MATLAB text editor automatically places the control statements in the indented positions illustrated in Listings 4.3 and 4.4.

2. It is good practice to include `otherwise` in a `switch` statement and `else` in an `if` statement to trap illegal values. The `otherwise` and `else` clauses should not be used in the main thread of your program unless you are confident that it is safe to use for all incoming values.

In Listing 4.4:

Line 1: All tests refer to the value of the variable `month`.

Line 2: This `case` specification is a cell array containing the numbers of the months with 30 days.

Line 4: The code blocks extend from the `case` statement to the next control statement (`case`, `otherwise`, or `end`).

Line 6: This code block contains an `if` statement to deal with the February case. It presumes that a Boolean variable `leapYear` has been created to indicate whether this month is in a leap year.

Line 11: The remaining months. The usual description of the logic suggests that this could be the `otherwise` clause. However, that would prevent you from being able to detect bad month number values, as this code does.

Listing 4.4 Example of a `switch` statement

```
1.  switch month
2.     case {9, 4, 6, 11}
3.         % Sept, Apr, June, Nov
4.            days = 30;
5.     case 2                % Feb
6.        if leapYear
7.              days = 29;
8.           else
9.              days = 28;
10.          end
11.    case {1, 3, 5, 7, 8, 10, 12}
12.       % other months
```

continued on next page

```
13.                 days = 31;
14.      otherwise
15.                 error('bad month index')
16. end
```

 Exercise 4.2 Using the `switch` statement

Do It Yourself

Write and test the script in Listing 4.4 using `input(...)` to request a numerical month value.

You will need to preset a value for `leapYear`.

Test your script by running it repeatedly for legal and illegal values of the month.

Modify your script to ask whether the current year is a leap year. (It's best to ask only for February.) You could use code like the following:

```
ans = input('leap year (yes/no)', 's');
leapYear = (ans(1) == 'y');
```

Test this new script thoroughly.

Try this script without the second parameter to `input(...)`. Can you explain what is happening?

Modify the script again to accept the year rather than yes/no, and implement the logic to determine whether that year is a leap year.

Line 15: A built-in MATALB function that announces the error and terminates the script.

Try using the `switch` statement in Exercise 4.2.

 ## 4.5 Iteration in General

Iteration allows controlled repetition of a code block. Control statements at the beginning of the code block specify the manner and extent of the repetition:

- The `for` loop is designed to repeat its code block a fixed number of times and largely automates the process of managing the iteration.
- The `while` loop is more flexible in character. In contrast to the fixed repetition of the `for` loop, its code block can be repeated a variable number of times, depending on the values of data being processed. It is much more of a "do-it-yourself" iteration kit.

The `if` and `switch` statements allow us to decide to skip code blocks based on conditions in the data. The `for` and `while` constructs allow us to repeat code blocks. Note, however, that the MATLAB language is designed to avoid iteration. Under most circumstances of processing numbers, the array processing operations built into the language make do-it-yourself loop constructs unnecessary.

4.6 `for` Loops

Figure 4.3 shows a simple `for` loop. The hexagonal shape illustrates the control of repetition. The repeated execution of the code block is performed under the control of a loop-control variable. It is first set to an initial value that is tested against a terminating condition. If the terminating test succeeds, the program leaves the `for` loop. Otherwise, the computations in the code block are performed using the current value of that variable. When one pass through the code block is finished, the variable is updated to its next value, and control returns to the termination test.

4.6.1 General `for` Loop Template

The general template for implementing `for` loops is shown in Template 4.3. All of the mechanics of iteration control are handled automatically in the variable specification section. In some languages—especially those with their origins in C—the variable specification is a formidable collection of statements that provide great generality of loop management. The designers of MATLAB, with its origins in matrix processing, chose a much simpler approach for specifying the variable range, as shown in the general template.

The repetition of the code block is managed completely by the specification of the loop control variable.

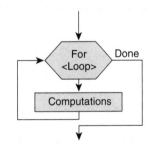

Figure 4.3 *Structure of a* `for` *loop*

Template 4.3 General template for the `for` statement

```
for <variable specification>
      <code block>
end
```

4.6.2 MATLAB Implementation

The core concept in the MATLAB `for` loop implementation is in the style of the variable specification, which is accomplished as follows:

```
<variable specification>: <variable> = <vector>
```

where `<variable>` is the name of the loop control variable and `<vector>` is any vector that can be created by the techniques discussed in Chapter 3. If we were to use the variable specification x = A, MATLAB would proceed as follows:

1. Set the value of x to A(1)
2. Evaluate the code block with that value of x
3. Advance x to the next value in A
4. Repeat Steps 2 and 3 until x exceeds the range of A

For a simple example of `for` loops, the code shown in Listing 4.5 solves a problem that should be done in a single MATLAB instruction: `max(A)` where A is a vector of integers. However, by expanding this into a `for` loop, we see the basic structure of the `for` loop at work.

In Listing 4.5:

Line 1: Creates a vector A with six elements.

Line 2: The tidiest way to find limits of a collection of numbers is to seed the result, `theMax`, with the first number, which avoids the problem of seeding the result with a value that is already outside the range of the vector. For example, we might think that `theMax = 0;` would be a satisfactory seed. However, this would not do well if all the elements of A were negative.

Line 3: The loop-control mechanism as described above.

Lines 4–6: The code block extends from the `for` statement to the associated `end` statement. The code will be executed the same number of times as the length of A *even if you change the value of x within the code block*. At each iteration the value of x will be set to the next element from the array A.

Listing 4.5 Example of a `for` statement

```
1. A = [6 12 6 91 13 6]  % initial vector
2. theMax = A(1);         % set initial max value
3. for x = A              % iterate through A
4.     if x > theMax      % test each element
5.             theMax = x;
6.     end
7. end
8. fprintf('max(A) is %d\n', theMax);
```

Line 8: The `fprintf(...)` function is a very flexible means of formatting output to the Command window. See the discussion in Chapter 8, or enter the following in the Command window:

```
> help fprintf
```

4.6.3 Indexing Implementation

The above for loop implementation may seem very strange to those with a C-based language background, in which the loop-control variable is usually an index into the array being traversed rather than an element from that array. In order to illustrate the difference, we will adapt the code from Listing 4.5 to solve a slightly different problem that approximates the behavior of `max(A)`. This time we need to know not only the maximum value in the array, but also its index. This requires that we resort to indexing the array in a more conventional style, as shown in Listing 4.6.

In Listing 4.6:

Line 1: Generalizes the creation of the vector A using the `rand(...)` function to create a vector with 10 elements each between zero and 100.

Lines 2 and 3: Initialize `theMax` and `theIndex`.

Line 4: Creates an anonymous vector of indices from 1 to the length of A and uses it to define the loop-control variable, `index`.

Line 5: Extracts the appropriate element from A to operate with as before.

Lines 6 and 7: The same comparison logic as shown in Listing 4.5.

Line 8: In addition to saving the new max value, we save the index where it occurs.

Line 11: This is the first occurrence of an example where a logical line of code extends beyond the physical limitations of a single line.

Listing 4.6 for statement using indexing

```
 1. A = floor(rand(1,10)*100)
 2. theMax = A(1);
 3. theIndex = 1;
 4. for index = 1:length(A)
 5.     x = A(index);
 6.     if x > theMax
 7.         theMax = x;
 8.         theIndex = index;
 9.     end
10. end
11. fprintf('the max value in A is %d at %d\n', ...
12.             theMax, theIndex);
```

Exercise 4.3 Producing `for` statement results

Do It Yourself

Enter and run the scripts in Listings 4.5 and 4.6. They should each produce the following results:

```
A =
   6  12  6  91  13  61  26  22  71  54
the max value in A is 91 at 4
>>
```

Since MATLAB normally uses the end of the line to indicate the end of an operation, we use the ellipses (. . .) to specify that the logic is continued onto the next line.

You can enter and run these scripts in Exercise 4.3.

Style Points

We wrote the `for` loop examples in two styles: the direct access style and the indexing style. Many people code in the indexing style even when the index value is not explicitly required. This is slightly tacky and demonstrates some ignorance of the full power of the MATLAB language.

4.6.4 Breaking a `for` Loop

If you are in a `for` loop and find a circumstance where you really do not want to continue iterating, the `break` statement will skip immediately out of the innermost containing `for` loop. If you want to continue iterating but omit all further steps of this iteration, you can use the `continue` statement.

 4.7 `while` Loops

We use `while` loops in general for more control over the number of times the iteration is repeated. Figure 4.4 illustrates the control flow for a `while` loop. Since the termination test is performed before the loop is entered, the loop control expression must be initialized to a state that will normally permit loop entry. It is possible that the code block is not executed at all—for example—if there is no data to process.

4.7.1 General `while` Template

Template 4.4 shows the general template for implementing `while` loops. The logical expression controlling the iteration is testing some state of the workspace; therefore, two things that were automatic in the `for` loop must be

Template 4.4 General template for the `while` statement

```
<initialization>
while <logical expression>
      <code block>    % must make some changes
            % to enable the loop to terminate
end
```

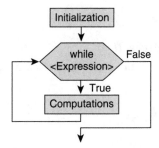

Figure 4.4 *Structure of a* while *Loop*

manually accomplished with the while loop: initializing the test and updating the workspace in the code block so that the test will eventually fail and the iteration will stop.

4.7.2 MATLAB while Loop Implementation

For the sake of consistency, Listing 4.7 shows you how to solve the same problem using the while syntax.

In Listing 4.7:

> Lines 1–3: Creates a test vector and initializes the answers as before.
>
> Line 4: Initializes the index value since this is manually updated.
>
> Line 5: This test will fail immediately if the vector A is empty.
>
> Line 6: Extracts the item x from the array (good practice in general to clarify your code).
>
> Lines 7–9: The same test as before to update the maximum value.
>
> Line 11: "Manually" updates the index to move the loop closer to finishing.

Enter and run the script as described in Exercise 4.4.

Listing 4.7 while statement example

```
1. A = floor(rand(1,10)*100)
2. theMax = A(1);
3. theIndex = 1;
4. index = 1;
5. while index <= length(A)
6.      x = A(index);
7.      if x > theMax
8.          theMax = x;
9.          theIndex = index;
10.     end
11.     index = index + 1;
12. end
13. fprintf('the max value in A is %d at %d\n', ...
14.             theMax, theIndex);
```

Exercise 4.4 Producing `while` statement results

Do It Yourself

Enter and run the script in Listing 4.7. It should produce the following results:

```
A =
  6 12 6 91 13 61 26 22 71 54
the max value in A is 91 at 4
>>
```

4.7.3 MATLAB Loop-and-a-Half Implementation

Listing 4.8 illustrates the implementation of the loop-and-a-half iteration style, in which we must enter the loop and perform some computation before realizing that we do not need to continue. Here we continually ask the user for the radius of a circle until an illegal radius is entered, which is our cue to terminate the iteration. For each radius entered, we want to display the area and circumference of the circle with that radius.

Style Points

The use of `break` and `continue` statements is frowned upon in programming circles for the same reason that the `goto` statement has fallen into disrepute —they make it more difficult to understand the flow of control through a complex program. It is preferable to express the logic for remaining in a `while` loop explicitly in its controlling Boolean expression, combined with `if` statements inside the loop to skip blocks of code. However, sometimes this latter approach causes code to be more complex than would be the case with judicious use of `break` or `continue`.

In Listing 4.8:

Line 1: Initializes the radius value to allow the loop to be entered the first time.

Line 2: We will remain in this loop until the user enters an illegal radius.

Line 3: The `input(...)` function shows the user the text string, translates what is typed, and stores the result in the variable provided. This is described fully in Chapter 8.

Line 4: We want to present the area and circumference only if the radius has a legal value. Since this test occurs in the middle of the `while` loop, we call this "loop-and-a-half" processing.

Try this script in Exercise 4.5.

Listing 4.8 Loop-and-a-half example

```
 1. R = 1;
 2. while R > 0
 3.     R = input('Enter a radius: ');
 4.     if R > 0
 5.         area = pi * R^2;
 6.         circum = 2 * pi * R;
 7.         fprintf('area = %f; circum = %f\n', ...
 8.             area, circum);
 9.     end
10. end
```

Exercise 4.5 Producing loop-and-a-half test results

Do It Yourself

Enter and run the script in Listing 4.8. It should produce the following results:

```
Enter a radius: 4
area = 50.265482; circum = 25.132741
Enter a radius: 3
area = 28.274334; circum = 18.849556
Enter a radius: 100
area = 31415.926536; circum = 628.318531
Enter a radius: 0
>>
```

4.7.4 Breaking a `while` loop

As with the `for` loop, `break` will exit the innermost `while` loop, and `continue` will skip to the end of the loop but remain within it.

 4.8 Engineering Example—Computing Liquid Levels

Figure 4.5 shows a cylindrical tank of height *H* and radius *r* with a spherical cap on each end (also of radius, *r*). If the height of the liquid is *h*, what is the volume of liquid in the tank?

Clearly, the calculation of the volume of liquid in the tank depends upon the relationship between *h*, *H*, and *r*:

- If *h* is less than *r*, we need the volume, *v*, of a partially filled sphere given by:

$$v = \frac{1}{3}\pi h^2 (3r - h)$$

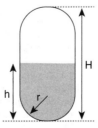

Figure 4.5 *A tank containing liquid*

- If h is greater than r but less than $H - r$, we need the volume of a fully filled hemisphere plus the volume of a cylinder of height $h - r$:

$$v = \frac{2}{3}\pi r^3 + \pi r^2(h - r)$$

- If h is greater than $H - r$, we need the volume of a fully filled sphere plus the volume of a cylinder of height $H - 2r$ minus the partially empty upper hemisphere of height $H - h$:

$$v = \frac{4}{3}\pi r^3 + \pi r^2(H - 2r) - \frac{1}{3}\pi(H - h)^2(3r - H + h)$$

The script to perform this calculation is shown in Listing 4.9. Rather than performing the computations for one liquid level only, we should write the script so that we continue to consider tanks of different dimensions and different liquid heights for each tank until the user indicates that he needs no more results.

In Listing 4.9:

Line 1: Initializes the value to keep it in the first `while` loop.

Lines 3 and 4: Get the tank sizes.

Line 5: Initializes the value to keep it in the inner `while` loop.

Line 7: Gets the liquid height.

Lines 8–14: Calculations for legal values of h. Notice that no dot operators are required here, because these conditional computations will not work correctly with vectors of H, r, or h.

Lines 15 and 16: Illegal h values end up here.

Line 17: Goes to the end of the loop, skipping the printout.

Lines 19–21: Print the result.

Line 22: More heights when "y" is entered.

Line 24: Another tank when "y" is entered.

Listing 4.10 shows some typical results.

Listing 4.9 Script to compute liquid levels

```
1. another_tank = true;
2. while another_tank
3.     H = input('Overall tank height: ');
4.     r = input('tank radius: ');
5.     more_heights = true;
6.     while more_heights
7.         h = input('liquid height: ');
8.         if h < r
9.             v = (1/3)*pi*h.^2.*(3*r-h);
```

continued on next page

```
10.        elseif h < H-r
11.            v = (2/3)*pi*r^3 + pi*r^2*(h-r);
12.        elseif h <= H
13.            v = (4/3)*pi*r^3 + pi*r^2*(H-2*r) ...
14.                - (1/3)*pi*(H-h)^2*(3*r-H+h);
15.        else
16.            disp('liquid level too high')
17.            continue
18.        end
19.        fprintf( ...
20.        'rad %0.2f ht %0.2f level %0.2f vol %0.2f\n', ...
21.                r,       H,         h,      v);
22.        more_heights = input('more levels? (y/n)','s')=='y';
23.    end
24.    another_tank = input('another tank? (y/n)','s')=='y';
25. end
```

| **Listing 4.10** Results for liquid levels

```
Overall tank height: 10
tank radius: 2
liquid height: 1
radius 2.00 height 10.00 level 1.00 vol 5.24
more levels? (y/n)y
liquid height: 2
radius 2.00 height 10.00 level 2.00 vol 16.76
more levels? (y/n)y
liquid height: 4
radius 2.00 height 10.00 level 4.00 vol 41.89
more levels? (y/n)y
liquid height: 8
radius 2.00 height 10.00 level 8.00 vol 92.15
more levels? (y/n)y
liquid height: 9
radius 2.00 height 10.00 level 9.00 vol 103.67
more levels? (y/n)y
liquid height: 10
radius 2.00 height 10.00 level 10.00 vol 108.91
more levels? (y/n)y
liquid height: 11
liquid level too high
liquid height: 10
radius 2.00 height 10.00 level 10.00 vol 108.91
more levels? (y/n)n
another tank? (y/n)y
Overall tank height: 8
tank radius: 4
liquid height: 4
radius 4.00 height 8.00 level 4.00 vol 134.04
more levels? (y/n)y
liquid height: 8
radius 4.00 height 8.00 level 8.00 vol 268.08
more levels? (y/n)
another tank? (y/n)
```

Chapter Summary

This chapter presented techniques for changing the flow of control of a program for condition execution and repetitive execution:

- The most general conditional form is the `if` statement, with or without the accompanying `elseif` and `else` statements
- The `switch` statement considers different cases of the values of a countable variable
- A `for` loop in its most basic form executes a code block for each of the elements of a vector
- A `while` loop repeats a code block a variable number of times, as long as the conditions specified for continuing the repetition remain true

 Special Characters, Reserved Words, and Functions

Special Characters, Reserved Words, and Functions	Description	Discussed in This Section
`false`	Logical false	4.2
`true`	Logical true	4.2
`break`	A command within a loop module that forces control to the statement following the innermost loop	4.6.4, 4.7.4
`case`	A specific value within a `switch` statement	4.1, 4.4.1
`continue`	Skips to the end of the innermost loop, but remains inside it	4.6.4, 4.7.4
`else`	Within an `if` statement, begins the code block executed when the condition is false	4.1, 4.3.2
`elseif`	Within an `if` statement, begins a second test when the first condition is false	4.1, 4.3.2
`end`	Terminates an `if`, `switch`, `for` or `while` module	4.1, 4.3.2, 4.4.1, 4.6
`for var = v`	A code module repeats as many times as there are elements in the vector `v`	4.1, 4.6
`if <exp>`	Begins a conditional module; the following code block is executed if the logical expression `<exp>` is true	4.1, 4.3.2
`input(str)`	Requests input from the user	4.3.2
`otherwise`	Catch-all code block at the end of a `switch` statement	4.1, 4.4.1
`switch(variable)`	Begins a code module selecting specific values of the `variable` (must be countable)	4.1, 4.4.1

Special Characters, Reserved Words, and Functions	Description	Discussed in This Section
while <exp>	A code module repeats as long as the logical expression <exp> is true	4.1
all(a)	True if all the values in a, a logical vector, are true	4.3.3
and(a, b)	True if both a and b are true	4.3.3
any(a)	True if any of the values in a, a logical vector, is true	4.3.3
not(a)	True if a is false; false if a is true	4.3.3
or(a, b)	True if either a or b is true	4.3.3

 ## Self Test

Use the following questions to check your understanding of the material in this chapter:

True or False

1. MATLAB keywords are colored green by the editor.

2. Indentation is required in MATLAB to define code blocks.

3. It is possible that no code at all is executed by if or switch constructs.

4. True is a valid logical expression.

5. When evaluating a sequence of logical && expressions, MATLAB will stop processing when it finds the first true result.

6. The for loop repeats the enclosed code block a fixed number of times even if you modify the index variable within the code block.

7. Using a break statement is illegal in a while loop.

8. The logical expression used in a while loop specifies the conditions for exiting the loop.

Fill in the Blanks

1. MATLAB uses _____ in the text to define the extent of code blocks.

2. The function _____ is implicitly called by MATLAB if you supply a vector of logical values to the if statement.

3. It is good practice to include _____ in a `switch` statement to trap illegal values entering the `switch`.

4. There is no reason to evaluate any more components of a logical or expression once a _____ result has been found.

5. A `while` loop can be repeated a _____ number of times, depending on the _____ being processed.

6. If you are in a _____ loop, you can use the `break` statement to skip immediately out of the _____ loop.

Programming Projects

1. Considering the following script:
   ```
   a = 1;
   b = 2;
   c = 3;
   if ( ( b * c ) == a )
        a = 5;
   else
        a = b + c;
   end
   b = a + (c^2);
   ```
   What is the value of `b` after this is run?

2. Which of the following evaluates to a Boolean `true`?
   a.   `( 5 > 4 ) & ( ( 8 + 4 ) < 11 )`
   b.   `~( ( ( 6 + 4 * 3 ) > 20 ) )`
   c.   `~( ( 4 ~= 4 ) | (~( 6 < ( 4 * 2 / 8 + 4 ) ) ) ) )`

3. You are given the following information: `A = true, B = false`.
   Evaluate:
   a.   `(A && B) || (A && B)`
   b.   `(A || B) && (A || B)`
   c.   `(~(A || B)) || (A && B)`

4. You have two Booleans, x and y. You do not know their values (yet).
   You *do* know the following:
   ```
   X && X = false
   X || Y = true
   ```
   What are the values of x and y?

5. Rewrite the following MATLAB expression using `if` statements in place of the the `or` (`|`) and `and` (`&`) operators.

```
ans = ((a > b) & (b > 100) ) | ( ~((a < b) & (b <100)));
```

6. Write a script that calculates the variable mode, the mode of transport used to travel a certain distance according to the following definition. You are given a variable called `distance` that represents the distance to be covered in feet (1 mile = 5,280 feet).

```
distance <= 2 miles: 'Walk'
2 miles < distance <= 10 miles: 'Bicycle'
10 miles < distance <= 30 miles: 'MARTA'
distance > 30 miles: 'Delta Airlines'
```

7. Rewrite the following MATLAB script using only one `if/else` statement:

```
if (b > 30)
        if (a > b)
                ans = 1;
        end
elseif (b < 30)
        if (b > a)
                ans = 1;
        end
else
        ans = 0;
end
```

Hint

Use the Boolean operators `&` and `|`.

8. Consider a client who wants you to write a simple script to calculate a GPA. Given a value between 0.0 and 4.0 as input, your script is expected to set the value of the variable `letterGrade` to a string according to the following:

```
'A'   for 3.5 <= value <= 4.0
'B'   for 2.5 <= value < 3.5
'C'   for 1.5 <= value < 2.5
'D'   for 0.5 <= value < 1.5
'F'   for 0.0 <= value < 0.5
```

If the input is not valid, your script should set `letterGrade` to 'NA'.

9. Fill in the blank with one of the choices to make this script evaluate so that b = 6:

```
a = 1;
b = 0;
if _____
    b = 6;
else
    b = 2;
end
```

a.   `b && a`

b.   `b || ~a`

c.   `~b`

d.   `~a`

e.   `a == b`

10.   You are given a variable named `sideCount` specifying the number of sides on a geometric figure. You need a string containing the name of the shape according to the value of `sideCount`. Write the instructions to calculate the variable `ans` using the following table:

Value of `sideCount`	Value of `ans`
Less than 3	`'Not a shape'`
3	`'Triangle'`
4	`'Quadrilateral'`
5	`'Pentagon'`
Greater than 5	`'Other'`

11.   You have a friend who has too many clothes to store in a tiny closet. Ready to lend a hand, you offer to help your friend decide whether each piece of clothing is worth saving. You write a script that will compute the value of each piece of clothing.

Each piece of clothing has five attributes that can be used to determine its value. The attributes are:

`condition, color, price, number of matches,` and `comfort.`

Each attribute will be rated on a scale of 1–5. Your script will analyze a vector v of length 5 containing the ratings for each attribute. The order of attributes in the vector is:

`[condition color price matches comfort]`

The script should calculate a variable value between 0 and 100; 100 represents a good piece of clothing, and 0 represents a bad piece of clothing. The points that should be given for each attribute are:

```
Condition:   1 => 0, 2 => 5, 3 => 10, 4 => 15, 5 => 20
Color:       1 => blue => 12
             2 => red (UGA Colors) => 2
             3 => pink => 15
             4 => yellow (GT Colors) => 20
             5 => white => 12
Price:       1 => 8, 2-3 => 16, 4-5 => 20
Matches:     1-2 => 8, 3-5 => 19
Comfort:     1 => 6, 2-3 => 13, 4-5 =>18
```

Note: If a number other than 1–5 is assigned for one of the attributes, then no points should be given.

12. You need a script to compute a normalized class average by the following steps:

Hint

See the built-in function max().

Given a vector of test scores, `tests`, first you compute a new vector, `normTests`, which will contain the test scores on a linear scale from 0 to 100. A zero still corresponds to a zero, and the highest test score will correspond to a 100.

Test this script with:

```
tests = [90 45 76 21 85 97 91 84 79 67 76 72 89 95 55];
```

Add to this script the calculation of the letter grade of the class average:

```
average>90        => A
80<=average<90    => B
70<=average<80    => C
60<=average<70    => D
    average<60    => F
```

Test your script with the following grade vectors:

```
[70 87 95 80 80 78 85 90 66 89 89 100] -> 'B'
[50 90 61 82 75 92 81 76 87 41 31 98] -> 'C'
[10 10 11 32 53 12 34 54 31 30 26 22] -> 'F'
```

13. Fill in the blanks with `for` or `while`:

A _____ loop can loop forever if the loop variable is not updated. A _____ loop always has an index variable.

14. What is the value of `k` at the end of the following code fragment?

```
k = 1;
for i = 1:50
    k = k + mod(i,2);
end
```

15. How many times will the following loop be executed?

```
c =0
i=10;
while i ~= 0
c=c+i;
i=i-3;
end
```

16.   Given below is a code fragment:

```
x = zeros(2*n-1,n);
if mod(n,2) == 0
    for i = 1:n
        x((n - (i - 1)) : (n + ( i - 1)),i) = i;
    end
else
    for i = 1:n
        x(n - (i - 1) : n + ( i- 1), (n - i + 1)) = i;
    end
end
```

What are the results for the following values of n:

```
n = 1:
n = 2:
n = 3:
n = 4:
```

17.   What will be the value of a when this script is executed?

```
a = 0;
b = [1 1 0 1 0];
for i = b(1:end-1)
  a = a + ~i;
end
```

18.   Assume you have the following code block in a script:

```
B = eye(6,6);
for counter = B
    disp(counter);
end
```

How many lines are printed when the code is run?

19.   What is printed when the following code block is run?

```
A = [1 2 3; 4 5 6; 7 8 9];
B = ones(3,3) * 2;
sizeA = size(A);
for pacific = 1:sizeA(1)
    for atlantic = 1:sizeA(2)
        arctic = A(pacific,atlantic);
        while arctic > 1
            B(pacific,atlantic) = B(pacific,atlantic) * 2;
            arctic = arctic - 1;
            if(B(pacific, atlantic) > 100)
                break;
            end
        end
    end
end
disp(B);
```

20.   Complete the following exercises in iteration. Although you will probably see ways to solve these problems without iteration, you must use it for all these solutions.

a. Iterate through the following vector, a, using a for loop, and create a new vector, b, of the same size containing Boolean values. The item in b should be true if the corresponding item in a is positive, and false for all other values.

```
a = [-300 2 5 -63 4 0 5 -23 46 0 896 -230 .23 -.01 22]
```

b. Iterate through the vector, a, using a while loop, and create a new vector, c, containing Boolean values by the same criteria as in exercise a.

c. Iterate through the following string array, d, using a for loop, and create a new vector, f. The item in f should be the character A wherever the corresponding item in d is G, and T wherever the item in d is B. All other characters should not be changed.

```
d =
'GBBBBBGGBGBABGBFBBGGGTGBGBGGBBGGJGGBGKGBLGBGTGGGB'
```

d. Iterate through the string array, d, using a while loop and create a new vector, g, under the same rules as exercise c.

e. Iterate through the following logical array, n, using a for loop, and create a new vector, m, whose item should be 2 wherever the corresponding item in n is true and −1 otherwise.

```
n = [true false false true true true false true...
     false true false false false false true false...
     true false false true true false true true false]
```

f. Iterate through the following array, z, using a while loop. Replace every element with the number 3 until you reach a number larger than 50. Leave the rest unchanged.

```
z = [1 3 4 5 45 7 3 6 7 8 50 4 64 34 32 56 43]
```

21. Now that you are comfortable with iteration, you must solve an interesting problem. It seems that UGA once again dropped the ball, and forgot the value of pi. You are to write a script that repeatedly asks the user for a number and computes an approximation to the value of pi. The script will stop when the user enters a number less than or equal to 0.

You are going to use the following algorithm based on geometric probability. You have a quarter circle inside of a unit square (the quarter circle has area pi/4). You pick a random point inside the square. If it is in the quarter circle, you get a "hit," and if not, you get a "miss." The approximate area of the quarter circle will be given by the number of hits divided by the number of points you chose.

Hint

Use the function `rand(...)` in this problem.

The number entered by the user is the number of points chosen, and the script computes the approximate value of `pi`. Try using 1,000, then 10,000, then 100,000 points and see how much closer you get to the value of `pi`.

22. Write a script that transforms a vector v by raising each element in the vector to the power of its index and then reversing the order of the elements.

Example:

```
V = [4 3 -6 5 2] -> [32 625 -216 9 4]
```

CHAPTER 5

Functions

Chapter Objectives

This chapter discusses the nature, implementation, and behavior of user-defined functions in MATLAB:

- How to define a function

- How data are passed into a function

- How to return data including multiple results

- How to include other functions not needed except as helpers to your own function

Writing a user-defined function allows you to isolate and package together a code block, so you can apply that code block to different sets of input data. We have already made use of some built-in functions like `sin(...)` and `plot(...)` by calling them; this chapter will deal with creating and using your own functions.

5.1 Concepts: Abstraction and Encapsulation

5.2 Black Box View of a Function

5.3 MATLAB Implementation

    5.3.1 General Template

    5.3.2 Function Definition

    5.3.3 Storing and Using Functions

    5.3.4 Calling Functions

    5.3.5 Returning Multiple Results

    5.3.6 Auxiliary Local Functions

    5.3.7 Encapsulation in MATLAB Functions

    5.3.8 Global Variables

5.4 Engineering Example— Measuring a Solid Object

5.1 Concepts: Abstraction and Encapsulation

A **function** is an implementation of procedural abstraction and encapsulation. **Procedural abstraction** is the concept that permits a code block that solves a particular subproblem to be packaged and applied to different data inputs. This is exactly analogous to the concept of data abstraction we discussed in Chapter 3 where individual data items are gathered to form a collection. We have already used a number of built-in procedural abstractions in the form of functions. All the mathematical functions that compute—for example, the sine of a collection of angles or the maximum value of a vector—are procedural abstractions. They allow us to apply a code block about which we know nothing to data sets that we provide. To make use of a built-in function, all we have to do is provide data in the form the function expects, and interpret the results according to the function's specification.

Encapsulation is the concept of putting a wrapper around a collection that you wish to protect from outside influence. Functions encapsulate the code they contain in two ways: the variables declared within the function are not visible from elsewhere, and the function's ability to change the values of variables (otherwise known as causing side effects) is restricted to its own code body.

5.2 Black Box View of a Function

The most abstract view of a function can be seen in Figure 5.1. It consists of two parts: the definition of the interface by which the user passes data items to and from the function, and the code block that produces the results required by that interface. A function definition consists of the following components:

- A name that follows the same syntactic rules as a variable name
- A set of 0 or more parameters provided to the function
- Zero or more results to be returned to the caller of the function

The basic operation of a function begins before execution of the function actually starts. If the function definition requires n parameters, the calling

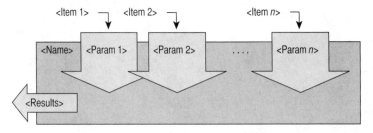

Figure 5.1 *Black box view of a function*

instructions first prepare *n* items of data from its workspace to be provided to the function. These data are then passed to the function, the code body is executed, and the results are returned to the caller.

5.3 MATLAB Implementation

In this section first we consider the general template for implementing functions and then the MATLAB implementation of that template.

5.3.1 General Template

The general layout of a function definition is shown in Template 5.1.

The `<return info>` section for most functions involves providing the name(s) of the results returned followed by an = sign. If more than one result is to be returned, they are defined in a vector-like container. If nothing is to be returned from this function, both the result list and the = sign are omitted.

The `<function name>` is a name with the same syntactic rules as a variable name, and will be used to invoke the code body.

The `<parameters>` section is a comma-separated list of the names of the data to be provided to the function.

The `<documentation>` section is one or more lines of comments that describe what the function does and how to call it. These lines will appear in two situations:

- All the documentation lines up to the first non-document line are printed in the Command window when you type the following:

  ```
  >> help <function name>
  ```

- The first line is listed next to the file name in the Current Directory listing

5.3.2 Function Definition

MATLAB functions must be stored in a separate file located in a directory accessible to any script or function that calls it. The file containing the definition of a function named `function_name` must be `<function_name>.m`. For the general user, the Current Directory is the normal place to store it. Listing 5.1 illustrates a typical MATLAB function called `cylinder` that consumes two parameters, the `height` and `radius` of a cylinder, and produces the return variable `volume`.

Template 5.1 General template for a function

```
function <return info> <function name> (<parameters>)
<documentation>
      <code body>    % must return the results
```

Listing 5.1 Function example

```
1. function volume = cylinder(height, radius)
2. % function to compute the volume of a cylinder
3. % volume = cylinder(height, radius)
4.    base = pi * radius^2;
5.    volume = base * height;
6.
```

In Listing 5.1:

> Line 1: The MATLAB function definition is introduced by the key word `function`, followed by the name of the return variable (if any) and the = sign.
>
> Line 2: All comments written immediately after the function header are available to the Command window when you enter:
>
>> `>>help <function_name>`
>
> The first comment line also appears in the Current Directory window as an indication of the basic purpose of the function.
>
> Line 3: It is a good idea to include in the comments a copy of the function header line, sometimes referred to as the Application Programmer Interface (API), to remind a user exactly how to use this function.
>
> Line 4: Although encapsulation rules forbid access to the caller's variables, the code body still has access to all built-in MATLAB names (for example, `pi`, as used here).
>
> Line 5: You must make at least one assignment to the result variable.
>
> Line 6: The function definition needs no `end` statement. The code body terminates either at the end of the file or at the next function definition in the same file.

Try saving and testing the cylinder function in Exercise 5.1.

 Exercise 5.1 Saving and testing the `cylinder` function

Do It Yourself

Enter the function definition from Listing 5.1 in the Text Editor and save it as `cylinder.m` in your Current Directory. Then enter the following experiments in the Command window. Notice that the first help line appears next to this file name in the Current Directory.

```
>> help cylinder
  function to compute the volume of a cylinder
    volume = cylinder(height, radius)
>> cylinder(1, 1)
ans =
    3.1416
>>
```

5.3.3 Storing and Using MATLAB Functions

All MATLAB functions must be created like scripts in an m-file. When the file is first created, it must be saved in an m-file with the same file name as the function. For example, the function in Listing 5.1 named `cylinder` must be saved in a file named `cylinder.m`.

Once the file has been saved, you may invoke the function by entering its name and parameters of the right type and number in the Command window, in a script, or in other function definitions. If you do not specify an assignment for the result of the function call, it will be assigned to the variable `ans`.

5.3.4 Calling Functions

When a function is defined, the user provides a list of the names of each data item expected to be provided by the caller. These are called the **formal parameters**. When this function is called from the Command window or a code block, the caller must provide the same number of data values expected by the function definition. These are the **actual parameters**, and can be generated in the following ways:

- Constants
- Variables that have been defined
- The result of some mathematical operation(s)
- The result returned from other functions

When the actual parameters have been computed, copies of their values are assigned as the values of the formal parameters the function is expecting. Values are assigned to parameters by position in the calling statement and function definition.

The process of copying the actual parameters into the formal parameters is referred to as "passing by value"—the only technique provided in MATLAB for passing data into a function. Some languages provide an alternative technique—"passing by reference"—wherein the storage location for the parameters remains in the caller's workspace. This is usually a bad thing, allowing deliberate or accidental assignments to "reach back" into the scope of the calling code and thereby perhaps causing undesirable side effects. However, restricting parameter access to passing by value can result in poor program performance.

Once the parameter names have been defined in the function's workspace, the function's code body is executed, beginning with the first instruction. If return variables have been defined for the function, every exit from the code body must assign valid values for the results.

Although the number of parameters is usually fixed, most languages, including MATLAB, provide the ability to deal with a variable number of parameters, both incoming and returning. The built-in MATLAB function `nargin` computes the actual number of parameters provided by the user in the current function call. If the function is sensitive to `nargin`, the user calling this function can provide any values he deems important, and allow the function to set default values for the unnecessary parameters.

Similarly, the function `nargout` computes the number of storage variables actually provided by the user. So if one or more of the results requires extensive computation or user interaction and the caller has not asked for that data, the computation can be omitted.

5.3.5 Returning Multiple Results

MATLAB is unique among programming languages in providing the ability to return more than one result from a function. The multiple results are specified as a vector of variable names: `[area, volume]`, as shown in Listing 5.2. Assignments must be made to each of the result variables. However, the calling program is not required to make use of all the return values.

In Listing 5.2:

> Line 1: Multiple results are specified as a vector of variable names, each of which must be assigned from the code body.

Exercise 5.2 shows how to invoke a function that can return multiple results.

Listing 5.2 `cylinder` function with multiple results

```
1.function [area, volume] = cylinder(height, radius)
2. % function to compute the area and volume
3. %                          of a cylinder
4. % usage: [area, volume]=cylinder(height, radius)
5.     base = pi .* radius.^2;
6.     volume = base .* height;
7.     area = 2 * pi * radius .* height + 2 * base;
```

 Exercise 5.2 Testing multiple returns

Do It Yourself

Adapt the original `cylinder` function as shown in Listing 5.2 and perform the following tests in the Command window:

```
>> [a, v] = cylinder(1, 1)
a =
    6.2832
v =
    3.1416
>> cylinder(1, 1)
ans =
    6.2832
```
continued on next page

```
>> a = cylinder(1, 1)
a =
    6.2832
>> v = cylinder(1, 1)
v =
    6.2832
>>
```

Notice that the normal method to access the multiple answers is to put the names of the variable to receive the results in a vector. The names may be any legal variable name, and the values are returned in the order of the results defined. If you choose less than the full number of results (or none at all), the answers that are specified are allocated from left to right from the available results. As with parameter assignment, the results are allocated by position in these vectors. Although we called the variable v in the last test, it still receives the value of the first result, area. If you really only want the second result value, you must provide a dummy variable for the first, by making the call something like this:

```
[junk, v] = cylinder(1, 1);
```

5.3.6 Auxiliary (Local) Functions

MATLAB uses the name of the file to identify a function; therefore, every function should normally be saved in its own m-file. However, there are times when auxiliary functions are needed to implement the algorithm contained in the main function in a file. If this auxiliary function is only used in the main function, it can be written in the same file as its calling function after the definition of the main function. By convention, many people append the word local_ to the name of local functions. These are also referred to as "helper functions." Calling code can reach only the first function defined in an m-file. Other functions in the m-file, the auxiliary functions, can only be called only from the first function or other auxiliary functions in the same file.

5.3.7 Encapsulation in MATLAB Functions

Encapsulation is accomplished in most modern languages, including MATLAB, by implementing the concept of variable scoping.

Variable scoping defines the locations within your Command window, MATLAB system, and m-files to which variables have access. It is related to the Current Workspace window. When using the Command window or running a script m-file, and you access the value of a variable, the system will reach into your Current Workspace and then into the MATLAB system libraries to find its current value. This is referred to as **Global Scope**. When you write a function, its local variables, including the internal names of its parameters, are not included in your Current Workspace, and it does not look into your Current Workspace for values of variables it needs. This is referred to as **Local Scope**, wherein the variables within a function are not visible from outside and the function is unable to cause side effects by making assignments to outside variables.

To illustrate variable scoping, do Exercise 5.3.

5.3.8 Global Variables

Because MATLAB always copies the input data into the function's workspace, there are occasions when it is very inefficient to pass data into and out of a function. Global variables must be defined in both the calling script and the function using the key word `global`. For example, suppose we collect a large volume of data in a variable `buffer` and do not want to copy the whole buffer into and out of a function that processes that data. In this case we must declare the variable to be global in both the calling space and the called function by placing the following line of code before the variable is first used in both places:

```
global buffer
```

The function will then be able to access and modify the values in `buffer` without having to pass it in and out as a parameter.

Style Points

1. Before you include a function in a complex algorithm, you should always test its behavior in isolation in a script. This test script should validate not only the normal operation of the function, but also its response to erroneous input data it might receive.

2. Although any legal MATLAB instruction is permitted within the code body of a function, it is considered bad form (except temporarily for debugging purposes) to display values in the Command window.

3. We also actively discourage the use of the `input(...)` function within the code body. If you need to input some values to test a function, do so from the Command window or a test script.

 Exercise 5.3 Observing variable scoping

Do It Yourself

Put a break point at Line 6 of your version of the code in Listing 5.2, and then re-run the function by entering:

```
>> [a, v] = cylinder(1, 1)
```

Notice that the logic stops at that break point and the Text Editor displays an arrow. The Workspace window shows you the values of `height`, `radius`, and `base` but none of the variables you left in the workspace for the Command window. The function has no access to other workspaces.

Observe that as you step through the function, the variables appear in the Workspace window and are updated. When you return from the cylinder function to display the results, the Workspace for the function disappears. The calling environment has no access to the variables within the function.

This feature must be used with caution, however, because any function with global access to data is empowered to change that data counter-intuitively.

5.4 Engineering Example—Measuring a Solid Object

Problem:

Consider the disk shown in Figure 5.2. It has a radius *R*, height *h*, and eight cylindrical holes each of radius *r* bored in it. This might be a component of a machine that must be painted and then assembled with other components. During the process of designing this machine, we may need to know the weight of this disk and the amount of paint required to finish it. The weight and the amount of paint for the machine is the sum of the values for each component. Since the weight of our disk is proportional to its volume and the amount of paint is proportional to its "wetted area," we need the volume and area of this disk.

Write a script to compute the volume of the disk and its wetted area.

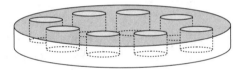

Figure 5.2 *Disk with holes*

Solution:

Listing 5.3 shows the code that solves this problem.

Listing 5.3 Volume and area of a disk

```
1. clear
2. clc

3. h = 1:5;      % set a range of disk thicknesses
4. R = 25;
5. r = 3;

6. [Area Vol] = cylinder(h, R)   % dimensions of large disk
7. [area vol] = cylinder(h, r)   % dimensions of the hole

8. % compute remaining volume
9. Vol = Vol - 8*vol
```

continued on next page

```
10.  % the wetted area is a little messier.  If we total the
11.  % large disk area and the areas of the holes, we get the
12.  % wetted area of the curved edges inside and out.
13.  % However, for each hole, the top and bottom areas have
14.  % been included not only in the top and bottom of the big
15.  % disk, but also as the contributions of each hole.
16.  % From the sum of the top areas, we therefore have to
17.  % remove 32 times the hole top area

18.  Area = Area + 8*(area - 2*2*pi*r.^2)
```

In Listing 5.3:

> Lines 3–5: Set up the disk sizes. Notice that the script works fine with a vector of disk thicknesses to check the behavior as thickness varies.
>
> Line 6: Area and volume of the large disk.
>
> Line 7: Area and volume of one hole.
>
> Line 9: Volume computation.
>
> Lines 10–17: Document the logic behind the area computation.
>
> Line 18: The area computation.

Hint

If you experiment with this script a little, you will discover the power of vector processing for rapidly determining the sensitivity of results to different parameters. The mathematics will not work if you provide vectors for more than one of the given data items. However, vectors supplied for each of them in turn provide insight into the sensitivity of the results to each parameter.

Listing 5.4 shows the results when this code is run. Notice that for thin disks, the area is smaller with the holes. However, as the thickness increases, the area with the holes is larger than without, as one would expect.

Listing 5.4 Volume and area results

```
Area = 4,084 4,241 4,398 4,555 4,712
Vol = 1,963 3,927 5,890 7,854 9,817
area = 75 94 113 132 151
vol = 28 57 85 113 141
Vol = 1,737 3,474 5,212 6,949 8,687
Area = 3,782 4,090  4,398 4,706 5,014
```

 Chapter Summary

This chapter showed you how to encapsulate a code block to allow it to be re-used:

- Functions are defined in a file of the same name using the key word `function` to distinguish them from scripts
- Parameters are copied in sequence into the function and given the names of the formal parameters

- Results are returned to the caller by assigning value(s) to the return variable(s)
- Variables within the function have scope only in the function's code block unless they are declared global
- Helper functions accessible only to functions within the same file may be added behind the main function and otherwise obey the same rules as the main function

 Special Characters, Reserved Words, and Functions

Special Characters, Reserved Words, and Functions	Description	Discussed in This Section
( )	Used to identify the formal and actual parameters of a function	5.3.2, 5.3.4
help	Invokes help utility	5.3.1
function	Identifies an m-file as a function	5.3.2
nargin	Determines the number of input parameters actually supplied by a function's caller	5.3.4
nargout	Determines the number of output parameters actually requested by a function's caller	5.3.4
global var	Defines a variable as globally accessible	5.3.8

 Self Test

Use the following questions to check your understanding of the material in this chapter:

True or False

1. All data used by a function must be passed in as parameters to the function.

2. The name of the first function in an m-file must match the name of the file containing its definition.

3. The first documentation line appears in the Current Directory listing.

4. Functions must consume at least one parameter.

5. The calling code must provide assignments for every result returned from a function.

6. The names of auxiliary functions must begin with `local_`.

Fill in the Blanks

1. _____ permits a code block to be packaged and referred to collectively rather than individually.

2. Values of the _____ parameters are copied to define the _____ parameters inside the function.

3. If more than one result is to be returned from a function, they are defined in a _____.

4. _____ describes the situation where the variables within a function are not visible from outside, and the function is unable to cause side effects by making assignments to outside variables.

5. Calling code can only reach the _____ function in an m-file. Other functions in the m-file can only be called from the _____ or _____.

 Programming Projects

1. Write a function called myMin4 that takes in four numbers and returns the minimum. You may not use the built-in min() function.

   Examples:
   ```
   myMin4(1,3,5,7) -> 1
   myMin4(8,9,3,4) -> 3
   ```

2. Write a function meansAndMedian that takes in a vector of numbers, v, and returns the arithmetic and geometric means, as well as the median. You can assume that the numbers in v are sorted in ascending order. You may not use the built-in functions mean() or median().

Hint
The geometric mean is the product of the terms raised to the power 1/n where n is the number of terms.

3. Write an iterative function called factorial that consumes a number and returns the factorial of the given number. The factorial of a number can be found using the following equation:

$$F(x) = x*(x - 1)*(x - 2)...*2*1$$

   Remember the factorial of 0 is equal to 1, and you must protect yourself from negative numbers. Call the function error(...) if this occurs.

Examples:

```
factorial(5) -> 120
factorial(0) -> 1
factorial(10) -> 3628800
```

4. This example will lead you through the steps to writing and using a function to find the roots of a quadratic equation. The question involves a ball thrown upwards with an initial velocity V. We need to know the times at which it will pass an altitude h.

    a. Set up the problem by writing a script to determine the parameters of the problem.

    b. Write a function roots that consumes the three coefficients A, B, and C that calculates the standard solution for the two roots of a quadratic equation:

    $$x = \frac{\left(-B \pm \sqrt{(B^2 - 4AC)}\right)}{2A}$$

    c. Run and test the script with various values of the velocity and distance.

    Should you do anything special if the roots are complex?

5. Your uncle Rico insists that at one time he could throw a football a quarter mile (1 mile = 5,280 feet). Write a MATLAB function called howFast that consumes an angle in degrees and returns the velocity in meters per second (m/s) that Uncle Rico would need to throw the ball a quarter mile.

    The distance that the ball travels is computed by the following formula:

    $$d = \left(\frac{v^2}{g}\right) \sin(2\vartheta)$$

    where is the speed the ball is initially thrown, ϑ, is the angle consumed by the function, and is 9.8 m/s^2 (1 m = 3.28 ft).

6. The U.S. Postal Service has given you the task of calculating the "check digit" of its Zip codes. The check digit is calculated by adding the digits of the five-digit Zip code and seeing what would have to be added to the sum to get a multiple of 10. For example, the check digit for the Zip code 51220 would be 0 (as $5 + 1 + 2 + 2 + 0 = 10$), whereas the check digit for 82125 would be 2 (as $8 + 2 + 1 + 2 + + 5 = 18$).

    Write a MATLAB function called checkDigit that takes in a vector of Zip code digits that range from 0 to 9 and returns the check digit.

Also check that the Zip code provided is a valid Zip code; that is, it is of length 5. If it is not a valid Zip code, return –1.

Examples:

```
checkDigit([9 8 0 3 4]) should return 6.
checkDigit([7 2 1 4]) should return -1.
```

7. The code for the function `magicCarpetRide` follows:

```
function answer = magicCarpetRide(x,y,z)
if x && z
    if (x || ~y)
        answer = 'Last night I held Aladdins lamp';
    elseif ~y
        answer = 'Let the sound take you away';
    else
        answer = 'Any place it goes is right';
    end
elseif y||z
    if z
        answer = 'You dont know';
    else
        answer = 'Right between the sound machine';
    end
else
    answer = 'Why dont you tell your dreams to me?';
end
```

What are the values of A, B, C, and D?

```
A = magicCarpetRide(1,0,0)
B = magicCarpetRide(1,0,1)
C = magicCarpetRide(0,0,1)
D = magicCarpetRide(0,1,0)
```

8. Write a function called `crazyVector` that take in a vector and two integers (v, m, n) respectively. This function returns a vector containing the mth, 2mth, 3mth, and so on elements from the original vector, each raised to the power n.

Examples:

```
crazyVector([2 3 5 6 7 8 3 5 6 7], 2, 3)
                        -> [27    216    512    125    343]
    crazyVector ([2 3 5 6 7 8 3 5 6 7], 3, 2) -> [25    64    36]
```

9. You are given an array of numbers representing the rainfall amounts for a certain period of time. As an example, consider the following array:

```
A = [3  6  -1  11  4  1.2  7  -1.7  5  1.3  -0.001]
```

a. Write a script that uses a `for` loop to display each rainfall amount contained in the array A on a different line in the Command window. You may assume that the array A already exists in the Workspace, and you may use the `disp( ...)` function.

b. You realize there are some negative values in the rainfall data that do not make sense, so you decide to exclude these erroneous values from your calculations. Write a function that will compute the average of all the *non-negative* values in the rainfall data array. You must allow for the fact that that there may not be any non-negative values in the array.

c. Add the instructions to test this function in your script.

10. A ternary logic system consists of three states: true (1), false (–1), and possibly true or false (0). Ternary expressions can be applied to values in the ternary system in the same manner as Boolean expressions in the binary system. The implementation of the ternary logic expressions tand(x,y) to compute the ternary logical 'and' and tor(x,y) to compute the ternary logical 'or' is as follows:

x	y	tand(x,y)	tor(x,y)
–1	–1	–1	–1
–1	0	–1	0
–1	1	–1	1
0	–1	0	0
0	0	0	0
0	1	0	1
1	–1	–1	1
1	0	0	1
1	1	1	1

a. Write the function tand(x,y) according to the above specification.

b. Write the function tor(x,y) according to the above specification.

c. Write a test script that thoroughly evaluates the capabilities of these two functions by iterating across all possible values of x and y.

11. You work for a chopstick company and have been appointed to take an overall inventory of chopsticks at every store location. Write a function called chopsticks that takes in an array of positive integers representing the number of *individual* chopsticks at each store. Unfortunately, one chopstick isn't very useful, so unpaired chopsticks do not count in the overall inventory. Your function chopsticks must return the total number of *complete pairs* of chopsticks in inventory.

Hint

The built-in MATLAB function mod(x, y) might be useful.

12. Write a function called `replace` that takes in a vector v and returns a modified vector of the same size. The function will replace all values in v greater than 60 with a –1 and all numbers in v perfectly divisible by 10 with the number 10. All other numbers in the vector should be changed to zeros.

> **Hint**
>
> `mod(30,10)` gives the remainder of 30/10.

Example:
```
replace([0 12 30 50 42 81 10] -> [0 0 10 10 0 -1 10]
```

13. You're playing a game where you roll a die 10 times. If you roll a 5 or 6 seven or more times, you win $2; four or more times, you win $1; and if you roll a 5 or 6 three or fewer times, you win no money.

Write a function called `diceGame` that takes in a vector representing the dice values and returns the amount of money won.

Examples:
```
diceGame([5 1 4 6 5 5 6 6 5 2]) should return 2
diceGame([2 4 1 3 6 6 6 4 5 3]) should return 1
diceGame([1 4 3 2 5 3 4 2 6 5]) should return 0
```

Note: This function should work for any length vector.

14. Write a function called `checkFactor` that takes in two numbers a and b, and checks whether a is divisible by b. Your function should return `true` if this is true and `false` if it is not. You may not assume that both numbers are positive.

Examples:
```
checkFactor(25, -6)— should return false.
checkFactor(-9, 3)— should return true.
checkFactor(3, 9)— should return false.
```

15. We need to generate a strange series of numbers. Here are the steps involved:

a. Write the function `squares` that consumes a positive integer, n, and returns a vector that contains the squares of the numbers from 1 to n, inclusive.

b. Write the code for the function `mysteryFunction` that consumes a vector and produces a vector of the same length. Each item in the new vector will be the sum of the corresponding item and its predecessor in the old vector.

Examples:
```
mysteryFunction(1:5) -> [1 3 5 7 9]
mysteryFunction(squares(12)) ->
                    [1   5 13 25   41   61   85 113 145 181 221 265]
```

16. Coming off a respectable 7–6 record last year, the Georgia Tech football team is looking to improve on that this season. They want you to write a function called `teamRecord` that takes in two parameters: `wins` and `losses`, and returns two values, `season` and `wPercentage`.

`wins` = numbers of wins for the season

`losses` = number of losses for the season

`season` = `1` for a winning season; that is, there are more wins than losses

       = `0` otherwise

`wPercentage` = the percentage of games won (ranging from 0 to 100)

Example:
```
[season,wPercentage] = teamRecord(3,9)
season =
    0
wPercentage =
   25
```

17. Write and test a function called `myFactor` that consumes a positive integer and returns the prime factors of that integer in a vector. If a factor is repeated, then it should be in the array for each time this factor appears. You may not use the built-in functions `primes()` or `factor()`, but you may use `isprime()`.

Note: The number 1 is not prime, but `myFactor(1)` should return `1`.

Examples:
```
myFactor(70) -> [2 5 7]
myFactor(24) -> [2 2 2 3]
```

CHAPTER 6

Character Strings

6.1 Character String Concepts: Mapping and Casting

6.2 MATLAB Implementation
6.2.1 Slicing and Concatenating Strings
6.2.2 Arithmetic and Logical Operations
6.2.3 Useful Functions

6.3 Format Conversion Functions
6.3.1 Conversion from Numbers to Strings
6.3.2 Conversion from Strings to Numbers

6.4 Character String Operations
6.4.1 Simple Data Output: The disp(...) Function
6.4.2 Complex Output
6.4.3 Comparing Strings

6.5 Arrays of Strings

6.6 Engineering Example—Encryption

Chapter Objectives

This chapter discusses the nature, implementation, and behavior of character strings in MATLAB:

■ The internal workings of character strings as vectors

■ Operations on character strings

■ Converting between numeric and character string representations

■ Input and output functions

■ The construction and uses for arrays of strings

To this point in the text, we have seen the use of character strings that we can store in variables and display in the Command window. In reality, we have already seen a significant amount of character manipulation that we have taken for granted. The m-files we use to store scripts and functions consist of lines of legible characters separated by an invisible "new-line" character.

Introduction

This chapter presents the underlying concept of character storage and the tools MATLAB provides for operating on character strings.

We need to distinguish two different relationships between characters and numbers:

1. *Individual characters have an internal numerical representation:* The visible character shapes we see in windows are created as a collection of white and black dots by special software called a **character generator**. Character generators allow us to take the underlying concept of a character—say, "w"— and "draw" that character on screen or paper in accordance with the rules defined by the current font. A complete study of fonts is beyond the scope of this discussion, but we need to understand how computers in general and MATLAB in particular represent that "underlying concept" of a character. This

is achieved by representing each individual character by a numerical equivalent. Not long ago, there were many different representations. Today, the dominant representation is the one defined by the American Standard Code for Information Interchange (ASCII). In this representation, the most common uppercase and lowercase characters, numbers, and many punctuation marks are represented by numbers between 0 and 127. A complete listing of the first 255 values is included in Appendix B.

2. *Strings of characters represent numerical values to the user:* Numerical values are stored in MATLAB in a special, internal representation for efficient numerical computation as described in Appendix C. However, whenever we need to see the value of that number in the Command window, that internal representation is automatically converted by MATLAB into a character string representing its value in a form we can read. For example, if the variable `a` contained the integer value 124, internally that number could be stored in a single byte (8 bits) with a binary value of 011111100. Not a very meaningful representation, but efficient internally for performing arithmetic and logical operations. For the user to understand that value, a MATLAB function must convert it to the three printable characters: `'124'`. Similarly, when we use the `input(...)` function, the set of characters that we enter is automatically translated to the internal number representation.

 ## 6.1 Character String Concepts: Mapping and Casting

Here we see the MATLAB tools that deal with the first relationship between characters and numbers: the numerical representation of individual characters. The basic idea of **mapping** is that it defines a relationship between two entities. The most obvious example of mapping is the idea that the function $f(x) = x^2$ defines the mapping between the value of x and the value of $f(x)$. We will apply that concept to the process of translating a character (like "A") from its graphical form to a numerical internal code. **Character mapping** allows each individual graphic character to be uniquely represented by a numerical value.

Casting is the process of changing the way a language views a piece of data without actually changing the data value. Under normal circumstances, a language like MATLAB automatically presents a set of data in the "right" form. However, there are times when we wish to force the language to treat a data item in a specific way. For example, if we create a variable containing a character string, MATLAB will consistently display it as a character string. However, we might want to view the underlying numerical representation as a number, in which case we have to cast the variable containing the characters to a numerical data type.

MATLAB implements casting as a function with the name of the data type expected. In essence, these functions implement the mapping from one character representation to another.

6.2 MATLAB Implementation

As illustrated, MATLAB's external specification of character strings uses the single quote mark (') to delimit character strings, and its editor colorizes the resulting string. This satisfies all the requirements except the question of how to include the delimiting quote mark within a string. This is accomplished by doubling the quote mark if it is intended to be included, thus: `'don''t do that!'`.

Exercise 6.1 illustrates the concept of casting between data types `char` and `double`.

In Exercise 6.1 the casting function `uint8(...)` takes a character or character string and converts its representation to a vector of the same length

---

Exercise 6.1 Character casting

Do It Yourself

Enter the following in the Command window and study the results:

```
>> uint8('A')  % uint8 is an integer data type
               % with values 0 - 255
ans =
    65
>> char(100)   % char is the character class
ans =
d
>> char([97 98 99 100 101])
ans =
abcde
>> double('fred')
ans =
   102    114    101    100
>> fred = 'Fred'
fred =
Fred
>> next = fred + 1
next =
    71   115   102   101
>> a = uint8(fred)
a =
    70   114   101   100
>> name = char(a + 1)
name =
Gsfe
```

as the original string. Then the casting function `char(...)` takes a number or vector and converts it to a string representation. The casting function `double(...)` appears to act in the same way as `uint8(...)`, but it actually uses 64 bits to store the values.

Single quotes delimit a string to be assigned to the variable `fred`. Notice that when a string is presented as a result, the delimiters are omitted. When you apply arithmetic operations to a string, the operation is illegal on characters; therefore, an implicit casting to the numerical equivalent occurs. You can perform any mathematical operation on the vector and use the cast, `char(...)` to cast it back to a string.

6.2.1 Slicing and Concatenating Strings

Strings are internally represented as vectors; therefore, we can perform all the usual vector operations on strings. Try it in Exercise 6.2.

6.2.2 Arithmetic and Logical Operations

Mathematical operations can be performed on the numerical mapping of a character string. If you do not explicitly perform that casting first, MATLAB will do the cast for you, and create a result of type double (not usually suitable for character values). Note that `char('a' + 1)` returning `'b'` is an accident of the character type mapping.

Logical operations on character strings are also exactly equivalent to logical operations on vectors, with the same automatic casting. Exercise 6.3 gives you an opportunity to try it yourself.

 Exercise 6.2 Character strings

Do It Yourself

Enter the following in the Command window and study the results:

```
>> first = 'Fred'
first =
Fred
>> last = 'Jones'
last =
Jones
>> name = [first, ' ', last]
name =
Fred Jones
>> name(1:2:end)
ans =
Fe oe
>> name(end:-1:1)
ans =
senoJ derF
```

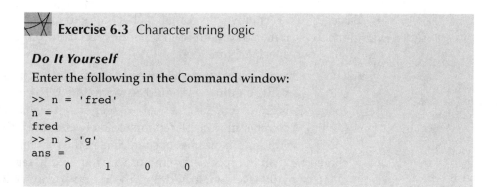

Exercise 6.3 Character string logic

Do It Yourself

Enter the following in the Command window:

```
>> n = 'fred'
n =
fred
>> n > 'g'
ans =
     0     1     0     0
```

6.2.3 Useful Functions

The following functions are useful in analyzing character strings:

- `ischar(a)` returns `true` if `a` is a character string
- `isspace(ch)` returns `true` if the character `ch` is the space character

6.3 Format Conversion Functions

Now we turn to the second relationship between characters and numbers: using character strings to represent individual number values. We need two separate capabilities: converting numbers from the efficient, internal form to legible strings, and converting strings provided by users of MATLAB into the internal number representation. MATLAB provides a number of functions that transform data between string format and numerical format.

6.3.1 Conversion from Numbers to Strings

Use the following built-in MATLAB functions for a simple conversion of a single number, x, to its string representation:

- `int2str(x)` if you want it displayed as an integer value
- `num2str(x, n)` to see the decimal parts; the parameter n represents the number of decimal places required—if not specified, its default value is 3

Frequently you need better control over the data conversion, and the function `sprintf(...)` provides fine-grained control. The MATLAB version of `sprintf(...)` is very similar to the C / C++ implementation of this capability. The first parameter to `sprintf` is a **format control string** that defines exactly how the resulting string should be formatted. A variable number of **value parameters** follow the format string, providing data items as necessary to satisfy the formatting.

Basically the format string contains characters to be copied to the result string; however, it also contains two types of special entry introduced by the following two special characters:

- The '`%`' character introduces a conversion specification, indicating how one of the value parameters should be represented. The most common conversions are `%d` (integer), `%f` (real), `%g` (general), `%c` (character) and `%s` (string). A number may be placed immediately after the `%` character to specify the minimum number of characters in the conversion. If more characters than the specified minimum are required to represent the data, they will be added. In addition, the `%f` and `%g` conversions can include '`.n`' to indicate the number of decimal places required. If you actually require a '`%`' character, it must be doubled, for example, '`%%`'. MATLAB processes each of the value parameters in turn, inserting them in the result string according to the corresponding conversion specification. If there are more parameters than conversion specifications in the format control string, the format control string is repeated.

- The '`\`' character introduces format control information, the most common of which are `\n` (new line) and `\t` (tab). If the '`\`' character is actually required in the result string, it should be doubled, for example, '`\\`'.

Consider the following statements:

```
A = [4.7 1321454.47 4.8];
index = 1;
v = 'values';
str = sprintf('%8s of A(%d) are \t%8.3f\t%12.4g\t%f\n'...
    v, index, A(index,1), A(index,2), A(index,3))
str =
  values of A(1) are      4.700      1.321e+006      4.800000
```

The first conversion, '`%8s`', took the value of the first parameter, `v`, allowed eight spaces for its conversion, and copied its contents to the result. Since this was a string conversion, the characters were merely copied. The characters ' `of A(`' were then appended to the output string. The second conversion, '`%d`', took the value of the second parameter, `index`, and converted it as an integer with the minimum space allocated. The characters ' `)are`' were then appended to the output string, followed by a tab character that inserted enough spaces to bring the next characters to a column that is an even multiple of eight. The following three conversions appended the next three value parameters converted with three decimal places, a general conversion with at least 12 spaces and 4 decimal places, and the default numerical conversion. Finally, a new line character was inserted into the string.

6.3.2 Conversion from Strings to Numbers

Conversion from strings to numbers is a much messier conversion, and it should be avoided if possible. When possible, allow MATLAB's built-in function `input(...)` to do the conversion for you. If you have to do the conversion yourself, use the function `sscanf(...)`.

The function `input(str)` presents the string parameter to the user in the Command window and waits for the user to type some characters and the ⌨Enter key, all of which are echoed in the Command window. Then it converts the input string according to the following rules:

- If the string begins with a numerical character, MATLAB converts the string to a number
- If it begins with a non-numeric character, MATLAB constructs a variable name and looks for its definition
- If it begins with an open bracket, '`[`', a vector is constructed
- If it begins with the single quote character, MATLAB creates a string

If a format error occurs, MATLAB repeats the prompt.

This behavior can be modified if '`s`' is provided as the second parameter, `input(str, 's')`, in which case the complete input character sequence is saved as a string. Exercise 6.4 demonstrates a number of capabilities of the `input(...)` function.

Exercise 6.4 The `input(...)` function

Do It Yourself

Enter the following into the Command window and notice the behavior:

```
>> fred = 'Fred';
>> n = input('Enter a number: ')
Enter a number: 5
n =
      5
>> n = input('Enter a number: ')
Enter a number: fred
n =
Fred
>> n = input('Enter a number: ')
Enter a number: 1sdf
??? 1sdf
Error: Missing MATLAB operator.
Enter a number: s1df
??? Error using ==> input
Undefined function or variable 's1df'.
Enter a number: char(fred - 2)
n =
Dpcb
>> n = input('Enter a number: ')
Enter a number: 'ABCD'
n =
ABCD
>> n = input('Enter a number: ', 's' )
Enter a number: ABCD
n =
```

In Exercise 6.4 first we define the variable fred. Then MATLAB attempts to interpret the result either as a number or as the name of an existing variable. Since the variable fred was defined (although not a number), it was assigned correctly to the variable n. MATLAB attempts to distinguish between a variable and a number by the first digit. Here, the information entered was an illegal variable name beginning with a number. When input(...) detects an error parsing the text entered, it automatically resets and requests a new entry.

On the second attempt, although this is a correctly formed variable name, its value is not known. On the third attempt, the input(...) function actually treats the string entered as an expression, to be evaluated by the same process as MATLAB parses the Command window entries.

If you actually want a string literal entered, it must be enclosed in the string delimiters. If you are sure you want a string literal entered, the second parameter, 's', forces MATLAB to return the string entered without attempting to parse it.

The function sscanf(...), unfortunately, is quite different from the C / C++ mechanization. In its simplest form, cv = sscanf(str, fmt) scans the string str and converts each data item according to the conversion specifications in the format string fmt. Each item discovered in str produces a new row on the result array, cv, a column vector. Unfortunately, if you convert strings this way, each character in the string becomes a separate numerical result in the output vector. A peculiar feature of MATLAB allows you to substitute the character '*' for the conversion size parameter to suppress any strings in the input string. For example:

```
str = 'are      4.700           1.321  4.800000'
B = sscanf( str, '%*s %f %f %f')

B =
    4.7000
    1.3210
    4.8000
```

 ## 6.4 Character String Operations

As with the string-to-number conversions, input and output in the Command window can be accomplished with simple functions that have little flexibility or with complex functions that have better control.

6.4.1 Simple Data Output: The disp(...) Function

We have already seen the use of the disp(...) function to present data in readable form in the Command window. As the exercises indicate, it can present the values of any variable, regardless of type, or of strings constructed

Exercise 6.5 The `disp(...)` function

Do It Yourself

Enter the following in the Command window:

```
>> a = 4;
>> disp(a)
      4
>> disp(['the answer is ', a])
the answer is □
>> disp(['the answer is ', int2str(a)])
the answer is 4
```

by concatenation. Note, however, that an explicit number conversion is required to concatenate variables with strings. Try Exercise 6.5.

Note that although you can concatenate strings for output, conversion from the ASCII code is not automatic; the second result produced a character whose ASCII code is 4. You must use the simple string conversion functions to enforce consistent information for concatenation.

6.4.2 Complex Output

The function `fprintf(...)` is similar to `sprintf(...)`, except that it prints its results to the Command window instead of returning a string. `fprintf(...)` returns the number of characters actually printed. Exercise 6.6 demonstrates this.

6.4.3 Comparing Strings

Since strings are readily translated into vectors of numbers, they may be compared in the obvious way with the logical operators we used on numbers.

Exercise 6.6 `fprintf(...)` and `sprintf(...)`

Do It Yourself

Enter the following into the Command window:

```
>> a = 42;
>> b = 'fried okra';
>> n = fprintf('the answer is %d\n cooking %s', ...
                              a,              b);
the answer is 42
 cooking fried okra
n =
    37
>> s = sprintf('the answer is %d\n cooking %s\n',    ...
                              a,              b)
```

continued on next page

```
s =
the answer is 42
 cooking fried Okra
>> str = input('Enter the data: ', 's');
Enter the data: 42 3.14159 -1
A = sscanf( str,'%f')
A =
    42.0000
     3.1416
    -1.0000
>>
```

However, there is the restriction that either the strings must be of the same length or one of them must be of length 1 before it is legal to compare them with these operators. To avoid this restriction, MATLAB provides the C-style function strcmp(<s1>, <s2>) that returns true if the strings are identical and false if they are not. Unfortunately, this is not quite the same behavior as the C version, which does a more rigorous comparison returning -1, 0, or 1. You can try a character string comparison in Exercise 6.7.

Common Pitfalls

The if statement uses a logical expression as its controlling test; therefore, it is bound by the same comparison rules as those applied to vectors. Two strings being compared must be of the same length, and all of the comparisons must match to result in a logical true. Frequently, we expect the if statement to compare strings of unequal length. However, this will cause an error the first time two strings of unequal length are compared. You should use the switch statement, which will correctly compare strings of unequal length in the case tests.

 Exercise 6.7 Character string comparison

Do It Yourself

Enter the following into the Command window and study the results:

```
>> 'abcd' == 'abcd'
     1    1    1    1
>> 'abcd' == 'abcde'
??? Error using ==> eq
Array dimensions must match for binary array op.
>> strcmp('abcd', 'abcde')
ans =
     0
>> strcmp('abcd', 'abcd')
ans =
     1
>> 'abc' == 'a'

ans =

     1    0    0
>> strcmpi('ABcd', 'abcd')
ans =
     1
```

In Exercise 6.7 we see that strings of the same length compare exactly to vectors returning a logical vector result. You cannot use the equality test on strings of unequal length. `strcmp(...)` deals gracefully with strings of unequal length. As with vectors, the equality test works if one of the inputs is a single character. For case-independent testing, use `strcmpi(...)`.

 ## 6.5 Arrays of Strings

Since a single character string is stored as a vector, it seems natural to consider storing a collection of strings as an array. The most obvious way to do this, as shown in previous examples, has some limitations, for which there are nice, tidy cures built into MATLAB. Consider the example shown in Exercise 6.8. Character arrays can be constructed by either of the following:

Common Pitfalls

Trying to concatenate strings of unequal length vertically into column arrays of strings will cause errors because the vertical concatenation must use rows of equal length. Use the version of the `char(...)` function that pads the strings with spaces.

- As a vertical vector of strings, all of which must be the same length
- By using a special version of the `char( & )` cast function that accepts a variable number of strings with different lengths, pads them with blanks to make all rows the same length, and stores them in an array of characters

---

 Exercise 6.8 Character string arrays

Do It Yourself

Enter the following into the Command window:

```
>> v = ['Character strings having more than'
        'one row must have the same number '
        'of columns just like arrays!      ']
v =
Character strings having more than
one row must have the same number
of columns just like arrays!
>> v = ['MATLAB gets upset'
        'when rows have'
        'different lengths']
??? Error using ==> vertcat
All rows in the bracketed expression must have the
same number of columns.

>>eng=char('Timoshenko','Maxwell','Mach','von Braun')
eng =
Timoshenko
Maxwell
Mach
von Braun
>> size(eng)
ans =
     4      10
```

6.6 Engineering Example—Encryption

The Problem:

As public access to information becomes more pervasive, there is increasing interest in the use of encryption to protect intellectual property and private communications from unauthorized access. The following discussion is based on no direct knowledge of the latest encryption technology. However, it illustrates a very simple approach to developing an algorithm that is immune to all but the most obvious, brute-force code-breaking techniques.

Background:

Historically, simple encryption has been accomplished by substituting one character for another in the message, so that 'Fred' becomes 'Iuhg' when substituting the letter three places down the alphabet for each letter in the message. More advanced techniques use a random letter selection to substitute new letters. However, any constant letter substitution is vulnerable to elementary code-cracking techniques based on the frequency of letters in the alphabet, for example.

The Solution:

We propose a simple algorithm where a predetermined random series is used to select the replacement letters. Since the same letter in the original message is never replaced by the same substitute, no simple language analysis will crack the code. The MATLAB rand(...) function is an excellent source for an appropriate random sequence. If the encryption and decryption processes use the same value to seed the generator, the same sequence of apparently random (**pseudo-random**) values will be generated. Since the seed can take on $2^{31}-2$ values, it is virtually impossible to determine the decryption without knowing the seed value. The seed (i.e., the decryption key) can be transmitted to anyone authorized to decrypt the message by any number of ways.

Furthermore, since there are abundant different techniques for generating pseudo-random sequences, the specific generation technique must be known in addition to the seed value for successful decryption. Listing 6.1 shows the code for encrypting and decrypting by this technique, and two attempts to decrypt—once with the wrong key and once with the wrong generator.

Listing 6.1 Encryption exercise

```
1. clear
2. clc
```

continued on next page

```
 3. disp('original text')
 4. txt = ['For example, consider the following:' 13 ...
 5.     'A = [4.7 1321454.47 4.8];' 13  ...
 6.     'index = 1;' 13  ...
 7.     'v = ''values'';' 13 ...
 8.     'str = sprintf(''%8s of A(%d) are \t%8.3f ' 13 ...
 9.     '    v, index, A(index,1) ' 13 ...
10.     'str =  ' 13 ...
11.     '  values of A(1) are    4.700' 13 ...
12.     'The first conversion, ''%8s'', took the value' ...
13.     ' of the first ' ...
14.     'parameter, v, allowed 8 spaces. ' 13 ]

%%% encryption section
15. rand('state', 123456)
16. loch = 33;
17. hich = 126;
18. range = hich+1-loch;
19. rn = floor( range * rand(1, length(txt) ) );
20. change = (txt>=loch) & (txt
21. enc = txt;
22. enc(change) = enc(change) + rn(change);
23. enc(enc > hich) = enc(enc > hich) - range;
24. disp('encrypted text')
25. encrypt = char(enc)

%% good decryption
26. rand('state', 123456);

27. rn = floor( range * rand(1, length(txt) ) );
28. change = (encrypt>=loch) & (encrypt
29. dec = encrypt;
30. dec(change) = dec(change) - rn(change) + range;
31. dec(dec > hich) = dec(dec > hich) - range;
32. disp('good decrypt');
33. decrypt = char(dec)

%% bad seed
34. rand('seed', 123457);

35. rn = floor( range * rand(1, length(txt) ) );
36. change = (encrypt>=loch) & (encrypt
37. dec = encrypt;
38. dec(change) = dec(change) - rn(change) + range;
39. dec(dec > hich) = dec(dec > hich) - range;
40. disp('decrypt with bad seed')
41. decrypt = char(dec)

%% different generator
42. rand('seed', 123456)
43. rn = mod(floor( range * abs(randn(1, length(txt) ))/10 ),
    ...
                                  range);
```

continued on next page

```
44. change = (encrypt>=loch) & (encrypt
45. dec = encrypt;
46. dec(change) = dec(change) - rn(change) + range;
47. dec(dec > hich) = dec(dec > hich) - range;
48. disp('decrypt with wrong generator')
49. decrypt = char(dec)
```

In Listing 6.1:

Lines 4–14: This is the original text taken from earlier in this chapter. Multiple lines of characters can be concatenated as shown. The number 13 inserted in the string is the numerical equivalent of the new line escape sequence, '\n'.

Line 15: Seeds the random generator with a known value.

Lines 16–18: Set the upper and lower bounds and the range of the characters we will convert. This range excludes 32, the space character, and 13, the new line character. This choice was deliberate—it leaves the encrypted text with the appearance of a character substitution algorithm since all the characters are printable, and seem to be grouped in words.

Line 19: Generates the random values between 0 and `range-1`.

Line 20: Identifies the indices of the printable characters.

Line 21: Makes a copy of the original text.

Line 22: Adds the random offsets to those characters we intend to change.

Line 23: If this pushes a character value above the maximum printable character, here it brings it back within range.

Lines 24 and 25: Display the encrypted text. Notice that no two characters of the original text are replaced by the same character.

Lines 26–29: Begin the decryption by seeding the generator with the same value, creating the same random sequence, finding the printable characters, and copying the original file to the decrypt string.

Lines 30 and 31: We must subtract the random sequence from the encrypted string and correct for the underflow. However, there are some numerical issues involved. It is best to add the `range` value to all the letters while subtracting the random offsets, and then bring back those values that remain above the highest printable character.

Lines 32 and 33: Display the decrypted valuestest that it is identical to the original.

Lines 34–41: Attempt to decrypt with the same code but a bad seed.

Lines 42–49: Attempt to decrypt with the right seed but a different generator—in this case, MATLAB's normal random generator limited to positive values within the letter range of interest.

Listing 6.2 shows the output from this encryption exercise.

Listing 6.2 Encryption exercise results

```
original text
txt =
For example, consider the following:
A = [4.7 1321454.47 4.8];
index = 1;
v = 'values';
str = sprintf('%8s of A(%d) are \t%.3f
   v, index, A(index,1)
str =
   values of A(1) are    4.700
The first conversion, '%8s', took the value
 of the first parameter, v, allowed 8 spaces.

encrypted text
encrypt =
@;J _a,Q/V_Q X/|IW?*q %;{ $Ctr:$&r3>
5 - v$zh uvqzmE@P(N Bh}.H
_31c> / b/
q ( <0"z<F[Wg
eWP _ )QrWEyeV153u 2} -H]7I gbM U>}U,5b
   km cof+:J 28K?d8`49{
Dkp m
   t.7[S\ Zh Lmk; v&<      .?&!S
:s6 #p.x5 W{aycv0$[n! M;sc:\ U[QT nfT ySET6
 fK ms_ @|MFn J,PSyKuM"+ G# 3`VL^sJ f .|2B8W?

good decrypt
decrypt =
For example, consider the following:
A = [4.7 1321454.47 4.8];
index = 1;
v = 'values';
str = sprintf('%8s of A(%d) are \t%.3f
   v, index, A(index,1)
str =
   values of A(1) are    4.700
The first conversion, '%8s', took the value
 of the first parameter, v, allowed 8 spaces.

decrypt with bad seed
decrypt =
tDQ <6VfMiS^ }1FI92/P c`@ eYrW%Q^2t+
6 L 4x5> B$rQ4XHpG# G;*<r
[8La^ ( $J
E 7 Mjpq~,I>(
GH4 1 ^YgRpX}]>0&v [$ n|pA| /}O OML-jKc
   3C f*q(WK (3oQQC\HpS
*a= +
  og>FK> .u Od]C :wf    J$"qQ
.&i wZwPo .=";~s6!-5g ~d7C}t >Q<z s}c HHZZh
 7u \uV f_h84 p(M&3kzGnP ci rljnRm| m t?!>FP;
```

continued on next page

```
decrypt with wrong generator
decrypt =
>1E o-P:'P=p :xLjV+bi {!d 3)[Az$~c7<
' l fny& tHWB Vve6o
(mRdc T W$
= Q Z"'$;e[@{
/<* / )tokB]h:;ODu o^ 4=A0- z@0 P"!+axV
    _U `LJsrj ^,Ia7]V3bq
 _P* 5
   |v^)Z+ ?! Ld`} 5$)    DKN54
o~U @^%'o u[YOzAV06JV i\(E^I X)cC -X` uu2.\
 dq 7:D diq#1 Y+sDW*FiF" $u eeF832} ? E,wc97*
```

Chapter Summary

This chapter discussed the nature, implementation, and behavior of character strings. We learned the following:

- Character strings are merely vectors of numbers that MATLAB presents to the user as single characters
- We can perform on strings the same operations as can be performed on vectors; if mathematical operations are performed, MATLAB converts the characters to double values
- We can convert between string representations of numbers and the numbers themselves using built-in MATLAB functions
- MATLAB provides functions that convert numbers to text strings for presentation in the Command window
- Arrays of strings can be assembled using the char(...) function

Special Characters, Reserved Words, and Functions

Special Characters, Reserved Words, and Functions	Description	Discussed in This Section
'...'	Encloses a literal character string	6.2
char(...)	Casts to a character type	6.2, 6.5
double(a)	Casts to type double	6.2
ischar(ch)	Determines whether the given object is of type char	6.2.3
isspace(a)	Tests for the space character	6.2.3
uint8(...)	Casts to unsigned integer type with 8 bits	6.2
int2str(a)	Converts an integer to its numerical representation	6.3.1

Special Characters, Reserved Words, and Functions	Description	Discussed in This Section
num2str(a,n)	Converts a number to its numerical representation with n decimal places	6.3.1
disp(...)	Displays matrix or text	6.4.1
fprintf(...)	Prints formatted information	6.4.2
input(...)	Prompts the user to enter a value	6.3.2
sscanf(...)	Formats input conversion	6.3.2
sprintf(...)	Formats a string result	6.3.1
strcmp(s1, s2)	Compares two strings; returns true if equal	6.4.3
strcmpi(s1, s2)	Compares two strings without regard to case; returns true if equal	6.4.3

 ## Self Test

Use the following questions to check your understanding of the material in this chapter:

True or False

1. Casting changes the value of a piece of data.

2. The ASCII code maps individual characters to their internal numerical representation.

3. Because the single quote mark (') delimits strings, you cannot use it within a string.

4. If you attempt mathematical operations on a character string, MATLAB will throw an error.

5. The function disp(...) can display multiple values to the Command window.

6. The function strcmp(...) throws an error if the two strings are of unequal length, unless one of them is a single character.

7. The switch statement will correctly compare strings of unequal length in the case tests.

Fill in the Blanks

1. Numerical values are stored in MATLAB in _____ for efficient numerical computation.

2. Most common _____, _____, and

    many _____ are represented in ASCII by the

    numbers _____.

3. The function _____ casts a string to a vector of the
    same length as the string containing the numerical mapping of

    _____.

4. The function `fprintf(...)` requires a _____ that
    defines exactly how the resulting string should be formatted and a
    variable number of _____.

5. Since the _____ statement tests a logical expression,

    it _____ test strings of unequal length.

6. A special version of the _____ cast function accepts

    strings with different lengths, _____,

    and stores them in an array of characters.

Hint

`find ( str == ' ' )` produces the
indices of the spaces in the sentence that
separate all the words, except the first and
the last.

Programming Projects

1. Write the function `myStrcmp(s1, s2)` according to the specification
    given by the MATLAB `help strcmp` command.

2. Write the function `nthWord(sentence, n)` that consumes a character
    string containing words separated by blanks and produces the *n*th
    word from that sentence.

3. Write and test a function called `DNAComplement` that consumes a set
    of letters as a character array that forms a DNA sequence, such as
    `'gattaca'`. The function will produce the complement of the
    sequence as follows:

    a `<->`t and g `<->` c (as become ts, gs become cs, and vice versa), so
    that `'gattaca'` becomes `'ctaatgt'`

Assume that all the letters in the sequence will be lowercase and that they will all be either a, t, g, or c.

Note: You may be tempted to use iteration for this problem, but you do not need it.

4. Write a function called firstLetters that consumes a string of words and returns an array containing the first letter of each word.

   Examples:
   ```
   >> firstLetters('Maybe this thing works as it is supposed to')
   >>    ans = 'Mttwaiist'
   >> firstLetters('OK')
   >>    ans = 'O'
   ```

   Assume that there are no punctuation marks in the input string.

5. We need a function called anagram that consumes two character strings and returns true if the two are anagrams of each other and false otherwise. (An anagram is a word or group of words whose letters can be rearranged to spell another word or group of words.)

   a. Write the function removeSpaces that consumes a character string and returns that same string with any spaces removed.
   b. Write the function anagram.

   Assume that all the characters will be lowercase, but you cannot assume that there will be only one word.

   Hint

   Each character has a numerical value, and you can also make use of the sort(...) function.

   Examples:
   ```
   >> a1 = anagram('dormitory', 'dirty room') ->
   true
   >> a2 = anagram('yes', 'no') -> false
   >> a3 = anagram('cat', 'dog') -> false
   >> a4 = anagram('conversation', 'conservation')
   -> true
   ```

6. Write a function called myContains that takes in two strings. This function checks to see whether the second string is located inside the first string and returns the starting point of that substring. If the substring is not located inside the primary string, then the function returns zero.

   ```
   myContains('George Burdell', 'dell') -> 11
   myContains('CS1371','131') -> 0
   myContains('GaTech', 'GaTech') -> 1
   ```

   Note: Spaces count as a character.

7. Write a function called tripFlip that takes in one string and switches each even-indexed character with the odd-indexed character immediately preceding it.

You must use iteration to complete this problem.

Examples:
```
tripFlip('orange') -> 'ronaeg'
tripFlip('Matlab is cool') -> 'aMltbai  soclo'
```

Assume that the string length is always greater than one.

Note: Spaces count as characters as well. If the string has an odd-numbered length, then the function ignores the last letter.

8. Write a function called `gibberish` that takes in a string of the lowercase characters `'a'`-`'z'` and produces a gibberish word. You get the gibberish word by moving every letter in the word forward six spaces in the alphabet. Also, the alphabet must wrap around so that the following is true:
```
a->g, b->h,   ... t->z, u->a, v-> b, w->c, x->d, y->e, z->f
```

Hint

You may find the **mod**(x,y) function useful.

Example:
```
gibberish('buzz') -> 'haff'
```

9. We need to count the vowels in a character string. Follow these directions:
   a. Write a function called `isConsonant` that takes in a letter of the alphabet. It returns `true` if the letter is a consonant, and `false` if it is a vowel. You can assume that only lowercase letters will be passed into the function, but you should not need to write out all the consonants!
   b. Write an iterative function called `countVowels` that takes in a character string and returns the number of vowels in the array. You *must* use `isConsonant` in this function.

10. Write a function called `middler` that consumes a character string that is a complete name and returns a numerical value of 1 or 0 depending on whether there is a middle name in the string. If there is a middle name or middle initial in the string, `middler` should return `true`; otherwise, the function should return `false`.

Examples:
```
middler('George Burdell') should return false
middler('Madonna') should return false
middler('Pamela Lee Anderson') should return true
```

11. You have a big problem! In one of your CS courses, your professor decides that the only way you will pass the class is if you write a function for him. All the grades in his class have been stored into one long string of characters as follows:

'ACFCABDFACAFBCDAFCBAWCBCBAWDDABWDDCCCFAAB'

a. Your job is to write a function called `CrazyGrade` that will take in the long string and flip the grades according to the following specifications:

- A becomes F
- B becomes D
- C remains unchanged
- D becomes B
- F becomes A
- And for kicks, W becomes Y

Your function should take in a string and return an inverted string. You may assume that the string will only consist of valid letter grades.

Examples:

`CrazyGrade('BADDAD')` should return `'DFBBFB'`
`CrazyGrade('BAWBAW')` should return `'DFYDFY'`

b. To make matters worse, the professor wants you to organize this modified grade set (see exercise a). Write a function called `GradeDist` to categorize similar grades (put all the AS next to each other, BS next to each other, and so on). Then calculate and return the professor's grade distribution. Your function should take in a string and return a string with all similar grades grouped together, along with an array containing percentage values from AS to FS.

Hint

Your header will be:

```
function [anstring dist] =
gradeDist(str)
```

Examples:

If there are 15% AS, 16% BS, 33% CS, 16% DS, 16% FS, and 4% YS, `GradeDist` should return [15 16 33 16 16 4].

CHAPTER 7

Cell Arrays and Structures

Chapter Objectives

This chapter discusses the nature, implementation, and behavior of collections that may contain data items of any class, size, or shape. We will deal with two different heterogeneous storage mechanisms:

■ Those accessed by index (cell arrays)

■ Those accessed by name (structures)

In addition, we will consider collecting structures into arrays of structures.

Introduction

This chapter covers data collections that are more general and flexible than the arrays we have considered so far. Heterogeneous collections may contain objects of any type, rather than just numbers. Consequently, none of the collective operations defined for numerical arrays can be applied to cell arrays or structures. To perform any operations on their contents, the items must be extracted one at a time and replaced if necessary. We will consider three different mechanisms for building heterogeneous collections: cell arrays index their contents with a numerical index; structures index their contents with a symbolic index; and structure arrays index structures with a numerical index.

7.1 Concept: Collecting Dissimilar Objects

7.2 Cell Arrays
   7.2.1 Creating Cell Arrays
   7.2.2 Accessing Cell Arrays
   7.2.3 Using Cell Arrays
   7.2.4 Processing Cell Arrays

7.3 MATLAB Structures
   7.3.1 Constructing and Accessing One Structure
   7.3.2 Constructor Functions

7.4 Structure Arrays
   7.4.1 Constructing Cell Arrays
   7.4.2 Accessing Structure Elements
   7.4.3 Manipulating Structures

7.5 Engineering Example— Assembling a Structure

7.1 Concept: Collecting Dissimilar Objects

Heterogeneous collections permit objects of different data types to be grouped in a collection. They allow data abstraction to apply to a much broader range of content. However, the fact that the contents of these collections may be of any data type severely restricts the operations that can be performed on the collections as a whole. Whereas a significant number of arithmetic and logical operations can be performed on whole number arrays, algorithms that process heterogeneous collections must deal with the data contents one item at a time.

 ## 7.2 Cell Arrays

Cell arrays, as the name suggests, have the general form of arrays and can be indexed numerically as arrays. However, each element of a cell array should be considered as a container in which one data object of any class can be stored. They can be treated as arrays of containers for the purpose of concatenation and slicing. However, if you wish to access or modify the contents of the containers, the cells must be accessed individually.

7.2.1 Creating Cell Arrays

Cell arrays may be constructed in the following ways:

- By assigning values individually to a variable indexed with braces:

```
>> A{1} = 42
A =
    [42]
```

- By assigning containers individually to a variable indexed with brackets:

```
>> B[1] = {[4 6]};
B =
    [1x2 double]
```

- By concatenating cell contents using braces {. . .}:

```
>> C = {3, [1,2,3], 'abcde'}
C =
    [3] [1x3 double] 'abcde'
```

- By concatenating cell containers:

```
>> D = [A B C {'xyz'}]
D =
    [42] [1x2 double] [3] [1x3 double] 'abcde' 'xyz'
```

Based on these examples, we observe the following:

- A cell array can contain any legal MATLAB object
- Just as with number arrays, cell arrays can be created "on the fly" by assigning values to an indexed variable

When the values from a cell array are displayed, their appearance is different from that of the contents of a number array. Individual numbers are shown in brackets, for example, `[3]`; larger numerical arrays display their size, for example, `[1x3 double]`; and character strings are displayed with the enclosing quotes, for example, `'abcde'`.

7.2.2 Accessing Cell Arrays

Since cell arrays can be considered as conventional arrays of containers, the containers can be accessed and manipulated normally. For example, continuing the previous examples, we have the following:

```
>> E = D(2)    % parentheses - a container
 E =
    [4 6]
```

However, braces are used to access the contents of the containers as follows:

```
>> D{2}        % braces - the contents
ans =
    4    6
```

If the right-hand side of an assignment statement results in multiple cell arrays, the assignment must be to the same number of variables. The built-in MATLAB function `deal(...)` is used to make these allocations. Exercise 7.1 shows its use.

 Exercise 7.1 Cell arrays

Do It Yourself

Enter the following commands in the Command window and study the results:

```
>> A = { 3, [1,2,3] 'abcde'}
 A =
    [3]    [1x3 double] 'abcde'
>> A{1:2}
 ans =
    3
 ans =
    1    2    3
>> [x y] = A{1:2}
 x =
    3
 y =
    1    2    3
>> B = A{1:2}
 ??? Illegal right-hand side in assignment.
         Too many elements.
>> B([1 3]) = A([1 2])
 B =
    [3]    []    [1x3 double]
```

continued on next page

```
>> B{[1 3]} = A{[1 2]}
??? Illegal right-hand side in assignment.
          Too many elements.
>> [a, b, c] = deal(A{:})
 a =
      3
 b =
      1     2     3
 c =
abcde
>> [a, b] = deal(A)
 a =
      [3]    [1x3 double]   'abcde'
 b =
      [3]    [1x3 double]   'abcde'
>> B = A(1:2)
 B =
      [3]    [1x3 double]
>> for i = 1:2
        s(i) = sum(A{i})
      end
s =
      3
s =
      3     6
>> F{2} = 42
F =
      []     [42]
>> F{3} = {42}
F =
      []     [42]      {1x1 cell}
```

Notice the following observations:

- When we extract the contents of multiple cells using A{1:2}, this results in multiple assignments being made. These multiple assignments must go to separate variables. This is the fundamental mechanism behind returning multiple results from a function.

- These multiple assignments cannot be made to a single variable; sufficient storage must be provided either as a collection of variables or explicitly as a vector.

- Cell arrays can be "sliced" with normal vector indexing assignments as long as the sizes match on the left and right sides of the assignment. Any unassigned array elements are filled with an empty vector.

- The assignment B{[1 3]} = A{[1 2]} that produced an error needs some thought. Since A{[1 2]} produces two separate assignments, MATLAB will not assign the answers, even to the right number of places in another cell array. The deal(...) function is provided to capture these multiple results in different variables. Notice the difference between A{:} and A as a parameter to deal(...). When deal(...) is provided with a parameter other than a collection of cells, it copies that parameter to each variable.

■ Assignments work normally if cell arrays are treated as vectors and the extraction of items can be indexed—s is a vector of the sums of the elements in A.

■ Finally, notice that when accessing cell arrays, it is normal to have braces on one side or the other of an assignment; it is rarely appropriate to have braces on both sides of an assignment. The result here is that a cell array is loaded into the third container in the cell array.

7.2.3 Using Cell Arrays

There are a number of uses for cell arrays in MATLAB, some of which will be evident in upcoming chapters. For now, the following examples will suffice:

■ Containing lists of possible values for switch/case statements, as we saw in Chapter 4

■ Substituting for parameter lists in function calls

For example, suppose you have a function largest(a, b, c) that consumes three variables and produces the largest of the three values provided. It can be used in the following styles, as shown in Listing 7.1.

In Listing 7.1:

Lines 1–3: Set the values of A, B, and C.

Line 4: A conventional function call that results in a value of 6 for N.

Line 5: The same function call implemented as a cell array, returning the same answer.

7.2.4 Processing Cell Arrays

The general template for processing cell arrays is shown in Template 7.1.

Listing 7.1 Using cell arrays of parameters

```
1. A = 4;
2. B = 6;
3. C = 5;
4. N = largest(A, B, C)
5. params = { 4, 6, 5 };
6. N = largest(params{1:3})
```

Template 7.1 General template for processing cell arrays

```
<initialize result>
for <index specification>
        <extract an element>
        <check the element accordingly>
        <process the element accordingly>
end
<finalize result>
```

Checking the class of the element can be achieved in one of two ways:

- The function `class(item)` returns a string specifying the item type that can be used in a `switch` statement
- Individual test functions can be used in an `if... elseif` construct; examples of the individual test functions are `isa(item, 'class')`, `iscell(...)`, `ischar(...)`, `islogical(...)`, `isnumeric(...)`, and `isstruct(...)`

For example, suppose you are provided with a cell array and have been asked for a function that finds the total length of all the vectors it contains. The function might look like that shown in Listing 7.2.

In Listing 7.2:

> Line 1: Typical function header accepting a cell array as input.
>
> Line 3: Initializes the result.
>
> Line 4: Traverses the whole cell array.
>
> Line 5: Extracts each item in turn.
>
> Line 6: Determines whether this item is of type `double`.
>
> If so, it proceeds to line 7.
>
> Line 7: Accumulates the number of items in this array. Recall that the `size(...)` function returns a vector of the sizes of each dimension. The total number of numbers is therefore the product of these values.

Listing 7.2 Cell array processing example

```
1. function ans = totalNums(ca)
2. % count the numbers in a cell array
3.     ans =  0 ;
4.     for in =  1 :length(ca)
5.         item = ca{i} ;      % extract the item
6.         if isnumeric(item) % check if a vector
7.             ans = ans + prod(size(item));
8.         end
9.     end
```

7.3 MATLAB Structures

Where cell arrays implemented the concept of homogeneous collections as
indexed collections, structures allow items in the collection to be indexed by
field name. Most modern languages implement the concept of a structure in
a very similar style. The data contained in a structure is referenced by field
name, for example, item1. The rules for making a field name are the same as
those for a variable. Fields of a structure, like the elements of a cell array, are
heterogeneous—they can contain any MATLAB object.

First we will see how to construct and manipulate one structure, and then
how to aggregate individual structures into an array of structures.

7.3.1 Constructing and Accessing One Structure

To set the value of items in a structure A, the syntax is as follows:

```
>> A.item1 = 'abcde'
 A =
    item1: 'abcde'
>> A.item2 = 42
A =
    item1: 'abcde'
    item2: 42
```

Notice that MATLAB displays the elements of an emerging structure by
name. Fields in a structure are accessed in the same way—by using the dotted
notation.

```
>> A.item2 = A.item2 ./ 2
 A =
    item1: 'abcde'
    item2: 21
```

You can determine the names of the fields in a structure using the built-in
function fieldnames(...). It returns a cell array containing the field names
as strings.

```
>> names = fieldnames(A)
 names =
    'item1'
    'item2'
```

Fields can also be accessed "indirectly" by setting a variable to the name of
the field, and then using parentheses to indicate that the variable contents
should be used as the field name:

```
>> fn = names{1};
 >> A.(fn) = [A.(fn) 'fg']
A =
    item1: 'abcdefg'
    item2: 21
```

Common Pitfalls

Be careful. `rmfield(...)` returns a new structure with the requested field removed. It does not remove that field from your original structure. If you want the field removed from the original, you must assign the result from `rmfield(...)` to replace the original structure:

```
>> A = rmfield(A, 'item1')
A =
    item2: 21
```

You can also remove a field from a structure using the built-in function `rmfield(...)`. Exercise 7.2 gives you an opportunity to understand how to build structures.

Here we build a typical structure that could be used as one entry in a telephone book. Since phone numbers usually contain punctuation, we could store them as strings. Notice that since a structure may contain any object, it is quite legal to make a structure containing

 Exercise 7.2 Building structures

Do It Yourself

Suppose that you want to use structures to maintain your address book in MATLAB. In the Command window, enter the following commands:

```
>> entry.first = 'Fred'
entry =
    first: 'Fred'
>> entry.last = 'Jones';
>> entry.phone = '(123) 555-1212'
entry =
    first: 'Fred''
     last: 'Jones'
    phone: '(123) 555-1212'
>> entry.phone
ans =
 (123) 555-1212
>> date.day = 31;
>> date.month = 'February';
>> date.year = 1965
date =
      day: 31
    month:'February'
     year: 1965
>> entry.birth = date
entry =
    first: 'Fred'
     last: 'Jones'
    phone: '(123) 555-1212'
    birth: [1x1 struct]
>> entry.birth
ans =
      day: 31
    month: 'February'
     year: '1965'
>> entry.birth.year
ans =
   1965
```

a date and insert that structure in the date field of the entry. The structure display function, however, does not display the contents of the structures.

7.3.2 Constructor Functions

This section discusses functions that assign their parameters to the fields of a structure and then return that structure. You do this, as opposed to "manually" entering data into structures, for the following reasons:

- Manual entry can result in strange behavior due to typographical errors or having fields in the wrong order
- The resulting code is generally more compact and easier to understand
- When constructing collections of structures, it enforces consistency across the collections

There are two approaches to the use of constructor functions: using built-in MATLAB capabilities and writing your own constructor. MATLAB has a built-in function, `struct(...)`, that consumes pairs of entries (each consisting of a field name as a string and a cell array of field contents) and produces a structure. If all the cell arrays have more than one entry, this actually creates a structure array, as discussed in Section 7.4.1.

The following command would construct the address book entry created in the previous section. Note the use of ellipses `(...)` to indicate to the MATLAB machinery that the logic is continued onto the next line.

```
>> struct('first','Fred', ...
'last','Jones', ...
'phone','(123) 555-1212', ...
'birth', struct( 'day', 31, ...
                 'month', 'February', ...
                 'year', 1965 ))
ans =
    first: 'Fred'
     last: 'Jones'
    phone: '(123) 555-1212'
    birth: [1x1 struct]
```

This is useful in general to create structures, but the need to repeat the field names makes this general purpose approach a little annoying. We can create a special purpose function that "knows" the necessary field names to create multiple structures in an organized way.

Listing 7.3 shows the code for a function that consumes parameters that describe a CD and assembles a structure containing those attributes by name.

In Exercise 7.3 you can try your hand at using this function to construct a CD structure and then verify the structure contents.

Listing 7.3 Constructor for a CD structure

```
function ans = makeCD(gn, ar, ti, yr, st, pr)
  % integrate CD data into a structure
     ans.genre = gn ;
     ans.artist = ar ;
     ans.title = ti;
     ans.year = yr;
     ans.stars = st;
     ans.price = pr;
```

 Exercise 7.3 A CD structure

Do It Yourself

In the Command window, enter the following commands to create one entry of CD information:

```
>> CD = makeCD('Blues', 'Charles, Ray',  &
'Genius Loves Company', 2004, 4.5, 15.35 )
CD =
      genre: 'Blues'
     artist: 'Charles, Ray'
      title: 'Genius Loves Company'
       year: 2004
      stars: 4.5000
      price: 15.3500
>> flds = fieldnames(CD)
flds =
     'genre'
     'artist'
     'title'
     'year'
     'stars'
     'price'
>> field = flds{2}
field =
artist
>> CD.(field)
ans =
     Charles, Ray
```

 ## 7.4 Structure Arrays

To be useful, collections like address books or CD collections require multiple structure entries with the same fields. This is accomplished by forming an array of data items, each of which contains the same fields of information. MATLAB implements the concept of structure arrays with the properties described in the following paragraphs.

7.4.1 Constructing Structure Arrays

Structure arrays can be created either by creating values for individual fields, as shown in Exercise 7.4; by using MATLAB's `struct(...)` function to build the whole structure array, as shown in Listing 7.4; or by using a custom function to create each individual structure, as shown in Listing 7.5. This latter listing illustrates these concepts by implementing a collection of CDs as a structure array using the function `makeCD(...)` from Listing 7.3.

In Listing 7.4:

Lines 1–5: Build cell arrays containing field values for five CDs.
Line 6: Uses the built-in `struct(...)` function to create the CD collection.

7.4.2 Accessing Structure Elements

Like normal arrays or cell arrays, items can be stored and retrieved by their index in the array. As structures are added to the array, MATLAB forces all

---

Exercise 7.4 Building a structure array "by hand"

Do It Yourself

```
>> entry(1).first = 'Fred';
>> entry(1).last = 'Jones';
>> entry(1).age = 37;
>> entry(1).phone = ' (123) 555-1212';
>> entry(2).first = 'Sally';
>> entry(2).last = 'Smith';
>> entry(2).age = 29;
>> entry(2).phone = '(000) 555-1212'
entry =
1x2 structure array with fields:
    first
    last
    age
    phone
```

Listing 7.4 Building a structure array using `struct(...)`

```
1. genres = {'Blues', 'Classical', 'Country' };
2. artists = {'Clapton, Eric', 'Bocelli, Andrea',  &
'Twain, Shania' };
3. years = { 2004, 2004, 2004 };
4. stars = { 2, 4.6, 3.9 };
5. prices = { 18.95, 14.89, 13.49 };
6. cds = struct( 'genre',  genres,  &
                 'artist', artists,  &
                 'year', years,  &
                 'stars', stars,  &
                 'price', prices);
```

Listing 7.5 Building a structure array using a custom constructor

```
% extracts from http://www.cduniverse.com/  12/30/04
cds(1) = makeCD('Blues', 'Clapton, Eric', ...
 'Sessions For Robert J', 2004, 2, 18.95 )
cds(2) = makeCD('Classical', ...
 'Bocelli, Andrea', 'Andrea', 2004, 4.6, 14.89 )
cds(3) = makeCD( 'Country', 'Twain, Shania', ...
 'Greatest Hits', 2004, 3.9, 13.49 )
cds(4) = makeCD( 'Latin', 'Trevi, Gloria', ...
 'Como Nace El Universo', 2004, 5, 12.15 )
cds(5) = makeCD( 'Rock/Pop', 'Ludacris', ...
 'The Red Light District', 2004, 4, 13.49 )
cds(6) = makeCD( 'R & B', '2Pac', ...
 'Loyal To The Game', 2004, 3.9, 13.49 )
cds(7) = makeCD( 'Rap', 'Eminem', ...
 'Encore', 2004, 3.5, 15.75 )
cds(8) = makeCD( 'Heavy Metal', 'Rammstein', ...
 'Reise, Reise', 2004, 4.2, 12.65 )
```

elements in the structure array to implement the same field names in the same order. Elements can be accessed either manually (not recommended) or by creating new structures with a constructor and adding them (recommended).

If you elect to manipulate them manually, you merely identify the array element by indexing, and use the .field operator. For example, for the CD collection cds, we could change the price of one of them as follows:

```
>> cds(3).price = 11.95
 cds =
1x31 struct array with fields:
    genre
    artist
    title
    year
    stars
    price
```

This is a little hazardous when making manual additions to a structure array. A typographical error while entering a field name results in all the structures having that bad field name. For example, consider this error:

```
>> cds(3).prce = 11.95
 cds =
1x31 struct array with fields:
    genre
    artist
    title
    year
    stars
    price
    prce
```

You have accidentally added a new field to the whole collection. You can check this by looking at one entry:

```
>> cds(1)
 ans =
     genre: 'Blues'
    artist: 'Sessions For Robert J'
     title: 'Clapton, Eric'
      year: 2004
     stars: 2
     price: 18.9500
      prce: []
```

If this happens, you can use the `fieldnames(...)` function to determine the situation, and then the `rmfield(...)` function to remove the offending entry.

```
>> fieldnames(cds)
  ans =

     'genre'
     'artist'
     'title'
     'year'
     'stars'
     'price'
     'prce'

>> cds = rmfield(cds,'prce')
cds =
1x32 struct array with fields:
    genre
    artist
    title
    year
    stars
    price
```

It is best to construct a complete structure and then insert it into the structure array. For example:

```
>> newCD = makeCD( 'Oldies', 'Greatest Hits', ...
 'Ricky Nelson', 2005, 5, 15.79 );
> cds(8) = newCD
cds =
1x8 struct array with fields:
    genre
    artist
    title
    year
    stars
    price
```

If you insert that new CD beyond the end of the array, as one might expect, MATLAB fills out the array with empty structures:

```
>> cds(50) = newCD
 cds =
1x50 struct array with fields:
```

Common Pitfalls

A few very understandable but sneaky errors occur when adding structures that have been created "manually" rather than by means of a standardized constructor function. If the new structure has fields not in the original structure, or extra fields, MATLAB gives a slightly obscure error: "Subscripted assignment between dissimilar structures." Perhaps more puzzling, this same error occurs if all the fields are present, but are in the wrong order. See the following example:

```
>> it = cds(1);
 >> it = rmfield(it,'price');
>> it = rmfield(it,'stars');
>> it.price = 19.95;
>> it.stars = 4
it =
genre: 'Blues'
artist: 'Sessions For Robert J'
title: 'Clapton, Eric'
year: 2004
price: 19.9500
stars: 4
>> cds(1) = it
??? Subscripted assignment between
dissimilar structures.
```

```
        genre
        artist
        title
        year
        stars
        price
>> cds(49)
ans =
        genre: []
       artist: []
        title: []
         year: []
        stars: []
        price: []
```

7.4.3 Manipulating Structures

Structures and structure arrays can be manipulated in the following ways:

Single values can be changed using the "." (dot) notation directly with a field name:

```
>> cds(5).price = 19.95;
```

or indirectly using the "." (dot) notation with a variable containing the field name:

```
>> fld = 'price';
>> cds(5).(fld) = 19.95;
```

or by using MATLAB's equivalent built-in functions:

nms = fieldnames(str) returns a cell array containing the names of the fields in a structure or structure array.

```
>> flds = fieldnames(cds)
```

if = isfield(str, <fldname>) determines whether the given name is a field in this structure or structure array.

```
>> if isfield(cds, 'price') ...
```

str = setfield(str, <fldname>, <value>) returns a new structure array with the specified field set to the specified value.

```
>> cds(1) = setfield(cds(1), ...
        'price', 19.95);
```

val = getfield(str, <fldname>) returns the value of the specified field.

```
>> disp(getfield(cds(1), 'price') );
```

str = rmfield(str, <fldname>) returns a new structure array with the specified field removed.

```
>> noprice = rmfield(cds, 'price');
```

Values across the whole array can be retrieved using the "." notation by accumulating them into arrays; either into cell arrays:

```
>> titles = {cds.title};
```

or if the values are all numeric, into a vector:

```
>> prices = [cds.price];
```

Exercise 7.5 provides some practice in manipulating structure arrays using the above CD collection as an example.

Notice that after extracting the price values into a vector, all the normal vector operations—in this case, sum(...)—can be utilized.

 Exercise 7.5 The CD collection

Do It Yourself

Retrieve and run the script named buildCDs.m from the Addison-Wesley Instructor Resource Center (www.aw.com/irc). In the Command window, enter the following commands to create your collection of CD information:

```
>> cds(5)
ans =
     genre: 'Rock/Pop'
    artist: 'Ludacris'
     title: 'The Red Light District'
      year: 2004
     stars: 4
     price: 13.4900
>> flds = fieldnames(collection)
flds =
    'genre'
    'artist'
    'title'
    'year'
    'stars'
    'price'
cds(5).strs = 0.5;
>> cds(5)
ans =
     genre: 'Rock/Pop'
    artist: 'Ludacris'
     title: 'The Red Light District'
      year: 2004
     stars: 4
     price: 13.4900
      strs: 0.5
```

continued on next page

```
>> cds(1)
ans =
     genre: 'Blues'
    artist: 'Clapton, Eric'
     title: 'Sessions For Robert J'
      year: 2004
     stars: 2
     price: 18.9500
      strs: []
>> cds = rmfield(cds, 'strs');
>> cds(1)
ans =
     genre: 'Blues'
    artist: 'Clapton, Eric'
     title: 'Sessions For Robert J'
      year: 2004
     stars: 2
     price: 18.9500
>> sum([cds.price])
ans =
  409.1100
```

7.5 Engineering Example—Assembling a Structure

Many large buildings today have steel frames as their basic structure.
Engineers perform the analysis and design work for each steel component
and deliver these designs to the steel company. The steel company
manufactures all the components, and prepares them for delivery to the
building site. At this point, each component is identified only by a unique
identifier string stamped and/or chalked onto that component. For even a
modest-sized building, this transportation may require a significant number
of truckloads of components.

The question we address here is how to decide the sequence in which the
components are delivered to the building site so that components are
available when needed, but not piled up waiting to be used.

Consider the relatively simple structure shown in Figure 7.1. The
components have individual labels, and we can obtain from the architect the
identities of the components that are connected together. The construction
needs to start from the fixed point A. We need to analyze this information
and compute the order in which the components would be used to assemble
the structure.

The data will be organized as a structure array with one entry for each
component. One of the fields in that structure will be a cell array of the
names of the components to which this component is connected.

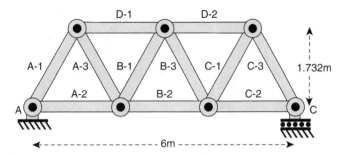

Figure 7.1 *Simple structure assembly*

The code in Listing 7.6 shows the solution to this problem.

Listing 7.6 Connectivity of a structure

```
clear
clc

 1. data(1) = beam('A-1', 0.866, 0.5, ...
       {'A','A-2','A-3','D-1'} );
 2. data(2) = beam('A-2', 0, 1, ...
       {'A','A-3','B-1','B-2'} );
 3. data(3) = beam('A-3', 0.866, 1.5, ...
       {'A-1','A-2','B-1','D-1'} );
 4. data(4) = beam('B-1', 0.866, 2.5, ...
       {'A-2','A-3','B-2','B-3','D-1','D-2'} );
 5. data(5) = beam('B-2', 0, 3, ...
       {'A-2','A-3','B-1','B-3','C-1','C-2'} );
 6. data(6) = beam('B-3', 0.866, 3.5, ...
       {'B-1','B-2','C-1','C-2','D-1','D-2'} );
 7. data(7) = beam('C-1', 0.866, 4.5, ...
       {'B-2','B-3','C-2','C-3','D-2'} );
 8. data(8) = beam('C-2', 0, 5, ...
       {'B-2','B-3','C-1','C-3','C'} );
 9. data(9) = beam('C-3', 0.866, 5.5, ...
       {'C-1','C-2','D-2','C'} );
10. data(10) = beam('D-1', 1.732, 2, ...
       {'A-1','A-3','B-1','B-3','D-2'} );
11. data(11) = beam('D-2', 1.732, 4, ...
       {'B-1','B-3','C-1','C-3','D-1'} )

12. conn = 'A';
13. clist = {conn};
14. while true
15.     index = 0;
     % find all the beams connected to conn
16.     for in = 1:length(data)
17.         str = data(in);
18.         if touches(str, conn)
19.             index = index + 1;
20.             found(index) = str;
21.         end
22.     end
```

continued on next page

```
        % eliminate those already connected
23.       for jn = index:-1:1
24.           if ison(found(jn).name, clist)
25.               found(jn) = [];
26.           else
27.               clist = [clist {found(jn).name}];
28.           end
29.       end
30.       if length(found) > 0
31.           conn = nextconn( found, clist );
32.       else
33.           break;
34.       end
35. end
36. disp('the order of assembly is:')
37. disp(clist)
```

In Listing 7.6:

> Lines 1–11: Construct the structure array using the `beam( ... )` constructor function below.
>
> Line 12: The current connection point, `conn`—originally, the point A.
>
> Line 13: Initializes the connection list, a cell array of names.
>
> Line 14: An infinite loop to be exited with break statements.
>
> Lines 15–22: Traverse the components to make a structure array, `found`, containing all the components connected to the current connection point, `conn`.
>
> Lines 23–29: Go through the `found` array, removing any component already on the connected list and appending the names of those not removed to the connected list.
>
> Lines 30–33: We will exit the `while` loop when there are no new components found; until then, choose the next component to connect to.

The support functions for this script are assembled for convenience into Listing 7.7.

Listing 7.7 Support functions

```
 1. function ans = beam( nm, xp, yp, conn )
% construct a beam structure with fields:
%   name - beam name
%   xp, yp - coordinates of its centroid
%   conn - cell array - names of adjacent beams
% useage: ans = beam( nm, xp, yp, conn )
 2. ans.name = nm;
 3. ans.pos = [xp, yp];
 4. ans.connect = conn;
```

continued on next page

```
 5. function res = touches(beam, conn)
% does the beam touch this connecting point?
% usage: res = touches(beam, conn)
 6. res = false;
 7. for in = 1:length(beam.connect)
 8.      item = beam.connect{in};
 9.      if strcmp(item,conn)
10.          res = true; break;
11.      end
12. end

13. function res = ison( nm, cl )
% is this beam on the connection list,
%          a cell array of beam names
% usage: res = ison( beam, cl )
14. res = false;
15. for in = 1:length(cl)
16.      item = cl{in};
17.      if strcmp(item, nm)
18.          res = true; break;
19.      end
20. end

21. function nm = nextconn( fnd, cl )
% find a connection name among
%          those found not already connected
% usage: nm = nextconn( fnd, cl )
22. for in = 1:length(fnd)
23.      item = fnd(in);
24.      cn = item.connect;
25.      for jn = 1:length(cn)
26.          nm = cn{jn};
27.          if ~ison(nm, cl)
28.              break;
29.          end
30.      end
31. end
```

In Listing 7.7:

Lines 1–4: Constructor for one structure defining one component.

Line 5: Function to determine whether a component is connected to the component with the name provided.

Line 6: Presume not connected.

Lines 7–8: Extract each item in turn from the component's connections

Lines 9–10: If this item matches the connection, return true.

Line 13: A similar function to determine whether a particular string is on the connection list, a cell array of strings.

Line 14: Presumes false.

Lines 15 and 16: Extract each item in turn from the cell array.

Lines 17 and 18: Check the item against the name provided, and return `true` if it matched.

Line 21: Functions to find the next connection to use based on the latest components found—the "outer edges" of the emerging structure—and its not being already on the connected list.

Lines 22–24: Extract one component at a time from the found list, and extract its connection list.

Lines 25 and 26: Extract each name in turn from that connection list.

Lines 27–29: If this component is not on the connected list, exit and return it. (Notice that the return variable `nm` has been set.)

Here is the resulting output:

```
data =

1x11 struct array with fields:
    name
    pos
    connect

the order of assembly is:
'A' 'A-2' 'A-1' 'D-1' 'A-3' 'B-2' 'B-1' 'D-2' 'B-3' 'C-2' 'C-1' 'C-3'
```

Chapter Summary

This chapter covered the nature, implementation, and behavior of two heterogeneous collections:

- Cell arrays are vectors of containers; their elements can be manipulated either as vectors of containers, or individually by inserting or extracting the contents of the container using braces in place of parentheses.
- The elements of a structure are accessed by name rather than by indexing, using the dot operator, '.', to specify the field name to be used.
- Structures can be collected into structure arrays whose elements are structures all with the same field names. These elements can then be indexed and manipulated in the same manner as the cells in a cell array.

Special Characters, Reserved Words, and Functions

Special Characters Reserved Words, and Functions	Description	Discussed in This Section
`{ }`	Defines a cell array	7.2
`.`	Used to access fields of a structure	7.3.1
`(variable)`	Used to allow a variable to be used as a structure field	7.3.1
`class(obj)`	Determines the data type of an object	7.2.4
`deal(...)`	Distributes cell array results among variables	7.2.2
`getfield (str,<fld>)`	Extracts the value of the field `<fld>`	7.4.3
`isa(obj, str)`	Tests for a given data type	7.2.4
`ischar(ch).`	Determines whether the given object is of type `char`	7.2.4
`iscell(...).`	Determines whether the given object is a cell	7.2.4
`isfield (str, <fld>)`	`true` if the string is a field in this structure	7.4.3
`islogical(...)`	Determines whether the given object is of type `logical`	7.2.4
`isnumeric(...).`	Determines whether the given object is of type `double`	7.2.4
`isstruct(...).`	Determines whether the given object is a structure	7.2.4
`str = setfield (str,<fld>, <value>)`	Constructs a structure in which the value of the field `<fld>` has been changed	7.4.3
`struct(...)`	Constructs a structure from `<fieldname> <value>` pairs of parameters	7.3.2

 Self Test

Use the following questions to check your understanding of the material in this chapter:

True or False

1. Of all the collective operations defined for numerical arrays, only logical operations can be applied to a whole cell array.

2. A cell array or a structure can contain any legal MATLAB object.

3. You gain access to the contents of a cell by using braces, `{...}`.

4. Since the contents of a structure are heterogeneous, we can store other structures in any structure.

5. The statement `rmfield(str, 'price')` removes the field `'price'` and its value from the structure `str`.

6. The statement `getfield(str, <fldname>)` returns the value of the specified field.

7. You cannot extract and process all of the values of a field in a structure array.

Fill in the Blanks

1. To perform any operations on the contents of a heterogeneous

    collection, the items must be _____ and

    _____ if necessary.

2. Cell arrays can be treated for the purpose of concatenation and slicing as _____ of _____.

3. The assignment `B{3}` = `{42}` results in the third entry in the cell array B to be a _____.

4. If a variable called field contains the value of a field of a structure str, the expression _____ will set the value of that field to 42.

5. MATLAB has a built-in function _____ that

    consumes pairs of entries, each consisting of a _____

    and a _____, and produces a structure array.

Programming Projects

1. Given the following code:
    ```
    a{1} = 'My favorite class';
    a{2} = 'is CS';
    a{3} = 1371;
    x = a{1};
    y = a{2}(2);
    z = a(3);
    ```

    what are the data types of x, y, and z respectively?

2. Consider the following code blocks. Decide which will run correctly, and predicts that code block's output.

   a. ```
      a = {3 3 3} ;
      a(2)*3
      ```

   b. ```
      x = {4 5 6 7} ;
      y = x{3}*7
      ```

   c. ```
      d = 0 :3 :21 ;
      e = 4234 ;
      f = d(0)*e
      ```

   d. ```
      g = 0:6:23;
      g
      ```

   e. ```
      m = [1 2 ; 2 3]
      m(2,2)*ones(4)
      ```

3. We need to be able to transform numerical vectors into cell arrays, and cell arrays to vectors.

   a. Write a function called `vecToCells` that converts a vector of numbers into a cell array of strings. Each item in the string will be the value of the cell array as generated by `sprintf(...)` using the format string `'%g'`.

   b. To test this function, build a vector with random length (between 20 and 100) of random numbers in the range (0 ... 1,000,000), and pass this vector to your `vecToCells` function, displaying the results in the Command window.

   c. Write and test a function that accepts a cell array of strings and builds a vector of numbers of the same length. Each item in the output vector will be the length of the strings in each cell array.

4. In this exercise, we will use a somewhat artificial cell array to build some fundamental cell array operations. We will use a cell array containing vectors with random sizes and contents, and then process it with a number of standard operations.

   a. Write a function called `randomVector` that first generates a random size (between 1 and 5) and then fills a vector of that size with random integers in the range (0 ... 100).

   b. Generate another random number between 5 and 25 that is the size of the cell array, and build a cell array `randVCells` of that size by calling `randomVector` that many times.

   c. Write a function called `traverse` that iterates across `randVCells` displaying each vector on a separate line in the Command window.
      ```

d.   Write a function called `map` that consumes `rvca`, a random vector cell array, and produces a new cell array of the same size with each of the vectors in `rcva` reversed. Test this new cell array with `traverse`.

e.   Write a function called `filter` that consumes `rvca`, a random vector cell array, and produces a new, shorter cell array containing only those cells from the original array whose lengths are greater than 3.

f.   Write a function called `fold` that consumes `rvca`, a random vector cell array, and produces a number that is the total value of all the items in all the vectors in the cell array.

g.   Write a function called `largest` that consumes `rvca`, a random vector cell array, and produces the largest vector. The largest vector is that with the greatest length. If two are of equal length, the vector with the greatest sum will be returned.

h.   Write a function called `search` that consumes `rvca`, a random vector cell array, and finds the first vector of length 1 (a scalar).

5.   The following script is run in MATLAB:

```
team1 = ...
   struct('name', 'Falcons', 'sport', 'Football');
team1.city = 'Atlanta';
team2 = ...
      struct('name', 'Fire', 'sport', 'Football', ...
                                 'city', 'Chicago');
team2.record = '2-2';
team2.sport = 'Soccer';
team1 = setfield(team1,'city', 'ATL');
team3 = rmfield(team2, 'record');
team4 = team2;
teams = [team1, team2, team3, team4];
A = isstruct(team2)
B = team(1).sport
C = isfield(team4,'record')
D = team(3).name
E = getfield(team3, 'sport')
```

What are the values of A, B, C, D, and E?

6.   The following script is run in MATLAB:

```
GT.Offense = 60;
GT.Defense = 45;
GT.QB = 'Ball';
NC.Offense = 85;
NC.Defense = 65;
NC.QB = 'Durant';
UGA.Offense = 3;
UGA.Defense = 4;
UGA.QB = 'Greene';
football = [GT NC UGA];
football(1).Factor = 2;
```

```
football(2).Factor = 4;
football(3).Rank = 5;
[m n o] = football(:).Offense;
[val, posn] = max([m n o]);
C = [];
for i = [3 1 2]
    C = [C football(i).Defense];
    D(i) = (football(i).Offense);
end
A = football(posn).Rank;
B = football(posn).QB;
```

What are the values of A, B, C, and D?

7. You are given an array of structures named Stats. Each structure contains the following fields:

   Name, BA, HomeRuns, Errors

   Write a function called MVP that takes in that array and returns the most valuable player (MVP) of the season. The MVP is defined as the player with the highest batting average (BA), given he has at least 25 home runs and at most 5 errors.

   For example, if the array were constructed as follows:

```
Stats(1).Name = 'Sleepy';
Stats(1).BA = 0.27;
Stats(1).HomeRuns = 19;
Stats(1).Errors = 4;
Stats(2).Name = 'Dopey';
Stats(2).BA = 0.03;
Stats(2).HomeRuns = 2;
Stats(2).Errors = 4;
Stats(3).Name = 'Grumpy';
Stats(3).BA = 0.46;
Stats(3).HomeRuns = 32;
Stats(3).Errors = 12;
Stats(4).Name = 'Doc';
Stats(4).BA = 0.29;
Stats(4).HomeRuns = 46;
Stats(4).Errors = 0;
Stats(5).Name = 'Happy';
Stats(5).BA = 0.31;
Stats(5).HomeRuns = 27;
Stats(5).Errors = 4;
```

   MVP(Stats) should return 'Happy'.

8. Suppose we have a car structure that has the following fields:

   basePrice a number representing the starting price of the car

   trim   the style of the car, represented as a string

   cc   a Boolean variable indicating that the car has cruise control

   dualAB   a Boolean variable indicating that the car has dual air bags

a. Write a function called `carOptions` that takes in a car structure and returns its final price from the base price and options:
   - The standard trim of the car is `'S'`
   - If the trim is `'LS'`, add $600
   - If the trim is `'LE'`, add $1200
   - If the car has cruise control, add $150
   - If the car has dual air bags, add $300

b. Now, write a function called `inventory` that consumes an array of car structures, and calculates the total value of the vehicles.

9. You have a structure array of friends. Each structure contains a Name, Age, Gender, Birthplace, and Zip code. An example of this structure might be as follows:

```
techFriend.Name = 'George P. Burdell';
techFriend.Age = 100;
techFriend.Gender = 'Male';
techFriend.Birthplace = 'Atlanta';
techFriend.ZipCode = 30332;
```

Write a function called `older` that will take in an array of the above structure type and an age. Your function should return a new structure array containing every friend whose age is higher than the provided age. If none of the friends contained in the structure array meets the age criteria, return the empty vector, `[ ]`.

10. We wish to create a "library" as an array of structures. Each structure has the following fields:

   - Title
   - Author
   - ISBN

a. Using MATLAB structures, create the first two entries for the "library" structure array, using data of your choosing.

b. Write a script that will display the titles of all the books in a library structure array. (You should be able to deal with libraries of all different sizes).

11. In terms of atomic physics, each electron has four numbers, called the quantum numbers, associated with it. They are principal (energy); azimuthal (angular momentum); magnetic (orientation of angular momentum); and spin (particle spin). Wolfgang Pauli hypothesized (correctly) that no two electrons in an atom can have the same set of four quantum numbers; that is, if the principal, azimuthal, and magnetic numbers are the same for two electrons, then it is necessary for the electrons to have different spin numbers.

Scientists from the University of Georgia have come to you for assistance with some research they are doing. They ask you to write a function called UGAhelper that takes in two structures. Each structure represents an electron in a hydrogen atom and has the following fields:

- Principal (this is always >0)
- Azimuthal
- Magnetic
- Spin

The first three fields are numbers, and the spin field is a string with either the value "up" or "down." Your function compares the values in the two structures and checks whether they all have the same values for the four fields. If true, you are required to switch the spin of one of the structures (it doesn't matter which one). You also have to add a field called "energy" to both structures. The value stored in this field must be $-2.18 * 10^{18}/n^2$, where n is the value of the principal quantum number for that electron. You have to return both structures with the energy field added to both, so that the one with the higher energy is first. If the energies are equal, return the one with the "up" spin first. If both have the same spin and the same energy, the order does not matter.

12. It turns out that since you've become an expert on rating clothing, Acme Clothing Company has hired you to rate their clothes. Clothes are now structures instead of vectors with the following fields (all of which are numbers between 0 and 5):

- Condition
- Color
- Price
- Matches
- Comfort

First we have to convert your old clothing rating system to their model. Write a function called convertGarment that consumes a vector of clothing values and produces a structure according to the Acme model.

a. Write a function called convertClothes that consumes an array (think of it as a vector of vectors) of clothing assessments and produces an array of Acme clothing structures. Your original data is:

```
clothes = [3 2 1 4 5; 1 5 4 3 2; 5 5 5 5 5; 4 1 3 4 3;
           0 1 0 0 1; 2 2 1 2 ; 2 0 1 4 3; 5 4 3 2 1]
```

b.   Acme has a much simpler way of rating their clothes than you used before:

5 * Condition + 3 * Color + 2 * Price + Matches + 9 * Comfort

Write a script called `rateClothes` that will add a Rating field and a Quality field to each of the structures in the `acmeClothes` array. The Rating field in each structure should contain the rating of that particular article of clothing. The Quality field is a string that is `premium` if the Rating is over 80, `good` if over 60, `poor` if over 20, and `liquidated` for anything else.

Note: You *must* use iteration to solve this problem.

13. A requirement for all freshmen classes is a progress "standing" during the middle of the term. The results are either a Satisfactory (S) or Unsatisfactory (U). You are the office employee in charge of issuing these grades, and you decide to write a function called `standing` to help you. You pull the grade file and discover that the grades are organized as follows:

Each student is a single element of a structure array, and each student has two fields: `name` and `classes`. The latter is itself a `struct` that contains the letter grade for five classes: `math`, `science`, `english`, `history`, and `cs`. Grades can be A, B, C, D, F, or W.

Your function should add two more tier-one fields for each student: `standings` and `status`.

- `standings` should be a string of S's (if grade is A, B, or C) and U's (if grade is anything else) for each of the five classes in alphabetical order
- `status` should be either GOOD if there are more S's than U's in the standings field, or BAD otherwise

Your function should take in a structure array and return the same structure array with the two added fields.

14. Georgia Tech has added a new award for students who were "almost there" last semester and just missed making the Dean's List.

a.   Write a function called `almost` that iterates through an array of student structures that it takes in, and that returns a cell array of names of those who have a semester GPA between 2.9 and 2.99 (inclusive). The student structure has the following fields:

- `Name`—string (e.g., 'George P. Burdell')
- `Semester_GPA`—decimal number (e.g., 2.97)
- `Cumulative_GPA`—decimal number (e.g., 3.01)

b.   Write a test script that populates an array of student structures and verifies that `almost` is working correctly.

File Input and Output

8.1 Concept: Serial Input and Output (I/O)
8.2 MATLAB Workspace I/O
8.3 High-level I/O Functions
   8.3.1 Exploration
   8.3.2 Excel Spreadsheets
   8.3.3 Delimited Text Files—Numerical Data Only
8.4 Low-level File I/O
   8.4.1 Opening and Closing Files
   8.4.2 Reading Text Files
   8.4.3 Examples of Reading Text Files
   8.4.4 Writing Text Files
8.5 Engineering Example—Spreadsheet Data

Chapter Objectives

This chapter discusses three levels of capability for reading and writing files in MATLAB, each including a discussion of the circumstances under which they are appropriate:

- Saving and restoring the workspace

- High-level functions for accessing files in specific formats

- Low-level file access programs for general-purpose file processing

Reading and writing data in data files is fundamental to the utility of programming languages in general, and MATLAB in particular. In addition to the obvious need to save and restore scripts and functions (covered in Chapter 2) here we consider three types of activities that read and write data files.

- MATLAB has the basic ability to save your workspace (or parts of your workspace) to a file and restore it later for further processing.

- There are high-level functions in MATLAB that consume the name of a file in any one of a number of popular formats and produce an internal representation of the data from that file in a form ready for processing. Almost all these functions have an equivalent write function that will write a new file in the same format after you have manipulated the data.

- However, we also need to deal with lower-level capabilities for manipulating text files that do not have recognizable structures.

Introduction

This chapter discusses files that contain workspace variables, spreadsheet data, and text files containing delimited numbers and plain text. Subsequent chapters will discuss image files and sound files. For information on the other file formats, consult the help documentation for details of their usage.

MATLAB also has the ability to access binary files—files whose data is not in text form—but the interpretation of binary data is beyond the scope of this text, and we will not consider binary files here. Refer to MATLAB help for information about binary files.

8.1 Concept: Serial Input and Output (I/O)

We frequently refer to the process of reading and writing data files as Input/Output (I/O). We have already seen and used examples of file I/O to store and retrieve data and programs. Your script and function files were stored in your current directory, and could be invoked from there by name from the Command window. In general, any computer file system saves and retrieves data as a sequential (serial) stream of characters, as shown in Figure 8.1. Mixed in with the characters that represent the data are control characters ("delimiters") that specify the organization of the data. When a program opens a file by name for reading, it continually requests values from the file data stream until the end of the file is reached. As the data is received, the program must identify the delimiting characters and reformat the data to reconstruct the organization of the data as represented in the file.

Similarly, when writing data to a file, the program must serialize the data, as shown in Figure 8.2. To preserve the organization of the data, the appropriate delimiting characters must be inserted into the serial character stream. The purpose of the file I/O functions discussed in this chapter is to encapsulate these fundamental operations into a single MATLAB function, or at least into a manageable collection of functions.

 ## 8.2 MATLAB Workspace (I/O)

MATLAB provides the tools to save your complete workspace to a file with the save command and reload it with the load command. If you provide a file name with the save command, a file of that name will be written into your current directory in such a form that a subsequent load command with that file name will restore the saved workspace. If you do not provide a file name, MATLAB saves the workspace as matlab.mat.

Figure 8.1 *An input stream*

Figure 8.2 *An output stream*

You can also identify specific variables that you want to save—either by listing them explicitly or by providing logical expressions to indicate the variable names. For example:

```
> > save mydata.mat a b c*
```

would save the variables a and b and any variable beginning with the letter c. For more details, consult the MATLAB help documentation.

In a practical sense, however, this is very rarely an appropriate approach to saving work because it saves the results but not the code that generated the results. It is almost always better to save the scripts and raw data that created the workspace. For example, this is a good idea when you have a lengthy computation (perhaps one run overnight) to prepare data for a display. You could split that script into two halves. The first half would do the overnight calculation and save the workspace. The second part can then read the workspace quickly, and you can develop sophisticated ways to display the data without having to re-run the lengthy calculations.

8.3 High-Level I/O Functions

We turn to the general case of file I/O in which we expect to load data from external sources, process that data, and perhaps save data back to the file system with enhancements created by MATLAB.

When you try to process data from some unknown source, it is difficult to write MATLAB code without some initial exploration of the nature and organization of the data. So a good habit is to explore the data in a file by whatever means you have available and then commit to processing the data according to your observations.

Most programming languages require the programmer to write detailed programs to read and write files, especially those produced by other application programs or data acquisition packages. Fortunately for MATLAB programmers, much of this messy work has been built into special file readers and writers. Table 8.1 identifies the type of data, the name of the appropriate reader and writer, and the internal form in which MATLAB returns the data.

8.3.1 Exploration

The types of data of immediate interest are text files and spreadsheets. In Table 8.1 notice that the delimited text files are presumed to contain numerical values, whereas the spreadsheet data may be either numerical data stored as doubles or string data stored in cell arrays. Typically, text files are delimited by a special character (comma, tab, or anything else) to designate the column divider, and a new-line character to designate the rows. Once the data is

Table 8.1 File I/O functions

File Content	File Extension	Reader	Writer	Data Format
Plain text	Any	`textscan`	`fprintf`	Specified in the function calls
Comma-separated numbers	CSV	`csvread`	`csvwrite`	Double array
Tab-separated text	TAB	`dlmread`	`dlmwrite`	Double array
General delimited text	DLM	`dlmread`	`dlmwrite`	Double array
Excel worksheet	XLS	`xlsread`	`xlswrite`	Double or cell array
Lotus 1-2-3 worksheet	WK1	`wk1read`	`wk1write`	Double or cell array
Scientific data in Common Data Format	CDF	`cdfread`	`cdfwrite`	Cell array of CDF records
Flexible Image Transport System data	FITS	`fitsread`		Primary or extension table data
Data in Hierarchical Data Format	HDF	`hdfread`		HDF or HDF-EOS data set
Extended Markup Language (XML)	XML	`xmlread`	`xmlwrite`	Document Object Model node
Image data	Various	`imread`	`imwrite`	True color, grayscale, or indexed image
Audio file	AU or WAV	`auread` or `wavread`	`auwrite` `wavwrite`	Sound data and sample rate
Movie	AVI	`aviread`		MATLAB movie

imported, all of MATLAB's normal array and matrix processing tools can be applied. The exception to this rule is the plain text reader that must be provided with a format specifier to define the data, and the names of the variables in which the data is to be stored.

So when you are approached with a file, the file extension (the part of the file name after the dot) gives you a significant clue to the nature of the data. For example, if it is the output from a spreadsheet, you should open the data in that spreadsheet program to explore its contents and organization. Typically, spreadsheet data will not open well in a plain text editor. If you do not recognize the file extension as coming from a spreadsheet, try opening the file in a plain text editor like Notepad, and see if the data is legible. You should be able to discern the field delimiters or the format of each line if the file contains plain text.

8.3.2 Excel Spreadsheets

Excel is a Microsoft product that implements spreadsheets. Spreadsheets are rectangular arrays containing labeled rows and columns of cells. The data in the cells may be numbers, strings, or formulae that combine the data values in other cells. Because of this computational capability, spreadsheets can be used to solve many problems, and most offer flexible plotting packages for presenting the results in colorful charts. There are occasions, however, when we need to apply the power of MATLAB to the data in a spreadsheet.

The MATLAB reader for Excel spreadsheets gives you a significant amount of flexibility in retrieving the data from the spreadsheet. Consider the typical set of data in an Excel spreadsheet named `grades.xls` shown in Table 8.2. The MATLAB `xlsread(...)` function does a good job of separating out the text and numerical portions of the spreadsheet. The parameter consumed by `xlsread(...)` is the name of the file; you can ask for up to three return variables: the first will hold all the numerical values in an array of doubles, the second will hold all the text data in cell arrays, and the third, if you request it, will hold both string and numerical data in cell arrays (try Exercise 8.1).

Table 8.2 Sample Excel spreadsheet

name	age	grade
fred	19	78
Joe	22	83
Sally	98	99
Charlie	21	56
Mary	23	89
Ann	19	51

 Exercise 8.1 Reading Excel data

Do It Yourself

Enter the following in the Command window and observe the results:

```
>> [nums txt raw] = xlsread('grades.xls')
nums =
    19    78
    22    83
    98    99
    21    56
    23    89
    19    51
```

continued on next page

```
txt =
    'name'          'age'      'grade'
    'fred'          ' '        ' '
    'joe'           ' '        ' '
    'sally'         ' '        ' '
    'charlie'       ' '        ' '
    'mary'          ' '        ' '
    'ann'           ' '        ' '
raw =
    'name'          'age'      'grade'
    'fred'        [ 19]      [   78]
    'joe'         [ 22]      [   83]
    'sally'       [ 98]      [   99]
    'charlie'     [ 21]      [   56]
    'mary'        [ 23]      [   89]
    'ann'         [ 19]      [   51]
    'ann'         [ 19]      [   51]
```

The reader first determines the smallest rectangle on the spreadsheet containing all of the numerical data; we will refer to this as the number rectangle. Then it produces the following results:

1. The first returned result is an array with the same number of rows and columns as the number rectangle and containing the values of all the numeric data in that rectangle. If there are non-numeric values within that rectangle, they are replaced by NaN, the built-in MATLAB name for something that is not a number.

2. The second returned result is a cell array with the same size as the original spreadsheet, containing only the string data; to ensure the consistency of this cell array, all numbers present are replaced by the empty string.

3. The third returned result is a cell array also with the same size as the original spreadsheet, containing both the strings and the numbers. Cells that are blank are presumed to be numerical, and are assigned as a cell containing NaN.

Frequently, after processing data with MATLAB, you are ready to write the results back to a spreadsheet. Excel spreadsheets can be written using:

```
xlswrite(<filename>, <array>, <sheet>, <range>)
```

where <filename> is the name of the file, <array> is the data source (a cell array), <sheet> is the sheet name, and <range> is the range of cells in Excel cell identity notation. The sheet name and range are optional.

8.3.3 Delimited Text Files—Numerical Data Only

If information is not available specifically in spreadsheet form, it can frequently be presented in text file form. If the data in a text file is numerical values only, and is organized in a reasonable form, MATLAB can read the file directly into an array. It is necessary that the data values are separated (delimited) by commas, spaces, or tab characters, as shown in Listing 8.1. Rows in the data are separated as expected by the new-line character. These values might be saved in a file named `nums.txt`. This type of numerical data (not strings) in general delimited form can be read using `dlmread(file, delimiter)`, where the delimiter parameter is a single character that can be used to specify an unusual delimiting character. However, the function can usually determine common delimiter situations without specifying the parameter.

Common Pitfalls

It is best not to provide the delimiter unless you have to. Without it, MATLAB will assume that repeated delimiters—like tabs and spaces—are single delimiters. If you do specify a delimiter, MATLAB will assume that repeated delimiter characters are separating different, absent field values.

This function produces a numerical array containing the data values. Try reading delimited files in Exercise 8.2.

Notice that the array elements where data is not supplied are filled with zero.

Delimited data files can be written using:

```
dlmwrite( <filename>, <array>, )
```

where `<filename>` is the name of the file, `<array>` is the data source (a numerical array), and `<dlm>` is the delimiting character. If the delimiting character is not specified, it is presumed to be a comma.

Listing 8.1 Sample delimited text file

```
19, 78,  42
22, 83, 100
98, 99,  34
21, 56,  12
23, 89
19, 51
```

 Exercise 8.2 Reading delimited files

Do It Yourself

Enter the following in the Command window and observe the results:

```
>> A = dlmread('nums.txt')
A =
      19      78      42
      22      83     100
      98      99      34
      21      56      12
      23      89       0
      19      51       0
```

8.4 Lower-Level File I/O

Some text files contain data in mixed format that are not readable by the high-level file reading functions. MATLAB provides a set of lower-level I/O functions that permit general purpose text file reading and writing. The following is a partial discussion of these functions that is sufficient for most text file processing. In general, the file must be opened to return a file handle to be used by subsequent functions. After the file contents have been manipulated, the file must be closed to complete the activity. Because these are lower-level functions used in combination to solve problems, we will need to present the behavior of several of them before we can show examples of their use.

8.4.1 Opening and Closing Files

To open a file for reading or writing, use:

```
fh = fopen( <filename>, <purpose>)
```

where `fh` is a file handle used in subsequent function calls to identify this particular I/O stream, `<filename>` is the name of the file, and `<purpose>` is a string specifying the purpose for opening the file.

The most common purposes are `'r'` to read the file, `'w'` to write it, or `'a'` to append to an existing file. See the MATLAB help files for more complex situations. If the purpose is `'r'`, the file must already exist; if `'w'` and the file already exists, it will be overwritten; if `'a'` and the file already exists, the new data will be appended to the end.

The consequence of failure to open the file is system dependent. In the standard version on a PC, this is indicated by returning a file handle of –1.

To close the file, use the following:

```
fclose( fh )
```

8.4.2 Reading Text Files

To read a file, three levels of support are provided: reading whole lines with or without the new line character, parsing into tokens with delimiters, or parsing into cell arrays using a format string.

- To read a whole line including the new line character, use:

  ```
  str = fgets( fh );
  ```

  which will return each line as a string until the end of the file, when the value –1 is returned instead of a string. To leave out each new-line character, use `fgetl(...)` instead (the last character is a lowercase `L`).

■ To parse each line into tokens (elementary text strings) separated by white space delimiters, use a combination of `fgetl(...)` and the tokenizer function:

```
[tk, rest] = strtok( ln );
```

where `tk` is string token, `rest` is the remainder of the line, and `ln` is a string to be parsed into tokens.

■ To parse a line according to a specific format string into a cell array, use:

```
ca = textscan( fh, <format> );
```

where `ca` is the resulting cell array, `fh` is the file handle, and `<format>` is a format control string we used for `sscanf(...)` in Chapter 6.

8.4.3 Examples of Reading Text Files

To illustrate the use of these functions for reading a text file, the script shown in Listing 8.2 shows a script that will list any text file in the Command window.

In Listing 8.2:

Line 1: Fetches the name of a file.

Line 2: Opens the file and returns the file handle.

Line 3: Initializes the `while` loop control variable.

Line 4: When the file read reaches the end of the file, it returns −1 instead of a string.

Line 5: Reads a string, including the end of line character.

Line 6: Classic loop-and-a-half logic that determines whether there is a line to process.

Listing 8.2 Script to list a text file

```
 1. fn = input( 'file name: ', 's' );
 2. fh = fopen( fn, 'r' );
 3. ln = '';
 4. while ischar( ln )
 5.      ln = fgets( fh );
 6.      if ischar( ln )
 7.          fprintf( ln );
 8.      end
 9. end
10. fclose( fh );
```

If so, it proceeds to line 7.

Line 7: Displays that line.

Line 10: Closes the file when finished.

As an example of the use of a tokenizer, consider the code shown in Listing 8.3, which performs the same function as Listing 8.2 but uses tokens.

Line 5: Uses `fgetl(...)` instead of `fgets(...)` because the tokenizer does not need the new line character.

Line 7: Initializes the resulting cell array.

Line 8: The tokenizer will be finished when it leaves an empty line as the result.

Line 9: Creates a token from the remains of the line and puts the remains back into the variable `ln`.

Practice using file listers in Exercise 8.3.

Exercise 8.3 shows the difference in output results between the conventional listing script and the tokenizing lister. With the tokenizer, we see each individual token (really, each word in a normal text file) separately listed.

Listing 8.3 Listing a file using tokens

```
1.  fn = input( 'file name: ' , 's' );
2.  fh = fopen( fn, 'r' );
3.  ln = '';
4.  while ischar( ln )
5.      ln = fgetl( fh );
6.      if ischar( ln )
7.          ca = [];
8.          while ~isempty( ln )
9.              [tk, ln] = strtok( ln );
10.             ca = [ca {tk}];
11.         end
12.         disp( ca );
13.     end
14. end
15. fclose( fh );
```

 Exercise 8.3 Using file listers

Do It Yourself

Enter the following in the Command window and observe the results:

```
>> listFile
file name: listFile.m
fn = input('file name: ','s');
fh = fopen(fn,'r');
ln = '';
while ischar(ln)
```

continued on next page

```
      ln = fgets(fh);
      if ischar(ln)
          fprintf(ln);
      end
end
fclose(fh);

>> tokenize
file name: listFile.m
    'fn' '=' 'input('file' 'name:' '','s');'
    'fh' '=' 'fopen(fn,'r');'
    'ln' '=' ''';'
    'while' 'ischar(ln)' '' '=' 'fgets(fh);'
    'if' 'ischar(ln)'
    'fprintf(ln);'
    'end'
    'end'
    'fclose(fh);'
```

Since the `textscan(...)` approach is data dependent, we will see practical examples of its use in Chapter 10.

8.4.4 Writing Text Files

Once a file has been opened for writing, the `fprintf(...)` function can be used to write to it by including its file handle as the first parameter. For example, Listing 8.4 is a minor alteration to Listing 8.2, copying a text file instead of listing it in the Command window.

In Listing 8-4:

> Line 2 Fetches the output file name.
>
> Line 4: Opens the output file.
>
> Line 9: Adds the `oh` parameter to direct the output to the specified file.
>
> Line 13: Closes the output file.

Listing 8.4 Script to copy a text file

```
1.   ifn = input( 'input file name: ', 's' );
2.   ofn = input('output file name: ', 's' );
3.   ih = fopen( ifn, 'r' );
4.   oh = fopen( ofn, 'w' );
5.   ln = '';
6.   while ischar( ln )
7.        ln = fgets( ih );
8.        if ischar( ln )
9.             fprintf( oh, ln );
10.       end
11.  end
12.  fclose( ih );
13.  fclose( oh );
```

8.5 Engineering Example—Spreadsheet Data

Frequently, engineering data is provided in spreadsheets. Here we will adapt the structure assembly problem from Chapter 7. The script for that solution constructed the data using a constructor function. Consider the situation in which the data is provided in a spreadsheet such as that shown in Figure 8.3. We have to start by considering the layout of the data and the process necessary to extract what we need. Bearing in mind the three results returned from `xlsread(...)`, first we determine which of the three is most appropriate:

- Numerical data is not really important in this application, and there are numbers in the first column as well as the columns we need. Consequently, the first result, an array of numbers, is really not what we need.

- However, this is not exclusively a text processing problem, since we need the numerical coordinates, so the second, text-only result is not what we need.

- Therefore, in this particular application, we will process the raw data provided by `xlsread(...)`, giving both the string and numerical data.

The other concern is that there are a different number of connections on each row of the sheet. When a connection is present, it is a string. When it is not there, we refer to the behavior of the raw data to discover that the contents of empty cells appear as `NaN` of type `double`.

We need a function that will read this file and produce the same model of the structure used in Chapter 7. Such a function is shown in Listing 8.5.

	A	B	C	D	E	F	G	H	I	J
1	Item	Name	X	Y	Connected to					
2	1	A-1	0.866	0.5	A		A-2	A-3	D-1	
3	2	A-2	0	1	A		A-3	B-1	B-2	
4	3	A-3	0.866	1.5	A-1	A-2	B-1	D-1		
5	4	B-1	0.866	2.5	A-2	A-3	B-2	B-3	D-1	D-2
6	5	B-2	0	3	A-2	A-3	B-1	B-3	C-1	C-2
7	6	B-3	0.866	3.5	B-1	B-2	C-1	C-2	D-1	D-2
8	7	C-1	0.866	4.5	B-2	B-3	C-2	C-3	D-2	
9	8	C-2	0	5	B-2	B-3	C-1	C-3	C	
10	9	C-3	0.866	5.5	C-1	C-2	D-2	C		
11	10	D-1	1.732	2	A-1	A-3	B-1	B-3	D-2	
12	11	D-2	1.732	4	B-1	B-3	C-1	C-3	D-1	

Figure 8.3 *Data in a spreadsheet*

Listing 8.5 Reading structure data

```
 1. function data = readStruct(filename)
% read a spreadsheet and produce a
%                       structure array:
%      name - the second column value
%       pos - columns 3 and 4 in a vector
%   connect - cell array with the remaining
%                       data on the row

 2. [no no raw] = xlsread(filename);
 3. [rows cols] = size(raw);
% ignore the first row and column
 4. out = 1;
 5. for row = 2:rows
 6.      str.name = raw{row,2};
 7.      str.pos = [raw{row,3} raw{row,4}];
 8.      cni = 1;
 9.      conn = {};
10.      for col = 5:cols
11.          item = raw{row, col};
12.          if ~ischar(item)
13.              break;
14.          end
15.          conn{cni} = item;
16.          cni = cni + 1;
17.      end
18.      str.connect = conn;
19.      data(out) = str;
20.      out = out + 1;
21. end
```

In Listing 8.5:

> Line 1: The function consumes the file name and produces a structure array with the fields described in the following comments.
>
> Line 2: Reads the spreadsheet and keeps only the raw data.
>
> Line 3: Gets the rows and columns in the raw data; we need to ignore the top row and left column.
>
> Line 4: Initializes the output index for the structure array.
>
> Line 5: Ignoring the first row, traverses all the remaining rows.
>
> Line 6: The component name is in the second column.
>
> Line 7: The coordinates of the component are in the third and fourth columns.
>
> Lines 8–9: Initializes the search for the connections for this component. It is important to empty the array conn before each pass to avoid "inheriting" data from a previous row.
>
> Lines 10–11: Extracts each item in turn from the row.

Lines 12–14: If the item is not of class char, this is the blank cell at the end of the row; the break command exits the for loop moving across the row.

Lines 15–16: Otherwise, it stores the connection and keeps going.

Lines 18–20: When the connections are complete, it stores them in the structure, stores the structure in the structure array, and continues to the next row.

Line 21: When the rows are completed, the data is ready to return to the calling script.

To test this function, replace the structure array construction in lines 1–11 of Listing 7.7 in Chapter 7 with the following line:

```
data = readStruct('Structure_data.xls');
```

The script will then produce the same results as before.

 ## Chapter Summary

We have described three levels of capability for reading and writing files in MATLAB:

- The save and load operators allow you to save variables from the workspace and restore them to the workspace
- Specialized functions read and write spreadsheets and delimited text files
- Lower-level functions provide the ability to open and close files, and to read and write text files in any form that is required

 ## Special Characters, Reserved Words, and Functions

Special Characters, Reserved Words, and Functions	Description	Discussed in This Section
NaN	Not a number	8.3.2
load	Loads the workspace from a file	8.2
save	Saves variables in a file	8.2
csvread(file)	Reads comma-separated text files	8.3
csvwrite (file, data)	Writes comma-separated text files	8.3
dlmread (file, dlm)	Reads text files separated by the given delimiting character(s)	8.3
dlmwrite (file, data, dlm)	Reads text files separated by the given delimiting character(s)	8.3

Special Characters, Reserved Words, and Functions	Description	Discussed in This Section
`[nums, txt, raw] = xlsread(file)`	Reads an Excel spreadsheet	8.3.2
`xlswrite (file, data, sheet, range)`	Writes an Excel spreadsheet in a specific row/column range	8.3.2
`fh = fopen (file, fl)`	Opens a text file for reading or writing	8.4.1
`fclose(fh)`	Closes a text file	8.4.1
`fgetl(fh)`	Reads a line, omitting the new-line character	8.4.2
`fgets(fh)`	Reads a line, including the new-line character	8.4.2
`[tk rest] = strtok(str, dlm)`	Extracts a token from a string and returns the remainder of the string	8.4.2
`ca = textscan (fh, format)`	Acquires and scans a line of text according to a specific format	8.3, 8.4.2
`fprintf(...)`	Writes to the console, or to plain text files	8.3, 8.4.4

 ## Self Test

Use the following questions to check your understanding of the material in this chapter:

True or False

1. All data files should be treated as a sequential series of characters.

2. When you save a workspace, you are actually saving the scripts that generate the data in the workspace.

3. MATLAB reads strings from tab- or comma-delimited files by recognizing the double quotes that delimit strings.

4. If you use `fopen(...)` to open an existing file and write to it, the original data in the file will be overwritten.

5. The function `fgets(fh)` does not always return a string.

Fill in the Blanks

1. In general, data files contain text that represents the

   _____ of the data and control characters that specify

   the _____ of the data.

2. The MATLAB `xlsread(...)` function returns three results: the

    _____ in a _____ , the

    _____ in a _____ , and

    _____ in a _____ .

3. When using `dlmread(...)` to populate a _____ , any

    unassigned values are _____ .

4. When using `fopen(...)`, the consequence of failure to open the file

    is _____ .

Programming Projects

1. You have a client who wants you to work on her old data files. She's
    an engineer, and wants you to use MATLAB for the project. Luckily,
    all of the old data is stored in simple tab-delimited text files.
    Unluckily, the first row of every data file is full of meaningless
    numbers. As a quick check to verify that you're capable of solving
    her problems, she has asked you to write a few MATLAB functions.

    a. Write a MATLAB function called `readData` that takes the name
        of a tab-delimited text file and returns a two-dimensional array
        of the data in the file, skipping the first row of data.

    b. Using your `readData` function from part a, write another
        function `maxMerge` that takes the name of two of these tab-
        delimited files and returns a single two-dimensional array
        where each element of the array is the larger of the
        corresponding elements from the two data files. For example:

File 1			File 2			maxMerge		
0	0	0	0	0	0			
10	20	30	2	4	8	10	20	30
45	55	63	16	32	64	45	55	64
80	90	99	128	56	512	128	90	512

    Notice that the first row is ignored, as specified by the requirements
    of the `readData` function.

2. You are provided with a file `data.xls`, which contains two columns of numbers. Each column contains 1,371 elements, starting from row 1. Create a script that does the following:

- The first column, A, represents your x values; read these numbers from the file and save to a vector called `xData`

- Column B contains your y values; read the numbers from the file and save them in the vector `yData`

- Make a plot of the x versus y values, and title your plot `Excel Plot`

3. You are provided with two files: `atlanta.txt` and `ttimes.txt`. Each is a delimited file that should read correctly using `dlmread()`. We need to explore and plot the data in these files.

4. You are provided with the Excel spreadsheet `World_Data.xls`. Do the following:

   a. Find the names of the 10 most populous countries.

   b. Plot the population growth for each for as many years as data is available. Do not forget a title, suitable axis labels, and a legend.

5. Write the equivalent of the UNIX `wc` utility that counts the characters, words, and lines in any arbitrary text file.

Recursion

9.1 Concept: The Activation Stack
    9.1.1 A Stack
    9.1.2 Activation Stack
    9.1.3 Function Instances
9.2 Recursion Defined
9.3 Implementing a Recursive Function in MATLAB
9.4 Exceptions
    9.4.1 Historical Approaches
    9.4.2 Generic Exception Implementation
    9.4.3 MATLAB Implementation
9.5 Wrapper Functions
9.6 Tail Recursion
9.7 Mutual Recursion
9.8 Generative Recursion
9.9 Examples of Recursion
    9.9.1 Detecting Palindromes
    9.9.2 Fibonacci Series
    9.9.3 Zeros of a Function
9.10 Engineering Example— Robot Arm Motion

Chapter Objectives

This chapter discusses the following basic ideas of recursive programming:

- Three basic characteristics must be present for a recursive function to work

- Exceptions are a powerful mechanism for detecting and trapping errors

- A wrapper function is used to set up the recursion

- Other forms of recursion occur in special circumstances

Introduction

Recursion is an alternative technique by which a code block can be repeated in a controlled manner. In Chapter 4, we saw repetition achieved by inserting control statements in the code (either `for` or `while`) to determine how many times a code block would be repeated. Recursion uses the basic mechanism for invoking functions to manage the repetition of a block of code.

While some problems are naturally solved by iterative solutions, there are many problems for which a recursive solution is elegant and easily understood.

Frequently, a recursive function needs a "wrapper function" to set up the recursion correctly, and to check for erroneous data conditions that might cause errors. The actual recursive function then becomes a private helper function.

◿ **9.1 Concept: The Activation Stack**

In order to understand recursive programming, we must look deeper into the mechanism by which function calls are mechanized. Calling any function depends on a special kind of stack built into the architecture of the Central Processing Unit (CPU). This is called the **activation stack**. It enables the CPU to determine which functions are active or suspended awaiting the completion of other function calls. To understand the activation stack, first we consider the basic concept of a stack.

9.1.1 A Stack

A stack is one of the fundamental data structures of computer science. It is best modeled by considering the trays at the front of the cafeteria line. You cannot see how many trays there are on the stack, and the only access you have to them is to take a tray off the stack or put one on. So a stack is a collection of objects of arbitrary size with a restricted number of operations we are allowed to perform on that collection (see Figure 9.1). Unlike a vector, where it is permissible to read, add, or remove items anywhere in the collection, we are only allowed the following operations with a stack:

- Push an object onto the stack
- Pop an object off the stack
- Peek at the top object without removing it
- Check whether the stack is empty

9.1.2 Activation Stack

The core concept that enables any function (especially a recursive function) to operate is the concept of an activation stack. The activation stack is the means by which the operating system allocates memory to functions for local storage. Typically, local storage is required by a function for the following reasons:

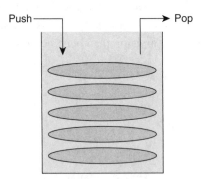

Figure 9.1 *Behavior of a stack*

- Storing the location of the function to be evaluated
- Storing the location in memory to return to when the function execution completes
- Storing copies of the function parameter values
- Providing space for the values of any local variables defined within the function

When the user starts a specific application program (in MATLAB terms, a script or an entry in the Command window), the operating system allocates enough memory to load the application and a block of memory to contain its activation stack. When that application calls a function, the information specific to that function call is assembled into an object called a **stack frame** and pushed onto the activation stack. The calling program is then suspended and control is passed to the function specified in the frame on the top of the stack. When that function completes, its frame is popped off the stack and destroyed, and control is returned to the frame beneath, which is now the top of the stack. If an active function calls another function, this process is repeated. The calling function is suspended, a stack frame is pushed onto the activation stack for the new function, and the original function is suspended until the new function completes.

Note that in a MATLAB implementation, the stack frame is the storage environment for the current workspace. Each new function call receives a fresh workspace from the activation stack that initially contains the copies of the actual parameters bearing the formal parameter names.

9.1.3 Function Instances

In Chapter 2 we discussed the difference between the type of data defined by its class, and an object—an instance of that class assigned to a variable. In the same way, we draw the distinction between the .m file that defines the behavior of a function and the instance(s) of that function that result when the function is called. Each new instance of a function has its own workspace that occupies a temporary stack frame allocated from the activation stack.

9.2 Recursion Defined

Following the previous logic, in principle there is no reason why a function could not in fact "call itself," and this is the logical basis for recursive programming. Of course, as with iterative programming, if there is no mechanism to stop the recursion, the process would repeat endlessly. In the case of endless recursion, since space is being consumed on the activation stack, the operating system will eventually terminate the process when the memory allocated for the activation stack is exhausted.

The canonical illustration of recursion is the computation of n factorial. We could view the calculation of 5! in the following ways:

```
5! = 5 * 4 * 3 * 2 * 1
5! = 5 * 4!
```

The second representation is the recursive view, which warrants a closer view as follows:

```
n! = n * (n-1)!
```

This definition would not be complete, however, without realizing that it must stop somewhere. This is easy with the factorial function because 0! is defined mathematically as 1.

In this example we see the three necessary characteristics of a recursive function:

1. There must be a terminating condition to stop the process
2. The function must call a clone of itself
3. The parameters to that call must move the function toward the terminating condition

The word *clone* is important here—a recursive function really does not "call itself," because it requests a new stack frame and passes different parameters to the instance of the function that occupies the new frame.

9.3 Implementing a Recursive Function in MATLAB

Template 9.1 shows the general template for recursive functions in MATLAB.

The following general guidelines indicate how the recursive template is implemented:

- The <function_name>, like the name of any other function, may be any legal variable name

Template 9.1 General template for a recursive function

```
function <result> = <function_name> (<formal_params>)
<documentation>
  if <terminating condition 1>
      <result> = <initial value 1>
  elseif <terminating condition 2>
      <result> = <initial value 2>
      . . .
  else
      <result> = <operation> ...
          (<formal_params>, ...
            <function_name> (<new_params>) )
  end
```

- The variable `<result>` may be any legal variable name or a vector of variable names
- As usual with functions, you should supply at least one line of `<documentation>` to define its purpose and implementation
- Each exit from the function must assign values to all the result variables
- The first design decision is to determine the condition(s) under which the recursive process should stop, and how to express this as the `<terminating condition N>` tests
- The `<initial value N>` entries are the value(s) of the result(s) at the terminating condition(s)
- The second design decision is to determine the `<operation>`—the specific mathematical or logical operation that must be performed to combine the current formal parameters with the result of the recursive call to create a new value of the `<result>`
- The last design decision is to determine how to compute the `<actual_params>` of the recursive call to ensure that the process moves towards at least one of the `<terminating condition N>` states

The MATLAB implementation of the factorial function is shown in Listing 9.1.

In Listing 9.1:

Line 3: Shows a diagnostic print call, which if not commented, enables you to observe the sequence of events.

Line 4: Shows the terminating condition.

Line 5: Shows the result at termination.

Line 7: Calls a clone of the function, which moves closer to termination by reducing N and computing the current result by multiplication.

Exercise 9.1 provides an analysis of recursive behavior. In particular, notice that all the mathematical operations are performed as the activation stack "unwinds."

Listing 9.1 Function to compute N factorial

```
1. function result = fact(N)
2. % recursive computation of N!
3. %    fprintf('fact( %d )\n', N); % testing only
4.    if N == 0
5.        result = 1;
6.    else
7.        result = N * fact(N - 1);
8.    end
```

Exercise 9.1 Analyzing recursive behavior

Do It Yourself

1. Create the `fact(...)` function from Listing 9.1 in MATLAB, uncomment the print line and run it from the Command window:

```
>> fact(4)
fact( 4 )
fact( 3 )
fact( 2 )
fact( 1 )
fact( 0 )
ans =
    24
```

2. Put a break point at Line 4, define some arbitrary variables in your main work space and run `fact(2)`. The function should pause in the first stack frame. The only variable in the workspace is N with a value 2.

3. Find the "step into" button and click it. Since N is not 0, the arrow should move to Line 7.

4. Click again, and the workspace should change to a new workspace with the value N = 1— you just called a clone of the original function with its own stack frame. There should be a second, transparent arrow at Line 7 to indicate that some clone of this function is waiting at that point for a result.

5. Continue stepping into functions until you return from the copy where N = 0. When this return happens you return to the frame with N = 1, the frame "underneath," at Line 7, and are then able to compute the first result.

6. Further stepping will return from each stack frame until you finally return to your script's workspace.

9.4 Exceptions

We digress here to discuss how programs deal with unexpected circumstances. Exceptions are a powerful tool for gracefully managing runtime errors caused by programming errors or bad data. The general need for an exception mechanism might best be established by way of an example. Suppose you write a program that requests some data from a user, and then launches a significant number of nested function calls—perhaps even a recursive function—to perform analysis on the data received. Somewhere in the depths of these function calls, the program divides something by a value, but in this instance that value is zero. The cause of this problem is probably bad data entered by the user. However, the effect is discovered deep in the activation stack in the middle of some obscure numerical computation.

9.4.1 Historical Approaches

Early languages attempted to deal with this problem in one of two equally unpleasant ways:

- Some languages require any mathematical function that might produce an error to return the status of that calculation to the calling function. They allow errors to be reported and processed, but they have two unpleasant consequences: using up the ability of a function to return a value and calling this function, which means choosing between testing for errors and solving the problem locally and passing the error condition back to its calling function in the hope that somewhere the error will be dealt with.

- Perhaps worse than this are the languages that use a globally accessible variable, such as `ierror`, to report status. For example, if `ierror` were normally set to `0`, an error could be announced by setting its value to something other than `0` to indicate the nature of the failure. This frees the function from needing to return status, but it does not relieve the calling function of the need to check whether the `ierror` value is bad, or solving the problem, or elevating it. Furthermore, if an error does occur within a function, since it is now still returning a value, what value should it return if it is unable to complete its assigned calculation?

9.4.2 Generic Exception Implementation

By contrast, most enlightened languages provide an exception mechanism whereby if an error occurs, regardless of how deep in the activation stack, program implementation is immediately suspended in the current stack frame. The activation stack below this frame is then searched for the frame of a program that has "volunteered" to process this type of exception. When it is found, all the stack frames above this frame are removed from the stack and the code in the exception handling mechanism is activated. If no such frame is discovered, the overall program aborts with an error code.

The following mechanisms are necessary to implement the exception mechanism effectively:

- *Throwing an exception*. Whenever a problem occurs, the operating system is asked to suspend operations at that point in the activation stack and go back down the stack without completing any of the functions looking for a function equipped to handle the specific exception. If no such function is found, the program is terminated and an exception is returned to the operating system.

- *Catching an exception*. A function that is able to deal with a specific exception uses a `try ... catch` construct to identify the suspect code and resolve the problem. Between `try` and `catch`, it puts a code block that contains the suspect code. After the `catch` statement that usually identifies the particular exception, there is a code block that should fix the problem.

Depending on the specific language implementation, the exception-catching mechanism usually offers facilities both for determining exactly where the exception occurred and for reconstructing the activation stack with all the variable values as they were at the time of the exception.

In the previous example, the general template for successfully interacting with the user is shown in Template 9.2. The successful Boolean flag will be set only if the data is processed without error. It does not matter how deep in the data processing code the error occurs—the user interface catches the error, reports it to the user, and prompts the user for better data.

9.4.3 MATLAB Implementation

MATLAB implements a simplified version of the most general form of exception processing. The `try` ... `catch` ... `end` construct is fully supported. However, unlike some languages, MATLAB does not distinguish between the kinds of exception that can be thrown.

- All built-in functions throw exceptions when they discover error conditions—attempting to open a nonexistent file for reading, for example—and expect the programmer to catch these exceptions if they are recoverable.

- To throw an exception manually, the program calls the `error(...)` function that takes one parameter, a string defining the error. If the exception is not caught, the string provided is displayed in red to the user. If the exception is caught, that string is ignored.

- To handle an exception, a code block we suspect might throw an exception is placed between `try` and `catch` statements. If no error occurs in the code block, the `catch` statement is ignored. If an

Template 9.2 General template for processing exceptions

```
successful = false
while <not successful>
    try
        <request data from the user>
        <process the data>
        successful = true
    catch
        <announce the error to the user>
    end
end
```

exception is thrown from that code block, however, execution is suspended at that point. No further processing is performed, no data are returned from functions, and the code in the closest `catch` block is executed up to the associated `end` statement. To determine the cause of the exception, you can use the `lasterror` function. It returns the textual information provided at the exception and a structure array describing the activation stack.

■ In more complex situations where this function may not be able to actually handle the error, a further exception can be thrown from the `catch` block. This exception will escape from this `try ... catch` block, and must be caught (if at all) by another function or script deeper in the activation stack.

Listing 9.2 illustrates a simple example. The objective is to have the user define a triangle by entering a vector of three sides, and to calculate the angle between the first two sides. The `acosd(...)` function computes the inverse cosine of a ratio. If that ratio is greater than one, there is something seriously wrong with the triangle, and `acosd` returns a complex number. This script detects that the answer is complex and throws an exception.

In Listing 9.2:

Lines 1 and 2: We will repeat the attempts to compute the angle of a triangle until successful.

Line 3: Begins the suspect code.

Line 8: Detects the problem with the data.

Line 9: Throws the exception. In this case, the exception occurs visibly in this script. However, the `try ... catch` behavior is the same if the exception occurs deep in a set of nested function calls.

Listing 9.2 MATLAB script using exception processing

```
1. OK = false;
2. while ~OK
3.      try
4.          side = input('enter a triangle: ');
5.          a = side(1); b = side(2); c = side(3);
6.          cosC = (c^2 - a^2 - b^2)/(2 * a * b);
7.          angle = acosd(cosC);
8.          if imag(angle) ~= 0
9.              error('bad triangle')
10.         end
11.     catch
12.         disp('bad triangle - try again')
13.     end
14.     OK = true;
15. end
16. fprintf('the angle is %f\n', angle)
```

Line 11: The end of the suspect code block and the beginning of the exception handler—in this case, it's a warning to the user that the data is bad.

Line 14: This line is reached only if the suspect code block executed correctly, in which case we can exit the `while` loop.

You have an opportunity to work with exception processing in Exercise 9.2.

You may have noticed that the `input(...)` function has its own internal exception handling. If you ever enter some data that causes a parsing error, you see that error announced, and are then offered another opportunity to enter correct data.

 Exercise 9.2 Processing exceptions

Do It Yourself

Put the code from Listing 9.2 in a script and execute it, using the following data:

```
enter a triangle: [3 4 8]
bad triangle - try again
enter a triangle: [3 4 6]
the angle is 62.720387
```

Then, edit the script to remove the `try` statement and the `catch` block and repeat the test.

Style Points

1. You should allow the exception-processing mechanism to simplify the structure of your code. Rather than attempting to detect every possible data error and return error condition, perhaps from deeply nested function calls, allow the exception mechanism to return control directly to the code that can deal with the problem.

2. Exception processing is for processing events that occur outside the normal thread of execution. It may be tempting at times to use the exception mechanism as a clever means of changing the normal flow of program control, but resist that temptation. It produces ugly, untraceable code and should be avoided.

 ## 9.5 Wrapper Functions

Consider the factorial function again for a moment—specifically, ask how you would deal with a user who accidentally called for the factorial of a negative number or of a number containing a fractional part. Our original recursive `fact(...)` function is not protected from these programmer errors. There are three possible strategies for dealing with this situation:

1. *The legalist approach* ignores the bad values, lets the user's program die, and then responds to user complaints by pointing out that the documentation clearly indicates that you should not call for the factorial of a negative number. Usually this is not the best approach from the customer relations viewpoint or from the technical support effort viewpoint, especially since recursive code that hangs up typically crashes with a stack overflow—not the easiest symptom to diagnose!

2. *In-line coding* builds into the code a test for N less than zero (or fractional) and exits with a meaningful error message. Although this is an improvement over the first choice because it exits gracefully, the test is in a bad place. The function is recursive; therefore, the code for that test is repeated as many times as the function is called. While modern computers are fast enough that one would probably not notice the difference, in general this is a poor implementation that punishes those who are using the function correctly with the same test each time the recursive function is called.

3. *A wrapper function* is the best solution.

A wrapper function is called once to perform any tests or setup that the recursion requires, and then to call the recursive function as a helper to the main function call. While there is a small computational cost to using a wrapper, it is only executed once rather than each time the recursive function is called. Template 9.3 illustrates this idea.

Template 9.3 General template for a wrapper function

```
function <result> = <function_name> (<formal_params>)
<documentation>
      if <bad_condition>
         <throw exception>
      else
         <result> = <private_name> (<actual_params>)
      end

function <result> = <private_name> (<formal_params>)
<documentation>
   if <terminating condition 1>
      <result> = <initial value 1>
   elseif <terminating condition 2>
      <result> = <initial value 2>

      . . .

   else
      <result> = <operation> ...
         (<formal_params>, ...
            <private_name> (<new_params>) )
   end
```

The first function named <function_name> is actually the wrapper function with the return result, parameters, and documentation expected by the caller. It makes whatever tests are necessary to validate the input data, clean it up if necessary, and call the helper function named <private_name>.

Listing 9.3 is the MATLAB implementation of the factorial function with protection from bad data.

In Listing 9.3:

Line 1: To the outside world, this is the function actually called. (Ugly secret: even if the name is not the same name as the file, the first function in the file is always executed first.)

Line 3: Checks for negative and fractional inputs.

Line 4: Throws an exception if the data is bad.

Line 6: Calls the recursive version if the data is valid.

Line 8: Blank line for clarity—not required by MATLAB.

Line 9: Definition of the recursive function. By convention, some MATLAB users tend to give the prefix local_ to private functions like this, but this has no significance to the system.

Exercise 9.3 gives you an opportunity to work with the protected factorial.

Listing 9.3 Wrapper implementation for the factorial function

```
1. function result = fact(N)
2. % computation of N!
3.     if (N < 0) || ((N - floor(N)) > 0)
4.         error('bad parameter for fact');
5.     else
6.         result = local_fact(N);
7.     end
8.
9. function result = local_fact(N)
10. % recursive computation of N!
11. %    fprintf('fact( %d )\n', N);
12.     if N == 0
13.         result = 1;
14.     else
15.         result = N * local_fact(N - 1);
16.     end
```

 Exercise 9.3 Writing the protected factorial

Do It Yourself

Write the fact(...) function as shown in Listing 9.3 and test it in the Command window:

```
>> fact(-1)
??? Error using ==> fact
```
continued on next page

```
bad parameter for fact
>> fact(.5)
??? Error using ==> fact
bad parameter for fact
>> fact(4)
ans =
    24
```

9.6 Tail Recursion

Although "normal" recursion is an effective way of using the function call mechanism to manage repetition, it can consume significant amounts of the activation stack. Tail recursion is a technique for accomplishing recursive behavior without consuming activation stack resources. It requires a wrapper function to initialize the recursion and uses an extra parameter in the function call to carry the emerging result of the recursion.

The driving characteristic of a tail recursive solution is that every exit from the recursive helper function must either return a result or be a standalone call to the recursive helper with no operations to be performed on it. All mathematical and logical operations must occur in computing the new parameters for the recursive call. When tail recursion is detected, almost all modern language compilers (including MATLAB) recognize this situation and construct the executable code to operate in place in the existing stack frame. This avoids pushing unnecessary duplicate stack frames onto the activation stack.

Template 9.4 is the general template for tail recursive processing. Notice that the wrapper function takes on the added responsibility of calling the helper function with an additional parameter that is the initial result.

Listing 9.4 is the MATLAB code for a tail recursive version of the factorial function.

Template 9.4 General template for tail recursive processing

```
function <result> = <function_name> (<formal_params>)
<documentation>
   <result> = <private_name> (<actual_params>, <init>)

function <result> = <private_name> (<params>, <current>)
<documentation>
  if <terminating condition>
     <result> = <current>
  else
     <result> = <private_name> (<new_params>, ...
                               <operation> (<params>) );
  end
```

Listing 9.4 Tail recursive factorial implementation

```
1. function ans = fact(N)
2. % computation of N!
3.     ans = local_fact(N, 1);
4.     end
5.
6. function ans = local_fact(N, res)
7. %     fprintf('local_fact( %d, %d )\n', N, res);
8.     if N == 0
9.         ans = res;
10.    else
11.        ans = local_fact(N - 1, N * res);
12.    end
```

In Listing 9.4:

> Line 3: The wrapper function calls the local, recursive factorial function with an extra parameter that is the initial value of the factorial result.

> Line 7: A diagnostic statement for use in determining the sequence of events.

> Line 8: Checks for the termination condition.

> Line 9: If we are terminating, then all the computation has been done—the second parameter is the answer!

> Line 11: Where all the work is done—the recursive call must stand by itself for tail recursion to work. The first parameter moves toward the termination as before and the second parameter is the computed ongoing result.

Try working with the tail recursive factorial in Exercise 9.4.

In Exercise 9.4 notice that all the computation is accomplished while "going forward" into the recursive process so that at the last recursive call the process is finished.

 Exercise 9.4 Writing the tail recursive factorial

Do It Yourself

Write the fact(...) function as shown in Listing 9.4 with the print function uncommented, and test it in the Command window:

```
>> fact(4)
local_fact( 4, 1 )
local_fact( 3, 4 )
local_fact( 2, 12 )
local_fact( 1, 24 )
local_fact( 0, 24 )
ans =
    24
```

9.7 Mutual Recursion

Recursion is not always accomplished by a function directly calling itself. On rare occasions, the logic of a solution calls for function A to call function B, and then function B calls function A. Of course, at least one of the functions must be seeking the terminating condition.

The canonical example of this situation is a pair of odd/even functions, although there are more direct ways to determine odd and even using the remainder when the number is divided by 2. The function odd(N) can test for 0 and 1 to terminate, and then call even(N-1). Similarly, the function even(N) can test for 0 and 1 to terminate, and then call odd(N-1).

 ## 9.8 Generative Recursion

A discussion of recursion would not be complete without at least mentioning the concept of generative recursion. Consider a program that models the behavior of a billiard ball rolling on a billiard table and bouncing off the cushions. Does it represent the basic characteristics of recursion?

- There is definitely a terminating condition in which the ball reaches one of the pockets.
- One could certainly represent the repetitive process of updating the position of the ball as a recursive, even tail recursive, function.
- Is this process always moving toward the terminating condition? In one sense, obviously not, because the ball is sometimes moving away from a pocket and sometimes toward it. In fact, if friction is suitably represented in the model, the ball may roll to a stop without ever reaching a pocket.

However, in a broader sense, we could argue that the ball is approaching the terminating condition to the degree that falling into a pocket is in the future, and as long as time is elapsing in the model, the ball is moving toward the time when it is in a pocket. The fact that physics may intervene and prevent that future event from actually occurring does not detract from the ball's hopeful search for a resting place. There would be two terminating conditions: one with the ball in the pocket and the other with the ball stationary. Therefore, generative recursion is a recursive process in which there is a terminating condition, but the model of the process permits an unsuccessful attempt to achieve that condition.

 ## 9.9 Examples of Recursion

We conclude this chapter with three examples of recursive programming: detecting palindromes, computing the Fibonacci series of numbers, and finding zeros of a function. The examples are followed by a practical engineering example of the use of zero finding.

9.9.1 Detecting Palindromes

We might want to determine whether a word or phrase received as a string is a palindrome, that is, whether it is spelled the same forward and backward. One could design a recursive function named `isPal(<string>)` as follows:

- The function `isPal(<string>)` terminates if the `<string>` has zero or one character, returning true.
- It also terminates if the first and last characters are not equal, returning `false`.
- Otherwise (first and last are equal), the function returns `isPal(<shorter string>)`, where the shorter string is obtained by removing the first and last characters of the original string.
- Clearly, since the string is always being shortened, the recursive solution is approaching the terminating condition.

The MATLAB implementation of the palindrome detector is shown in Listing 9.5.

In Listing 9.5:

> Line 3: The successful terminating condition is when the length of the string is under 2.
>
> Line 5: The failure condition is when the first and last characters do not match.
>
> Line 8: To move toward termination, remove the first and last characters that have already been checked.

We should observe further that a serious student of palindromes might know that real palindromes contain spaces, punctuation marks, and uppercase and lowercase characters. We leave it as an exercise for you to write a wrapper function that cleans up strings containing these issues before passing the string to the recursive palindrome detector.

Listing 9.5 Recursive palindrome detector

```
1. function ans = isPal(str)
2. % recursive palindrome detector
3.     if length(str) < 2
4.         ans = true;
5.     elseif str(1) ~= str(end)
6.         ans = false;
7.     else
8.         ans = isPal(str(2:end-1));
9.     end
```

9.9.2 Fibonacci Series

The Fibonacci series was originally named for the Italian mathematician Leonardo Pisano Fibonacci, who was studying the growth of rabbit populations in the eleventh century. He hypothesized that rabbits mature one month after birth, after which time each pair would produce a new pair of rabbits each month. Starting with a pair of newborn rabbits free in a field, he wanted to calculate the rabbit population after a year. Figure 9.2 illustrates the calculation for the first six months, counting rabbit pairs. It soon becomes clear that the number of rabbits in month N comprises the number in month N-1 (since in this ideal example, none of them die) plus the new rabbits born to the mature pairs (shown in boxes in the figure). Since the rabbits mature after a month, the number of mature pairs that produce a new pair is the number of rabbits in the month before, N-2. So the algorithm for computing the population of pairs after N months, fib(N), is recursive:

- There is a terminating condition: when N = 1 or N = 2, the answer is 1
- The recursive condition is: fib(N) = fib(N-1) + fib(N-2)
- The solution is moving toward the terminating condition, since as long as N is a positive integer, computing N-1 and N-2 will move towards 1 or 2.

The MATLAB implementation of the Fibonacci function is shown in Listing 9.6.

The algorithm produces the Fibonacci series: 1, 1, 2, 3, 5, 8, 13, 21, 34, 55, 89, 144, 233, …, giving a population after a year of 144.

Truthfulness requires pointing out that while computing the Fibonacci series recursively is a very nice, conceptually simple approach, it is a nightmare as far as the computational load on your processor. Do not try to compute beyond about 27 numbers in the series. An iterative solution, while less elegant, runs in linear time rather than exponential.

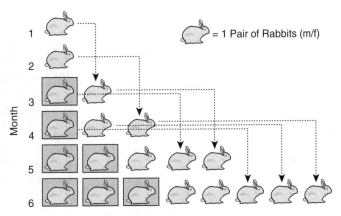

Figure 9.2 *Computing rabbit populations*

Listing 9.6 The Fibonacci function

```
1. function result = fib(N)
2. % recursive computation the Nth Fibonacci number
3.     if N == 1 || N == 2
4.         result = 1;
5.     else
6.         result = fib(N-1) + fib(N-2);
7.     end
```

A closely related phenomenon is the golden ratio or golden number computed as the limit of the ratio of successive Fibonacci series values—approximately 1.618034—that has been found to occur in nature. To the surprise of naturalists, this series of numbers occurs in nature in a remarkable number of circumstances. Consider Figure 9.3 for example, where a set of squares placed side by side in a rotating sequence is drawn using the Fibonacci series for the size of each square. The resulting geometric figure is a close approximation to the logarithmic spiral so frequently found in nature, such as the nautilus shell pictured in the figure.

9.9.3 Zeros of a Function

Frequently we need to solve nonlinear equations by seeking the values of the independent variable that produced a zero result. There are a number of well-known numerical techniques for achieving this goal. We will examine a recursive approach to determining the zeros of functions. However, especially when there are multiple zero crossings, it is very helpful to have a good initial estimate of the location(s) of the crossing(s). As an example, consider a function $f(x)$. We will use the function given by:

$$f(x) = 0.0333x^6 - 0.3x^5 - 1.3333x^4 + 16x^3 - 187.2x$$

as plotted in Figure 9.4. However, this algorithm will work for any function of x. We assume that the continuous line describes the exact function, and the

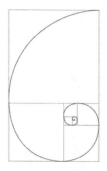

Figure 9.3 *Fibonacci in nature*

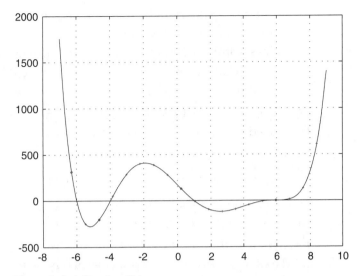

Figure 9.4 *A function f(x)*

plus marks indicate locations for which we have measurements. Clearly, there are a number of zero crossings of this function, including a very messy looking crossing at around $x = 6$.

We will find the exact value of one of the zeros of this function by first estimating the zero crossings, and then using a recursive technique for refining a better estimate to arbitrary levels of accuracy.

Estimating Critical Points of a Function First, we need to compute an approximation to the roots of this equation. These approximations will be found by finding the x values at which adjacent values of the function change sign. The technique for determining where adjacent points change sign is simply to multiply adjacent values of $f(x)$ and find where that product is not positive, as shown in Listing 9.7.

In Listing 9.7:

> Line 1: Establishes samples of x.
>
> Line 2: Computes $y = f(x)$.
>
> Line 3: Detects the indices where the zero crossings occur by

Listing 9.7 Initial zero crossings

```
1. px = linspace(-6.3, 8.4, 19);
2. py = f(px);
3. zeros = find(py(1:end-1) .* py(2:end) <= 0)
4. disp('zeros occur just after')
5. px(zeros)
6. root = findZero([px(zeros(3)) px(zeros(3)+1)])
```

shifting y to the right by one slot, and shortening the original by one to keep the vector size equal.

Lines 4 and 5: Displays the zero crossing estimates.

Line 6: Calls the recursive function to refine the third root of this equation.

Listing 9.7 produces the following results, which can be verified by observing the circled data points shown in Figure 9.4:

```
zeros occur just after
ans =
    -6.3000    -4.6667    0.2333    5.9500
```

Having observed these results, we decide to compute the exact value of the first positive root, occurring at the third crossing.

Recursive Refinement of the Estimate   The recursive function to find the third root of $f(x)$ works on the principle of binary division. It consumes a vector of adjacent values of x that are guaranteed to have values of $f(x)$ of opposite sign. The three characteristics of recursion implemented here are as follows:

- The terminating condition is when the two x values are within acceptable error—in this case, 0.001
- Otherwise, we find the middle of this x range, mx, find its f(mx), and then make the recursive call either with [x(1) mx] or [mx x(2)], depending on the sign of mx
- This will always converge because each recursive call halves the distance between the x limits

In general, this method is a little slower than Newton's method, which uses the slope of $f(x)$ to compute the next estimate. However, it is very strong and immune from the instability suffered by Newton's method on undulating data. The function that solves this problem is shown in Listing 9.8.

Listing 9.8   Recursive root finding

```
 1. function pt = findZero(x)
% x is a lower-upper pair guaranteed to have
%                   y values of opposite sign
%       return the x coordinate of the root
 2. if abs(x(1)-x(2)) < .001
 3.       pt = x(1);
 4. else
 5.       mx = sum(x)/2;
 6.       my = f(mx);
 7.       if my*f(x(1)) <= 0
 8.             pt = findZero([x(1) mx]);
 9.       else
10.             pt = findZero([mx x(2)]);
11.       end
12. end
```

In Listing 9.8:

> Line 1: The function consumes a pair of x limits and produces the x root.
>
> Lines 2–4: Check for the terminating condition and return the x root.
>
> Lines 5 and 6: Calculate the x and y values of the midpoint of the x range.
>
> Line 7: Checks the sign of the y value of the midpoint.
>
> Line 8: If different from the first limit, it makes the recursive call with the first limit and the midpoint.
>
> Lines 9 and 10: Otherwise, it uses the range from the midpoint to the second limit.

This function computes the correct crossing at $x = 1.00$.

 ## 9.10 Engineering Example—Robot Arm Motion

Here we consider the problem of programming the arm of a robot to move in a straight line. Consider the arm shown in Figure 9.5. It consists of two jointed limbs of length r_1 and r_2 at angles α and β, respectively, to the horizontal.

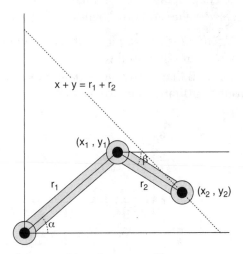

Figure 9.5 *The robot arm problem*

Overall Objective

The ultimate challenge of this situation is to calculate the sequence of values of α and β that will guide the end of the arm along the straight line:

$$x + y = r_1 + r_2 \tag{1}$$

However, this complete problem is more complex than necessary for this point in the text. First we will address a necessary component of the problem.

Immediate Objective

The subproblem we address here is to determine for a given value of α, the value β that will place the end of the arm at some place on the line. The algebra and trigonometry of this problem are quite simple. The position of the end of the arm, $[x_2\ y_2]$, is expressed as:

$$x_2 = r_1 \cos \alpha + r_2 \cos \beta \tag{2}$$

$$y_2 = r_1 \sin \alpha + r_2 \sin \beta \tag{3}$$

Combining these two relationships with Equation (1) gives the equation for $F(\beta)$, the difference between the end point derived from β and the straight line. We need to solve this for $F(\beta) = 0$:

$$F(\beta) = r_1 \cos \alpha + r_2 \cos \beta + r_1 \sin \alpha + r_2 \sin \beta - (r_1 + r_2) \tag{4}$$

If we are given values for r_1, r_2, and the angle α, we will use the method of Section 9.9.3 to find the value(s) of β that satisfies this equation. By inspecting Figure 9.5, we might expect two answers—one with a small negative value and one "bending backwards" at an angle greater than 90°.

Figure 9.6 shows a plot of this function for $r_1 = 4$, $r_2 = 3$, and $\alpha = 30°$. The zero crossings of this function confirm our intuition that there are two values of β that satisfy the equation for small, positive values of α: one around –30° and one around 110°.

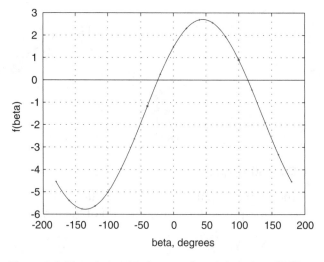

Figure 9.6 *The relationship between β and the value of $F(\beta)$*

The Solution to the Subproblem

As before, since there is no analytical solution to this function, we will find the approximate location of the zero crossings and then use a recursive function to find the exact roots. The script that accomplishes this is shown in Listing 9.9.

In Listing 9.9:

> Lines 3–8: Establish the parameters of the problem as global variables to avoid the overhead cost of passing them into recursive functions.
>
> Lines 9 and 10: Sample the possible range of beta values with enough values to identify the zero crossings, and compute the corresponding values of F(β).
>
> Lines 11–13: Estimate the zero locations by multiplying adjacent function values and display the results.
>
> Line 14: Calls the recursive function to find the zero crossing.

Running this script produces the following:

```
r1 =
      4
r2 =
      3
alpha =
     0.5236
zeros =
      8     15
zeros occur just after
ans =
    -0.6981    1.7453
zero =
    -0.4152   -0.0009
```

Listing 9.9 Finding arm position

```
 1. clear
 2. clc

 3. global r1
 4. r1 = 4
 5. global r2
 6. r2 = 3
 7. global alpha
 8. alpha = pi/6    % 30 deg
 9. beta = linspace(-pi, pi, 19);
10. pf = fab(beta);
11. zeros = find(pf(1:end-1) .* pf(2:end) <= 0)
12. disp('zeros occur just after')
13. beta(zeros)
 %
14. zero = findZeroAB([beta(zeros(1)) ...
                        beta(zeros(1)+1)])
```

The function for which we are seeking the zero is shown in Listing 9.10.

In Listing 9.10:

> Lines 2–4: Gain access to the global parameters.
>
> Line 5: Computes the left-hand side of Equation (4).

The function that finds the zero crossings of `fab(beta)` is shown in Listing 9.11.

In Listing 9.11:

> Line 2: Computes the y values corresponding to the x limits.
>
> Lines 3 and 4: Check the terminating condition and return the [x y] coordinates of the result.
>
> Lines 6 and 7: Find the x and y values of the midpoint.
>
> Lines 8 and 9: If the midpoint is on the opposite side of the x axis from the lower limit, make a recursive call using these limits.
>
> Line 11: Otherwise, makes the recursive call using the midpoint and the upper limit.

Listing 9.10 Function for zeros

```
1. function res = fab(beta)
% f(beta) = r1 (cos(alpha) + sin(alpha) - 1)
%           + r2 (cos(beta) + sin(beta) - 1)
2. global r1
3. global r2
4. global alpha
5. res =  r1 * (cos(alpha) + sin(alpha) - 1) ...
            + r2 * (cos(beta) + sin(beta) - 1);
```

Listing 9.11 Recursive zero finder

```
1. function pt = findZeroAB(x)
% x is a lower-upper pair guaranteed to have
%                    y values of opposite sign
2. y = fab(x);
3. if abs(x(1)-x(2)) < .001
4.     pt = [x(1) y(1)];
5. else
6.     mx = sum(x)/2;
7.     my = fab(mx);
8.     if my*y(1) < 0
9.         pt = findZeroAB([x(1) mx]);
10.    else
11.        pt = findZeroAB([mx x(2)]);
12.    end
13. end
```

Reflection

A modest amount of code is all that is required to create an elegant solution to a nontrivial problem. The structure of the recursive function shown in Listing 9.9 clearly reflects the standard recursive template, and that function can be used to find zeros of any continuous function defined in `fab(x)`.

 ## Chapter Summary

This chapter discussed the three basic principles of recursive programming that must be present for a recursive program to succeed:

- There must be a terminating condition
- The function must call a clone of itself
- The parameters of that clone must move the function toward the terminating condition

We have also seen some other important capabilities as follows:

- Exceptions are declared either within MATLAB system functions or by the user using the `error(...)` function; they are trapped and perhaps remedied using `try ... catch` code blocks
- A wrapper function is used to set up a recursive solution by validating the incoming data
- Tail recursion is a programming style that enables the recursive computation to happen on the way onto the stack, and usually results in no stack usage at all
- Mutual recursion can happen in rare circumstances, and must still obey the fundamental tenets of recursion

 ## Special Characters, Reserved Words, and Functions

Special Characters, Reserved Words, and Functions	Description	Discussed in This Section
catch	End of a suspect code block where the exception is trapped	9.4.3
error(str)	Announces an error with the string provided	9.4.3
global var	Defines a variable as globally accessible	9.10
lasterror	Provides a structure describing the environment from which an exception was thrown	9.4.3
try	Begins a block of suspect code from which an exception might be thrown	9.4.3

Self Test

Use the following questions to check your understanding of the material in this chapter:

True or False

1. We limit the functionality of a stack in order to protect the data from corruption.

2. The only way to remove a stack frame from the activation stack is to exit from the function instance hosted by that frame.

3. All the math operations in a recursive function are performed as the activation stack unwinds.

4. Exception processing can be used as a clever means of changing the normal flow of program control.

5. The name of the first function in a function definition m-file must match the name of the file.

Fill in the Blanks

1. Recursion is _____ by which a code block can be repeated in a controlled manner.

2. Very frequently, a recursive function needs a _____

   to set up the recursion correctly and to _____.

3. Exceptions are a powerful tool for managing _____

   caused by either _____ or _____.

4. A wrapper function is called once to perform _____ that the recursion requires, and then to call the recursive function

   _____.

5. Every exit from a tail recursive function must return either a

   _____ or the result of a _____.

Programming Projects

1. We will write the recursive function *oddTotal* to solve the following problem: the user will input a positive integer N, and your function is expected to add up all the *odd integers* between 1 and N.
    a. Identify specifically the three aspects of recursion as they apply to this problem.
    b. Write this function in recursive style.
    c. Write a script to repeatedly ask the user for a number, compute oddTotal of that number if it is positive, or otherwise stop the iteration.

2. You know that Σ refers to the function "summation of." For example:

$$\sum_{x=2}^{6} x(x-1) = (2*1) + (3*2) + (4*3) + (5*4) = 40$$

Similarly, the symbol Π is used to represent "product of." For example:

$$\prod_{x=2}^{5} x(x-1) = (2*1)*(3*2)*(4*3)*(5*4) = 2880$$

    a. Identify specifically the three aspects of recursion as they apply to this problem.
    b. Write a recursive function called myMultiOf that takes in n and returns y evaluated as the following:

$$y = \prod_{x=2}^{n} x(x-1)$$

You may assume that **n** is an integer that is greater than 1.

3. Ackermann's Function is "a function to end all functions." The work done by the function ack grows much faster than polynomials or exponentials.

    Given the following recursive method:

```
ans = ack(x, y)
    if x == 0
                ans = y + 1;
        elseif y == 0
                ans = ack(x - 1, 1);
        else
                ans = ack(x - 1, ack(x, y - 1));
    end
```

Hint

Tracing this on the activation stack simplifies things.

what is the result of ack(1, 4)?

4. Starting with the first line below, write a recursive function that takes in a positive integer N and displays the following message N times without returning anything:

    ```
    'I love Computer Science!'
    ```

    Your function *must* utilize numerical recursion.

    ```
    function myRecursive (N)
    ```

5. Write a function called GCD to find the greatest common divisor of two numbers. You must use recursion and no iteration of any kind to solve this problem. Recall that the GCD of m and n is the largest integer that divides both m and n with no remainder. You may assume both m and n will be positive.

    Hint

    You may need to call a recursive helper function and pass it m, n, and a third parameter that is initially the smaller of m and n.

6. For this problem you will be required to write three recursive functions: recurSum, recurProd, and recurFact.

    a. recurSum will take in a vector and compute the sum of the elements of the vector with the following header:

    ```
    function ans = recurSum(arr)
    ```

    b. recurProd will take in a vector and compute the product of the elements of the vector with the following header:

    ```
    function ans = recurProd(arr)
    ```

    c. recurFact will take in a number and return the factorial of the number with the following function header:

    ```
    function ans = recurFact(num)
    ```

7. Write a function called tracker that takes in a structure and returns the number of levels at which it has a field called Inner. Each field named Inner can also be a structure having a field called Inner, but at each level there can be only one field called Inner. The innermost structure will not contain a field called Inner. You must use recursion. Your function header should be as follows:

    ```
    function num = tracker(astruct)
    ```

Hint

Use the isfield(...) function.

Principles of
Problem Solving

10.1 Solving Simple Problems

10.2 Assembling Solution Steps

10.3 Summary of Operations

    10.3.1 Basic Arithmetic Operations

    10.3.2 Inserting into a Collection

    10.3.3 Traversing a Collection

    10.3.4 Building a Collection

    10.3.5 Mapping a Collection

    10.3.6 Filtering a Collection

    10.3.7 Summarizing a Collection

    10.3.8 Searching a Collection

    10.3.9 Sorting a Collection

10.4 Solving Larger Problems

10.5 Engineering Example— Processing Geopolitical Data

Chapter Objectives

This chapter presents an overview of framing the solutions to problems:

- We begin with simple problems that can be solved in a single step

- We continue to strategies for solving more complex problems involving data collections by dividing the solution into the following fundamental operations that can be performed on any collection of data:

  - Inserting
  - Traversing
  - Building
  - Mapping
  - Filtering
  - Summarizing
  - Searching
  - Sorting

Then we will briefly discuss how to combine these fundamental tools to solve more complex data manipulation problems.

Introduction

Programming is really all about applying the computer as a tool to solve problems. One of the most difficult tasks facing novice programmers is the blank sheet of paper. Faced with a problem you have never seen before, how do you start to solve it? The problem-solving style recommended in this text is first to identify the basic character of the data and the basic operation(s) we are asked to perform. If these two ideas are clear, we can create a template or outline of the solution, and begin to fill in the blanks.

As we gain more experience with the language, we have more computing tools to apply, and we can attack larger, more complex problems. We now have sufficient tools available to consider a more principled approach to data manipulation and problem solving. We will begin with the typical plan for solving simple problems in one step, and then continue to consider assembling multiple steps to solve more complex problems.

10.1 Solving Simple Problems

In Chapter 2 we saw the basic plan for solving simple problems:

- Define the input data
- Define the output data
- Discover the underlying equations to solve the problem
- Implement the solution
- Test the results
- Repair the code until it conforms to the specifications

This plan works whenever the problem is simple enough to be able to visualize the complete solution. Typically, however, problems are more complex and require a number of steps to be assembled.

10.2 Assembling Solution Steps

Problem complexity frequently comes in the form of data collections that need to be transformed into other collections or summarized as intermediate results. Identifying the operation(s) that will create the output from the input requires some experience. The rest of this chapter provides some guidelines for identifying elementary solution steps that can be combined to create solutions to many complex problems.

10.3 Summary of Operations

First, we document the operations we expect to be able to perform on collections. Table 10.1 lists the generic operations, a brief description of each, and a discussion of the consequences. The following paragraphs illustrate these fundamental operations, using the array of structures from Chapter 7 as examples. The discussion of each step takes the form of a written description, a flowchart, and a template for writing the code.

Style Points

It is conceivable—and in fact, a common practice—to combine multiple operations into one computing module, but it is poor abstraction and leads to code that is hard to understand and/or debug.

Table 10.1 Taxonomy of solution steps		
Operation	**Description**	**Consequence**
Insert	Inserts one item into a collection	An updated collection of data
Traverse	Touches each item of data in the collection	The collection is unchanged—frequently used to display or copy a collection
Build	Creates a collection from a data source (external file or traversing another collection); usually accomplished by inserting one item at a time	A new collection of data
Map	Changes the content of some or all of the items in the collection	A new collection of the same length, but the content of some or all items is changed
Filter	Removes some items from the collection	A new collection with reduced length, but the content of the items remains unchanged
Fold	Touches the entire collection, summarizing the contents with a single result	A single result summarizing the collection in some way (e.g., sum, max, or mean)
Search	Traverses the collection until an item matches a given search criterion and then stops, returning a result	A single result or the indication that the result was not achieved
Sort	Puts the collection in order by some specific criterion	A new collection of the same length in order

10.3.1 Basic Arithmetic Operations

The simple problem solution described in Section 10.1 frequently needs to be used as part of a larger problem solution. We include this activity in this list for completeness.

10.3.2 Inserting into a Collection

Inserting an item into a collection is a process usually used to build or maintain a collection of information. In MATLAB, we have seen four basic data collection types to which insertion applies: vectors, arrays, cell arrays, and structure arrays. We will discuss the peculiarities of each collection, and then the common processing algorithm that can be used to insert a new entry into the collection.

- **Vectors** are very flexible collections in MATLAB, and suffer only from the obvious limitation that one can add only numbers to a vector

- **Arrays** are as flexible as vectors, except that they require that new data be inserted a row or column at a time, and that the size of the row or column must match the existing array dimensions
- **Cell arrays** can be indexed like number arrays, and can contain any object; however, to compare one element to another usually requires a special-purpose comparison function
- **Structure arrays** as a collection behave like cell arrays, except that any structure inserted must have the same fields in the same order as those in the existing structure

In general, inserting into any of these collections involves insertion into the front of the collection, the back of the collection, or at some position in the middle by a specific comparison method.

Inserting into the front is accomplished by concatenating the new element before the existing collection. For example, adding `item` to the front of an existing cell array, `ca`, is accomplished as follows:

```
>> ca = [{item} ca] % note the braces needed for a cell array
```

Inserting at the back is accomplished by concatenating the new element after the existing collection. For example, adding `item` to the back of an existing cell array, `ca`, is accomplished as follows:

```
>> ca = [ca {item}]   % note the braces needed for a cell array
```

Inserting in order is usually accomplished using a `while` loop. If we are inserting `item` into a collection `coll`, we will use a `while` loop to find the index of the insertion point, `ins`, and then concatenate the three parts of the new collection. Figure 10.1 shows the flowchart that applies here, and Template 10.1 shows the template for the general solution.

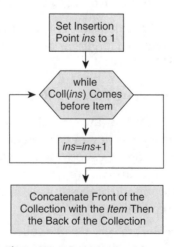

Figure 10.1 *Inserting in order*

Template 10.1 Template for inserting

```
%inserting item into a collection coll

<set insert point, ins, at the front>
while <insertion point in coll and
        item comes before coll(ins)>
    <move insertion point forward>
<end of the while loop>
<concatenate coll before ins with item and
        coll at and beyond ins>
```

For example, adding `item` in order to a vector, `v`, is accomplished as follows:

```
ins = 1;
while ins <= length(v) && before(item, v(ins))
    ins = ins + 1;
end
v = [v(1:ins-1) item v(ins:end)]
```

where `before(a,b)` is a generic comparator that determines whether `a` comes before `b` in the ordering scheme. Notice that this covers the cases where `item` must be the first or last item in the collection. Consequently, we could include the case of front or back insertion by having `before(a,b)` return `true` for inserting in the front and `false` for inserting at the back.

10.3.3 Traversing a Collection

Traversal involves moving across all elements of a collection and performing some step (not necessarily the same step) on each element without changing that element. Figure 10.2 and Template 10.2 illustrate the flowchart and basic template for traversing a collection. They assume that you are doing something like writing a file that needs to be initialized and finalized. These two steps may not always be required.

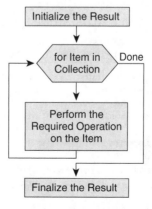

Figure 10.2 *Traversing a collection*

Template 10.2 Template for traversing

```
<initialize the result>
for item <across the whole collection>
   <operate on the item>
<end of the loop>
<finalize the result>
```

Listing 10.1 illustrates a function to write to a text file a selected attribute for all the CDs in a collection. Since some attributes are numeric and some strings, we need a helper function that is sensitive to the type of data to convert the data to string form. Such a helper function is listed in Listing 10.2. This function could be invoked with the following line:

```
>> printCDs(collection, 'artists.txt', 'artist');
```

In Listing 10.1:

> Line 6: We open the file of the name provided for writing, and return a file handle, fh, to be supplied to subsequent functions to identify the file.
>
> Line 7: Shows the simplest form of the for loop, taking each item in turn from the CD collection.
>
> Line 8: Shows the general form of the fprintf(...) usage where the first parameter is the handle of the file to which the output will be sent. As we have already seen, if this handle is omitted, the output goes to the Command window.
>
> Line 9: We invoke the helper function toString(...) to convert the attribute to a string before being written to the output file. Structure fields can be accessed indirectly via a variable by putting the variable in parentheses when selecting the structure attribute (CD.(attrib)).
>
> Line 11: This closes the file to make it accessible to any text editor.

Listing 10.2 shows the basic form of a helper function that will convert data objects of any class to the string representation you select.

Listing 10.1 Listing one field to a text file

```
 1. function printCDs(CDs, filename, attrib)
 2. % usage: printCDs(CDs, attrib, type)
 3. % print the specified attribute of all the CDs
 4. %    attrib must be one of the attributes as
 5. %                           a character string
 6. fh = fopen(filename, 'w');
 7. for CD = CDs
 8.     fprintf( fh, '%s: %s\n'], ...
 9.             attrib, toString(CD.(attrib)) );
10. end
11. fclose(fh);
```

Listing 10.2 The toString(...) helper function

```
 1. function str = toString(item)
 2. % convert an object of any class to string form
 3. if isa(item, 'char')
 4.     str = ['''' item ''''];
 5. elseif isa(item, 'double')
 6.     if length(item) == 1
 7.         str = sprintf('%g', item );
 8.     else
 9.         str = '[';
10.         for in = 1:length(item)
11.             str = [str sprintf(' %g', item(in) )];
12.         end
13.         str = [str ' ]'];
14.     end
15. elseif isa(item, 'struct')
16.     nms = fieldnames(item);
17.     str = [];
18.     for in = 1:length(nms)
19.         nm = nms{in};
20.         str=[str nm ': ' toString(item.(nm)) 13];
21.     end
22. else
23.     str = 'unknown data';
24. end
```

In Listing 10.2:

> Lines 3 and 4: We first form character strings by surrounding them with single quotes.
>
> Lines 5–7: Scalars are shown with %g conversion without punctuation.
>
> Lines 8–14: Vectors are surrounded by brackets (this version does not deal gracefully with arrays of more than one dimension).
>
> Lines 15–21: Each field of a structure is listed by name, using recursive calls to toString(...). The function does not follow the normal recursive template, because it depends on the natural character of structures eventually to terminate (not contain other structures).
>
> Line 23: A trap for data classes not yet covered by this function.

For a second traversal example, consider the need to save a collection to a text file after making modifications to the original collection. This is a little tricky because the modifications may include adding or deleting fields. Therefore, the text file must contain the field names and types. The function shown in Listing 10.3 accomplishes this. It is called by the following line:

```
>> writeCDs(collection, 'myCDs.txt');
```

Listing 10.3 Function to write CDs to a text file

```
1. function writeCDs(CDs, ilename)
2. % write a text file from which a general
3. % structure can be retrieved
4. fh = fopen(ilename, 'w');
5. attribs = fieldnames(CDs);
6. fprintf(fh,'%d\t%d\n', ...
                    length(CDs),length(attribs) );
7. for index = 1:length(attribs)
8.     fprintf(fh, '%s\t', attribs{index} );
9. end
10. fprintf(fh,'\n');
11. for index = 1:length(attribs)
12.     att = attribs{index};
13.     type{index} = class(CDs(1).(att));
14.     fprintf(fh, '%s\t', type{index} );
15. end
16. fprintf(fh,'\n');
17. for CD = CDs
18.     for index = 1:length(attribs)
19.         switch class(CD.(attribs{index}))
20.             case 'char'
21.                 str = ['"' CD.(attribs{index}) '"'];
22.             case 'double'
23.                 str=sprintf('%g', ...
                            CD.(attribs{index}) );
24.         end
25.         fprintf(fh, '%s\t', str );
26.     end
27.     fprintf(fh,'\n');
28. end
29. fclose(fh);
```

In Listing 10.3:

> Line 4: Opens the file for writing.
>
> Line 5: Retrieves the field names.
>
> Line 6: Writes the number of records and fields.
>
> Lines 7–10: Write the field names.
>
> Lines 11–16: Fetch and write the class of each field.
>
> Lines 17–28: Write the data for each structure.
>
> Line 29: Closes the file.

10.3.4 Building a Collection

In practice, frequently we combine traversal of one collection and building of another to copy data from one collection into another. Building a collection is the process of beginning with an empty collection and assembling data elements by inserting them one at a time into the new collection. The size of the collection increases continually until the process is finished. Figure 10.3 and Template 10.3 illustrate the algorithm for building a collection.

Template 10.3 Template for building

```
<initialize the new collection>
for item <across the data source>
   <extract the item>
   <insert item in new collection>
<end of the loop>
<finalize the new collection>
```

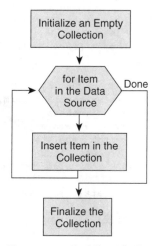

Figure 10.3 *Building a collection*

For example, the CD collection can be built by applying a custom read function to a text file containing the CD information with the following command:

```
>> collection = readCDs('myCDs.txt');
```

This function expects the data file—which was originally written by traversing a CD collection (see Listing 10.4)—in a specific format, as described in its header. The custom function to read the file is shown in Listing 10.4.

Listing 10.4 Custom structure read function

```
1.  function CDs = readCDs(filename)
2.  % read a text file describing the CD collection.
3.  % The first line specifies the number of CDs and
4.  % attributes
5.  % The second line lists the attributes
6.  % The 3rd line lists the class of each attribute
7.  % Subsequent lines list the data for each CD,
8.  %    one line per CD
9.  fh = fopen(fileName, 'r');
10. ns = textscan(fh, '%d %d', 1);
11. noCDs = ns{1};
12. noAtts = double(ns{2});
```
continued on next page

```
13. temp = textscan(fh, '%s\t', noAtts );
14. att = temp{1};
15. temp = textscan(fh, '%s\t', noAtts );
16. type = temp{1};
17. form = '';
18. for at = 1:noAtts
19.     switch type{at}
20.         case 'char'
21.             form = [form '%q'];
22.         case 'double'
23.             form = [form '%f'];
24.     end
25.     if at < noAtts
26.         form = [form ' '];
27.     end
28. end
29. for line = 1:noCDs
30.     temp = textscan(fh, form, 1 );
31.     for at = 1:noAtts
32.         value = temp{at};
33.         switch type{at}
34.             case 'char'
35.                 value = value{1};
36.         end
37.         CD.(att{at}) = value;
38.     end
39.     CDs(line) = CD;
40. end
41. fclose(fh);
```

In Listing 10.4:

Line 1: This function consumes a file name and produces an array of structures.

Lines 2–8: Description of the expected file format.

Line 9: Opens the file for reading—the result is a file handle, `fh`, to be used in subsequent file I/O calls.

Line 10: Uses `textscan(...)` to extract two numbers: the number of CDs and the number of attributes. The results are returned in a cell array.

Lines 11 and 12: Extract the sizes.

Lines 13 and 14: These lines read in and save the field names. When `textscan(...)` is provided with a third, numerical parameter, it performs a limited number of applications of the format string. Without that limitation, it would attempt to read the whole file. The results from each specified field in the format string are nested in the same cell array. So we find each field name in the first cell of the information returned.

Lines 15 and 16: These lines return the data types of each field in the same way.

Lines 17–28: These lines build the format string for reading each data record: `'%q'` for character strings and `'%f'` for numerical values. `'%q'` is a format parameter designed for `textscan(...)` to allow quoted strings to be read.

Lines 25–27: These lines provide for the spaces between format control parameters.

Lines 29–40: These lines actually extract and store the data values for each structure. If the data are characters, they must be extracted from the containing cell array (Lines 33–36).

Line 41: Close the data file.

Style Points

A simpler example of collection building occurred when we built the CD collection initially by repeated calls to the `makeCD` method, as shown in Chapter 7, Table 7.9, inserting each item at the end of the collection. However, while that example seems to simplify the process of building the collection, it really did not. The data for the function calls had to be extracted from a CD listing and edited to construct the function calls—normally not an efficient or effective way to compose a collection. Such hard-wiring should generally be avoided.

Because of the generality of the data, this is a slightly complex example of code to build a structure array. However, do not lose sight of the fact that it really is just scanning through a data file, extracting each structure in turn, and inserting that structure into the resulting collection.

10.3.5 Mapping a Collection

The purpose of mapping is to transform a collection by changing the data in some or all of its elements according to some functional description without changing its length. It is distinct from traversal because its intent is to change the data elements. While many languages permit collections to be modified in place, MATLAB usually requires you to create a new collection. However, this is still considered mapping. The scalar mathematical and logical operations on vectors are good examples of mapping. Figure 10.4 and Template 10.4 illustrate the basic algorithm for mapping. As illustrated in the example of operations on vectors, mapping may involve combining two or more collections of the same length.

Template 10.4 Template for mapping

```
<initialize the result>
for item <across the whole collection>
   <extract the item>
   <modify the item>
   <insert modified item in the result>
<end of the loop>
<finalize the result>
```

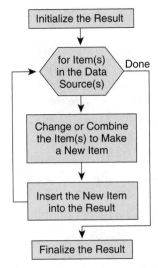

Figure 10.4 *Mapping a collection*

Listing 10.5 shows a function that will add an attribute to all the CDs reflecting the value of each CD as the ratio of the number of stars to the price. This function would be invoked by the following:

```
>> addedCDs = addValue(collection);
```

In Listing 10.5:

Line 4: Notice the use of the indexed form of the `for` loop in order to be able to store the new CD in the new collection.

Line 6: Notice the use of `eps` to guard against free CDs in the collection.

10.3.6 Filtering a Collection

Filtering involves removing items from a collection according to specified selection criteria. The data contents of the remaining items in the collection should not be changed, and the collection will usually be shorter than before. Typically, we filter vectors by applying built-in logical operations and then indexing with the results to produce new, shorter arrays. Figure 10.5 and Template 10.5 illustrate the general algorithm for filtering a collection.

Listing 10.5 Adding value to a CD collection

```
1. function newCDs = addValue( CDs )
2. %  newCDs = addValue( CDs )
3. % add the value attribute
4. for index = 1:length(CDs)
5.     CD = CDs(index);
6.     CD.value = CD.stars / (CD.price + eps);
7.     newCDs(index) = CD;
8. end
```

Template 10.5 Template for filtering

```
<initialize the new collection>
for item <across the whole collection>
    <extract the item>
    if <keep the item>
        <insert item in new collection>
    <end if>
<end for>
<finalize the new collection>
```

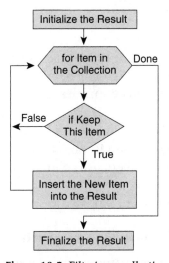

Figure 10.5 *Filtering a collection*

Listing 10.6 is the code for a generic function to filter CDs by a given attribute and value. It needs the auxiliary function illustrated in Listing 10.7 to compare two values uniformly. It could be invoked by this call:

```
>> noRayCharles = filterCDs(collection, 'artist', 'Charles, Ray');
```

Listing 10.6 Filtering a CD collection

```
1. function newCDs = filterCDs( CDs, attrib, value )
2. %   newCDs = filterCDs( CDs, attrib, value )
3. % get rid of all CDs with the attribute
4. %                     equaling the given value
5. index = 1;
6. for CD = CDs
7.     if ~valueEq( CD.(attrib), value )
8.         newCDs(index) = CD;
9.         index = index + 1;
10.     end
11. end
12. if index == 1
13.     newCDs = [];
14. end
```

In Listing 10.6:

> Line 1: The good news is that this function will filter by removing any item that matches the given value of any attribute.
>
> Line 5: This is a different technique for saving the new collection by keeping a separate index that is incremented when a new item is saved.
>
> Line 7: The bad news is that generality brings a little complexity—we need a helper function to test for equality between objects of various types.
>
> Lines 8 and 9: This is the process of saving an item to the new collection.
>
> Lines 12–14: Protect us from the case where we have removed all the items, keeping none. Without this, MATLAB will throw an exception because newCDs is not defined until the first item is saved.

In Listing 10.7:

> Line 1: A and B could be any data type. We address only the most common here. All common data types respond correctly to the normal equality test, except for strings.
>
> Lines 4 and 5: Take care of string comparison.

10.3.7 Summarizing a Collection

Folding is the name given to summarizing a collection. It is a special case of traversal where all of the items in the collection are summarized as a single result. The collection is not altered in size or values by the operation. Totaling, averaging, or finding the largest element in a vector are typical examples of folding. For example, having mapped the CD collection to add a value field, we might want to find the CD with the best value. Figure 10.6 and Template 10.6 show the basic algorithm for folding a collection. The general form of a fold should be to initialize the summary value and then traverse the whole collection, updating the summary.

Listing 10.7 Helper function with a generic quality test

```
1. function ans = valueEq( A, B )
2. % are A and B equal, regardless of data type?
3. switch class(A)
4.     case 'char'
5.         ans = strcmp(A, B);
6.     otherwise
7.         ans = (A == B);
8. end
```

Template 10.6 Template for folding

```
<initialize the summary value>
for item <across the whole collection>
   <extract the item>
   <update the summary value>
<end for>
<finalize the summary value>
```

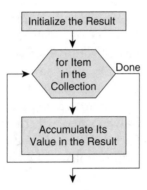

Figure 10.6 *Folding a collection*

The function shown in Listing 10.8 finds the CD with the highest value in a collection. Note that we carefully avoided generality here by not letting the user specify the attribute. Had we permitted this, we would need another type-independent helper function to determine which of two values was greater.

When the summary involves calculating the maximum or minimum of something, it can be difficult to choose the right starting value. This function illustrates a tidy solution to this dilemma: picking the value of the first item, then comparing that to all the rest. The function would be called by the following:

```
>> bestCD = bestValue(collection);
```

Listing 10.8 Finding the best CD

```
1. function theCD = bestValue(CDs)
2. % find the CD with best value
3. theCD = CDs(1);
4. bestVal = theCD.value;
5. for index = 2:length(CDs)
6.      CD = CDs(index);
7.      if CD.value > bestVal
8.           theCD = CD;
9.           bestVal = CD.value;
10.     end
11. end
```

In Listing 10.8:

> Lines 3 and 4: Set the first CD as the result.
>
> Lines 6–10: Extract and test each item.

10.3.8 Searching a Collection

Searching is the process of traversing the collection and applying a specified test to each element in turn, terminating the process as soon as the test is satisfied. This is superficially similar to filtering, except that it is not necessary to touch all the elements of the collection; the search stops as soon as one element of the collection matches the search criteria. If the criteria are extremely complex, it is sometimes advisable to perform a mapping or folding before the search is performed. Figure 10.7 and Template 10.7 show one way to implement searching a collection using a `for` loop with a break exit. There are always two exit criteria from a search—finding what you seek or failing to find it. It can also be implemented with a `while` loop, but the multiple exit criteria make the code generally more complex.

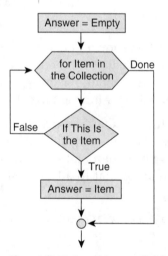

Figure 10.7 *Searching a collection*

Template 10.7 Template for searching

```
<initialize result to not succeeded>
for <item in the collection>
    if <found criteria>
        <set result to succeeded>
        <break the loop>
    <end if>
<end for>
<check for failure>
```

Listing 10.9 Searching for a specific CD

```
1.  function theCD = findCD(CDs, attrib, value)
2.  % find the specific CD
3.  index = 1;
4.  found = false;
5.  while (index <= length(CDs)) && ~found
6.        CD = CDs(index);
7.        if valueEq(CD.(attrib), value)
8.              found = true;
9.              theCD = CD;
10.       else
11.             index = index + 1;
12.       end
13. end
14. if ~found
15.       theCD = [];
16. end
```

Listing 10.9 illustrates the search for a particular CD, using the helper function created to test for equality. It could be invoked by the following:

```
>> joshCD = findCD(addedCDs, 'artist', 'Groban, Josh')
```

In Listing 10.9:

> Lines 3 and 4: Initialize terminating conditions.
>
> Line 5: Notice the use of a `while` loop because we intend to terminate the search at success. There are two possible exits from the `while` loop—when the index passes the end of the collection, indicating failure, or when the CD has been found.
>
> Line 6: Extracts the item.
>
> Line 7: Checks for equality.
>
> Line 11: Moves through the collection.
>
> Lines 14 and15: If we should exit the `while` loop without finding the CD, we need to return something to the user—null, the empty vector, is usually a good choice. The user can check for this by calling `isempty(...)`.

10.3.9 Sorting a Collection

Sorting involves reordering the elements in a collection according to a specified ranking function that defines which item "comes before" another. Sorting is computationally expensive. However, if a large collection of data is stable—items are added or removed infrequently—but is frequently searched for specific items, keeping the data sorted can greatly improve the efficiency of the searches. Chapter 16 is devoted to the details of sorting, but the concept is included here to complete the list of operations we can perform on a collection.

10.4 Solving Larger Problems

Problem statements are rarely simple enough to be able to seize one of the above steps and solve the whole problem. Usually, the solution involves choosing a number of known operations and performing those operations in order to solve the complete problem. Solution steps are combined in one of two ways—in sequence or nested. When considering the overall strategy for solving a problem, one might identify steps A and B as contributing to the solution. Your logical statement might say either "do A and then B" sequential steps—or "for each part of A, do B"—nested steps.

For example, consider the baseball card problem originally proposed in Chapter 1. You have collected over the years a huge number of baseball cards and you wish to find the names of the 10 "qualified" players with the highest lifetime batting average. To qualify, the players must have been in the league at least five years, had at least 100 plate appearances per year, and made less than 10 errors per year.

You have built a structure array containing the relevant information on the cards for each player, and we need to operate on this collection to solve the problem. Consider again the overall problem situation, as shown in Figure 10.8. The original data is a structure array containing all the player data. The final result is a list of 10 names of the qualified players with the highest batting averages. There may be more than one sequence of operations to solve this problem; some may be more efficient than others.

First, consider the operations that could be performed on the original data. Since the end result is a collection, it is unlikely that the first step would reduce the collection to one answer. This eliminates folding and searching. Since the collection is already built, we do not need to insert or build, leaving four possible operations to consider—traversal, mapping, filtering, and sorting (see Figure 10.9).

Now, consider the last operation—it seems reasonable that the last thing to do is a mapping—taking the 10 selected structures and extracting the names. Figure 10.10 shows this step. Here, we think about how to find these 10 structures. If we had a collection of qualified players sorted by their batting

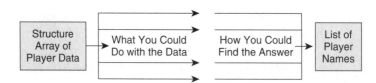

Figure 10.8 *Generalized problem solving*

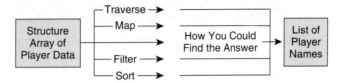

Figure 10.9 *First step*

average, we could accomplish this with a special filter taking the first 10 from these sorted, qualified players, as shown in Figure 10.11. Backing up one more step, we can see that the sorted collection we need is just a sort of the qualified players, as shown in Figure 10.12. Figure 10.13 shows the connection from the front to the back.

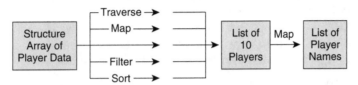

Figure 10.10 *Step N*

Figure 10.11 *Step N-1*

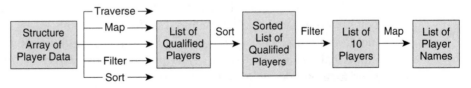

Figure 10.12 *Step N-2*

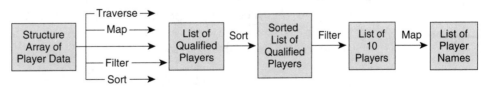

Figure 10.13 *Connecting the dots*

10.5 Engineering Example—Processing Geopolitical Data

Imagine that the U.S. government has still not passed the Fair Tax and you have decided to move your prosperous business overseas to the country with the most business-friendly environment. After considerable study, you decide that the best measure of friendliness would be to compute the rate of growth of the gross domestic product for candidate countries, subtract their rate of population growth, and use this measure to choose the best country. An Internet search provides an interesting source of data. Figure 10.14 shows an excerpt from a spreadsheet containing historical data for 154 countries from Penn World Table Version 6.1[1]. The data columns of interest to us contain the following information:

- Country—Country name
- Code—Country code
- Year—Year in which the data in this row was recorded
- POP—Population that year
- XRAT—Exchange rate versus U.S. currency that year
- PPP—Purchasing power parity over GDP that year
- Cpdp—Real gross domestic product per capita that year

Figure 10.14 also illustrates one of the weaknesses of spreadsheets: they are inherently two dimensional, and the data in this case is three dimensional; each country has several sets of data as functions of the year when the information was recorded. Therefore, the data must be massaged into a form more useful to us. A careful examination of the data also reveals the following challenges:

- The years in which the data was available vary from country to country—most have data from 1950 to 2000
- There are some places within the numerical data where the values are not available, signified by the letters "na" at those locations

Our algorithm must take into account the variable number of years and the potential presence of strings within the data. Fortunately, the `xlsread(...)` function discussed earlier recognizes this situation and inserts NaN in the numerical data fields. To ensure clarity and reliability in our solution, we need a careful design for this data processing task as follows.

- Looking at the end result desired, eventually we need to fold a collection of data about each country, and choose the friendliest one.
- The information describing each country must include not only its name, but also vectors of the population and CGDP as a function of the year. It seems that a structure array by country would be an appropriate form for the data.

---

[1] Credit: Alan Heston, Robert Summers and Bettina Aten, Penn World Table Version 6.1, Center for International Comparisons at the University of Pennsylvania (CICUP), October 2002.

	A	B	C	D	E	F	G	H	I	J	K	L	M	N	O	P
1	Country	Code	Year	POP	XRAT	PPP	cgdp	cc	ci	cg	P	pc	pg	pi	openc	cgnp
2	Angola	AGO	1960	4816.00	0.03	0.01	542.68	76.75	8.84	9.45	17.51	13.07	24.03	49.11	36.98	na
3	Angola	AGO	1961	4884.19	0.03	0.00	564.37	74.23	7.92	9.85	17.36	13.18	23.65	48.67	35.23	na
4	Angola	AGO	1962	4955.35	0.03	0.00	573.94	75.48	6.76	10.55	17.28	13.41	23.65	50.44	38.79	na
5	Angola	AGO	1963	5028.69	0.03	0.01	593.72	73.68	5.72	13.56	17.73	13.90	24.04	52.06	38.69	na
⋮	⋮	⋮	⋮	⋮	⋮	⋮	⋮	⋮	⋮	⋮	⋮	⋮	⋮	⋮	⋮	⋮
36	Angola	AGO	1994	10627.18	59.51	53.32	1095.94	34.66	9.09	46.75	89.59	70.34	76.84	228.63	160.87	47.86
37	Angola	AGO	1995	10972.00	2750.23	1007.53	1244.73	41.86	9.43	57.65	36.63	29.58	31.91	96.85	146.58	48.19
38	Angola	AGO	1996	11316.94	128029.20	54873.28	1362.32	37.17	8.57	56.75	42.86	34.35	37.77	113.51	134.87	52.97
39	Angola	AGO	1997	na	na	na	na	na	na	na	na	na	na	na	na	59.09
40	Angola	AGO	1998	na	na	na	na	na	na	na	na	na	na	na	na	50.08
41	Angola	AGO	1999	na	na	na	na	na	na	na	na	na	na	na	na	44.52
42	Angola	AGO	2000	na	na	na	na	na	na	na	na	na	na	na	na	53.81
43	Albania	ALB	1991	3277.00	15.63	3.13	1605.36	82.81	6.92	36.66	20.04	23.78	12.02	17.70	54.89	98.10
44	Albania	ALB	1992	3225.00	75.03	10.53	1566.99	136.94	5.11	35.08	14.03	15.59	7.88	14.42	108.94	95.94
45	Albania	ALB	1993	3179.00	102.06	19.33	2031.94	109.39	12.54	25.73	18.94	20.80	10.51	20.01	77.14	99.02
⋮	⋮	⋮	⋮	⋮	⋮	⋮	⋮	⋮	⋮	⋮	⋮	⋮	⋮	⋮	⋮	⋮
5795	Zambia	ZMB	1998	9665.71	1862.07	744.91	800.69	85.12	13.75	14.14	40.00	39.54	33.22	49.87	68.86	93.36
5796	Zambia	ZMB	1999	9881.21	2388.02	941.87	765.24	91.82	15.30	12.54	39.44	39.02	31.89	48.14	66.55	94.97
5797	Zambia	ZMB	2000	10089.00	3110.84	1157.63	840.97	86.33	15.38	12.34	37.21	37.70	29.54	40.65	70.45	95.88
5798	Zimbabwe	ZWE	1954	3011.69	0.71	0.37	400.19	66.89	41.48	4.03	50.97	60.59	135.99	29.92	77.30	na
5799	Zimbabwe	ZWE	1955	3127.52	0.71	0.36	429.04	65.87	50.95	3.47	50.40	60.80	136.52	31.10	78.43	na
5800	Zimbabwe	ZWE	1956	3264.42	0.71	0.36	471.08	63.51	54.77	3.53	50.08	62.11	136.86	30.53	74.27	na
⋮	⋮	⋮	⋮	⋮	⋮	⋮	⋮	⋮	⋮	⋮	⋮	⋮	⋮	⋮	⋮	⋮
5842	Zimbabwe	ZWE	1998	12153.85	23.68	4.06	2799.85	77.66	10.75	13.39	17.16	14.97	22.03	26.87	91.96	93.25
5843	Zimbabwe	ZWE	1999	12388.32	38.30	6.12	2770.48	76.89	10.73	12.81	15.98	14.35	19.01	24.02	92.99	93.75
5844	Zimbabwe	ZWE	2000	12627.00	44.42	9.48	2607.03	69.23	8.62	22.44	21.33	19.26	23.63	31.96	62.61	96.62

Figure 10.14 *Spreadsheet samples*

- Therefore, before actually solving the problem, we have to build this structure.
- Having built the structure, the folding operation to find the friendliest country follows the folding template shown in Section 10.3.7.

Listing 10.10 shows the script that accomplishes this analysis, although most of the work is actually done in the following functions.

Listing 10.10 Country analysis

```
% build the country array

1. worldData = buildData('World_data.xls');

2. best = findBest(worldData);

3. fprintf('best country is %s\n', ...
                 worldData(best).name)
```

Line 1: `worldData` will be a structure array containing the relevant data from the spreadsheet.

Line 2: `best` will be the index of the friendliest country according to the criteria defined in the function `findBest(...)`.

Line 3: Here we can look up and print the name of the best country.

Listing 10.11 lists the function that builds the country data. The algorithm violates the best style by taking advantage of the logical ordering of the data in the spreadsheet to traverse the data from the spreadsheets simultaneously, filter out the data for each country in turn, and then map the available data for that country into the emerging structure array.

In Listing 10.11:

Line 2: Reads the Excel spreadsheet—we need the numerical data and the text part for the names of the countries.

Listing 10.11 Building the country data

```
1. function worldData = buildData(name)

% read the spreadsheet into a data array
%                 and a text cell array
2. [data txt] = xlsread(name);
3. country = ' '; % force the first data row
%                 % to change the country
4. cntry_index = 0;
%   Traverse the data and cell arrays producing
%      an array of structures,
%      one for each country

5. for row = 1:length(data)
      % Because the text data in txt contains
      %   the header row of the spreadsheet,
      %   the data at a given row belongs to the country
      %                 whose name is at txt{row+1}.
      % if the country name changes,
      %                 begin a new structure.
6.      if ~strcmp(txt{row+1}, country)
7.          col = 1;
8.          country = txt{row+1};
9.          cntry_index = cntry_index + 1;
10.         cntry.year = 1;
11.         cntry.pop = 1;
12.         cntry.gdp = 1;
13.     end
14.     cntry.name = country;
15.     cntry.year(col) = data(row, 1);
16.     cntry.pop(col)  = data(row, 2);
17.     cntry.gdp(col)  = data(row, 5);
18.     col = col + 1;
19.     worldData(cntry_index) = cntry;
20. end
```

Lines 3 and 4: Initialize the results of the traversal, setting an unknown country name and the initial country count.

Line 5: Traverses the rows of the numerical data.

Line 6: Since the numerical data skipped the header row, the name of the country corresponding to each row of data is in the text file at row+1. When the country changes, we step to the next country index, reset the year counter, col, for that country, and empty the structure used to accumulate the country data.

Line 7: Resets the counter that indexes the year storage for the current country.

Line 8: Saves the name of the new country to continue retrieving its data.

Line 9: Increases the country count.

Lines 10–12: Reset the structure used to store the vectors of data. This is crucial because the number of annual data items for all countries is not the same.

Lines 14–17: Add this row of data to the structure. Column 1 is the year, column 2 is the population, and column 5 is the CGDP.

Line 18: Moves to the next year.

Line 19: Saves all this in the structure array.

Listing 10.12 shows the function that finds the best country by folding the country structure array, together with the two supporting functions that provide the comparison criteria. Notice that the complexity of the data has forced the solution into nested folds: to fold the country data array, we have to summarize (fold) the annual data for each country.

In Listing 10.12:

Lines 2 and 3: As with any folding function that is looking for the maximum or minimum of a collection, the best place to start is the first item in the collection. The remaining items can then be compared to this one.

Listing 10.12 Folding the country data

```
1. function besti = findbest(worldData)
% find the index of the best country
% according to the criterion in the function
%   fold
2. best = fold(worldData(1));
3. besti = 1;
4. for ndx = 2:length(worldData)
5.      cntry = worldData(ndx);
6.      tryThis = fold(cntry);
7.      if tryThis > best
8.          best = tryThis;
9.          besti = ndx
10.     end
11. end
```

continued on next page

```
12. function ans = fold(st)
% s1 is the rate of growth of population
13. pop = st.pop(~isnan(st.pop));
14. yr = st.year(~isnan(st.pop));
15. s1 = slope(yr, pop)/mean(pop);
% s2 is the rate of growth of the GDP
16. gdp = st.gdp(~isnan(st.gdp));
17. yr = st.year(~isnan(st.gdp));
18. s2 = slope(yr, gdp)/mean(gdp);
% Measure of merit is how much faster
%    the gdp grows than the population
19. ans = s2 - s1;

20. function s1 = slope(x, y)
% Estimate the slope of a curve
21. if length(x) == 0 || x(end) == x(1)
22.     error('bad data')
23. else
24.     s1 = (y(end) - y(1))/(x(end) - x(1));
25. end
```

Line 4: Loops through the remaining countries in the array.

Line 5: Extracts one structure.

Line 6: Computes its friendliness value.

Lines 7–10: If the result is improved, these lines update the stored values. The index besti is returned when the loop finishes.

Line 12: This function computes the measure of friendliness for each country. The goal is to subtract the rate of population growth from the rate of growth of the GDP. So first we compute the rate of population growth.

Lines 13 and 14: These lines establish two local vectors containing the population value and the corresponding year without the values that are NaN, the places where "na" appears in the spreadsheet.

Line 15: Calls the helper function for the slope of this relationship, and non-dimensionalizes the result by dividing by the mean population.

Lines 16–18: Repeat the same logic for the non-dimensional rate of increase of the GDP.

Line 19: Returns the difference in growth rates.

Line 20: The function that estimates the rates of growth.

Lines 21 and 22: We have a problem if there is no data or if the value we will subsequently use as a divisor is zero.

Line 24: A very crude measure of the slope is to divide the difference between the first and last data points by the difference between the first and last x values. (We will be able to improve on this approach later.)

When we run this program, we see the following result:

```
>> best country is Equatorial Guinea
```

This may not be exactly the result we were hoping for. In Chapter 16 we will revisit this example with some better tools that will allow us to apply additional criteria to the best countries.

 ## Chapter Summary

This chapter presented the fundamental operations that can be applied to problem solving:

- Using normal arithmetic operations with specific input and output values
- Inserting new elements in a collection
- Traversing a collection
- Building a collection by repetitive insertion
- Mapping a collection—changing the values of the data items in the collection, but not the number of them
- Filtering a collection—reducing the number of entries, but not changing the data contents of the collection
- Folding—summarizing the values in a collection into a single quantity
- Searching for a specific match in a collection
- Sorting a collection

Then we briefly discussed how to combine these fundamental tools to solve more complex data manipulation problems.

 ## Self Test

Use the following questions to check your understanding of the material in this chapter:

True or False

1. Copying the elements of a structure array into a cell array is a combination of traversal and insertion.

2. If you map a collection, you must change at least one of its elements.

3. When you filter a collection, at least one data element is changed.

4.   The function `max(...)` is not folding because it returns two values.

5.   You can use a `for` loop to search a collection even if you need to stop the search when you find the answer.

6.   Sorting must involve putting the items in a collection in numerical order (ascending or descending).

Fill in the Blanks

1.   The problem-solving style recommended in this text is to identify the _____ and the _____ .

2.   Building is the process of _____ and

     _____ .

3.   Mapping may involve combining _____ of the same length.

4.   We _____ vectors by applying built-in logical operations and then indexing with the results to produce new, shorter arrays.

5.   Totaling, averaging, or finding the smallest element in a vector are typical examples of _____ .

6.   There are almost always two exit criteria for a search:

     _____ or _____ .

7.   To save a collection to a text file, you _____ the

     collection _____ to the file.

Programming Projects

For these projects, you will need to do the research to find a set of data about vehicles for sale. Search the Internet for vehicles for sale, and assemble the information in a text file or spreadsheet. You may have to generate suitable random numbers if some of the data you need is not readily available.

1. *Building:* Write a script that will read your data file and makes a structure array where each entry has the following fields:

   - Manufacturer
   - Model
   - Body Style
   - Year
   - Price
   - Seats
   - Gas Mileage
   - Odometer

2. *Traversing:* Write a script that lists the following information about each vehicle: the year, manufacturer, model, and price.

3. *Traversing:* Adapt the readCD(...) and writeCD(...) functions to save and restore text files with the results of the following problems. (Do you really have to change anything but the function name?)

4. *Mapping:* Assume that your collection of vehicle data is the inventory at a car dealership. Write a script that will reduce the prices of all the vehicles by 10 percent, except for the convertibles, whose prices you will raise by 5 percent.

5. *Filtering:* The manager has decided that older vehicles do not enhance the appearance of the dealership. Write a script that removes all vehicles made before 2002 from your collection.

6. *Folding:* Write a script to calculate the total inventory cost of the vehicles. Assume that the inventory cost is 75 percent of each vehicle price.

7. *Searching:* Write a script that a customer could use to do the following:

   - Enter a manufacturer's name
   - Enter a year
   - Find the first vehicle on the list made by that manufacturer in that year

8. *Complex Solution:* Now you want to use the data set for something
    practical. You want a script that does the following:
    - Asks you for a year and odometer reading
    - Searches the collection for vehicles (there may be more than one)
      made on or after the given year and that have less than the
      specified odometer reading and that have the highest gas mileage
    - Displays the year, manufacturer, model, and price of these
      vehicles

Plotting

Chapter Objectives

This chapter presents the principles and practice of plotting in the following forms:

- Basic two-dimensional line plots

- Two-dimensional parametric plots

- Three-dimensional line and parametric plots

- Basic three-dimensional surface plots

- Parametric surface plots

- Bodies of rotation

There is a much quoted expression that "a picture is worth a thousand words," and this is never more appropriate than when talking about data. In previous chapters we used some simple plot commands to display data to illustrate its behavior. The ability of MATLAB to present data reaches far beyond ordinary data plotting, and far beyond the limited confines of a textbook. This chapter will present the fundamental concepts of the different forms in which data can be presented, but it leaves to the reader the challenge of exploring the full range of capabilities available. You only really discover the power of MATLAB's plotting capabilities when you have some unusual data to visualize.

11.1 Plotting in General
   11.1.1 A Figure—The Plot Container
   11.1.2 Simple Functions for Enhancing Plots
   11.1.3 Multiple Plots on One Figure—Subplots
   11.1.4 Manually Editing Plots

11.2 2-D Plotting
   11.2.1 Simple Plots
   11.2.2 Plot Options
   11.2.3 Parametric Plots
   11.2.4 Other 2-D Plot Capabilities

11.3 3-D Plotting
   11.3.1 Linear 3-D Plots
   11.3.2 Linear Parametric 3-D Plots
   11.3.3 Other 3-D Plot Capabilities

11.4 Surface Plots
   11.4.1 Basic Capabilities
   11.4.2 Simple Exercises
   11.4.3 3-D Parametric Surfaces
   11.4.4 Bodies of Rotation
   11.4.5 Other 3-D Surface Plot Capabilities
   11.4.6 Assembling Compound Surfaces

11.5 Engineering Example— Visualizing Geographic Data
   11.5.1 Analyzing the Data
   11.5.2 Displaying the Data

11.1 Plotting in General

Before considering the details of how each plotting mode works, we should set the context. In this section we will discuss the general container for all graphical types, the figure, and some basic operations that apply to all figures—functions that enhance them, the ability to assemble subplots into a single figure, and the advisability of making manual changes to plots.

11.1.1 A Figure—The Plot Container

The fundamental container for plotting is a MATLAB figure. In a simple script, if you just start plotting data, *figure number 1* is automatically generated to present the data. You can manage the figures by calling the `figure` function. Each time `figure` is called, a new figure is made available, with the next higher figure number. The `figure` function actually returns a reference called a handle with which, in advanced plotting circumstances, you can change the attributes of the figure.

To clear the current figure, put the key word `clf` in the header of your script. To remove all the figures, put the key phrase `close all` at the beginning of your script.

11.1.2 Simple Functions for Enhancing Plots

We have already introduced `plot(x, y)`, the basic function that creates a simple plot of x versus y. The following functions can be used to enhance any of the plots discussed in this chapter. Note that they enhance an existing plot; they should all be called after the fundamental function that creates a plot figure.

- `axis <param>` provides a rich set of tools for managing the appearance of the axes including the following:
  - `tight` reduces the axes to their smallest possible size
  - `equal` sets the x and y scales to the same value
  - `square` makes the plot figure of equal width and height
  - `off` does not show the axes at all
- `axis([xl xu yl yu zl zu])` overrides the automatic computation of the axis values, forcing the x-axis to reach from `xl` to `xu`, the y-axis from `yl` to `yu`, and the z-axis from `zl` to `zu`. For 2-D plots, the z values should be omitted.
- `colormap <specification>` establishes a sequence of colors, the color map, to be used under a number of circumstances to cycle through a series of colors automatically. The legal specification values are listed in Appendix A.

- `grid on` puts a grid on the plot; `grid off` (the default) removes grid lines.

- `hold on` holds the existing data on the figure to allow subsequent plotting calls to be added to the current figure without first erasing the existing plot; `hold off` (the default) redraws the current figure, erasing the previous contents.

- `legend(...)` takes a cell array of strings, one for each of the multiple plots on a single figure, and creates a legend box. By default, that box appears in the top-right corner of the figure. However, this default can be overridden by explicitly specifying the location of the legend. See the MATLAB help files for a complete discussion of the legend options.

- `shading <spec>` defines the method for shading surfaces. See the MATLAB help files for a complete discussion of the shading specification options.

- `text(x, y, {z,}, str)` places the text provided at the specified (x, y) location on a 2-D plot, or at the (x, y, z) location on a 3-D plot.

- `title(...)` places the text provided as the title of the current plot.

- `view(az, el)` sets the angle from which to view a plot. The parameters are `az`, the azimuth, an angle measured in the horizontal plane, and `el`, the elevation, an angle measured upward from the horizontal. Both angles are measured in degrees.

- `xlabel(...)` sets the string provided as the label for the x-axis.

- `ylabel(...)` sets the string provided as the label for the y-axis.

- `zlabel(...)` sets the string provided as the label for the z-axis. (As we will see, all plots actually have a third axis.)

11.1.3 Multiple Plots on One Figure—Subplots

Within the current figure, you can place multiple plots with the `subplot` command, as shown in Figure 11.1.

The function `subplot(r, c, n)` divides the current figure into r rows and c columns of equally spaced plot areas, and then establishes the nth of these (counting across the rows first) as the current figure. You do not have to draw in all of the areas you specify. Figure 11.1 was generated by the code shown in Listing 11.1.

| **Listing 11.1** Creating a subplot

```
1. clf
2. x = -2*pi:.05:2*pi;
3. subplot(2,3,1)
4. plot(x, sin(x))
5. title('1 - sin(x)');
```

continued on next page

```
 6. subplot(2,3,2)
 7. plot(x, cos(x))
 8. title('2 - cos(x)');

 9. subplot(2,3,3)
10. plot(x, tan(x))
11. title('3 - tan(x)');

12. subplot(2,3,4)
13. plot(x, x.^2)
14. title('4 - x^2');

15. subplot(2,3,5)
16. plot(x, sqrt(x))
17. title('5 - sqrt(x)');

18. subplot(2,3,6)
19. plot(x, exp(x))
20. title('4 - e^x');
```

In Listing 11.1:

> Line 1: clf clears the parameters of the current figure.
>
> Line 2: Specifies a suitable range of x values.
>
> Line 3: Sets the first subplot region.
>
> Line 4: This is the simple version of the plot(...) function introduced earlier, plotting x against y and automatically creating the axes, creating subplot 1, the plot in the top-left corner. Note that although in the figure seen here the line is gray, when you run the script, the line will appear in its default color, blue.
>
> Line 5: The title(...) function puts the specified string at the top of the plot as its title.
>
> Lines 6–8: Create subplot 2, the second plot on the first row.
>
> Lines 9–11: Create subplot 3, the first plot on the second row.
>
> Lines 12–14: Create subplot 4, the second plot on the second row.
>
> Lines 15–17: Create subplot 5, the first plot on the bottom row.
>
> Lines 18–20: Create subplot 6, the second plot on the bottom row.

Style Points

All of these capabilities are also available to the script that creates the plots, and you are very likely to want to generate a plot more than once. Therefore, it is unwise to put a significant amount of manual effort into adjusting a plot. It is better to experiment with the manual adjustments and then find out how to make the same adjustments in the script that creates the plots. This also leaves you a permanent record of how the plot was generated.

11.1.4 Manually Editing Plots

When a figure has been created, you are free to manipulate many of its characteristics by using its menu items and tool bars. They provide the ability to resize the plot, change the view characteristics, and annotate it with legends, axis labels, lines, and text callouts.

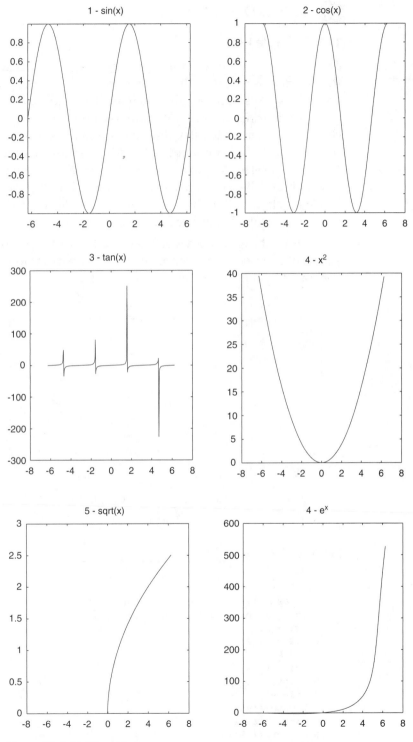

Figure 11.1 *Plotting effects*

11.2 2-D Plotting

11.2.1 Simple Plots

The basic function to use for 2-D plots is `plot(...)`. The usual way to use this function is to give it three parameters, `plot(x, y, str)`, where x and y are vectors of the same length containing the x and y coordinates, respectively, and `str` is a string containing one or more optional line color and style control characters. A complete list of these control characters is included in Appendix A. If the vector x is omitted, MATLAB assumes that the x coordinates are 1:N, where N is the length of the y vector. If the `str` is omitted, the default line is solid blue. The function also permits multiple (x, y, str) data sets in a single function call. In this case, if the line style is not specified, the default line colors rotate through the active color map.

Since we have already seen basic 2-D plotting at work, it should be sufficient to observe and comment on the simple example seen in Figure 11.2, generated by the code shown in Listing 11.2.

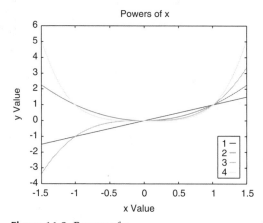

Figure 11.2 *Powers of x*

Listing 11.2 Simple 2-D plots

```
 1. clear
 2. clc
 3. close all
 4. x = linspace(-1.5, 1.5, 30);
 5. y1 = x;
 6. y2 = x.^2;
 7. y3 = x.^3;
 8. y4 = x.^4;
 9. plot(x,y1,x,y2,x,y3,x,y4)
10. xlabel('x')
11. ylabel('value')
12. title('powers of x')
13. legend({'1', '2', '3', '4'}, ...
14. 'Location','SouthEast')
```

In Listing 11.2:

> Line 3: Clears all previous plot results.
>
> Lines 4–8: Create four curves to plot.
>
> Line 9: Plots all four curves in one call. You might be wondering why we use this ponderous form of the plot function, where all the curves are generated with one call. It would indeed have been much simpler to iterate across the powers of x, and overlay the plots one at a time, using `hold on` to allow multiple plots to be overlaid. However, with individual plot calls, the colors of each line must then be set manually. Plotting in this form automatically cycles the colors and generates the data for the legend.
>
> Lines 10–13: Add enhancements to the plot as noted above.
>
> Line 14: One of many possible parameters to the `legend(...)` function—this one forces its location to the lower-right corner of the figure, out of the way of the data.

11.2.2 Plot Options

Figure 11.3 illustrates some of the options available to enhance 2-D plots. This figure was generated using the code shown in Listing 11.3. Study the code and the comments that follow.

Listing 11.3 Demonstrating plot options

```
1.  clear
2.  clc
3.  close all

4.  x = linspace(0, 2*pi);
5.  subplot(2, 3, 1)
6.  plot(x, sin(x))
7.  axis([0 2*pi -0.5 0.5])
8.  title('Changing Data Range on an Axis')

9.  subplot(2, 3, 2)
10. plot(x, sin(x))
11. hold on
12. plot(x, cos(x))
13. axis tight
14. title('Multiple Plots with hold on')

15. subplot(2, 3, 3)
16. plot(x, sin(x), '-')
17. hold on
18. plot(x, cos(x), 'r:')
19. axis tight
20. title('Multiple Plots with hold on')
```

continued on next page

```
21. subplot(2, 3, 4)
22. N = 16;
23. xr = linspace(0, 1, N);
24. yr = xr + rand(1,N) - 0.5;
25. plot(xr, yr, 'r+')
26. title('Symbols for Real Data')

27. subplot(2, 3, 5)
28. x = 0:0.01:20;
29. y1 = 20*exp(-0.05*x).*sin(x);
30. y2 = 0.8*exp(-0.5*x).*sin(3*x);
31. plotyy(x,y1,x,y2, 'plot');
32. xlabel('Zero to 20 \musec.')
33. title('plotting on the Second Axis')

34. subplot(2, 3, 6)
35. pow = linspace(0, 1);
36. w = 10.^pow;
37. fr = complex(0, w);
38. h = (fr.^2 + 0.1*fr + 7.5) ...
        ./ (fr.^4 + 0.12*fr.^3 + 9*fr.^2);
39. loglog(w, abs(h))
40. title('log - log plots')
```

In Listing 11.3:

Lines 4–8: The first plot using `axis(...)` to override the default axis limits.

Lines 9–14: Plot multiple curves on one figure using `hold on` and `axis tight` to minimize the white space.

Lines 15–20: Multiple plots distinguished by line style, using the third parameter on `plot(...)` to control the color and line style: `'--'` specifies a dashed line in the default color, blue; `'r:'` specifies a dotted line in red.

Lines 21–26: Simulated real data plotted with symbols but no line: `'r+'` specifies red plus signs for the symbols. Adding a line specification such as `'r+-'` or `'r+--'` would draw both the symbols at each data point and the lines, solid and dashed, respectively.

Lines 27–33: Plot on the same figure with two sets of data with widely differing data ranges. Depending on the exact version of MATLAB, the axis control and label functions are complex and may not work well. See the MATLAB help documentation for `plotyy(...)` for details.

Lines 34–40: To plot data with a wide range of values, you can use logarithmic scales on either axis or, as in this case, both. For logarithmic axes only in x or y, use `semilogx(...)` or `semilogy(...)`.

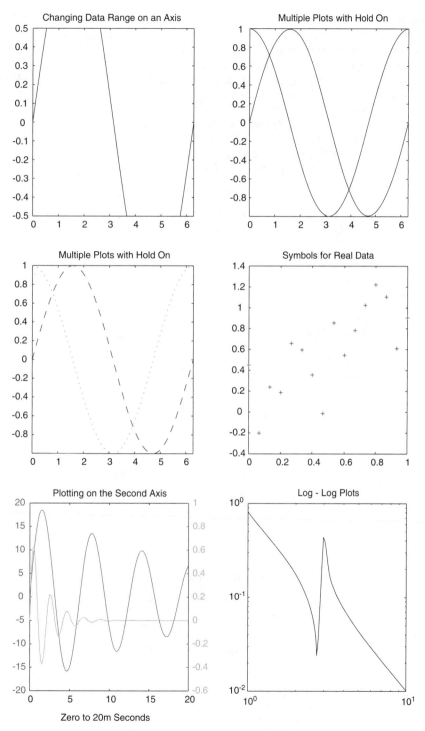

Figure 11.3 *Examples of plotting styles*

11.2.3 Parametric Plots

MATLAB plotting is not restricted to the situation where one axis is an independent variable and one is dependent. Parametric plots allow the variables on each axis to be dependent on a separate, independent variable. That independent variable will define a path on the plotting surface. Consider the plot shown in Figure 11.4, which presents a simple exercise in transforming a specific circle into an airfoil. It was generated using the code shown in Listing 11.4.

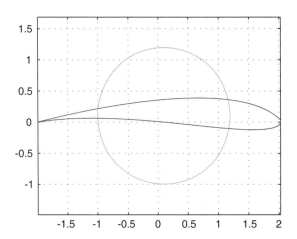

Figure 11.4 *Parametric 2-D plot*

Listing 11.4 Parametric plots

```
1. th = linspace(0, 2*pi, 40);
2. r = 1.1;  g = .1;
3. cx = sqrt(r^2-g^2) - 1;   cy = g;
4. x = r*cos(th) + cx;
5. y = r*sin(th) + cy;
6. plot( x, y, 'r' )
7. axis equal
8. grid on
9. hold on
10. z = complex(x, y);
11. w = z + 1./z;
12. plot( real(w), imag(w), 'k' );
```

In Listing 11.4:

> Line 1: The independent variable in this case is the angle `th` varying from 0 to 2π.

> Line 2: The particular transformation we use here requires a circle with a radius, `r`, slightly greater than 1 offset by a small distance, `g`, from the x-axis, passing through the point $(-1, 0)$.

> Line 3: We compute the center of the circle passing through the point $(-1, 0)$.

> Lines 4–5: Show a standard polar-to-Cartesian coordinate transformation computing the coordinates of the circle.

> Line 6: Plots the two dependent variables `x` and `y` with a red line.

> Line 7: Equalizes the axes and forces the circle to be drawn correctly.

> Line 8: Displays the grid and simplifies the assessment that the circle passes through the important point $(-1, 0)$.

> Line 9: Here we want to add a second plot to the figure.

> Lines 10–11: The Joukowski transformation is easiest when expressed in complex terms: if `z` is the path around the required circle, `w = z + 1/z` traces a very credible looking airfoil shape.

> Line 12: Adds the plot of `w`, and reverts from the complex plane to plot the real and imaginary parts colored in black.

11.2.4 Other 2-D Plot Capabilities

MATLAB can also create two dimensional pie charts, histograms, and bar graphs with the following functions:

- `bar(x, y)` produces a bar graph with the values in `y` positioned at the horizontal locations in `x`. The options available can be studied with `>> help bar`.

- `barh(x, y)` produces a bar graph with the values in `y` positioned at the horizontal locations in `x`. The options available can be studied with `>> help barh`.

- `fill(x,y,n)` produces a filled polygon defined by the coordinates in `x` and `y`. The fill color is specified by indexing `n` into the color map. The options available can be studied with `>> help fill`.

- `hist(y, x)` produces a histogram plot with the values in `y` counted into bins defined by `x`. The options available can be studied with `>> help hist`.

- `loglog(x, y)` plots `x` versus `y` on a log-log scale. For more options, see `>> help loglog`.

- `pie(y)` makes a pie chart of the values in `y`. For more options, see `>> help pie`.

- `polar(th, y)` makes polar plot of the angle `th` (radians) with the radius r specified for each angle. For more options, see >> `help polar`.
- `semilogx(x, y)` plots x versus y with the x scale logarithmic. For more options, see >> `help semilogx`.
- `semilogy(x, y)` plots x versus y with the y scale logarithmic. For more options, see >> `help semilogy`.

11.3 3-D Plotting

Before attacking the details of plotting in three dimensions, it should be noted that even two-dimensional plots in MATLAB are actually 3-D plots. Consider the picture shown in Figure 11.5, which was generated originally as a 2-D plot of `sin(x)` versus x. By selecting the Rotate 3D icon on the tool bar and moving the mouse on your figure, it becomes apparent that what appeared to be a 2-D plot in the x-y plane is really a 3-D plot in the x-y-z plane "suspended in space" at z = 0.

11.3.1 Linear 3-D Plots

The simplest method of three-dimensional (3-D) plotting is to extend our 2-D plots by adding a set of z values. In the same style as `plot(...)`, `plot3(x, y, z, str)` consumes three vectors of equal size and connects the points defined by those vectors in 3-D space. The optional `str` specifies the color and/or line style. If the `str` is omitted, the default line is solid blue. The function also permits multiple `(x, y, z, str)` data sets in a single function call. In this case, if the line style is not specified, the default line colors rotate through the active color map.

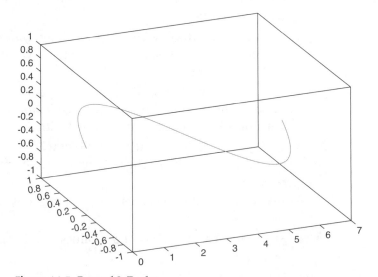

Figure 11.5 *Rotated 2-D plot*

Figure 11.6 shows three curves plotted in three dimensions, using the script shown in Listing 11.5. Each plot is in the z-x plane: the red curve at y = 0; the blue curve at y = 0.5; and the green curve at y = 1.

In Listing 11.5:

> Line 1: Each plot has the same set of x values.
>
> Lines 2–3: The y values for the first plot are all 0.
>
> Lines 4–5: The second and third plots are sin(x) at different frequencies.
>
> Lines 6–7: The y values of the second and third plots are all 0.5 and 1, respectively.

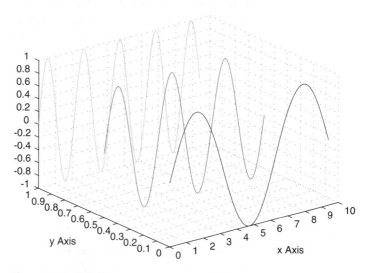

Figure 11.6 *3-D lines*

Listing 11.5 Simple 3-D line plots

```
 1. x=0:0.1:3.*pi;
 2. y1=zeros(size(x));
 3. z1=sin(x);
 4. z2=sin(2.*x);
 5. z3=sin(3.*x);
 6. y3=ones(size(x));
 7. y2=y3./2;
 8. plot3(x,y1,z1, 'r',x,y2,z2, 'b',x,y3,z3, 'g')
 9. grid on
10. xlabel('x-axis')
11. ylabel('y-axis')
12. zlabel('z-axis')
```

11.3.2 Linear Parametric 3-D Plots

We can generalize the concept of parametric plots to 3-D, as shown in Figure 11.7, in which the x, y, and z values are mappings of some linear parameter. As with 2-D parametric plots, 3-D parametric plots allow the variables on each axis to be dependent on a separate, independent variable that defines a path in the plotting space.

On the left side, we draw a spiral as an example of a 3-D plot where two of the dimensions, x and y, are dependent on the third, independent parameter. The independent parameter in this example is the rotation angle, θ, varying from 0 to 10π (five complete revolutions). The x and y values are mapped as $\sin(\theta)$ and $\cos(\theta)$—the classic means of describing a circle. The spiral effect is accomplished by plotting θ on the z-axis.

The right half of Figure 11.7 illustrates a fully parametric plot, where the values of all three coordinates are mappings of an independent parameter, t. This particular example is a plot of the 3-D motion of a particle receiving random impulses in all three axes. Note the use of text anchored in x-y-z space to label points on the graph. The figure is drawn using Listing 11.6.

In Listing 11.6

> Lines 2–5: Draw the spiral plot with a simple `plot3(...)` call.
>
> Lines 8–10: Define random velocity increments in x, y, and z.

Listing 11.6 Linear parametric 3-D plots

```
1.  subplot(1, 2, 1)
2.  theta = 0:0.1:10.*pi;
3.  plot3(sin(theta),cos(theta),theta)
4.  title('parametric curve based on angle');
5.  grid on

6.  subplot(1, 2, 2)
7.  N = 20;
8.  dvx = rand(1, N) - 0.5    % random v changes
9.  dvy = rand(1, N) - 0.5
10. dvz = rand(1, N) - 0.5
11. vx = cumsum(dvx);         % integrate to get v
12. vy = cumsum(dvy);
13. vz = cumsum(dvz);
14. x = cumsum(vx);           % integrate to get pos
15. y = cumsum(vy);
16. z = cumsum(vz);
17. plot3(x,y,z)
18. grid on
19. title('all 3 axes varying with parameter t')
20. text(0,0,0, 'start');
21. text(x(N),y(N),z(N), 'end');
```

Parametric Curve Based on Angle

All Three Axes Varying with Parameter T

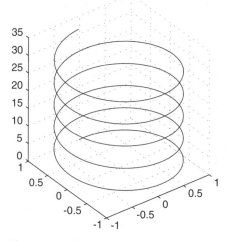

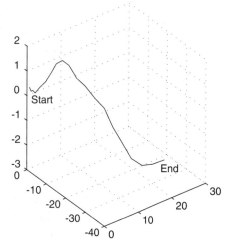

Figure 11.7 *Parametric 3-D plots*

Lines 11–13: Integrate to obtain the velocities, starting at 0. There will be a full discussion of integration in Chapter 15, Section 15.3.

Lines 14–16: Integrate again to compute the position in x, y, z space.

Lines 17–19: Plot and enhance the time history of the particle.

Lines 20 and 21: Add labels to indicate the start and end of the trace.

11.3.3 Other 3-D Plot Capabilities

MATLAB can also create three-dimensional pie charts, histograms, and bar graphs with the following functions:

- `bar3(x, y)` produces a bar graph with the values in `y` positioned at the horizontal locations in `x`. The options available can be studied with `>> help bar3`.

- `barh3(x, y)` produces a bar graph with the values in `y` positioned at the horizontal locations in `x`. The options available can be studied with `>> help barh`.

- `pie3(y)` makes a 3-D pie chart of the values in `y`. For more options, see `>> help pie3`.

 11.4 Surface Plots

In Section 11.3.2 we saw that data can be generated for all three axes based on one linear parameter. However, the most dramatic graphics are produced by a different group of 3-D graphics functions that produce images based on mapping a 2-D surface. The underlying surface is sometimes referred to as *plaid* because of its conceptual similarity to a Scottish tartan pattern. To design such a pattern, one needs only to specify the color sequence of the horizontal and vertical threads. In the same way, we specify a plaid by defining vectors of the row and column data configurations. The simplest surface plots are obtained by defining a z value for each point on an x-y plaid.

11.4.1 Basic Capabilities

Three fundamental functions are used to create 3-D surface plots:

- `meshgrid(x, y)` accepts the $x_{1 \times m}$ and $y_{1 \times n}$ vectors that bound the edges of the plaid, and replicates the rows and columns appropriately to produce $xx_{m \times n}$ and $yy_{m \times n}$, containing the x and y values (respectively) of the complete plaid. This enables us in general to compute mappings for the 3-D coordinates of the figure we want to plot.

- `mesh(xx, yy, zz)` plots the surface as white facets outlined by colored lines. The line coloring uses one of many color maps (listed in Appendix A), where the color is selected in proportion to the `zz` parameter. You can turn the white facets transparent with the command `hidden off`.

- `surf(xx, yy, zz)` plots the surface as colored facets outlined by black lines. The line coloring by default is selected in proportion to the `zz` parameter. You can remove the lines by using one of a number of `shading` commands listed in Appendix A.

11.4.2 Simple Exercises

We will consider some simple situations that illustrate many of the features of surface drawing.

Drawing a Cube In the first example, in order to understand the underlying logic, we will develop the basic concept of drawing surfaces *without* the help of the `meshgrid(...)` function. Figure 11.8 shows the coordinates of a cube of side 2 units centered at the origin. Listing 11.7 shows the code that plots two cubes from scratch—one with no top or bottom, and the other with a top and bottom added. Figure 11.9 shows the results from this script. On the left is the basic core of the solid cube. The `surf(...)` function works by drawing the line defined by the top row of the `xx`, `yy`, and `zz` arrays. Then it locates the line defined by the next row and makes a smooth surface between the two lines.

To add the top and bottom as illustrated on the right side, we add the points P and Q to the array. Although only one point each is required to define P and Q, the array must have the same number of columns in each row.

Therefore, P and Q must be replicated five times to keep the arrays rectangular. Physically, this has the following effect:

- Beginning at point P, drawing expanding squares until they reach ABCD
- "Sliding down" the sides of the cube to EFGH
- Shrinking that square down to the point Q

In Listing 11.7:

Lines 1–6: Establish the plaid defining the A-B-C-D plane (the first rows of each array) and the E-F-G-H plane (the second rows). Notice that the first corner is repeated on each row to close the figure shape.

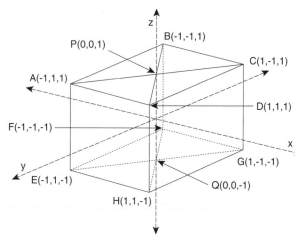

Figure 11.8 *A simple cube*

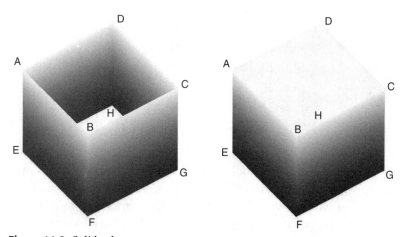

Figure 11.9 *Solid cubes*

Listing 11.7 Simple solid cube

```
 1. xx = [-1 -1  1  1 -1     % A-B-C-D-A
 2.        -1 -1  1  1 -1]    % D-E-F-G-D
 3. yy = [ 1 -1 -1  1  1      % A-B-C-D-A
 4.         1 -1 -1  1  1]    % D-E-F-G-D
 5. zz = [ 1  1  1  1  1      % A-B-C-D-A
 6.        -1 -1 -1 -1 -1]    % D-E-F-G-D
 7. subplot(1, 2, 1)
 8. surf(xx, yy, zz)
 9. axis equal
10. shading interp
11. view(-36, 44)
12. axis off

13. xx = [ 0  0  0  0  0      % P-P-P-P-P
14.        -1 -1  1  1 -1     % A-B-C-D-A
15.        -1 -1  1  1 -1     % D-E-F-G-D
16.         0  0  0  0  0]    % Q-Q-Q-Q-Q
17. yy = [ 0  0  0  0  0      % P-P-P-P-P
18.         1 -1 -1  1  1     % A-B-C-D-A
19.         1 -1 -1  1  1     % D-E-F-G-D
20.         0  0  0  0  0]    % Q-Q-Q-Q-Q
21. zz = [ 1  1  1  1  1      % P-P-P-P-P
22.         1  1  1  1  1     % A-B-C-D-A
23.        -1 -1 -1 -1 -1     % D-E-F-G-D
24.        -1 -1 -1 -1 -1]    % Q-Q-Q-Q-Q
25. subplot(1, 2, 2)
26. surf(xx, yy, zz)
27. axis equal
28. shading interp
29. view(-36, 44)
30. axis off
```

Line 7: Selects the first plot.

Lines 8–12: Plots the cube sides.

Line 13: The x value of P.

Line 16: The x value of Q.

Line 17: The y value of P.

Line 20: The y value of Q.

Line 21: The z value of P.

Line 24: The z value of Q.

Line 25: Selects the second plot.

Lines 26–30: Plot the cube top, sides, and bottom.

A Simple Parabolic Dish We will continue with a simple example illustrating the use of meshgrid(...) to define the plaid. Consider how we might plot the data shown in Figure 11.10. Before we look at the code, consider what the picture represents. Clearly, the independent variables are x and y, each covering the

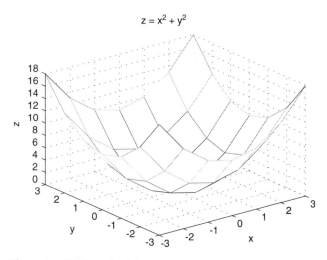

Figure 11.10 *A mesh plot*

range from –3 to 3, each having seven discrete values. As the label indicates, the z values are calculated as the sum of x^2 and y^2. There are not, however, 14 z values as the range of x and y values might suggest, but 49! In order to plot the 3-D shape of our parabolic bowl, we must have a z value for every point on the x-y surface. Each of these points has a value of x corresponding to the reading on the x-axis, and a value of y from the y-axis.

Therefore, the process of creating this plot has three parts:

1. Develop the underlying plaid specifying the x-y location of every point on the x-y plane.
2. Calculate the z values from the plaid
3. Call some function that will accept the plaid and these z values to produce the required plot

The code to accomplish this is shown in Listing 11.8.

In Listing 11.8:

Line 1: The x and y vectors define the edges of the plaid.

Listing 11.8 Simple surface plot

```
1. x=-3:3; y = x ;
2. [xx,yy]=meshgrid(x,y);
3. zz=xx.^2 + yy.^2;
4. mesh(xx,yy,zz)
5. axis tight
6. title('z = x^2 + y^2')
7. xlabel('x'),ylabel('y'),zlabel('z')
```

Line 2: Generates the plaid.

Line 3: In this particular example, we map only the z coordinate, leaving the plaid (xx and yy) as the x and y coordinates of the figure.

Line 4: `mesh(...)` is one of many functions that represent 3-D mappings of a plaid in different ways. Notice in the figure that the faces between line segments are solid white, and the line colors change with the z coordinate.

Try Exercise 11.1 and make your observations.

 Exercise 11.1 Output from `meshgrid(...)`

Do It Yourself

Run the script shown in Listing 11.8 without the semicolon on Line 2, and observe the following:

xx =

-3	-2	-1	0	1	2	3
-3	-2	-1	0	1	2	3
-3	-2	-1	0	1	2	3
-3	-2	-1	0	1	2	3
-3	-2	-1	0	1	2	3
-3	-2	-1	0	1	2	3
-3	-2	-1	0	1	2	3

yy =

-3	-3	-3	-3	-3	-3	-3
-2	-2	-2	-2	-2	-2	-2
-1	-1	-1	-1	-1	-1	-1
0	0	0	0	0	0	0
1	1	1	1	1	1	1
2	2	2	2	2	2	2
3	3	3	3	3	3	3

Examine the values of xx and yy. Notice that in general, if x is length m and y is length n, the xx values consist of the x vector in rows replicated n times, and the yy values consist of the y vector as a column replicated m times. Together, they provide the underlying x and y values for the "floor" of the bowl plot from which the z values are computed to draw the picture.

Manipulating Plots Exercise 11.2 provides an opportunity for you to work with plotting.

 Exercise 11.2 Plotting

Do It Yourself

To begin to discover the range of rendering capabilities available, perform the following simple exercise, based on the code shown in Listing 11.8:

1. Insert the line `hidden off` after `mesh(xx, yy, zz)`.

continued on next page

2. Change `mesh(xx, yy, zz)` to `surf(xx, yy, zz)`. Notice that the panels are now colored and the lines are black. This form is also insensitive to the `hidden` parameter.

3. Replace `hidden off` with `shading flat`, and notice that the lines have disappeared.

4. Replace `shading flat` with `shading interp`, and notice that the surface is now smoothly contoured.

5. Insert the line `colormap 'summer'` after `mesh(xx, yy, zz)`. There are a number of built-in color maps to handle the shading. Look up `help colormap` for details.

6. Do not forget to rotate your images and examine them from different points of view using the 3D rotate tool bar icon.

For the next few exercises, we will replace our do-it-yourself data with one of MATLAB's many built-in data sets. Figure 11.11 shows a picture of the peaks data set created by the script shown in Listing 11.9.

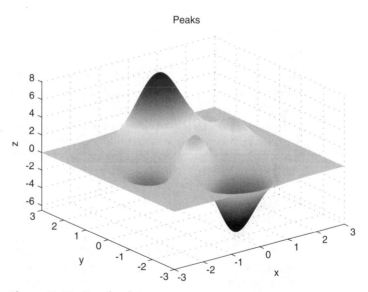

Figure 11.11 *A peaks plot*

Listing 11.9 Basic `peaks(...)` plot

```
1. [xx,yy,zz]=peaks(30);
2. surf(xx,yy,zz)
3. colormap 'default'
4. shading interp
5. axis tight
6. title('peaks')
7. xlabel('x'),ylabel('y'),zlabel('z')
```

In Listing 11.9:

> Line 1: The function `peaks(n)` returns the complete `xx`, `yy`, `zz` data sets for drawing this odd-shaped function with `n` facets along each axis. Note that `meshgrid` is done internally in the `peaks(...)` function.
>
> Line 3: The color map can be restored if necessary by specifying `'default'`.

Exercise 11.3 provides an opportunity to work with `peaks(...)`.

11.4.3 3-D Parametric Surfaces

Thus far, we have drawn beautiful pictures of typical 3-D plots in a Cartesian axis system where the x-y plaid was passed directly to the plotting function. The only coordinate actually mapped was the z-axis. We now return to the concept briefly introduced in Section 11.3.2 when discussing Figure 11.9. In that case, all three coordinate values were mappings of one parameter, `t`.

Exercise 11.3 `peaks(...)`

Do It Yourself

Continue with the next exercise using Listing 11.9 as your code baseline.

1. Change the `surf(xx, yy, zz)` call to `surfc(xx, yy, zz)`. Notice the contour lines plotted on the x-y plane base.

2. Add the line `view(-45, 60)`, which changes the viewing angle. This can program a different angle rather than having to manually rotate the image after it is drawn. If you rotate the image manually, the azimuth and elevation numbers in the lower-left corner are the values you need to enter in the `view(...)` function to replicate that view.

3. Add a color bar by inserting the command `colorbar`—see the help menu for code that labels the color bar.

4. Change the `surfc(xx, yy, zz)` call to `surf(xx, yy, zz, yy)`. Here, we override the default color direction z with the y direction by supplying a fourth parameter to the `surfc(...)` function, specifying the color values explicitly rather than implicitly.

5. Change `surf(xx, yy, zz, yy)` to `surf(xx, yy, zz, del2(zz),)`. The `del2(...)` function computes the second derivative, or curvature, of the plot, so now the coloring highlights the areas of maximum curvature.

6. For an eye-catching effect, change the parameter to `peaks` to `120`, and add the line `lightangle(60, 45)` at the bottom of the script. This illuminates the surface with a light at the specified azimuth and elevation angle (degrees). Figure 11.12 shows the results.

7. Try this effect without increasing the peaks parameter. You will see that the lighting effect highlights the facets on the figure due to the courser resolution of the raw data.

Peaks

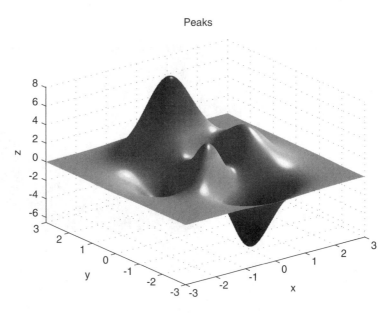

Figure 11.12 *Curvature color and lighting*

Consider first the construction of a cylinder as illustrated in Figure 11.13. One could consider this figure as a sheet of paper rolled up in a circular shape. We could visualize that piece of paper as a plaid of values, not of x-y in this case, but perhaps x − θ. The range of x would be from 0 to the length of the cylinder, and the range of θ would be 0 to 360°.

To plot this, one would then merely need to create a plaid in x and θ, and then decide on the mapping from θ to the y and z values of the cylinder. The resulting picture is shown in Figure 11.14, and the code is shown in Listing 11.10.

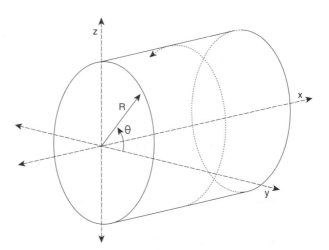

Figure 11.13 *Creating a cylinder image*

Figure 11.14 *A cylinder plot*

In Listing 11.10:

> Line 1: Constants to define the smoothness of the cylinder.
>
> Lines 2–4: Define a plaid in x and θ. Note that only two points are needed in the x direction because that contour is straight.
>
> Lines 5 and 6: The circular cross-section is achieved by using the parametric definition of a circle of a given radius.
>
> Line 9: Changes the color to a pleasant metallic scale.
>
> Line 10: Squares up and removes the axes.
>
> Line 11: Illuminates the figure.
>
> Line 12: Sets the transparency of the surface so that a portion of the hidden details can show through.

Listing 11.10 Constructing a cylinder

```
1. facets = 120;  len = 2;  radius = 1;
2. thr = linspace(0, 2*pi, facets);
3. xr = [0 len];
4. [x, th] = meshgrid( xr, thr );
5. y = radius * cos(th);
6. z = radius * sin(th);
7. surf(x, y, z);
8. shading interp
9. colormap bone
10. axis equal,axis tight,axis off
11. lightangle(60, 45)
12. alpha(0.8)
13. view(-20, 35)
```

Figure 11.15 *A copper sphere*

Now, we construct a sphere as shown in Figure 11.15, starting with the cylinder. However, instead of using a constant radius in the x direction, we will calculate the radius in that direction by rotating a second angle, φ, from 0 to 180°. Think of this as mapping or "wrapping" a plaid with two angles as the independent variables around the sphere. The coordinate in the x direction would be r cos, and the radii of the y-z circles would be r sinφ. The code for drawing this sphere is shown in Listing 11.11.

In Listing 11.11:

> Line 1: The `radius` set here is the sphere radius.
>
> Lines 2 and 3: Set the ranges of θ and φ.
>
> Line 4: Builds the plaid in θ and φ.
>
> Line 5: As φ rotates, the value of x varies as its cosine.
>
> Lines 6 and 7: The radius of rotation about the x-axis varies as the sine of φ.

Listing 11.11 Constructing a sphere

```
 1. facets = 120; radius = 1;
 2. thr = linspace(0, 2*pi, facets); % range of theta
 3. phir = linspace(0, pi, facets); % range of phi
 4. [th, phi] = meshgrid( thr, phir );
 5. x = radius * cos(phi);
 6. y = radius * sin(phi) .* cos(th);
 7. z = radius * sin(phi) .* sin(th);
 8. surf(x, y, z);
 9. shading interp
10. colormap copper
11. axis equal, axis tight, axis off
12. lightangle(60, 45)
```

11.4.4 Bodies of Rotation

The cylinder and sphere drawn in the above section are special cases of a more general form of solid body. Bodies of rotation are created by rotating a linear curve about a specified axis, that is, by rotating a general function z = f(x) defined over a range of x values about the x or z axes. Note: this is perfectly general because rotating such a function about the y-axis would result merely in "sliding" the function across a flat surface in the x-z plane. We use z rather than y for the dependent variable here because in MATLAB 3-D plots, the z-axis is vertical.

Rotating Continuous Functions   First we consider rotating a continuous function z = f(x) about the x and z axes.

- To rotate z = f(x) about the x-axis, we should rewrite this equation as r = f(x). Figure 11.16 shows the logic of this rotation. The independent variable is x, and the values of y and z are computed as the usual polar-to-Cartesian conversion:

   ```
   y = r cos(θ)
   z = r sin(θ)
   ```

   Notice that these are the two axes about which we are not rotating.

- To rotate z = f(x) about the z-axis, we should rewrite this equation as z = f(r). Figure 11.17 shows the logic of this rotation. The independent variable is now r, and the values of x and y are computed as the usual polar-to-Cartesian conversion:

   ```
   x = r cos(()
   y = r sin(()
   ```

   Notice again that these are the two axes about which we are not rotating. Notice also a simple rule of thumb: if you rewrite z = f(x)

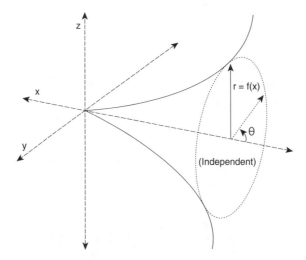

Figure 11.16 *Rotating* f(x) *about the x-axis*

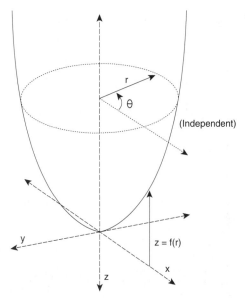

Figure 11.17 *Rotating* `f(x)` *about the z-axis*

correctly for each rotation, the independent variable is always the
parameter to `f(...)`.

Figure 11.18 shows the result of these rotations generated by the code
shown in Listing 11.12.

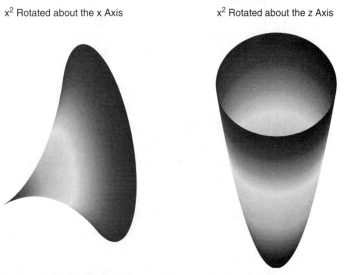

Figure 11.18 *Rotation of x squared*

Listing 11.12 Rotating $z = x^2$ about the x and z axes

```
1. facets = 100;
2. x = linspace(0, 5, facets);
3. th = linspace(0, 2*pi, facets);
4. [xx tth] = meshgrid(x, th);

5. % rotate about the x-axis
6. subplot(1, 2, 1)
7. rr = xx.^2;
8. yy = rr .* cos(tth);
9. zz = rr .* sin(tth);
10. surf(xx, yy, zz, xx);
11. shading interp, axis tight
12. xlabel('x'), ylabel('y'), zlabel('z')
13. title('x^2 rotated about the x-axis')
14. % rotate about the z-axis
15. subplot(1, 2, 2)
16. rr = xx;
17. zz = rr.^2;
18. xx = rr .* cos(tth);
19. yy = rr .* sin(tth);
20. surf(xx, yy, zz);
21. shading interp, axis tight
22. xlabel('x'), ylabel('y'), zlabel('z')
23. title('x^2 rotated about the z-axis')
```

In Listing 11.12:

Lines 1–4: Set up the plaid of x, the independent variable for the function, and θ for the rotations.

Lines 6–13: Compute the rotation about the x-axis. Notice that when rotating about a specific axis, that axis must be treated separately; the other two axes will always have the form of a polar-to-Cartesian transformation. In rotating about the x-axis, since x is the independent variable for our function, we only need to compute the yy and zz values.

Line 10: We use the fourth parameter to surf(...) to set the direction of color variation.

Lines 15–23: Compute the z-axis rotation. Some apparent sleight of hand is necessary here. In this case, the axis containing the independent variable is being rotated about the z-axis. Because the radius of the rotated surface is the original independent variable, xx, we copy xx to the variable radius. Then we promptly redefine xx together with yy as the polar-to-Cartesian transformation to achieve the rotation. In this case, the z value of the surface is f(x), x^2.

Rotating Discrete Functions   There is no need to restrict ourselves to continuous functions as the profiles for bodies of rotation. Figure 11.19 shows

2-D Profile

Rotated Object

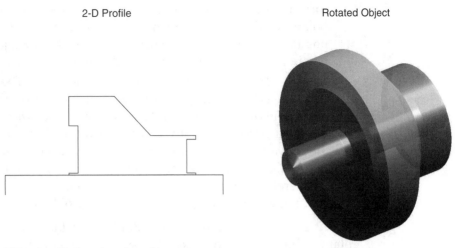

Figure 11.19 *Rotation of machine part*

the 2-D profile of a fictitious machine part and the picture created when that profile is rotated about the x-axis. The figure was generated by the code shown in Listing 11.13.

In Listing 11.13:

> Lines 1–9: Define and plot the initial 2-D profile. Notice that although this is a continuous curve, MATLAB has accomplished

Listing 11.13 Rotating an irregular shape

```
1. x = [0 0 3 3 1.75 1.75 2 2 1.75 1.75 3 4 ...
2.     5.25 5.25 5 5 5.25 5.25 3 3 6 6];
3. y = [0 .5 .5 .502 .502 .55 .55 1.75 1.75 ...
4.        2.5 2.5 1.5 1.5 1.4 1.4 ...
5.        .55 .55 .502 .502 .5 .5 0];
6. subplot(1, 2, 1)
7. plot(x, y)
8. axis ([-1 7 -1 5]), axis off
9. title('2-D profile')

10. facets = 200;
11. subplot(1, 2, 2)
11. [xx tth] = meshgrid( x, linspace(0, 2*pi, facets) );
12. radius = meshgrid( y, 1:facets);
13. yy = radius .* cos(tth);
14. zz = radius .* sin(tth);
15. surf(xx, yy, zz);
16. shading interp
17. axis square, axis tight, axis off
18. colormap bone
19. lightangle(60, 45)
20. alpha(0.8)
21. title('rotated object')
```

something very strange. The coordinates of the third and fourth points are identical to those of the (end-fourth) and (end-third) points. Therefore, MATLAB has ignored the segment joining these two points in the profile picture and in the 3-D rendering.

Lines 10–21: Perform the rotation about the x-axis. The only unusual idea here is how to turn this discrete collection of points into the equivalent of z = f(x). Line 12 shows an elegant way to solve this dilemma. After going through the meshgrid(..) to produce a plaid, the conversion zz = f(xx) would result in zz having the same plaid dimensions as xx. Since we already have all the y values available, we merely need to force it to conform to the dimensions of xx by running meshgrid(...) again, but keeping only the first result.

Rotating about an Arbitrary Axis Bodies of rotation are not confined to rotating about the x, y, or z axes. The simplest approach to rotating z = f(x) about an arbitrary axis is as follows:

- Calculate the matrix that will place your axis of rotation along the x-axis (see Chapter 12)
- Transform x and z with that rotation
- Rotate the results about the x-axis
- Invert the transformation on the resulting surface

11.4.5 Other 3-D Surface Plot Capabilities

MATLAB can also create special-purpose plots with the following functions:

- alpha(x) sets the transparency of the surfaces. 0<=x<=1, where 0 means completely transparent and 1 is opaque. The options available can be studied with >> help alpha.
- contour(z) produces a contour plot of the plaid surface defined by z. The options available can be studied with >> help bar3.
- [x,y,z] = cylinder(n) constructs the meshgrid for a cylinder with n facets in each direction. For more options, see >> help cylinder.
- [x,y,z] = ellipsoid(n) constructs the meshgrid for an ellipsoid with n facets in each direction. For more options, see >> help ellipsoid.
- lightangle(az,el) sets the angle of a light source (angles in degrees). For more options, see >> help lightangle.
- meshc(x,y,z) makes a mesh plot with contours below. For more options, see >> help meshc.
- meshz(x,y,z) makes a mesh plot with vertical line extensions. For more options, see >> help meshz.
- pie3(y) makes a 3-D pie chart of the values in y. For more options, see >> help pie3.

- [x,y,z] = sphere(n) constructs the `meshgrid` for a sphere with n facets in each direction. For more options, see >> `help sphere`.
- surfc(x,y,z) makes a surface plot with contours below. For more options, see >> `help surfc`.
- surfz(x,y,z) makes a surface plot with vertical line extensions. For more options, see >> `help surfz`.
- waterfall(x,y,z) makes a mesh plot with vertical line extensions only in the x direction. For more options, see >> `help surfz`.

11.4.6 Assembling Compound Surfaces

We can assemble more complex solid bodies by constructing simple surfaces and concatenating the data before submitting it to the rendering machine. The solid disk shown in Figure 11.20 was constructed by first drawing the front face as a body of rotation, then the curved surface, and then the back face. If the angles of rotation are maintained in a consistent direction, the three sets of [x y z] arrays can be concatenated and submitted to the rendering software as before. The code for this figure is shown in Listing 11.14.

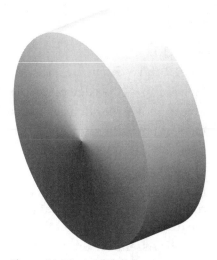

Figure 11.20 *A solid disk*

Listing 11.14 Drawing a solid disk

```
1. %basic parameters
2. facets = 200;
3. len = 2; radius = 3;
4. radial = [0, radius];
5. th = linspace(0, 2*pi, facets);
6. along = [0 len];
```

continued on next page

```
 7. %build the front face
 8. [r1, tth] = meshgrid( radial, th );
 9. x1 = zeros(size(r1));
10. y1 = r1.*cos(tth);
11. z1 = r1.*sin(tth);

12. % build the curved surface
13. [l, tth] = meshgrid(along, th);
14. x2 = l;
15. y2 = radius*cos(tth);
16. z2 = radius*sin(tth);

17. % build the back face
18. x3 = len*ones(size(r1));
19. [r3, tth] = meshgrid(radial(end:-1:1), th);
20. y3 = r3.*cos(tth);
21. z3 = r3.*sin(tth);

22. % assemble and draw the three parts
23. x = [x1 x2 x3]; y = [y1 y2 y3]; z = [z1 z2 z3];
24. surf(x, y, z);
25. shading interp
26. colormap copper
27. axis equal, axis tight, axis off
```

In Listing 11.14:

> Lines 2 and 3: Show the basic parameters of the disk.
>
> Line 4: Shows the edge of the plaids in the radial direction.
>
> Line 5: Shows the edge of the plaids around the cylinder.
>
> Line 6: Shows the edge of the plaids along the cylinder.
>
> Lines 8–11: Build a disk for the front face from the center outward.
>
> Lines 13–16: Build a cylindrical surface along the x-axis.
>
> Lines 18–21: Build the back face from the rim inward to ensure continuity of the flow of data along the cylinder from the center of the front disk finishing at the center of the back disk.
>
> Line 23: Assembles the pieces by concatenating the x, y, and z values.
>
> Lines 24–27: Render the complete object.

Shapes of considerable complexity can be assembled this way. Consider, for example, the Klein bottle, a well-documented example of topological curiosity. The particular example shown in Figure 11.21 was constructed in the manner indicated above by assembling individually mapped articles.

The code is a little too complex to be included here, and is left as an exercise for the reader.

Figure 11.21 *A Klein bottle*

 11.5 Engineering Example—Visualizing Geographic Data

You have been given two files of data: `atlanta.txt`, which presents the streets of Atlanta in graphical form, and `ttimes.txt`, which gives the travel times between Atlanta suburbs and the city center. You have been asked to present these data sets in a manner that will help to visualize and validate the data.

11.5.1 Analyzing the Data

First we proceed to determine the nature of the data by opening the files in a text editor and examining their format and content.

1. *Determine the file format:* The first step is to open the data files in a plain text editor (the MATLAB editor would work fine). The format appears to be consistent with that of a text file delimited by tab characters. Since there are no strings in the file, it should be suitable to be read using MATLAB's built-in `dlmread(...)` function.

2. *Discern the street map file content:* Table 11.1 shows the first few lines of the file `atlanta.txt` simplified by omitting certain irrelevant columns. The numbers in columns 3–6 are pairs, the first of the pair being a large negative number, and the second a smaller positive number. Assuming that each row of this file is a street segment, these could be the x-y coordinates of the ends of a line. A little thought confirms this guess when we realize that the latitude of Atlanta is –84° 42' relative to the Greenwich meridian, and its longitude is 33° 65'—clearly, the values in these columns are 1,000,000 times the latitude and longitude of points within the city, probably each end of street segments. Column 7 contains numbers mostly in the range 1–6,

Table 11.1 Street map data

... ... −84546100.00	33988160.00	−84556050.00	33993620.00	1.00 ...
... ... −84546080.00	33988480.00	−84558400.00	33995480.00	1.00 ...
... ... −84243880.00	33780010.00	−84249980.00	33800840.00	1.00 ...
... ... −84243590.00	33780060.00	−84249740.00	33800840.00	1.00 ...
... ... −84509920.00	33944340.00	−84517200.00	33958190.00	1.00 ...
... ... −84510420.00	33944930.00	−84516490.00	33957280.00	1.00 ...
... ... −84252840.00	33895840.00	−84247360.00	33899290.00	1.00 ...
... ... −84247360.00	33899290.00	−84240250.00	33903630.00	1.00 ...
... ... −84240250.00	33903630.00	−84216090.00	33911010.00	1.00 ...
... ... −84216090.00	33911010.00	−84203990.00	33913990.00	1.00 ...

which could indicate the type of street. We could explore this idea by coloring each line according to that value.

3. *Discern the travel time file content:* Table 11.2 shows the first few lines of the file `ttimes.txt` simplified by omitting certain irrelevant columns. The same latitude/longitude values occur in columns 4 and 5, but they are not repeated, suggesting that the data in this file are in a different form. Examining the first two columns, the numbers in column 2 cycle repeatedly from 1 to 75, with column 1 counting the number of cycles up to 75. Furthermore, the values in column 5 are the same whenever column 1 is the same, and the values in column 4 are the same whenever the value in column 2 matches. This seems to

Table 11.2 Travel time data

1	1	...	−84575725	33554573	14.34
1	2	...	−84569612	33554573	0
1	3	...	−84563499	33554573	0
1	4	...	−84557387	33554573	0
1	5	...	−84551274	33554573	51.66
1	6	...	−84545161	33554573	50.2
1	7	...	−84539049	33554573	49.4
1	8	...	−84532936	33554573	49.65
1	9	...	−84526823	33554573	0
1	10	...	−84520710	33554573	0

be much like the plaid that results from a meshgrid(...) function call. The values in column 6 then become evident—they would be the z values of the plaid, and it seems reasonable to assume that they represent the travel time in minutes.

11.5.2 Displaying the Data

With this much understanding of the data sources, we proceed to solve the problem of presenting the data. The script shown in Listing 11.15 shows the code used to visualize these data files.

In Listing 11.15:

> Line 1: Reads the street map data.
>
> Lines 2–3: Extract the relevant columns and determine the size of the array.

Listing 11.15 Map analysis script

```
% draw the streets
1.  raw = dlmread('atlanta.txt');
2.  streets = raw(:,3:7);
3.  [rows,cols] = size(streets)
4.  colors = 'rgbkcmo';
5.  for in = 1:rows
6.        x = streets(in,[1 3])/1000000;
7.        y = streets(in,[2 4])/1000000;
8.        col = streets(in,5);
9.        col(col < 1) = 7;
10.       col(col > 6) = 7;
11.       plot(x,y,colors(col));
12.       hold on
13. end

% plot the travel times
14. tt = dlmread('ttimes.txt');
15. [rows,cols] = size(tt)
16. for in = 1:rows
17.       r = tt(in, 1); c = tt(in, 2);
18.       xc(r,c) = tt(in, 4)/1000000;
19.       yc(r,c) = tt(in, 5)/1000000;
20.       zc(r,c) = tt(in, 6);
21. end
22. surf(xc, yc, zc)
23. shading interp
24. alpha(.5)
25. grid on
26. axis tight
27. xlabel('Longitude')
28. ylabel('Latitude')
29. zlabel('Travel Time (min)')
30. view(-30, 45)
```

Line 4: Color symbols to use for the lines.

Line 5: Traverses the rows of the file.

Lines 6 and 7: Extract the longitude and latitude in degrees.

Lines 8–10: Extract and limit the line colors.

Lines 11 and 12: Plot the street lines on the same figure.

Line 14: Read the travel times.

Line 15: Sizes the array.

Line 16: Constructs the plaid by traversing the array.

Line 17: Extracts the row and column numbers.

Lines 18–20: Extract the plaid values.

Lines 22–30: Plot and display the results.

Figure 11.22 shows the resulting plot. As a credibility check, the plot can be rotated to look straight down on the map. The travel time surface shows valleys of low travel times that follow the paths of the major expressways through the city.

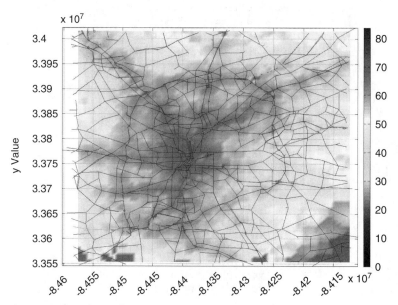

Figure 11.22 *Atlanta travel times*

Chapter Summary

This chapter presented the principles and practice of plotting:

- Basic two-dimensional line plots are accomplished by using `plot(x,y)`, where x is the independent variable and y the dependent variable
- Two-dimensional parametric plots are accomplished by using `plot(x,y)`, where both x and y are dependent on another independent variable
- Three-dimensional line and parametric plots are accomplished by using `plot3(x,y,z)`
- Basic three-dimensional surface plots are accomplished by building a plaid using `[xx yy] = meshgrid(x,y)`, computing the zz layer as a function of xx and yy, then plotting the surface using `mesh(xx, yy, zz)` or `surf(xx, yy, zz)`
- Parametric surface plots, like parametric line plots, are achieved by building the plaid with two independent variables and making xx, yy, and zz functions of those independent variables
- Bodies of rotation are a special case of parametric surface plots where one of the independent variables is an angle with values between 0 and 2π.

 Special Characters, Reserved Words, and Functions—2-D

Special Characters, Reserved Words, and Functions	Description	Discussed in This Section
`axis(...)`	Freezes the current axis scaling for subsequent plots or specifies the axis dimensions	11.1.2
`bar`	Generates a bar graph	11.2.5
`barh`	Generates a horizontal bar graph	11.2.5
`clf`	Clears the current figure	11.1.1
`close all`	Closes all graphics windows	11.1.1
`colormap <spec>`	Specifies a sequence of colors to be used when a cycle of color values is required	11.1.2
`figure`	Opens a new figure window	11.1.1
`fill(x,y,n)`	Fills a polygon defined by x and y with color index n	11.2.5
`grid off`	Turns the grid off	11.1.2
`grid on`	Adds a grid to the current and all subsequent graphs in the current figure	11.1.2

Special Characters, Reserved Words, and Functions	Description	Discussed in This Section
`hist`	Generates a histogram	11.2.5
`hold off`	Instructs MATLAB to erase figure contents before adding new information	11.1.2
`hold on`	Instructs MATLAB not to erase figure contents before adding new information	11.1.2
`loglog`	Generates an x-y plot, with both axes scaled logarithmically	11.2.5
`pie`	Generates a pie chart	11.2.5
`semilogx`	Generates an x-y plot, with the x-axis scaled logarithmically	11.2.5
`semilogy`	Generates an x-y plot, with the y-axis scaled logarithmically	11.2.5
`plot(...)`	Creates an x-y plot	11.1.2
`polar`	Creates a polar plot	11.2.4
`legend(ca)`	Adds a legend to a graph	11.1.2
`shading <spec>`	Shades a surface according to the specification	11.1.2
`subplot(plts, n)`	Divides the graphics window into sections available for plotting	11.1.3
`text(x,y,{z,} str)`	Adds a text string to a graph	11.1.2
`title(str)`	Adds a title to a plot	11.1.2
`view(az,el)`	Sets the angle from which to view a plot; the parameters are `az`, the azimuth, and `el`, the elevation, both angles measured in degrees	11.1.2
`xlabel(str)`	Adds a label to the x-axis	11.1.2
`ylabel(str)`	Adds a label to the y-axis	11.1.2
`zlabel(str)`	Adds a label to the z-axis	11.1.2

 Special Characters, Reserved Words, and Functions—3-D

Special Characters, Reserved Words, and Functions	Description	Discussed in This Section
`alpha(x)`	Sets the transparency of the surfaces; `0<=x<=1`, where 0 means completely transparent and `1` is opaque	11.3.3
`bar3`	Generates a three-dimensional bar graph	11.3.3
`barh3`	Generates a horizontal three-dimensional bar graph	11.3.3

Special Characters, Reserved Words, and Functions	Description	Discussed in This Section
contour	Generates a contour plot	11.4.5
cylinder(n)	Constructs the plaid for a cylinder with n facets	11.4.5
ellipsoid(n)	Constructs the plaid for an ellipsoid with n facets	11.4.5
cylinder(n)	Constructs the plaid for a cylinder with n facets	11.4.5
lightangle(az,el)	Sets the angle of a light source, angles in degrees	11.4.5
mesh(x,y,z)	Generates a mesh plot of a surface	11.4.1
meshc(x,y,z)	Generates a mesh plot of a surface with a contour below it	11.4.5
meshz(x,y,z)	Generates a mesh plot of a surface with vertical line extensions	11.4.5
meshgrid(r, c)	Creates a plaid for 3-D plots	11.4.1
peaks	Creates a sample matrix used to demonstrate graphing functions	11.4.2
pie3	Generates a three-dimensional pie chart	11.3.3
plot3(...)	Generates a three-dimensional line plot	11.3.1
sphere	Example function used to demonstrate graphing	11.4.5
surf(x,y,z)	Generates a surface plot	11.4.1
surfc(x,y,z)	Generates a combination surface and contour plot	11.4.5
waterfall(x,y,z)	Generates a mesh plot of a surface with vertical line extensions in the x direction only	11.4.5

 ## Self Test

Use the following questions to check your understanding of the material in this chapter:

True or False

1. The plot(...) function needs only one parameter to function correctly.

2. Plot enhancement functions may be called before or after the function that plots the data.

3. You must provide plots for all the specified subplot areas.

4. When multiple data sets are used in a single plot(...) or plot3(...) call, all the lines are black

5. `meshgrid(...)` accepts vectors of length m and n that bound the edges of the plaid and produces two arrays sized m × n giving the complete plaid.

6. To construct a parametric surface, both independent parameters must be angles.

7. When rotating a function about the y-axis, the variables along the x and y axes are computed from a classic polar-to-Cartesian conversion.

8. To compute a body of rotation, the curve must be a continuous, differentiable function.

9. Bodies of rotation are confined rotating about the x, y, or z axes.

Fill in the Blanks

1. Each time `figure` is called, a _____ is made available, with _____ figure number.

2. To prepare for plotting, put _____ or _____ at the beginning of your script.

3. Parametric plots allow the variables on each axis to be _____ on a _____, _____ variable.

4. The simplest surface plots are obtained by defining a _____ value for each point on _____.

5. We construct a sphere by wrapping a _____ with two _____ as the independent variables around the sphere.

6. Bodies of rotation are created by rotating a _____ about a _____.

Programming Projects

1. Write the MATLAB commands to plot the equation $z = \cos(x^2 - y^2)$ with the following restrictions:
   - Vary x and y between –2 and 2 with an increment of .1
   - The faces should be colored with no lines visible

   Make sure the plot is suitably labeled and titled.

2. We need to plot a hyperbolic paraboloid. This is special in mathematics due to the existence of a *saddle point* or *minimax* that exists at the origin. This function can be created from the equation:

$$z = \frac{x^2}{4} - \frac{y^2}{4}.$$

   Write a MATLAB script to plot this function with the following restrictions:
   a. Vary x and y between –3 and 3, incremented in steps of .1
   b. Draw the picture as a wire frame with the lines colored to indicate the y value
   c. Put a color bar on the plot identifying the colors to values of y

   Make sure the plot is appropriately labeled and titled.

3. Write and test a function called `sineGraph` that graphs a sine function four times between the interval [start,stop] on the same graph. The values `start` and `stop` will be parameters of the function. The number of points per interval will vary across the plots. More specifically:
   a. The first time you graph the sine function you should have two evenly spaced points, that is, start and stop
   b. The next plot should have four evenly spaced points—start, stop, and two in between
   c. The third has eight evenly spaced points
   d. The fourth has 256 points

   Make sure to put a legend (title), " Multiple graphs on one plot, " and to label the axes. Make sure each line has a different color.

   Test your function with the following intervals:
   $[0,\pi/2],[0,2\pi],[0,4\pi],[0,16\pi]$

4. We want to plot the top half of a sphere, which can be created from the equation $x^2 + y^2 + z^2 = r^2$, where r is the radius of the

hemisphere. Write a MATLAB script to plot this function with the following restrictions:

a. The hemisphere has a radius of three units
b. Vary x and y between –3 and 3, incremented in steps of .1
c. The surface should be smoothly colored in shades of gray with no lines apparent

Make sure the plot is appropriately labeled and titled.

5. Plot the shape generated when you rotate around the x-axis the curve $y = x^2 - 2x + 1$, with x values from 0 to 2 in steps of 0.1.

6. Repeat Programming Project 5, plotting the same curve rotated around the y axis.

7. The equation:

$$r = \sin\left(\frac{11\theta}{10}\right)$$

creates a plot that looks similar to a "Slinky." Write a MATLAB script to plot the Slinky for $0 < \theta < 10\pi$. Make sure the plot is fully labeled and titled.

The x and y axes are defined as follows:

```
x = r * cos(θ)
y = r * sin(θ)
```

8. Write a script that will plot the function $f(x) = sin(x)$ for a user-specified range of values. Specifically, prompt the user for the start point and end point to use for the plot's x-axis, calculate the sine function over the values of x in the interval, and then plot those values. There should be 100 evenly spaced points along the plot's x-axis, including the start and end points.

You should also prompt the user for the title of this plot. Use this answer for the plot title and the y-axis label. Label the x-axis 'x values'.

Hint

Put 's' as the second parameter to input(...) in order to avoid entering the quote marks.

You may assume that the value of the end point will always be greater than the value of the start point.

9. Write a script to plot the toroid shape that is the body of rotation produced by rotating the curve $(x - R)^2 + y^2 = r^2$ about the y axis. Use suitable values for r and R, where r should be less than R.

Hint

It is probably a good idea to use the polar form of the circle:

$x - R = r \cos(\theta)$
$y = r \sin(\theta)$

10. You just realized that February 14th has passed and you haven't bought anything for your Valentine. Since you are in the CS1371 class and your date is a CS major, sending the lucky person a MATLAB coded heart would seem like a cool and sincere thing to do. Make sure you follow each and every instruction carefully, or your heart will turn out broken. Trust us.

    a. Create a new script called *valentine.m*

    b. Create two variables, x and y, with range (0 to 2pi, interval 0.05) and (0 to 1, interval 0.05), respectively.

    c. Use the `meshgrid` function to generate the matrices xx and yy from x and y

    d. Define: c = [0.1 + 0.9 * (pi (abs(xx - pi))/pi] .* yy

    e. Define: aa = c .* cos(xx)

    f. Define: bb = c.* sin(xx)

    g. Define: zz = (–2)*aa.^3 + (3/2)*c.^2 + 0.5

    h. Plot zz against aa and bb.

Voilá! You are now all set to present your heart to your Valentine.

11. In this problem you will be creating two 3-D plots for comparison using `subplot(...)` in one row and two columns. Label all axes accordingly (X-axis, Y-axis, and so forth). Give a title to your plot corresponding to the problem statement. Create the following plots in a script:

- In the first subplot, plot the function f(x,y)=x^2*cos(y) in the range x = –5:5 and y = –5:5 using `mesh`. Title this plot *Using Mesh*.

- In the second subplot, plot the same function as above, in the same range, but using `surf`. Title this plot *Using Surf*.

12. Georgia Tech wants to tear down the Campanile and build a new one that is ridiculously tall. However, before construction begins they need you to model it in MATLAB. Using the equation z = 1/(x^2 + y^2) as the model, write a script that will plot the Campanile.

- Plot the function with both x and y between –0.75 and 0.75 in steps of 0.05

- Set your axes such that all of the x,y domain is seen and z runs from 0 to 300

- You must account for dividing by 0 (hint: look up `eps` in the MATLAB help documentation)

- Make sure you use `surf` to plot your surface
- Title the plot *Campanile* and label the axes

13. Write a script to use the Joukowski airfoil section to draw a 3-D picture of a complete wing. The wing should have a sweep angle of 30°, and the chord (length of the wing section) at the tip should be half of the root chord.

Matrices

Chapter Objectives

This chapter shows matrices as logical extensions of arrays. You will learn about two specialized operations performed with matrices:

- Multiplication for coordinate rotation

- Division for solving simultaneous equations

Although the matrix operations that are the subject of this chapter can be performed on pairs of vectors or arrays that meet certain criteria, when using these operations, we tend to refer to the data objects as matrices. In most mathematical discussions, the words matrix and array can be used interchangeably, and rightly so, because they store data in exactly the same form. Moreover, almost all of the operations we can perform on an array can also be performed on a matrix—logical operations, concatenation, slicing, and most of the arithmetic operations behave identically. The fact that some of the mathematical operations are defined differently gives us a chance to think about an important concept that will increase in importance when we begin to consider object-oriented programming.

12.1 Concept: Behavioral Abstraction

12.2 Matrix Operations
12.2.1 Matrix Multiplication
12.2.2 Matrix Division
12.2.3 Matrix Exponentiation

12.3 MATLAB Implementation
12.3.1 Matrix Multiplication
12.3.2 Matrix Division

12.4 Rotating Coordinates
12.4.1 2-D Rotation
12.4.2 3-D Rotation

12.5 Solving Simultaneous Linear Equations
12.5.1 Intersecting Lines
12.5.2 Curve Fitting

12.6 Engineering Examples
12.6.1 Ceramic Composition
12.6.2 Analyzing an Electrical Circuit

12.1 Concept: Behavioral Abstraction

Recall the following concepts:

- *Abstraction* is the ability to ignore specific details and generalize the description of an entity
- *Data abstraction* is the specific example of abstraction that we first considered whereby we could treat vectors of data (and later other collections like structures and arrays) as single entities rather than enumerating their elements individually
- *Procedural abstraction* are functions that collect multiple operations into a form; once they are developed, we can overlook the specific details and treat them as a "black box," much as we treat MATLAB's built-in functions

Behavioral abstraction combines data and procedural abstraction, encapsulating not only collections of data, but also the operations that are legal to perform on that data. One might argue that this is a new, irrelevant concept best ignored until "we just have to!" But consider the rules we have had to establish for what we can and cannot do with data collections we have seen so far. For example, can I add two arrays together? Yes, but only if they have the same number of rows and columns, or if one of them is a scalar (a 1×1 array). Can I add two character strings? Almost the same answer, except that each string is first converted to a numerical quantity and the result is a vector of numbers and not a string. Can I add two cell arrays? No.

So at least some, and maybe all, MATLAB data collections also "understand" the set of operations that are permitted on the data. This encapsulation of data and operations is the essence of behavioral abstraction. Therefore, we can distinguish arrays from matrices not by the data they collect, but by the operations that are legal to perform on them.

12.2 Matrix Operations

The arithmetic operations that differ between arrays and matrices are multiplication, division, and exponentiation.

12.2.1 Matrix Multiplication

Previously, when we considered multiplying two arrays, we called this scalar multiplication, and it had the following typical array operation characteristics:

- Either the two arrays must be the same size, or one of them must be scalar
- The multiplication was indicated with the .* operator

- The result was an array with the same size as the larger original array
- Each element of the result was the product of the corresponding elements in the original two arrays

This is best illustrated in Figure 12.1. Scalar division and exponentiation have the same constraints. Matrix multiplication, on the other hand, performed using the normal * operator, is an entirely different logical operation, as shown in Figure 12.2. The logical characteristics of matrix multiplication are as follows:

- The two matrices do not have to be the same size. The requirements are either:
  - One of the matrices is a scalar, in which case the matrix operation reduces to a scalar multiply.
  - The number of columns in the first matrix must equal the number of rows in the second. We refer to these as the **inner dimensions**. The result is a new matrix with the column count of the first matrix and the row count of the second.
- If, as illustrated, A is an $m \times n$ matrix and B is an $n \times p$ matrix, the result of A * B is an $m \times p$ matrix.
- The item at (i, j) in the result matrix is the sum of the scalar product of the ith row of A and the jth column of B.

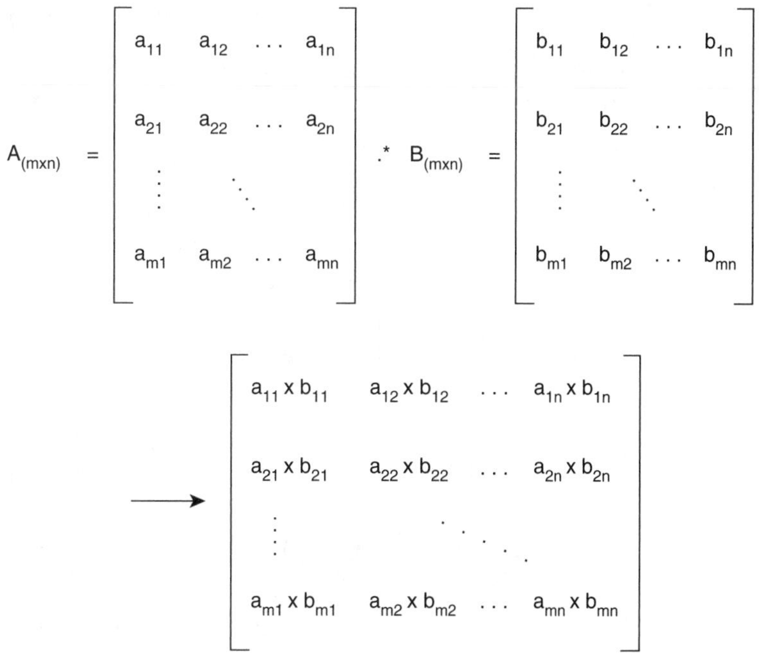

$$A_{(mxn)} = \begin{bmatrix} a_{11} & a_{12} & \cdots & a_{1n} \\ a_{21} & a_{22} & \cdots & a_{2n} \\ \vdots & & \ddots & \vdots \\ a_{m1} & a_{m2} & \cdots & a_{mn} \end{bmatrix} .* B_{(mxn)} = \begin{bmatrix} b_{11} & b_{12} & \cdots & b_{1n} \\ b_{21} & b_{22} & \cdots & b_{2n} \\ \vdots & & \ddots & \vdots \\ b_{m1} & b_{m2} & \cdots & b_{mn} \end{bmatrix}$$

$$\longrightarrow \begin{bmatrix} a_{11} \times b_{11} & a_{12} \times b_{12} & \cdots & a_{1n} \times b_{1n} \\ a_{21} \times b_{21} & a_{22} \times b_{22} & \cdots & a_{2n} \times b_{2n} \\ \vdots & & \ddots & \\ a_{m1} \times b_{m1} & a_{m2} \times b_{m2} & \cdots & a_{mn} \times b_{mn} \end{bmatrix}$$

Figure 12.1 *Matrix dot multiply*

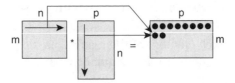

Figure 12.2 *Mechanics of matrix multiplication*

■ Whereas with scalar multiplication A .* B gives the same result as B .* A, this is not the case with matrix multiplication. In fact, if A * B works, B * A will not work unless both matrices are square, and even then the results are different. (Proof of this can be derived immediately from Figure 12.3 by eliminating the third row and column and exchanging a for b. All four terms of the result of A * B are different from B * A.)

■ Whereas with scalar multiplication the original array A can be recovered by dividing the result by B, this is not the case with matrix multiplication unless both matrices are square.

■ The **identity matrix**, sometimes given the symbol I_n, is a square matrix with n rows and n columns that is zero everywhere except on its major diagonal, which contains the value 1. I_n has the special property that when pre-multiplied by any matrix A with n columns, or post-multiplied with any matrix A with n rows, the result is A. We will need this property to derive matrix division below. (The MATLAB function eye(...) generates the identity matrix.)

Figure 12.3 illustrates the mathematics for the case where a 3 × 2 matrix is multiplied by a 2 × 3 matrix, resulting in a 3 × 3 matrix.

$$A_{(mxn)} = \begin{bmatrix} a_{11} & a_{12} \\ a_{21} & a_{22} \\ a_{m1} & a_{m2} \end{bmatrix} * B_{(mxn)} = \begin{bmatrix} b_{11} & b_{12} & b_{13} \\ b_{21} & b_{22} & b_{23} \end{bmatrix}$$

$$\rightarrow \begin{bmatrix} (a_{11} \times b_{11} + a_{12} \times b_{21}) & (a_{11} \times b_{12} + a_{12} \times b_{22}) & (a_{11} \times b_{13} + a_{12} \times b_{23}) \\ (a_{21} \times b_{11} + a_{22} \times b_{21}) & (a_{21} \times b_{12} + a_{22} \times b_{22}) & (a_{21} \times b_{13} + a_{22} \times b_{23}) \\ (a_{31} \times b_{11} + a_{32} \times b_{21}) & (a_{31} \times b_{12} + a_{32} \times b_{22}) & (a_{31} \times b_{13} + a_{32} \times b_{23}) \end{bmatrix}$$

Figure 12.3 *Matrix multiplication*

12.2.2 Matrix Division

Matrix division is the logical process of reversing the effects of a matrix multiplication. The goal is as follows: given $A_{n\times n}$, $B_{n\times p}$ and $C_{n\times p}$, where c = A * B, we wish to define the mathematical equivalent of c/A that will result in B.

Since c = A * B, we are actually searching for some matrix $K_{n\times n}$ by which we can multiply each side of the above equation:

K * C = K * A * B

This multiplication would accomplish the division we desire if K * A were to result in I_n, the identity matrix. If this were the case, pre-multiplying c by K would result in I_n * B, or simply B by the definition of I_n above. The matrix K is referred to as the inverse of A, or A^{-1}. The algebra for computing this inverse is messy but well defined. In fact, Gaussian Elimination to solve linear simultaneous equations accomplishes the same thing. MATLAB has both functions (inv(A)) and operators ("back divide," \) that accomplish this. However, two things should be noted:

- This inverse does not exist for all matrices—if any two rows or columns of a matrix are linearly related, the matrix is singular and does not have an inverse
- Only nonsingular, square matrices have an inverse (just as a set of linear equations is soluble only if there are as many equations as there are unknown variables)

12.2.3 Matrix Exponentiation

For completeness, we mention here that matrix operations include exponentiation. However, this does not suggest that one would encounter $A_{n\times n}{}^{B_{n\times n}}$ in the scope of our applications. Rather, our usage of matrix exponentiation will be confined to A^k where k is any non-zero integer value. The result for positive k is accomplished by multiplying A by itself k times (using matrix multiplication). The result for negative k is accomplished by inverting A^{-k}. (There is, in fact, meaning in matrix exponentials with non-scalar exponents, but this involves advanced concepts with eigen values and eigenvectors. See the MATLAB help files for more detail.)

12.3 MATLAB Implementation

In this section, we see how MATLAB implements matrix multiplication and division. However, since applications that require matrix exponentiation are beyond the scope of this text, we will not look at its implementation in MATLAB.

12.3.1 Matrix Multiplication

Matrix multiplication is accomplished by using the "normal" multiplication symbol, as illustrated in Exercise 12.1.

Exercise 12.1 Matrix multiply

Do It Yourself

In the Command window, enter the following:

```
1. >> A = [2 5 7; 1 3 42]
A =
        2       5       7
        1       3       42
2. >> B = [1 2 3]'
B =
        1
        2
        3
3. >> A * B
ans =
        33
        133
4. >> (1:2) * A
ans =
        4       11      91
5. >> I2 = eye(2)
I2 =
        1       0
        0       1
6. >> I2 * A
ans =
        2       5       7
        1       3       42
7. >> A*I2
??? Error using ==> mtimes
Inner matrix dimensions must agree.
8. >> A*eye(3)
ans =
        2       5       7
        1       3       42
```

In Exercise 12.1 we make the following observations:

- Entry 1 creates a 2 × 3 matrix, A
- Entry 2 creates a 3 × 1 matrix, B, a column vector
- Entry 3 indicates that this multiplication is legal because the columns in A match the rows in B
- Entry 4 shows that, likewise, it is legal to multiply a 1 × 2 vector by a 2 × 3 matrix
- Entry 5 creates an identity matrix
- Entry 6 shows that pre-multiplying A by this is legal because the inner dimensions match
- Entry 7 shows that post-multiplying A by I_2 does not work because the inner dimensions do not match
- Entry 8 uses I_3 to post-multiply legally

12.3.2 Matrix Division

Matrix division is accomplished in a number of ways, all of which are equivalent. Returning to the division problem described in Section 12.2.2, we know that A, B, and C are square matrices and C = A * B. If we are actually given the matrices C and B, we can compute A in one of the following ways:

- A = C * inv(B)—using the MATLAB inv(...) function to compute the inverse of B
- A = B \ C—"back dividing" B into C to produce the same result
- A = C / B—apparently performing the same operation, but giving different answers

According to the MATLAB help system, the third way really computes (C'\B')'.

The order in which the matrix multiply is done affects the value of the result; therefore, care must be taken to ensure that the appropriate inversion or division is used. Both multiplying by the inverse and the normal divide nullify the effect of the array that did the post-multiplication. Back dividing nullifies the effect of the matrix that did the pre-multiplication. See Exercise 12.2.

Exercise 12.2 Matrix divide

Do It Yourself

Create a script containing the following:

```
1. >> A = magic(3)
A =
     8     1     6
     3     5     7
     4     9     2
2. >> B = [1 26 24; 9 22 20; 5 12 16]
B =
     1    26    24
     9    22    20
     5    12    16
3. >> AB = A * B
AB =
    47   302   308
    83   272   284
    95   326   308
4. >> BA = B * A
BA =
   182   347   236
   218   299   248
   140   209   146
5. >> AB * inv(B)
ans =
    8.0000    1.0000    6.0000
    3.0000    5.0000    7.0000
    4.0000    9.0000    2.0000
```

continued on next page

```
6. >> AB / B
ans =
     8.0000    1.0000    6.0000
     3.0000    5.0000    7.0000
     4.0000    9.0000    2.0000
7. >> B \ BA
ans =
     8.0000    1.0000    6.0000
     3.0000    5.0000    7.0000
     4.0000    9.0000    2.0000
8. >> BA/B
ans =
    -4.3000   29.2000  -15.3000
    -9.9667   27.5333   -3.9667
    -5.7333   20.7667   -8.2333
```

In Exercise 12.2 we make the following observations:

- Entries 1 and 2 construct two 3 × 3 matrices, A and B
- Entries 3 and 4 pre-multiply and post-multiply B and A; recall that we expect this to produce different answers
- Entry 5 shows that since we defined inv(B) as that function that produces the result B*inv(B)=I, this should produce a matrix with the same values as A
- Entry 6 reveals that normal division by B should also produce a matrix with the same values as A
- Entry 7 shows that back dividing B into BA should also produce a matrix equal to A
- Entry 8 verifies that dividing BA by B works but does not return the matrix A

12.4 Rotating Coordinates

A common use for matrix multiplication is for rotating coordinates in two or three dimensions. Previously we have seen the ability to rotate a complete picture by changing the viewing angle. We can move and scale items on a plot by adding coordinate offsets or multiplying them by scalar quantities. However, frequently the need arises to rotate the coordinates of a graphical object by some angle. We can use matrix multiplication to rotate individual items in a picture in two or three dimensions.

12.4.1 2-D Rotation

The mathematics implementing rotation in two dimensions is relatively straightforward, as shown in Figure 12.4. If the original point location is (x, y) at angle α to the x axis and you wish to rotate that point by the angle θ about the origin of coordinates, the mathematics are as follows:

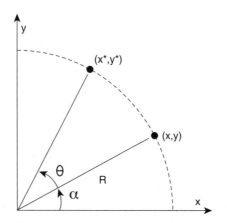

Figure 12.4 *Rotating Cartesian coordinates*

$$x^* = x\cos\theta - y\sin\theta$$

$$y^* = x\sin\theta + y\cos\theta$$

This can be expressed as a matrix multiplication as follows:

$$\begin{bmatrix} x^* \\ y^* \end{bmatrix} = \begin{bmatrix} \cos\theta & -\sin\theta \\ \sin\theta & \cos\theta \end{bmatrix} * \begin{bmatrix} x \\ y \end{bmatrix}$$

To rotate the x-y coordinates of a graphic object in the x-y plane about some point, P, other than the origin, you would do as follows:

1. Translate the object so that P is at the origin by addition
2. Perform the rotation by matrix multiplication
3. Translate the rotated object back to P by subtraction

Rotating a Line Listing 12.1 illustrates a simple script to rotate a line about the origin. It uses the function shown in Listing 12.2 to build the appropriate rotation matrix.

Listing 12.1 Script to rotate a line

```
1. pts =    [3, 10
2.           1, 3];
3. plot(pts(1,:), pts(2,:))
4. axis ([0 15 0 15])
5. hold on
6. for angle = 0.05:0.05:1
7.     A = rotation(angle);
8.     pr = A * pts;
9.     plot(pr(1,:), pr(2,:))
10. end
```

Listing 12.2 Compute a rotation matrix

```
1. function transformation = rotation(angle)
2. % rotate by the angle (radians)
3. transformation = [ cos(angle), -sin(angle)
4.                    sin(angle),  cos(angle) ];
```

In Listing 12.1:

> Lines 1 and 2: Considering the form of the rotation equations, we need to define the points where the x values are in the first row and the y values are in the second row.
>
> Line 3: Plots the line in its original location from (3, 1) to (10, 3).
>
> Lines 4 and 5: Fix the axes at a suitable size.
>
> Line 6: Iterates across a selection of angles (in radians).
>
> Line 7: Uses the function in Listing 12.2 to define the matrix of rotation.
>
> Line 8: Rotates the original line by the current angle.
>
> Line 9: Plots the rotated line.

Figure 12.5 shows the plot resulting from this script.

Twinkling Stars As a second example, consider the problem of simulating twinkling stars. One way to accomplish this is to draw two triangles for each star rotating in opposite directions. The script shown in Listing 12.3 accomplishes this.

In Listing 12.3:

> Line 1: Sets the number of stars and the initial rotation angle.
>
> Lines 2–6: Establish the location, size, and rotation speed of each star.

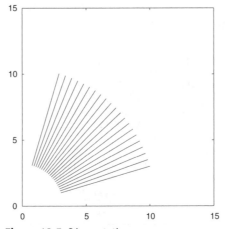

Figure 12.5 *Line rotations*

Listing 12.3 Simulating stars

```
1.  nst = 20; th = 0;
2.  for ndx = 1:nst
3.      pos(ndx,:) = rand(1,2)*10;
4.      scale(ndx) = rand(1,1) * .9 + .1;
5.      rate(ndx) = rand(1,1) * 3 + 1;
6.  end
7.  while true
8.      for str = 1:nst
9.              star(pos(str,:), ...   % location
10.                 scale(str), ...     % scale
11.                 th,   ...           % basic angle
12.                 rate(str))          % angle multiplier
13.     end
14.     colormap autumn
15.     axis equal; axis([-.5 10.5 -.5 10.5])
16.     axis off;   hold off
17.     th = mod(th + .1, 20*pi);
18.     pause(0.1)
19. end
```

Line 7: Continues drawing until interrupted by Ctrl-C.

Lines 8–13: Draw each star at the current rotation (see Listing 12.4 for the star(...) function).

Line 14: Chooses a color map with yellow as the first color.

Line 15 and 16: Show the normal display environment setup.

Line 17: Updates the angle of rotation.

Line 18: Waits for the figure to be displayed.

Listing 12.4 Drawing one star

```
1.  function star(pt, sc, v, th)
%  draw a star at pt(1), pt(2),
%          scaled with sc, at angle v*th

2.  triangle(1, v*th, pt, sc)
3.  hold on
4.  triangle(-1, v*th, pt, sc)

5.  function triangle( up, th, pt, sc )
6.  pts = [-.5    .5    0   -.5;      % x values
7.         -.289 -.289 .577 -.289];   % y values
%  rotation matrix
8.  A = sc * [cos(th), -sin(th); sin(th), cos(th)];
9.  thePts = A * pts;
10. fill(   thePts(1,:) + pt(1), ...
11.      up*thePts(2,:) + pt(2), 1);
```

In Listing 12.4:

> Line 1: Draws one star at location [pt(1), pt(2)] with scale sc, rotation speed v, and angle th.
>
> Lines 2–4: Invoke the helper function triangle(...) to draw two triangles rotating in opposite directions.
>
> Line 5: Draws one triangle with the following parameters: up, with values 1 for upright and -1 for point down; th, the scaled rotation angle; and pt and sc, which are passed directly through from the star(...) function.
>
> Lines 6 and 7: Are coordinates of an equilateral triangle.
>
> Line 8: Computes the rotation matrix and applies the scaling factor.
>
> Line 9: Rotates and scales the points of the triangle.
>
> Lines 10 and 11: Call the function fill(...) to fill the triangle, offsetting the x and y coordinates by the original location of the triangle, and scaling y by the up multiplier to invert the triangle if necessary.

The results of this script are shown in Figure 12.6.

12.4.2 3-D Rotation

The mathematics implementing rotation in three dimensions is a natural extension of the 2-D rotation case. We present here a simple way to make this extension. The 2-D rotation in Section 12.4.1 that rotates by the angle θ in the x-y plane is actually rotating about the z axis. The 3-D equivalent of this transformation is as follows:

$$\begin{bmatrix} x^* \\ y^* \\ z^* \end{bmatrix} = \begin{bmatrix} \cos\theta & -\sin\theta & 0 \\ \sin\theta & \cos\theta & 0 \\ 0 & 0 & 1 \end{bmatrix} * \begin{bmatrix} x \\ y \\ z \end{bmatrix}$$

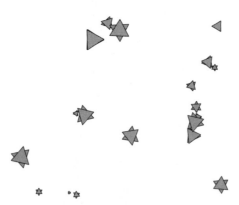

Figure 12.6 *Stars*

We can establish similar transformations by the angle ϕ about the y-axis, and ψ about the x-axis as follows:

$$\begin{bmatrix} x^* \\ y^* \\ z^* \end{bmatrix} = \begin{bmatrix} \cos\phi & 0 & -\sin\phi \\ 0 & 1 & 0 \\ \sin\phi & 0 & \cos\phi \end{bmatrix} * \begin{bmatrix} x \\ y \\ z \end{bmatrix}$$

and:

$$\begin{bmatrix} x^* \\ y^* \\ z^* \end{bmatrix} = \begin{bmatrix} 1 & 0 & 0 \\ 0 & \cos\psi & -\sin\psi \\ 0 & \sin\psi & \cos\psi \end{bmatrix} * \begin{bmatrix} x \\ y \\ z \end{bmatrix}$$

Once these matrices are constructed, the rotations can be combined by multiplying the matrices together:

$$x* = R_x * R_y * R_z * x$$

where R_x, R_y, and R_z are the matrices of rotation about the x, y, and z axes, respectively.

An example of a script to rotate the solid cube drawn in Chapter 11 is shown in Listing 12.5. The major problem with rotating solid objects is that the coordinates of the object are defined as arrays of points. However, the rotation matrices need each set of coordinates in single rows. To accomplish this, we will use the `reshape(...)` function to translate the coordinates to and from the row vectors necessary for the coordinate rotation.

Listing 12.5 Rotating a solid cube

```
1. xx = [ 0   0   0   0   0;
2.        -1  -1   1   1  -1;
3.        -1  -1   1   1  -1;
4.         0   0   0   0   0]
5. yy = [ 0   0   0   0   0;
6.        -1   1   1  -1  -1;
7.        -1   1   1  -1  -1;
8.         0   0   0   0   0]
9. zz = [ 1   1   1   1   1;
10.        1   1   1   1   1;
11.       -1  -1  -1  -1  -1;
12.       -1  -1  -1  -1  -1]
13. [r c] = size(xx);
14. ln = r*c; % length of reshaped vector
15. th = 0; ph = 0; ps = 0;
16. dth = 0.05; dph = 0.03; dps = 0.01;
17. go = true
18. while go
19.     surf(xx+4, yy, zz)
20.     shading interp; colormap autumn
```

continued on next page

```
21.      hold on; alpha(0.5)
22.      Rz = [cos(th) -sin(th)   0
23.            sin(th)  cos(th)    0
24.               0        0       1];
25.      Ry = [cos(ph)    0    -sin(ph)
26.             0         1        0
27.            sin(ph)    0     cos(ph)];
28.      Rx = [ 1         0        0
29.             0      cos(ps) -sin(ps)
30.             0      sin(ps)  cos(ps)];
31.      P(1,:) = reshape(xx, 1, ln);
32.      P(2,:) = reshape(yy, 1, ln);
33.      P(3,:) = reshape(zz, 1, ln);
34.      Q = Rx*Ry*Rz*P;
35.      qx = reshape(Q(1,:), r, c);
36.      qy = reshape(Q(2,:), r, c);
37.      qz = reshape(Q(3,:), r, c);
38.      surf(qx, qy, qz)
39.      shading interp
40.      axis equal; axis off; hold off
41.      axis([-2 6 -2 2 -2 2])
42.      lightangle(40, 65); alpha(0.5)
43.      th = th+dth; ph = ph+dph; ps = ps+dps;
44.      go = ps < pi/4
45.      pause(0.03)
46. end
```

In Listing 12.5:

> Lines 1–12: Build the coordinates of the cube centered at the origin.
>
> Lines 13 and 14: Determine the length of the linearized row vector for the reshape(...) function.
>
> Lines 15 and 16: Set up the three rotation angle parameters—the initial values and the increments.
>
> Line 17 and 18: Repeat the drawing loop until the variable go is reset.
>
> Lines 19–21: Draw one cube not rotated four units down the x-axis.
>
> Lines 22–30: Set up the rotation matrices.
>
> Lines 31–33: Reshape the x, y, and z arrays into linear form.
>
> Line 34: Performs the rotation.
>
> Lines 35–37: Reshape the original arrays.
>
> Lines 38–42: Draw the rotated cube.
>
> Line 43: Updates the rotation angles.
>
> Line 44: Shows the terminating condition.
>
> Line 45: Pauses to give the figure time to draw.

The results after running this script are shown in Figure 12.7. Notice that the mechanization of the top face has caused a "wrapped parcel" effect on the light reflections off that surface.

Figure 12.7 *Solid cubes*

 ## 12.5 Solving Simultaneous Linear Equations

A common use for matrix division is for solving simultaneous linear equations. To be soluble, simultaneous linear equations must be expressed as N independent equations involving N unknown variables, x_i. The equations will also involve $N * (N + 1)$ constant values, A_{ij} and c_i, where i and j each take on values from 1 to N. They are usually expressed in the following form:

$$A_{11} \ x_1 + A_{12} \ x_2 + \ldots + A_{1N} \ x_N = c_1$$

$$A_{21} \ x_1 + A_{22} \ x_2 + \ldots + A_{2N} \ x_N = c_2$$

$$\cdot \qquad \cdot \qquad \qquad \cdot \qquad \cdot$$

$$\cdot \qquad \cdot \qquad \qquad \cdot \qquad \cdot$$

$$A_{N1} \ x_1 + A_{N2} \ x_2 + \ldots + A_{NN} \ x_N = c_N$$

In matrix form, they can be expressed as follows:

$$A_{N \times N} \ * \ X_{N \times 1} = C_{N \times 1}$$

from which, since all of the values in A and C are constants, we can immediately solve for the column vector X by back division:

```
X = A\C
```

or by using the matrix inverse function:

```
X = inv(A) * C
```

12.5.1 Intersecting Lines

A typical example of a simultaneous equation problem might take the following form. Consider two straight lines on a plot with the following general form:

$$A_{11} x + A_{12} y = c_1$$

$$A_{21} x + A_{22} y = c_2$$

These lines intersect at some point [x, y] that is the solution to both of these equations. The equations can be rewritten in matrix form as follows:

```
A * V = c
```

where c is the column vector `[c1 c2]'` and v is the required result, the column vector `[x y]'`. The solution is obtained by eliminating A from the left side of the equation using the back divide operator as follows:

```
V = A \ c
```

Recall that back divide, like the `inv(...)` function, will fail to produce a result if the matrix is singular, that is, has two rows or columns that have a linear relationship. In the specific example of two intersecting lines, this singularity occurs when the two lines are parallel, in which case there is no point of intersection. Listing 12.6 shows one solution to a pair of simultaneous equations.

Listing 12.6 Plotting line intersections

```
1. % equations are y = m1 x + c1
2. %                y = m2 x + c2
3. %    in matrix form:
4. %       [ -m1 1;   *  [xp;  =  [c1
5. %         -m2 1 ]      yp]       c2]
6. ax = [-0.5 6]; ay = [-4.5 18];
7. % plot the two lines
8. m1 = 3; c1 = -2;
9. y1 = m1*ax + c1;
10. m2 = -2; c2 = 9;
11. y2 = m2*ax + c2;
12. plot(ax, y1)
13. hold on
14. plot(ax, y2, 'b--')
15. % solve for the intersection point
16. A = [-m1 1; -m2 1];
17. c = [c1; c2];
18. P = A\c;
19. % draw intersection identification lines
20. ix = P(1); iy = P(2);
21. plot([ix ix], [0 iy*1.2], 'r:')
22. plot([0 ix*1.2],[iy iy], 'r:')
23. % draw the axes
24. plot(ax, [0 0], 'k');
```

continued on next page

```
25. axis([ax ay])
26. plot([0 0], ay, 'k');
27. legend({'Line 1','Line 2','Intersect'}, ...
                'Location','NorthWest' )
```

In Listing 12.6:

> Line 6: Sets the x and y limits of the plot.
>
> Lines 8–14: Plot the original lines.
>
> Line 16: Sets the simultaneous equation matrix.
>
> Line 17: Shows the right-hand side of the equation.
>
> Line 18: Solves the linear equations—P(1) is the x value; P(2) is the y value.
>
> Lines 21 and 22: Plot the lines identifying the intersection point.
>
> Lines 24–27: Complete the plot.

Figure 12.8 shows the result of this script.

12.5.2 Curve Fitting

A specific example of simultaneous equation solution occurs when seeking the best polynomial fit to a set of data points. This fitting a polynomial equation of order n to a set of x and y values involves a search for the $n + 1$ coefficients C_1 of x^n through x^0 that minimize the sum of the squares of the difference between actual y values and the y values of the polynomial at the given x values. The polynomial is of the form:

$$y = C_n x^n + C_{n-1} x^{n-1} \ldots + C_1 x + C_0$$

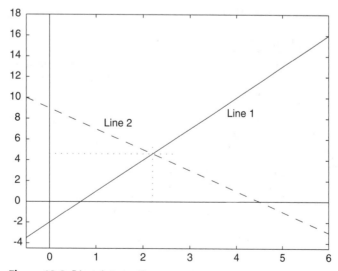

Figure 12.8 *Lines intersecting*

The solution, found in any good calculus book, produces the following set of simultaneous equations:

$$
\begin{bmatrix}
\acute{O}x^{2n} & \acute{O}x^{2n-1} & \cdots & \acute{O}x^{n+2} & \acute{O}x^{n+1} & \acute{O}x^{n} \\
\acute{O}x^{2n-1} & \acute{O}x^{2n-2} & \cdots & \acute{O}x^{n+1} & \acute{O}x^{n} & \acute{O}x^{n-1} \\
\vdots & & \ddots & & & \vdots \\
\acute{O}x^{n+1} & \acute{O}x^{n} & \cdots & \acute{O}x^{3} & \acute{O}x^{2} & \acute{O}x \\
\acute{O}x^{n} & \acute{O}x^{n-1} & \cdots & \acute{O}x^{2} & \acute{O}x & n
\end{bmatrix}
*
\begin{bmatrix}
C_n \\ C_{n-1} \\ \vdots \\ C_1 \\ C_0
\end{bmatrix}
=
\begin{bmatrix}
\acute{O}x^{n}y \\ \acute{O}x^{n-1}y \\ \vdots \\ \acute{O}xy \\ \acute{O}y
\end{bmatrix}
$$

This is an equation of the general form $A_{(n+1) \times (n+1)} * C_{(n+1) \times 1} = B_{(n+1) \times 1}$. To solve this, we merely perform the back divide in the usual way:

```
C = A \ B
```

The example shown in Listing 12.7 illustrates the computation of a linear fit to a set of data. It reads a file of fuel consumption records and computes the curve fit of order 1, a linear curve fit. The resulting plot is shown in Figure 12.9; the crosses show the raw data, and the line is the least squares linear fit.

In Listing 12.7:

> Line 3: Reads in the data.
>
> Lines 4 and 5: Extract the data.
>
> Lines 6–10: Plot the original data as red x's.
>
> Line 11: Builds the simultaneous equation matrix.
>
> Line 12: Builds the right-hand side of the equation.
>
> Line 13: Solves for the coefficients. The best fit is
> `y = a(1) * x + a(2)`.

Listing 12.7 Linear curve fit

```
1. % the file gasoline.dat contains two data
2. % columns:   the miles driven and the gas used.
3. r = dlmread('gasoline.dat');
4. x = r(:,2)';
5. y = r(:,1)';
6. plot(x, y, 'rx');
7. hold on
8. title('gas vs miles');
9. ylabel('miles');
10. xlabel('gallons');
11. c = [ sum(x.^2) sum(x); sum(x) 1];
12. rhs = [sum(x.*y); sum(y)]
13. a = c \ rhs;
14. plot(x, a(1)*x + a(2))
15. fprintf('average mpg = %f\n', a(1) );
```

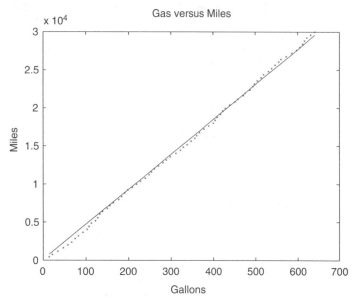

Figure 12.9 *Linear curve fit*

Line 14: Plots the best fit line.

Line 15: The slope happens to be the average fuel consumption.

As we will see later, MATLAB has built-in functions that perform polynomial curve fits.

 ## 12.6 Engineering Examples

The following examples illustrate applications of the matrix capabilities discussed in this chapter.

12.6.1 Ceramic Composition

Industrial ceramics plants require mixtures with precise formulations in order to produce products of consistent quality. For example, a factory might require 100 kg of a mix consisting of 67 percent silica, 5 percent alumina, 2 percent calcium oxide, and 26 percent magnesium oxide. However, the raw material provided is not pure quantities of these materials. Rather, they are delivered as batches of material that consist of the required components in different proportions. Each batch of raw materials is analyzed to determine their composition, and we will need to do the analysis to determine the proportions of the raw materials to mix in order to accomplish the appropriate formulation. The raw materials we will use here are feldspar, diatomite, magnesite, and talc. Table 12.1 illustrates a typical analysis of the composition of these compounds.

Table 12.1 Compound compositions				
	Silica	**Alumina**	**CaO**	**MgO**
Feldspar	0.6950	0.1750	0.0080	0.1220
Diatomite	0.8970	0.0372	0.0035	0.0623
Magnesite	0.0670	0.0230	0.0600	0.8500
Talc	0.6920	0.0160	0.0250	0.2670

For example, if we mixed W_f kg of feldspar, W_d kg of diatomite, W_m kg of magnesite, and W_t kg of talc, the amount of silica would be $0.695\,W_f + 0.897\,W_d + 0.067\,W_m + 0.692\,W_t$. Repeating this equation for the other components produces a matrix equation that reduces to:

$$\begin{bmatrix} 67 \\ 5 \\ 2 \\ 26 \end{bmatrix} = \begin{bmatrix} 0.695 & 0.897 & 0.067 & 0.692 \\ 0.175 & 0.0372 & 0.023 & 0.016 \\ 0.008 & 0.0035 & 0.06 & 0.025 \\ 0.122 & 0.0623 & 0.025 & 0.267 \end{bmatrix} * \begin{bmatrix} W_f \\ W_d \\ W_m \\ W_t \end{bmatrix}$$

which is an equation of the form:

$$C = A * W$$

We find the appropriate amounts of the raw material by solving these equations:

$$W = A\backslash B$$

A script that works this problem is shown in Listing 12.8.

In Listing 12.8:

> Lines 1–4: Matrix A is the transpose of the original data table.
>
> Line 5: Shows the required composition in kg.
>
> Line 6: Shows the computed weights of the raw materials in kg, which produces the following result:
> ```
> W =
>      16.0083    35.3043    15.1766    33.5108
> ```

Listing 12.8 Analyzing ceramic composition

```
1. A = [0.6950    0.8970    0.0670    0.6920
2.         0.1750    0.0372    0.0230    0.0160
3.         0.0080    0.0035    0.0600    0.0250
4.         0.1220    0.0623    0.8500    0.2670]

5. B = [67 5 2 26]'

6. W = (inv(A) * B)'
```

12.6.2 Analyzing an Electrical Circuit

Figure 12.10 illustrates a typical electrical circuit with two voltage sources connected to five resistors with three closed loops. The voltages and resistances are given. We are asked to determine the voltage drop across R_1. Solution techniques apply Ohm's Law to the voltage drops around each closed circuit. When this technique is applied, the equations are as follows:

$$V_1 = i_1 * R_1 + (i_1 - i_2) * R_4$$
$$0 = i_2 * R_2 + (i_2 - i_3) * R_5 + (i_2 - i_1) * R_4$$
$$-V_2 = i_3 * R_3 + (i_3 - i_2) * R_5$$

When these three equations are manipulated to isolate the three currents, we have the following matrix equation:

$$\begin{bmatrix} V_1 \\ 0 \\ -V_2 \end{bmatrix} = \begin{bmatrix} R_1 + R_4 & -R_4 & 0 \\ -R_4 & R_2 + R_4 + R_5 & -R_5 \\ 0 & -R_5 & R_3 + R_5 \end{bmatrix} * \begin{bmatrix} i_1 \\ i_2 \\ i_3 \end{bmatrix}$$

which is in the form V = A * i, and can be solved as usual by:

i = A \ V

The script to accomplish this is shown in Listing 12.9.

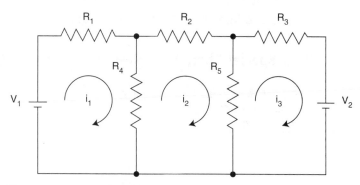

Figure 12.10 *Typical electrical circuit*

Listing 12.9 Analyzing an electrical circuit

```
1. R1 = 100; R2 = 200; R3 = 300
2. R4 = 400; R5 = 500
3. V1 = 10; V2 = 5
4. A = [R1+R4    -R4       0
5.        -R4    R2+R4+R5  -R5
6.         0     -R5       R3+R5]
7. B = [V1; 0; -V2]
8. curr = inv(A) * B
9. fprintf('drop across R1 is %6.2f volts\n', ...
10.    curr(1) * R1 );
```

In Listing 12.9:

> Line 1–3: Set up the parameters of the problem.
> Lines 4–7: Set up the coefficient matrices.
> Lines 8–10: Solve the problem.
> Running this script produces the following printout:

```
curr =
        0.0283
        0.0104
        0.0003
    drop across R1 is    2.83 volts
```

Chapter Summary

This chapter presented two specialized operations performed with matrices:

- Matrix multiplication can be used for two- and three-dimensional coordinate rotations by building the appropriate rotation matrices
- Matrix division is used for solving simultaneous equations by setting up the equations in the general form B = A * x, where the known matrix A is n × n and the known column vector B is n × 1; the unknown vector x is then found by x = A\B or x = inv(A) * B

Special Characters, Reserved Words, and Functions

Special Characters, Reserved Words, and Functions	Description	Discussed in This Section
*	Matrix multiplication	12.2.1
/	Matrix division	12.2.2
\	Matrix back division	12.2.2
^	Matrix exponentiation	12.2.3
eye(n)	Computes the identity matrix	12.2.1
inv(a)	Computes the inverse of a matrix	12.2.3
reshape(a,r,c)	Changes the row/column configuration of the array a	12.4.2

Self Test

Use the following questions to check your understanding of the material in this chapter:

True or False

1. All MATLAB classes exhibit some form of behavioral abstraction.

2. Matrix multiplication requires that the inner dimensions match.

3. The results of A * B and B * A are identical.

4. Both A * A^{-1} and A^{-1} * A return the identity matrix.

5. Multiplying inv(A) * B is logically equivalent to B / A.

6. Fitting a polynomial to a set of data always reduces to a set of simultaneous linear equations.

Fill in the Blanks

1. Behavioral abstraction combines _____ abstraction and _____ abstraction.

2. The result of a matrix multiplication is a new matrix with the _____ count of the first matrix and the _____ count of the second.

3. To rotate a graphic object in the x-y plane about some point, P, other than the origin, you first _____, then _____, and then _____.

4. To be soluble, simultaneous linear equations must be expressed as _____ equations involving _____ variables, x$_i$, and _____ values.

 Programming Projects

1. Do the following matrix exercises:
    a. Create a 5 × 6 matrix A that contains random numbers between 0 and 10.
    b. Create a 6 × 5 matrix B that contains random numbers between 0 and 10.

    c.   Find the inverse of matrix A * B and store it in the variable, C.

    d.   Create a new matrix D that is the same as A except that all values less than 5 are replaced by zero. (Do not use iteration to create D.)

    e.   Create a new matrix F that is the same as A except that all values less than 5 are replaced by zero; use iteration to create F.

    f.   Create a new matrix G that is the "horizontal" reverse of A. For example:

```
[1 2 3           [3 2 1
 3 2 5    =>      5 2 3
 1 7 4]           4 7 1]
```

    g.   Find the minimum value among all the elements in A and store your answer in the variable H.

2.   Which of the following statements is true?

    a.   `eye(5)` is equivalent to `eye(5, 5)`

    b.   `size(eye(size(A)))` is equal to `size(A)`

    c.   Typing "eye" at the command prompt will produce an error

3.   Write a short script to solve the system of linear equations:

$$2x + 5y + 7z = 9$$
$$3x + 2y + 3z = 2$$
$$x + 3y + 2z = 5$$

4.   As an enthusiastic and motivated student, you decided to buy plenty of pens for all your classes this semester. This spending spree occurred at the unfortunate time before you realized that your engineering classes required little use for "ink." So now you're left with four different types of pens and no receipt—you only remember the total amount you spent, and not the price of each type of pen.

You decide to get together with three of your friends who coincidentally did the same thing as you, buying the same four types of pens and knowing only the total amount. In order to find the price of each individual pen, you create the following matrix called data, where each column represents a different type of pen and each row represents a different person.

	pen1	pen2	pen3	pen4	
data =	3	6	2	5	<-you
	4	7	5	2	<-friend 1
	1	3	12	6	<-friend 2
	2	8	2	4	<-friend 3

Then you generate a column vector `totals`, which contains the totals each of you spent on the pens.

```
totals =    19.60
            18.78
            25.59
            19.26
```

Using the matrix `data` and the vector `totals`, find the column vector `prices` that contains the price of each type of pen.

5. World Leaders have decided to come up with a single currency for the world. This new currency, called the eullar, is defined by the following:

    - Seven dollars and three euros equals seventy-one eullars
    - One dollar and two euros equals twenty eullars

    As a reputed economist, your job is to determine the value of a dollar in terms of eullars. Write a script to compute and print the value of the dollar in eullars. For example, your script might print

    `1 dollar = 4.64 eullars.`

Images

Chapter Objectives

This chapter covers:

- The basic representation of images

- How to read, display, and write JPEG image files

- Some basic operations on images

- Some advanced image processing techniques

Introduction

The graphical techniques we have seen so far have been two- and three-dimensional plots, whose basic concept is to write in places on the screen where data are required and to leave the rest of the screen blank. These images are easily generated when we have a mathematical model of the data and wish to represent it graphically. However, many sensors observing the world do not have that underlying model of the data. Rather, they passively generate two-dimensional representations that we see as images, leaving the interpretation of those images to a human observer.

This chapter discusses some of the elementary processes that can be applied to images in order to begin to extract meaning from them.

13.1 Nature of an Image
13.2 Image Types
    13.2.1 True Color Images
    13.2.2 Gray Scale Images
    13.2.3 Color Mapped Images
    13.2.4 Preferred Image Format
13.3 Reading, Displaying, and Writing Images
13.4 Operating on Images
    13.4.1 Stretching or Shrinking Images
    13.4.2 Color Masking
    13.4.3 Making a Collage
    13.4.4 Creating a Kaleidoscope
    13.4.5 Images on a Surface
13.5 Engineering Example— Detecting Edges

13.1 Nature of an Image

Before we confine ourselves to practical, computational reality, we need to understand the general nature of an image. The easiest answer would be that an image is a two-dimensional sheet on which the color at any point can have essentially infinite variability. However, since we live in a digital world, we will immediately confine ourselves to the conventional representation of images required for most digital display processors, as shown in Figure 13.1. We can represent any image as a 2-D, M × N array of points usually referred to as picture elements, or **pixels**, where M and N are the number of rows and columns respectively. Each pixel is "painted" by blending variable amounts of the three primary colors: red, green, and blue. (Notice that this is not the same blending process used in painting with oils or water colors, where the third primary color is yellow and the combination process is reversed—increasing amounts of the primary colors tends toward black, not white.)

The resolution of a picture is measured by the number of pixels per unit of picture width and height. This governs the fuzziness of its appearance in print, and controls the maximum size of good-quality photo printing. The color resolution is measured by the number of bits in the words containing the red, green, and blue (RGB) components. Since one value generally exists for each of the M × N pixels in the array, increasing the size of the pixel color will have a significant effect on the stored size of the image. Typically, 8 bits (values 0–255) are assigned to each color.

MATLAB has a data type, `uint8`, which uses 8 bits to store an unsigned integer in the range 0–255. It is unsigned because we are not interested in negative color values, and to specify the sign value would cost a data bit and reduce the resolution of the data to 0–127. By combining the three color values, there are actually 2^{24} different combinations of color available to a true-color image—many more possible combinations than the human eye can distinguish.

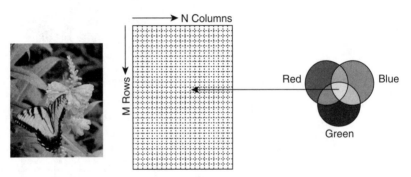

Figure 13.1 *The nature of images*

13.2 Image Types

Our sources for images to process are data files captured by imaging devices such as cameras, scanners, and graphic arts systems, and these image files are provided in a wide variety of formats. According to the MATLAB documentation, it recognizes files in TIFF, PNG, HDF, BMP, JPEG (JPG), GIF, PCX, XWD, CUR, and ICO formats. The various file formats are usually identified by their file extensions.

While this seems a bewildering collection of formats, MATLAB provides one image reading function that converts these file formats to one of three internal representations: true color, gray scale, or color mapped images.

13.2.1 True Color Images

True color images are stored according to the scheme shown in Figure 13.2 as an M × N × 3 array where every pixel is directly stored in three layers of the 3-D array. The first layer contains the red value, the second layer the green value, and the third layer the blue value. The advantage of this approach, as the name suggests, is that every pixel can be represented as its true color value without compromise. The only disadvantage is the size of the image in memory because there are three color values for every pixel.

13.2.2 Gray Scale Images

Gray scale images are also directly stored, but save the black-to-white intensity value for each pixel as a single `uint8` value rather than three values.

13.2.3 Color Mapped Images

Color mapped, or indexed, images keep a separate color map either 256 items long (for maximum economy of memory) or up to 32,768 items long. Each item in the color map contains the red, blue, and green values of a color, respectively.

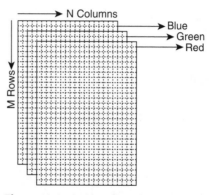

Figure 13.2 *A true color image*

As illustrated in Figure 13.3, the image itself is stored as an M × N array of indices into the color map. So, for example, a certain pixel index might contain the value 143. The color to be shown at that pixel location would be the 143rd color set (RGB) on the color map.

If the color map is restricted to 256 colors, each pixel can be drawn at the same color resolution as a true color image, as three 8-bit values, but the choice of colors is very restricted, and normal pictures of scenery—sky, for instance—take on a "layered color" appearance. Color mapped images can be used effectively, however, to store cartoon pictures economically where limited color choices are not a problem. Using a larger color map provides a larger, but still sometimes restrictive, range of color choices, but since the indices in the picture array must be 16-bit values and the color map is larger, the memory size advantages of this method of storage are diminished.

Computationally, it is possible to convert a color mapped image to true color, but true color or black and white images cannot normally be converted to color mapped format without loss of fidelity in the color representation.

13.2.4 Preferred Image Format

In order to avoid confusion in the format of images, we will confine our discussions to one specific image file format that is prevalent at the time of writing, and provides a nice compromise between economy of storage as an image file and accessibility within MATLAB. We will discuss files compressed according to a standard algorithm originally proposed by the Joint Photographic Experts Group (JPEG). When MATLAB reads JPEG images, they are decoded as true color images; when MATLAB writes them, they are again encoded in compressed form. If you take the time to look, the file size for a typical JPEG file is 30 times less than the size you would need to store the M × N × 3 bytes of the image. As we will see later, this compression does not come without cost.

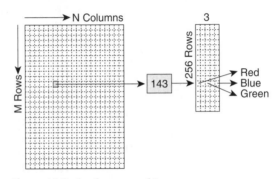

Figure 13.3 *A color mapped image*

13.3 Reading, Displaying, and Writing Images

MATLAB uses one image reading function, imread(...), for all image file types. We will not attempt to describe its behavior for all the image file types—the MATLAB help file for imread(...) is extremely detailed if you need to read files other than the most common.

To read a file named *myPicture.jpg*, we use the following command:

```
>> pic = imread('myPicture.jpg', 'jpg')
```

where the result, pic, is an M × N × 3 uint8 array of pixel color values, and the second parameter, 'jpg', provides the format of the file explicitly. This parameter is optional; MATLAB usually infers the file format correctly from the file contents.

Once the picture has been read into MATLAB, you can display it in a figure window with fixed size, just like a plot with the image(...) function. To display the picture represented by pic, for example, use the following command:

```
>> image(pic)
```

The image(...) function actually stretches or shrinks the image to fit the size of the normal plot figure, a behavior you normally desire. However, occasionally, you want the plot figure to match the actual image size. Most MATLAB editions provide the imshow(...) function, which presents the image without stretching or shrinking (unless the figure window is too small).

Similarly, there is one function for writing files: imwrite(...), which can be used to write most common file formats. If we have made some changes to pic, the internal representation of the image, we could write a new version to the disk by using the following:

```
>> imwrite( pic, 'newPicture.jpg', 'jpg')
```

where the third parameter, 'jpg', is required to specify the output format of the file. Reading and writing color mapped images is more complicated. Refer to the MATLAB help files for these operations, and for the many options available in writing JPEG files.

 13.4 Operating on Images

Since images are stored as arrays, it is not surprising that we can employ the normal operations of creation, manipulation, slicing, and concatenation. We will note one particular matrix operation that will be of great value before examining some applications of array manipulation related to image processing.

13.4.1 Stretching or Shrinking Images

In earlier chapters we have seen the basic ability of MATLAB to use index vectors to extract rows and columns from an array. Now we extend these ideas to understand how to uniformly shrink or stretch an array to match an exact size. Consider, for example, A, a rows × cols array. Assume for a moment that the vertical size is good, but we want to stretch or shrink the image horizontally to newRows—a number that might be larger or smaller than rows. We use linspace(...) to create an index vector as follows:

```
>> rowVector = linspace(1, rows, newRows)
```

where the third parameter is the required size of the new array. In general, this will contain fractional values, and MATLAB will accept these for indexing but will issue warnings. Therefore we need to round the results as follows:

```
>> rowVector = round(rowVector)
```

Then we can use this vector to shrink or stretch the array A as follows:

```
>> newA = A(rowVector,:)
```

Clearly, this can be applied to both dimensions simultaneously, as shown in Exercise 13.1.

Exercise 13.1 Working with image stretching

Do It Yourself

```
>> m = magic(7); m = m(1:5,:)
m =
      30    39    48     1    10    19    28
      38    47     7     9    18    27    29
      46     6     8    17    26    35    37
       5    14    16    25    34    36    45
      13    15    24    33    42    44     4
>> [rows, cols] = size(m)
rows =
       5
cols =
       7
>> a = m(2:2:end, 3:3:end)
a =
       7    27
      16    36
>> RFactor = 1.43; CFactor = 0.75
RFactor =
    1.4300
CFactor =
    0.7500
>> rowVec = ...
```

continued on next page

```
  round(linspace(1, rows, RFactor*rows))
rowVec =
      1      2      2      3      4      4      5
>> colVec = ...
  round(linspace(1, cols, CFactor*cols))
colVec =
      1      3      4      6      7
>> m(rowVec, colVec)
ans =
      30     48      1     19     28
      38      7      9     27     29
      38      7      9     27     29
      46      8     17     35     37
       5     16     25     36     45
       5     16     25     36     45
      13     24     33     44      4
>>
```

In this exercise, first we create a 5×7 array m and determine its size. Then we illustrate the "normal" slicing operations by extracting the array a as the even rows, and every third column of m. Next we generalize this array slicing by stretching the number of rows by a factor 1.43 and shrinking the number of columns by a factor 0.75, which should give us an array 7.15×5.25.

This is accomplished by building a row index vector, rowVec, and a column index vector, colVec, according to the algorithm above. Notice that the stretching is achieved by repeating selected values in the index vector, and shrinking is achieved by omitting some. When these index vectors are applied to the original array, m, the result is a new array with the anticipated size rounded down to the nearest whole number.

13.4.2 Color Masking

As an example of image manipulation, consider the image shown in Figure 13.4. This is a 2400×1600 JPEG image that can be taken with any good digital camera. However, the appearance of the Vienna garden is somewhat marred by the fact that the sky is gray, not blue. Fortunately, we have a picture of a cottage, as shown in Figure 13.5, with a nice, clear blue sky. So our goal is to replace the gray sky in the Vienna garden with the blue sky from the cottage picture.

Initial Exploration Before we can do this, however, we need to explore the Vienna picture to determine how to distinguish the gray sky from the rest of the picture. In particular, there are patches of sky visible between the tree branches that must be changed as well as the open sky. Listing 13.1 illustrates a good way to accomplish this. Here we display the image in one figure, choose a representative row in the image that includes some sky showing through the tree (we chose row 350), and then plot the red, blue, and green values of the pixels across that row. Figure 13.6 shows the resulting plot.

Figure 13.4 *A garden in Vienna*

Figure 13.5 *A cottage in Oxfordshire*

Listing 13.1 Exploring the sky situation

```
 1. clear
 2. clc
 3. close all

 4. v = imread('Vienna.jpg');
 5. image(v)
 6. figure
 7. row = input('which row? ');
 8. red = v(row, :, 1);
 9. gr  = v(row, :, 2);
10. bl  = v(row, :, 3);
11. plot(red, 'r');
12. hold on
13. plot(gr, 'g');
14. plot(bl, 'b');
```

In Listing 13.1:

Lines 1–3: The usual graphics setup.

Line 4: Reads the image.

Line 5: Displays the image.

Line 6: Determines a suitable row (350 is a good choice).

Line 7: Makes a new plotting figure.

Lines 8–10: Extract the three color layers for the chosen row.

Lines 11–14: Plot the three colors. Since we omitted one of the axis values, MATLAB makes the correct assumption that the x values are the integers `1:length(y)`, which give us the horizontal pixel number across the row.

Initial Analysis As we examine Figure 13.6, we see that the red, green, and blue values for the open sky are all around 250 because the sky is almost white. However, the color "spikes" that correspond to the color values of the sky elements that show through the tree are actually lower. We could decide, for example, to define the sky as all those pixels where the red, blue, and green values are all above a chosen threshold, and we could comfortably set that threshold at 160.

There is one more important consideration. It would be unfortunate to turn the hair of the lady (the author's wife) blue, and there are fountains and walkways that might also logically appear to be "sky." We can prevent this embarrassment by limiting the color replacement to the upper portion of the picture above row 700.

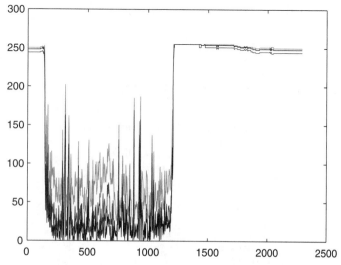

Figure 13.6 *Plot of the color values on one row of the Vienna image*

Final Computation So we are ready for the code that will replace the gray sky with blue. The code in Listing 13.2 accomplishes this, and Figure 13.7 shows the resulting image.

In Listing 13.2:

Lines 1–3: Clear the environment.

Lines 4 and 5: Read the two images.

Line 6: Sets the arbitrary threshold.

Lines 7–13: Build a logical mask to replace the appropriate pixels from the cottage picture into the Vienna picture. This is the only

Figure 13.7 *The Vienna garden with a blue sky*

Listing 13.2 Replacing the gray sky

```
1. clear
2. clc
3. close all

4. v = imread('Vienna.jpg');
5. w = imread('Witney.jpg');
6. thres = 160;
7. layer = (v(:,:,1) > thres) ...
8.         & (v(:,:,2) > thres) ...
9.         & (v(:,:,3) > thres);
10. mask(:,:,1) = layer;
11. mask(:,:,2) = layer;
12. mask(:,:,3) = layer;
13. mask(700:end,:,:) = false;
14. nv = v;
15. nv(mask) = w(mask);
16. image(nv);
17. imwrite(nv, 'newVienna.jpg', 'jpg')
```

messy part of the solution. We need to build a logical, 3-D array of the same size as both images. However, since the criterion for detecting the sky is a 2-D layer, we have to build that first and then populate each color of the mask with that layer.

Lines 7–9: Determine which pixels are sky as a 2-D layer.

Lines 10–12: Build the required mask by putting this logical layer in each color plane.

Line 13: Refuses to replace any pixels below row 700.

Line 14: Copies the original image.

Line 15: Replaces the sky.

Line 16: Shows the image.

Line 17: Writes out the JPEG result.

Post Operative Analysis We realize that this is not quite the end of the story, because a wire has suddenly become evident in the picture. Furthermore, if we take a close look at the wire in Figure 13.8, we see a number of disturbing things:

- The sky is by no means uniform in color—justifying the assertion that color mapped images do not have enough different colors to draw a true sky effectively

- The color of the wire is not far removed from the color of some parts of the blue sky—so replacing slightly darker blue would be problematic

- There is a light colored "halo" around the wire that is actually a result of the original JPEG compression of the image so that even if we did replace the darker colors, the ghost of the wire would still be visible

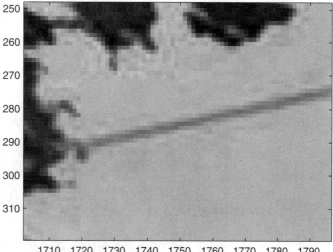

Figure 13.8 *Magnified image of the wire*

So pixel replacement will probably not solve our wire problem. We will take a different approach to solve this problem in Chapter 15.

13.4.3 Making a Collage

As a second example of image manipulation, consider the two images shown in Figures 13.9 and 13.10, each of which is a 1600×1200 JPEG image. However, the cute factor is a little low. What we really want for our family album is a collage consisting of the author's cute dog without most of the background and the lake picture. Furthermore, it would be nice to have a brown frame and a light yellow mat setting off the two pictures.

Figure 13.9 *The original cute dog picture*

Figure 13.10 *The original lake scene*

Before we begin coding, we draw a diagram in detail to understand what we are trying to achieve. The design diagram is shown in Figure 13.11, the resulting collage is shown in Figure 13.12, and the code is shown in Listing 13.3.

Notice that two different manipulations are required. Cropping will eliminate the extraneous background in the dog picture; however, since the lake picture is twice the size of the dog picture, it has to be shrunk by a factor of two in each dimension. The easiest way to accomplish that is to eliminate every other row and every other column of the lake picture. This will reduce its resolution, but still retain enough detail to be pleasant to the eye. If these parameters had not been exact, the technique discussed in Section 13.4.1 could be used to provide a generalized shrinking of the image.

Study the notes in the code for a full understanding of the implementation of this picture. In Listing 13.3:

Lines 4 and 5: Read the JPEG files that are stored as 8-bit unsigned integers of type `uint8`.

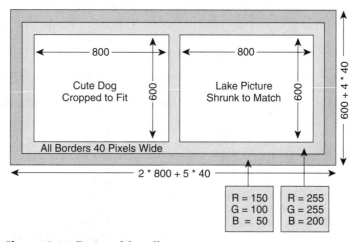

Figure 13.11 *Design of the collage*

Figure 13.12 *The final collage*

Listing 13.3 Making a collage

```
 1. clear
 2. clc
 3. clf

 4. dog = imread('Pep.jpg');
 5. lake = imread('Lake.jpg');

 6. [rows, cols, clrs] = size(dog);
 7. pheight = rows/2; pwidth = cols/2
 8. border = 40;
 9. overallw = 2*pwidth + 5*border;
10. overallh =  pheight + 4*border;
11. frameR = 150; frameG = 100; frameB = 50;
12.  matR = 255;  matG = 255;  matB = 200;
13. % make the outside frame
14. frame = uint8(ones( overallh, overallw ));
15. collage = uint8(zeros( overallh, overallw, 3 ));
16. collage(:, :, 1) = frame * frameR;
17. collage(:, :, 2) = frame * frameG;
18. collage(:, :, 3) = frame * frameB;
19. % insert the mat
20. mat = uint8(ones( overallh - 2*border, ...
21.                   overallw - 2*border ));
22. collage(border+1:overallh-border,...
23.         border+1:overallw-border,1) = mat*matR;
24. collage(border+1:overallh-border,...
25.         border+1:overallw-border,2) = mat*matG;
26. collage(border+1:overallh-border,...
27.         border+1:overallw-border,3) = mat*matB;
28. % crop the dog picture
29. left = 180; % a judgment call
30. dogCr = dog( end - pheight + 1: end,...
31.               left + 1: left + pwidth, :);
32. collage(2*border+1:2*border + pheight,...
33.         2*border+1:2*border + pwidth, :) = dogCr;
34. % shrink the lake picture
35. lakeSh = lake( 1:2:end, 1:2:end, :);
36. collage(2*border+1:2*border + pheight, ...
37.         3*border+pwidth+1:3*border+2*pwidth,:) ...
38.                           = lakeSh;
39. image(collage)
40. axis equal
41. axis off
42. imwrite(collage, 'collage.jpg', 'jpg' )
```

Line 6: Obtains the size of the dog picture.

Line 7: Gives the height and width of each picture.

Lines 9 and 10: Compute the overall height and width of the image using the design shown in Figure 13.11.

Lines 11 and 12: Set the colors of the frame and mat between the pictures.

Line 13: Now we build the collage starting from the outside and working inwards.

Line 14: Makes the 2-D layer that is the size of the overall picture. Since `ones(...)` naturally produces an array of type `double`, we have to cast it to type `uint8` by calling the function `uint8(...)`.

Line 15: Creates an empty collage of the right shape.

Lines 16–18: Load the three color layers with the color values specified for the frame.

Lines 19–27: Repeat the process for the mat. The rectangle for the mat is two borders smaller (one each side/end) than the frame, and must be positioned one border in from the frame edge in the collage.

Lines 28–31: Looking at the dog picture, we must decide where to cut off the background. Considering the rows, it is pretty clear that the bottom rows should be kept. However, we need to cut off a little to the left and a lot to the right, so setting a variable for the left cutoff allows one to look at the results and adjust the position of the dog in the clipped picture.

Lines 32 and 33: The clipped dog picture is inserted into the collage two borders from the top and two borders from the left.

Line 35: Shrinks the lake picture by removing every other row and every other column.

Lines 36–38: The shrunken lake picture is inserted into the collage two borders from the top and three borders plus the width of the dog picture from the left.

Lines 39–42: In cleaning up, the two axis commands make sure that the x and y scales are equal to avoid distortion in the image, and turn off the unwanted numerical boundaries. The image is then written out as a JPEG file.

Common Pitfalls

Be careful requesting the size of 3-D (and more) arrays. If you leave off variables—as here, you might be tempted not to ask for the number of colors because you know it's three—the `size(...)` function multiplies together the remaining dimension sizes. So `[r,c] = size(dog)` would return `r = 1200` and `c = 4800`!

13.4.4 Creating a Kaleidoscope

Figure 13.13 illustrates the geometric manipulation necessary to create a particular kaleidoscope picture. We start with a square image, *sqbutter.jpg*. A non-square image can always be made square by stretching or clipping, as defined in Section 13.4.1. We will divide the picture into four quadrants and then halve each quadrant with a diagonal toward the center of the picture.

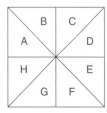 

Figure 13.13 *Layout of the collage*

We will keep those halves that touch the horizontal centerline, and overwrite the other half of the quadrant with its mirror image reflected in the diagonal.

Two of MATLAB's built-in functions make this process quite simple:

- `tril(A)` takes a 2-D array and returns its lower-left diagonal half, with zeros in the triangle above the diagonal
- `rot90(A, n)` takes a 2-D array and rotates it by n*90° counter-clockwise; if n is not specified, it is assumed to be 1

Figure 13.14 shows the results. The overall logic flow of the solution matches that shown in Figure 13.13:

- Disassemble the picture into four quadrants
- Rotate each quadrant the appropriate number of 90° turns
- Mirror the quadrant
- Rotate the mirrored quadrant back to its original orientation
- Reassemble the picture

Listing 13.4 shows the code that manages the overall logic.

Figure 13.14 *The butterfly kaleidoscope*

Listing 13.4 Making a kaleidoscope

```
1. sb  = imread('sqbutter.jpg');
2. subplot( 1, 2, 1);
3. image(sb);
4. cols = length(sb);
5. mid = cols/2
6. subplot( 1, 2, 2);
7. img = [diagMirror( sb(1:mid,     1:mid, :), 0 ) ...
8.          diagMirror( sb(1:mid,     mid+1:end, :), 3 );
9.          diagMirror( sb(mid+1:end, 1:mid, :), 1 ) ...
10.         diagMirror( sb(mid+1:end, mid+1:end, :), 2 )];
11. image(img);
```

In Listing 13.4:

> Line 1: Reads the butterfly image.
>
> Line 2: Starts the left subplot.
>
> Line 3: Shows the original image in the left half of the plot.
>
> Line 4: Finds the largest dimension to use as the number of columns (the image might not initially be square).
>
> Line 5: Computes the center point of the picture.
>
> Line 6: Switches to the right picture.
>
> Lines 7–10: These lines simultaneously do the work of dividing the picture into quadrants, calling the function that mirrors each one, and reassembling the quadrants by concatenation to build the new picture.

Listing 13.5 shows the detailed code for rotating and reflecting each quadrant.

In Listing 13.5:

> Line 5: Unfortunately, since our built-in tools operate in only two dimensions, we have to rotate each color plane separately.
>
> Line 7: Extracts a color layer.

Listing 13.5 Mirroring on a diagonal

```
1. function sq = diagMirror(A, code)
2. % mirror this square image diagonally
3. % the parameter code represents the number of
4. %                   90 deg left rotations

5. for c = 1:3  % tacky to do a layer at a time, but
6.               % tril must see a 2-D array
7.     layer = A(:,:,c);
8.     trin = tril(rot90(layer, code));
9.     % rotate the image back after mirroring
10.    sq(:,:,c) = rot90(trin + trin', 4 - code);
11. end
```

Line 8: Rotates the image the specified number of times (depends on the original quadrant) and strips out the lower triangle.

Line 10: The transpose operator performs the required mirroring about the diagonal and the addition merges the original and the mirror because the other triangle is zero. Finally, it rotates the image back to its original orientation and replaces the original color layer in the image.

13.4.5 Images on a Surface

In Chapter 11 we saw how to create a surface representing solid objects and, in particular, how to create a spherical image that rotates with lighting. Spectacular effects can be created by "pasting" images onto these surfaces, as will be illustrated in this last example. Here, we are given an image of the surface of the earth using Mercator projection, shown in Figure 13.15.[1]

It is important to use the Mercator projection, named for the sixteenth-century Flemish cartographer Gerardus Mercator, because this projection keeps the lines of latitude and longitude on a rectangular grid. This allows a correct representation of the map as it is pasted onto the spherical surface. However, it also presents a challenge because in this projection, the north and south poles would be stretched unreasonably across the top and bottom of the map. These maps, therefore, leave off the region near the poles, and we have to replace those regions.

The objective of this exercise is to paste this image onto a rotating globe. The trick to accomplishing this is to use a feature of the surf(...) function whereby the image is supplied in a specific form as the fourth parameter, as follows:

```
surf(xx, yy, zz, img)
```

It will replace the normal coloring scheme of the surface with the image under the following conditions:

Figure 13.15 *Map projection*

---

[1] The file *earth_s.jpg* is provided as part of the MATLAB system.

- The rows and columns of the image match the rows and columns of the xx, yy, zz plaid
- The image supplies the red, green, and blue layers in the same form as true color images
- The color values, however, must be of type double in the range 0..1

We use the following MATLAB tricks to improve the appearance of the image on the globe:

- material dull reduces the reflectivity of the surface.
- handle = light('Color',[1,1,1]) creates a custom light source with a source with the specified properties. The handle provided by this function is passed as the first parameter to the lightangle(...) function to manipulate the position of this light rather than the default light. See MATLAB help light for more options on this function.

In the following code, rather than stretching the image to the size of the plaid, we choose to size the plaid to the image, thereby preserving all the image resolution. Clearly, in different circumstances where the size of the plaid is specified, the image can be stretched to suit those dimensions. The code to accomplish this is shown in Listing 13.6

Listing 13.6 Rotating a globe

```
 1. WM = imread('figure_13_15_map_projection.jpg');
 2. WM(:,end+1,:) = WM(:,1,:);
 3. snow = mean(mean(WM(1,:,:)));
 4. [WMr, WMc, clr] = size(WM);
 5. rowsperdeglat = WMr/170
 6. add = floor(rowsperdeglat * 5)
 7. addlayer = uint8(ones(add, WMc) * snow);
 8. toAdd(:,:,1) = addlayer;
 9. toAdd(:,:,2) = addlayer;
10. toAdd(:,:,3) = addlayer;
11. worldMap = [toAdd; WM; toAdd];
12. [nlat nlong clr] = size(worldMap)
13. lat =  double(0:nlat-1)  * pi / nlat;
14. long = double(0:nlong-1) * 2 * pi / (nlong-1);
15. [th  phi] = meshgrid(long, lat);
16. radius = 10;
17. zz = radius * cos(phi);
18. xx = radius * sin(phi) .* cos(th);
19. yy = radius * sin(phi) .* sin(th);
20. wM = double(worldMap) / 256;
21. surf(xx, yy, zz, wM);
22. shading interp
23. axis equal, axis off, axis tight
24. material dull
25. handle = light('Color',[1,1,1]);
26. th = 0;
```

continued on next page

```
27. while true
28.      th = th - 1;
29.      view([th 20]);
30.      lightangle(handle, th+50, 20)
31.      pause(.001)
32. end
```

In Listing 13.6:

Line 1: Reads the JPEG image.

Line 2: Enables good closure at the image edge by copying the first column of the map beyond the last column.

Line 3: Computes the mean image intensity of the snow on the top edge of the image. This will be used to fill the circle at the north and south poles.

Line 4: Fetches the size of the map.

Line 5: To calculate the size of the circles at the poles, we assume that the map takes us to ±85° of latitude, so we need the equivalent of 5° at the top and bottom of the map. This line calculates how many rows represent 1° of latitude.

Line 6: Shows the number of rows to add to the map.

Line 7: Computes the values of a single color layer by making an array with ones(...) using the number of rows to add and the number of map columns, and multiplying by the snow intensity.

Lines 8–10: Build the strips to add to the globe map by copying this layer to the red, green, and blue layers of a new image array.

Line 11: Prepares the complete map by concatenating this image to the top and bottom of the map.

Line 12: Retrieves the size of this map.

Lines 13 and 14: Prepare the vectors defining the plaid by spreading the map dimensions across π radians in latitude and 2π radians in longitude.

Lines 15–19: Prepare the sphere.

Line 20: Scales the image to double values between 0 and 1 as required by surf(...).

Lines 21–23: Draw the surface as usual, using the image as the color distribution.

Lines 24 and 25: With the usual lightangle(...) implementation with the default light, the globe does not look right. These two lines set the reflectivity of the surface and create a custom light with a lower intensity.

Lines 26–29: The perpetual rotation with the angle `th` moving backward one degree at a time.

Line 30: This keeps the custom light in the same position relative to the observer.

Line 31: The usual `pause` to allow the drawing to take place for each iteration.

A snapshot of the globe as it is rotating is shown in Figure 13.16.

Figure 13.16 *Globe*

13.5 Engineering Example—Detecting Edges

While images are powerful methods of delivering information to the human eye, they have limitations when being used by computer programs. Our eyes have an astonishing ability to interpret the content of an image, such as the one shown in Figure 13.17. Even a novice observer would have no difficulty

Figure 13.17 *C-130 in flight*

seeing that it is a picture of an aircraft in flight. An experienced observer would be able to identify the type of aircraft as a Lockheed C-130, and perhaps some other characteristics of the aircraft.

While our eyes are excellent at interpreting images, computer programs need a lot of help. One operation commonly performed to reduce the complexity of an image is edge detection, in which the complete image is replaced by a very small number of points that mark the edges of "interesting artifacts."

Figure 13.18 shows the results from a simple program attempting to paint the outline of the aircraft in black by putting a black pixel at an identified edge. The key element of the algorithm is the ability to determine unambiguously whether a pixel is part of the object of interest or not. An edge is then defined as a pixel where some of the surrounding pixels are on the object and some are not. The image selected for this exercise makes edge detection simple since the aircraft is everywhere darker than the surrounding sky.

Figure 13.18 *Result of edge detection*

The script used to generate this picture is shown in Listing 13.7. The basic approach of the algorithm is to use MATLAB's built-in array processing to detect the edges across the whole image at once. To accomplish this, we create four arrays, each one row and one column less than the original image, and each offset by one pixel, as illustrated in Figure 13.19. The array pix is in the original location, pt is one row up from that location, pl is one row left, and ptl is one row left and up. If we now collapse these arrays on top of each other, we are simultaneously comparing the values of a square of four pixels across the whole image (less one row and one column).

Listing 13.7 Edge detection

```
1. pic = imread('C-130.jpg');
2. [rows, cols, cl] = size(pic);

3. amps = uint16(pic(:,:,1))...
4.     + uint16(pic(:,:,2))...
5.     + uint16(pic(:,:,3));
```

continued on next page

```
 6. up = max(max(amps))
 7. dn = min(min(amps))
 8. fact = .5
 9. thresh = uint16(dn + fact * (up - dn))

10. pix = amps(2:end, 2:end);
11. ptl = amps(1:end-1, 1:end-1);
12.  pt = amps(1:end-1, 2:end);
13.  pl = amps(2:end, 1:end-1);

14. alloff= and(and((pix > thresh), ( pt  > thresh)),...
15.              and(( pl > thresh), (ptl > thresh)));
16. allon = and(and((pix <= thresh), ( pt <= thresh)),...
17.              and(( pl <= thresh), (ptl <= thresh)));
18. edges = and(not(allon), not(alloff));
19. layer = uint8(ones(rows-1, cols-1) *255);
20. layer(edges) = 0;
21. outline(:,:,1) = layer;
22. outline(:,:,2) = layer;
23. outline(:,:,3) = layer;
24. image(outline)
25. imwrite(outline, 'c-130 edges.jpg', 'jpg')
```

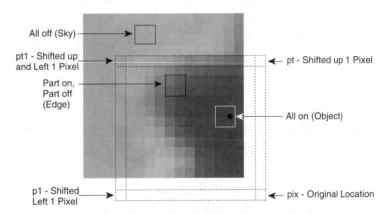

Figure 13.19 *Overlapping picture layers*

In Listing 13.7:

Lines 1 and 2: Read the original image and determine its size.

Lines 3–5: Construct an array of size rows x cols containing the total color intensity of each pixel. The class uint16, using two bytes instead of one, is big enough for the sum of three units8s.

Lines 6–9: Rather than guess an amplitude threshold, we compute a threshold halfway between the maximum and minimum intensities across the picture.

Lines 10–13: Set up the four overlapping arrays offset by a pixel each.

Lines 14 and 15: The logical array `alloff` will be true wherever all four adjacent pixels have an intensity above the threshold—these are on the sky.

Lines 16 and 17: The logical array `allon` will be true wherever all four adjacent pixels have an intensity below the threshold—these are on the aircraft.

Line 18: The pixels we are looking for are those where the pixel is neither completely sky nor completely aircraft.

Line 19: Makes a white image the same size as the logical arrays.

Line 20: Sets the edges to black.

Lines 21–25: Put that layer into the RGB layers, show the image, and write it to the disk.

Observation   Clearly, while there is much more to be done with this data for it to be useful, the complexity of this image has been reduced from 12 million `uint8` values with no real meaning to a small number of data values that outline an object of interest. Algorithms beyond the scope of this text could be used to convert these outlining points to polynomial shapes. These shapes could then be matched against projections of 3-D models to actually identify the object in the picture.

 Chapter Summary

This chapter covered the following:

- Images represented internally in MATLAB in bit-mapped, gray scale, or true color form
- Image files that come in a large variety of formats; MATLAB provides a single reader function and a single writer function to manipulate all the common image types
- Common operations on images, including cropping, stretching or shrinking, and concatenating and pasting an image onto a surface
- An engineering example showing how edge detection begins the process of extracting meaning from an image

Special Characters, Reserved Words, and Functions

Special Characters, Reserved Words, and Functions	Description	Discussed in This Section
`image(pic)`	Displays an image in a figure of fixed dimensions with axes	13.3
`imread(file)`	Reads an image file	13.3
`imshow(pic)`	Displays an image in a figure of variable dimensions without axes (not available in all MATLAB versions)	13.3
`imwrite(data, file, format)`	Writes an image file	13.3
`handle = light ('Property', 'value', ...)`	Creates a light source with the specified properties	13.4.5
`linspace(from, to, n)`	Defines a linearly spaced vector	13.2.1, 13.4.1
`material <spec>`	Sets the material quality of a surface	13.4.5
`rot90(A,n)`	Rotates A by 90° clockwise n times	13.4.4
`tril(A)`	Reduces A to its lower triangular half with zeros in the upper triangle	13.4.4
`uint8/16`	Unsigned integer type with the specified number of bits	13.1

 Self Test

Use the following questions to check your understanding of the material in this chapter:

True or False

1. An image whose color values are all 0 will be all white on the screen.

2. MATLAB uses one image reader for all image file types.

3. The normal operations of creation, slicing, and concatenation can be used to manipulate images.

4. `rot90(A)` rotates a 3-D array by 90° clockwise.

5. Edge detection dramatically reduces the amount of data to be processed by image identification software.

Fill in the Blanks

1. Each pixel of a true color image is stored as _____ values of type _____ containing values _____.

2. Gray scale images store the black-to-white intensity value for each _____ as a _____.

3. When MATLAB reads JPEG files, they are _____ as _____ images containing _____.

4. Once a picture has been read into MATLAB, you can display it in a _____ with the _____ function.

5. _____ an image discards pixels around one or more edges; _____ an image discards pixels within its borders; _____ an image involves replicating pixels.

6. The _____ operator mirrors an array about its _____.

 Programming Projects

1. Consider the following image (assume it is a perfect square), saved under the file *mysquare.jpg*:

A	B
C	D

And the following code:
```
b = imread('mysquare.jpg');
[n,m,l] = size(b);
a = b(1:end, 1:n/2, :);
c = b(1:end, (n/2 + 1):end, :);
b = [c a];
imshow(b);
```

Which of these will the picture shown on the last line most resemble?

C	D
A	B

a.

B	A
D	C

b.

A
C
B
D

c.

B
D
A
C

d.

2. Given an image file called *american_flag.jpg* in which the colors are red, white, and blue, and the code as follows:

```
af = imread('american_flag.jpg');
[r1,c1] = find(af(:,:,1) == 255 ...
              && af(:,:,2) == 0 ...
              && af(:,:,3) == 0);
[r2,c2] = find(af(:,:,1) == 0 ...
              && af(:,:,2) == 0 ...
              && af(:,:,3) == 255);
[r3,c3] = find(af(:,:,1) == 255 ...
              && af(:,:,2) == 255 ...
              && af(:,:,3) == 255);
af(r1,c1,:) = 0;
af(r2,c2,:) = 255;
af(r3,c3,2:3) = 0;
image(af)
```

what happens in the resulting image?

3. Given the following code:

```
buzz = imread('GTBuzz.jpg');
```

which of the following lines of code would cause buzz to be displayed in the greenest color?

```
a.   buzz(:, :, 1) = 0;
b.   buzz(:, :, 1) = 255;
c.   buzz(:, :, 2) = 0;
d.   buzz(:, :, 2) = 255;
e.   buzz(:, :, 3) = 0;
g.   buzz(:, :, 3) = 255;
```

4. The edge detection algorithm in Section 13.5 applies only to true color images. Rewrite it to apply it to bit-mapped images.

5. Write a script that reads the image *uselessTA.jpg* and converts it into an RGB matrix. The script then displays a sub-image of *uselessTA.jpg*. The sub-image starts at pixel number 50 on both the x and y axes. The height and width of the sub-image are each 50 pixels.

6. Consider this code that reads in an image saved as *myimage.jpg*:

```
b = imread('myimage.jpg');
[m,n,l] = size(b);
count = 0;
for i = 1:m
    for j = 1:n
        if ( <A> (double(b(i, j, <B> )))) == <C>
            count = count + 1;
        end
    end
end
```

What would you put in the place of <A>, <B>, and <C> to give you the number of completely white pixels in the image?

7. You are provided an image and your job is to convert the full-sized image to one that is one-fourth of the original size. Normally when image processing software is required to resize an image, a complex resizing algorithm is used to accomplish the conversion. We will attempt to duplicate this conversion.

Write a function called resizeMe that takes in a string as an input corresponding to an image file name. The function should then resize the image to one-fourth its original size and display it.

Additionally, your function should use the built-in function imwrite to create an image file containing the new image, named with the original file name preceded by 'SM'. For example, if the original file is called *yellow_bird.jpg*, the new file should be called *SMyellow_bird.jpg*.

> **Hint**
>
> To generate a pixel in the smaller image, take the average of four pixels that make up a square at that position in the original image.

Note: Your function should work with ALL .jpg files! So be sure to test it with multiple files of different sizes. Remember image matrices have to be of type uint8, so make sure to cast the result at the end.

You must use iteration to accomplish this task.

8. Write a function called IMrotate that takes in an image matrix and a number. The number represents the number of times the function will rotate the image by 90°. A negative number signifies counter-clockwise rotation, and a positive one signifies clockwise rotation. You are not allowed to use the built-in function rot90(...).

> **Hint**
>
> Rotating counter-clockwise once is the same as rotating clockwise three times.

Processing Sound

Chapter Objectives

This chapter discusses the following:

- How sound is physically recorded and played back, and MATLAB's internal storage of sound

- Operations that can be performed with the original time trace

- The ability to transform the data into the frequency domain, and the physical significance of the transformed data

- Operations that can be performed in the frequency domain

14.1 The Physics of Sound
14.2 Recording and Playback
14.3 MATLAB Implementation
14.4 Time Domain Operations
    14.4.1 Slicing and Concatenating Sound
    14.4.2 Musical Background
    14.4.3 Changing Sound Frequency Poorly
    14.4.4 Changing Sound Frequency Well
14.5 The Fast Fourier Transform
    14.5.1 Background
    14.5.2 MATLAB Implementation
    14.5.3 Simple Spectral Analysis
14.6 Frequency Domain Operations
    14.6.1 Analyzing Instrument Sound
    14.6.2 Adding Sounds to the Spectrum
    14.6.3 Manipulating the Spectrum
14.7 Engineering Example—Oil Rig Structural Integrity

14.1 The Physics of Sound

Any sound source produces sound in the form of pressure fluctuations in the air. While the air molecules move infinitesimal distances in order to propagate the sound, the important part of sound propagation is that pressure waves move rapidly through the air by causing air molecules to "jostle" each other. These pressure fluctuations can be viewed as analog signals—data that has a continuous range of values. These signals have two attributes: their amplitude and their frequency characteristics.

In absolute terms, sound is measured as the **amplitude** of pressure fluctuations on a surface like an ear drum or a microphone. However, the primary characteristic of this data is its dynamic range. Our ears are able to detect small sounds with amplitudes around 10^{10} (10 billion) times smaller than the loudest comfortable sound. Sound intensity is therefore usually reported logarithmically, measured in decibels where the intensity of a sound in decibels is calculated as follows:

$$I_{DB} = 10 \log_{10}(I / I_0)$$

where I is the measured pressure fluctuation and I_0 is a reference pressure usually established as the lowest pressure fluctuation a really good ear can detect, 2×10^{-4} dynes/cm^2.

Also, sounds are pressure fluctuations at certain **frequencies**. The human ear can hear sounds as low as 50 Hz and as high as 20 kHz. Voices on the telephone sound odd because the upper frequency is limited by the telephone equipment to 4 kHz. Typically, hearing damage due to exposure to excessive sound levels causes an ear to lose sensitivity to high and/or low frequencies.

14.2 Recording and Playback

Early attempts at sound recording concentrated first on mechanical, and later magnetic, methods for storing and reproducing sound. The phonograph/record player depended on the motion of a needle in a groove as a cylinder or disk rotated at constant speed under the playback head. Not surprisingly, when you see the incredible dynamic range required, even the best stereos could not reproduce high-quality sound. Later, analog magnetic tape in various forms replaced the phonograph, offering less wear on the recording and better, but still limited, dynamic range. Digital recording has almost completely supplanted analog recording, and will be the subject of this chapter.

Of course, sound amplitude in analog form is unintelligible to a computer—it must be turned into an electrical signal by a microphone, amplified to suitable voltage levels, digitized, and stored, as shown in Figure 14.1. The key to successful digital recording and playback—whether by digital tape machines, compact disks, or computer files—is the design of the analog-to-digital (A/D)

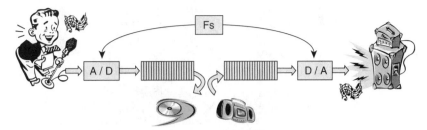

Figure 14.1 *Mechanics of sound recording and playback*

and digital-to-analog (D/A) devices. The reader should remember that this is still low-level data. Each word coming out of the A/D or going into the D/A merely represents the pressure on the microphone at a point in time.

The primary parameter governing the sound quality is the **recording rate**—how quickly they record samples of the sound (the sampling rate). The background theory of sampling is too deep for this text. Interested readers should research Nyquist on a good search engine. For our purposes, we want the sampling rate to be twice the highest frequency you are likely to encounter, usually around 20,000 samples per second.

The other parameter, the **resolution** of the recorded data, has remarkably little effect on the quality of the recording to an untrained ear. The resolution is usually either 8 bits (−128 to 127) or 16 bits (−32,768 to 32767). While 8-bit resolution ought to offer very limited dynamic range, and theoretically should be used only for recording speech, in practice it produces excellent reproductions of music also. However, 16-bit resolution, which still does not have sufficient resolution to capture the complete 100dB range discussed above, reproduces high-quality music superbly.

These parameters must be received from the functions that read pre-recorded files of sound data. To be able to play such a file, we must receive not only the data stream, but also information indicating the sample frequency, Fs, and the word size.

14.3 MATLAB Implementation

MATLAB offers the tools for reading sound files in two formats: `.wav` files (`wavread(...)`), and `.au` files (`auread(...)`). Both return three variables: the vector of sound values in the range (−1 ... 1), the sampling frequency in Hz (samples per second), and the number of bits used to record the data (8 or 16).

To play a sound file, MATLAB provides the function `sound(data, rate)` where `data` is the vector of sound values, and `rate` is the playback frequency, usually the frequency at which the sound values were recorded.

We will see that the function `sound(...)` passes the data directly to the computer's sound card, and does not wait for the card to finish playing the

Exercise 14.1 The effect of data resolution

Do It Yourself

Enter the following commands in the Command window:

```
>> [b16, F16, n] = wavread('brooklyn16.wav');
>> sound(b16, F16)
>> [b8, F8, n] = wavread('brooklyn8.wav');
>> sound(b8, F8)
```

sound. A number of .wav files are included at the Addison-Wesley Instructor Resource Center (www.aw.com/irc) to demonstrate certain aspects of sound files. Try Exercise 14.1, which compares two recordings of the identical sound bite recorded at 16-bit and 8-bit resolution, respectively.

Exercise 14.1 compares sound files stored in 8-bit and 16-bit form by reading and playing each version. Unless you have very good audio equipment and a really good musical ear, in spite of the discussion of the ideal physics, it is very hard to distinguish between 8-bit and 16-bit recording quality.

 ## 14.4 Time Domain Operations

First we consider three kinds of operation, on sound files in the time domain: slicing, playback frequency changes, and sound file frequency changes.

14.4.1 Slicing and Concatenating Sound

Consider the problem of constructing an "audio ransom note" by choosing and assembling words from published speeches. This exercise is strictly experimental in nature, but can produce some interesting results. There are a number of Web sites that offer free .wav files containing memorable speech fragments from movies, TV shows, and cartoons.

The resource center (www.aw.com/irc) contains a sampling of such files. In particular, it has the *Apollo 13* speech, "Houston, we have a problem"; "Frankly, my dear ..." from *Gone with the Wind*; and "You can't handle the truth" from *A Few Good Men*. Exercise 14.2 describes the process of assembling parts of these speeches into a semi-coherent conversation. Consider the following exercises that could be turned into scripts.

The first part of Exercise 14.2 reads the *Apollo 13* speech, plays the speech, and plots the data (with the data index as x-axis). The resulting plot is shown in the left half of Figure 14.2. Since the sound actually includes more than we need, the next step is to crop this file to keep only the words we need. By listening to the speech using the function sound(...), and judiciously zooming and panning the plot, it is possible to narrow down the location in

Exercise 14.2 Locating the first part of the speech

Do It Yourself

Step 1: Find the location of problem speech.

```
>> [houston, Fsh] = wavread('al3prob.wav');
>> subplot(1, 2, 1)
>> plot(houston);
>> sound(houston, Fsh);
```

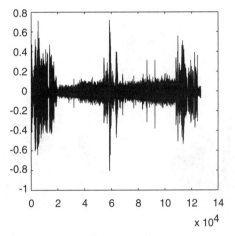 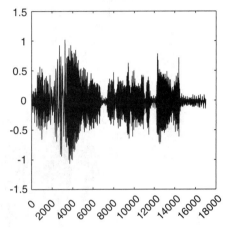

Figure 14.2 *Apollo 13 speech*

the file where the problem speech starts, at about 111000. In Exercise 14.3 you will extract the first part of the speech.

In Exercise 14.3 we truncate the speech file to the words we need and also, realizing that the amplitude of these words is a little low, raise its amplitude by a factor of 2.

In Exercise 14.4, by a similar process, we remove "my dear" from the "frankly, my dear ..." speech, reducing its amplitude by one-half, which results in Figure 14.3.

 Exercise 14.3 Extracting the first part of the speech

Do It Yourself

Step 2: Extract the problem speech.

```
>> clip = 110000;
>> prob = houston(clip:end)*2;
>> subplot(1, 2, 2)
>> plot(prob)
```

Exercise 14.4 Extracting the second part

Do It Yourself

Step 3: Remove "my dear".

```
>> figure
>> [damn, Fsd] = wavread('givdamn2.wav');
>> subplot(1, 2, 1)
>> plot(damn);
>> lo = 4500;
>> hi = 8700;
>> sdamn = [damn(1:lo); damn(hi:end) ] * .5;
>> subplot(1, 2, 2)
>> plot(sdamn);
```

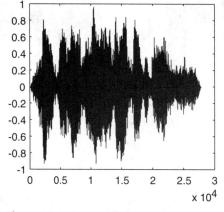
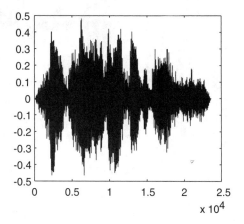

Figure 14.3 *Gone with the Wind speech*

Finally, in Exercise 14.5, we assemble the complete speech by concatenating these two fragments with the speech from *A Few Good Men*. The resulting picture is shown in Figure 14.4.

Exercise 14.5 Completing the speech

Do It Yourself

Step 4: Assemble the speech.

```
>> [truth, Fst] = wavread('truth1.wav');
>> speech = [prob; sdamn; truth * .7];
>> figure
>> plot(speech);
>> sound(speech, Fst);
```

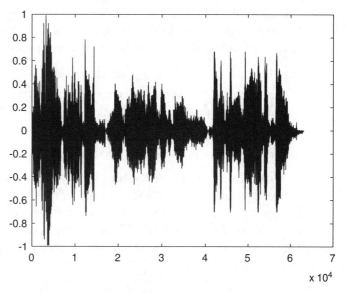

Figure 14.4 *The complete speech*

14.4.2 Musical Background

For good historical reasons, music is usually described graphically on a music score. The graphics describe for each note to be played its pitch and its duration, together with other notations indicating how to introduce expression and quality into the music. However, this graphical notation is not amenable to the simple representation of music we need for these experiments. Rather, we will use the representation illustrated in Figure 14.5. The right side of this figure shows a standard piano keyboard, the index of each white note, and the number of half steps necessary to achieve the pitch of each note. On the left side of the figure, we see the method to be used in this text to describe simple tunes. It will consist of an array with two columns and n rows, where n is the number of notes to be played for each tune. The first column is the key number to play, and the second column is the number of beats each note should be held.

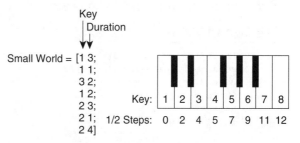

Figure 14.5 *Musical notes*

The examples to follow will manipulate the file `piano.wav` to produce a snippet of music. This file is a recording[1] of a single note played on a piano. Other files provided in the resource center are the same note played on a variety of instruments. There are two ways to accomplish this, as follows:

1. Playing each note at a different playback frequency
2. Stretching or shrinking each note to match the required note pitch and playing them all at the same playback frequency

The first way is easier to understand and code, but very inflexible; the second method is a little more difficult to implement, but completely extensible.

Musically speaking, if a sound is played at twice its natural frequency, it is heard as one musical octave higher. The steps from one note to the next higher octave are divided into 7 increments: 5 whole note steps and 2 half note steps, for a total of 12 half note steps. These 12 half steps are logarithmically divided where the frequency change between half-note steps is $2^{1/12}$.

14.4.3 Changing Sound Frequency Poorly

We begin by implementing a scale and a tune by changing the playback frequency. There are a few practical issues to deal with in this simple example:

- Since different notes are played at different frequencies, we cannot concatenate different notes in the same sound file.
- Changing the playback frequency also changes the duration of the note because it consumes more or less data items in a given period of time. Therefore, we have to manage the number of data items sent to the `sound(...)` function.
- Since the `sound(...)` function starts playing the sound, but immediately continues to the next line of code, it is necessary to pause until the sound is finished playing before continuing to process the next sound.

Play a Scale First, we examine one way to play a scale—keys 1–8 played in order at a steady pace. Consider the code shown in Listing 14.1 that plays a major scale on the piano (the white notes seen in Figure 14.5) and saves the frequencies and durations for subsequent use.

Listing 14.1 Playing a scale poorly

```
1. [note, Fs] = wavread('instr_piano.wav');
2. count = floor(length(note)/8);
3. wait = count / Fs;
4. whole = 2^(1/6);
5. half = 2^(1/12);
6. for i = 1:8
```

continued on next page

---

[1] http://chronos.ece.miami.edu/~dasp/samples/samples.html.

```
 7.      cnt(i) = count;
 8.      freq(i) = Fs;
 9.      sound(note(1: count), Fs);
10.      pause(wait)
11.      if (i == 3) || (i == 7)
12.          Fs = Fs * half;
13.          count = round(count * half);
14.      else
15.          Fs = Fs * whole;
16.          count = round(count * whole);
17.      end
18. end
```

In Listing 14.1:

Line 1: Reads the piano note file.

Line 2: We arbitrarily decide that the duration of each note will be one-eighth of the length of the piano note.

Line 3: We compute the wait time in seconds between notes.

Lines 4 and 5: Compute the frequency ratios for half notes and whole notes.

Line 6: Plays the eight white notes one at a time.

Lines 7 and 8: Save the length and frequency of each note.

Line 9: Plays the note.

Line 10: Pauses to allow the sound to be completed.

Lines 11–17: Update the duration and frequency. Referring to Figure 14.5, after the third and seventh notes, there is a half-note step; for all the others, it is a whole-note step. We increase the playback frequency by that factor, and to maintain the duration of the note, we also increase the number of samples played by the same factor.

Play a Simple Tune Now we extend the above script by using an array of note frequencies and durations to play the simple tune diagrammed in Figure 14.5. A script that extends the code from Listing 14.1 to play this tune is shown in Listing 14.2.

Listing 14.2 Play a tune fragment poorly

```
1. smallworld = [ 1 3; 1 1; 3 2; 1 2; 2 3; 2 1; 2 4]
2. l = length(smallworld);
3. for i = 1:l
4.     f = freq(smallworld(i,1));
5.     n = cnt(smallworld(i,1)) * smallworld(i,2);
6.     sound(note(1:n), f);
7.     pause(wait*smallworld(i,2));
8. end
```

In Listing 14.2:

> Line 1: Shows the tune array diagrammed in Figure 14.5.
>
> Lines 2 and 3: Play the notes for each row in the array.
>
> Line 4: Extracts the frequency for the current note previously stored in the vector `freq(...)`.
>
> Line 5: Computes the note duration as the stored duration multiplied by the number of note steps required by the tune.
>
> Lines 6 and 7: Play the note and pause as before.

14.4.4 Changing Sound Frequency Well

This time-domain exercise is to manipulate the piano note file to produce a snippet of music at the same playback frequency throughout. In order to change the note frequency without changing the playback frequency, we have to remove or add the appropriate number of data samples from or to the original data file. This is exactly the same process as we used to stretch or shrink images in Section 13.4.1. Use Exercise 14.6 to experiment with this technique for playing notes at different pitches.

In Exercise 14.6, first we read and play the note at its natural frequency. Then we raise its pitch by removing about one-third of the samples, and then lower the pitch by an octave by doubling the number of samples.

Play a Scale Listing 14.3 shows a script that uses this capability to play the same scale as before on the piano. It repeatedly shortens the vector `newNote` to increase the frequency of the note played.

In Listing 14.3:

> Lines 1–3: Read the note and set the step multipliers.
>
> Line 4: Plays eight notes of the scale.
>
> Lines 5 and 6: Play the note and pause.
>
> Lines 7–11: Choose the appropriate factor.
>
> Line 12: Shrinks the note file by the chosen factor.

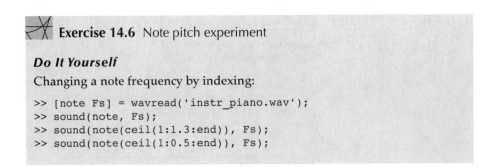

Exercise 14.6 Note pitch experiment

Do It Yourself

Changing a note frequency by indexing:

```
>> [note Fs] = wavread('instr_piano.wav');
>> sound(note, Fs);
>> sound(note(ceil(1:1.3:end)), Fs);
>> sound(note(ceil(1:0.5:end)), Fs);
```

Listing 14.3 Play a scale by shrinking the note

```
1.  [note, Fs] = wavread('instr_piano.wav');
2.  half = 2^(1/12);
3.  whole = half^2;
4.  for index = 1:8
5.      sound(note, Fs);
6.      pause(.5);
7.      if (index == 3) || (index == 7)
8.          mult = half;
9.      else
10.         mult = whole;
11.     end
12.     note = note(ceil(1:mult:end));
13. end;
```

Play a Simple Tune We now use that same technique illustrates a script to build a playable .wav file using the note shrinking technique. The script is shown in Listing 14.4. It uses the array steps to decide how many half-tone steps are necessary to reach the nth note on the scale, and uses the array doremi to define the tune. The array doremi is illustrated in Figure 14.5—the first column specifies the pitch (the note on the scale), and the second the duration in "beats." The script sets the beat time to be 0.2 seconds.

The goal of the script is to put the notes into a single sound array called tune, as illustrated in Figure 14.6, rather than playing the notes "on the fly."

This is accomplished as follows:

- Create an empty array, tune, of the appropriate length (the length of the original note plus the total number of beats in the song)
- Initialize storeAt to store the first note at the start of the tune
- Iterate across the tune definition array doremi with the following steps:

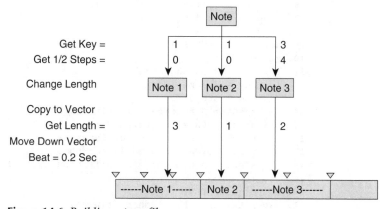

Figure 14.6 *Building a tune file*

- Start with the original `note`
- Get the key index to decide how many times to raise the `note` array by half a step
- Raise the `note` to the right pitch and save it as `theNote`
- Add that `theNote` vector to the `tune` vector, starting at `storeAt`
- Move the `storeAt` variable down the `tune` vector a distance equivalent to the duration of that note

When all the notes have been added to the tune file, play the tune and save it as a `.wav` file.

In Listing 14.4:

Lines 1–6: Read the file and set up the parameters.

Line 7: A vector defining how may half-steps it takes to set the frequency of notes 1–8.

Line 8: The time between notes of length 1—the beat of the tune.

Line 9: The number of samples to play for one beat of the tune.

Line 10: Begins storing notes at the beginning of the tune.

Line 11: Inserts each note in the song file into the tune file.

Line 12: Fetches the key number.

Line 13: Extracts the number of half-steps required for this note.

Line 14: Stretches the bass note by this multiplier.

Lines 15 and 16: Compute where the end of the note will be stored.

Listing 14.4 Building a tune file

```
1. [note, Fs] = wavread('instr_piano.wav');
2. half = 2^(1/12);
3. doremi = [1 3; 2 1; 3 3; 1 1; 3 2; 1 2; 3 4; 2 3;
4.           3 1; 4 1; 4 1; 3 1; 2 1; 4 8; 3 3; 4 1;
5.           5 3; 3 1; 5 2; 3 2; 5 4; 4 3; 5 1; 6 1;
6.           6 1; 5 1; 4 1; 6 4 ];
7. steps = [0 2 4 5 7 9 11 12];
8. dt = .2;
9. nCt = floor(dt*Fs);
10. storeAt = 1;
11. for index = 1:length(doremi)
12.     key = doremi(index,1);
13.     pow = steps(key);
14.     theNote = note(ceil(1:half^pow:end));
15.     noteLength = length(theNote);
16.     noteEnd = storeAt + noteLength - 1;
17.     tune(storeAt:noteEnd,1) =  theNote;
18.     storeAt = storeAt + doremi(index,2) * nCt;
19. end
20. sound(tune, Fs)
21. wavwrite(tune, Fs, 'dohAdeer.wav')
```

Line 17: Copies the note into the tune file.

Line 18: Advance the `storeAt` index down the tune file by the beat count multiplied by the beats required for this note.

Lines 20 and 21: Play the complete tune and save it as a `.wav` file.

 ## 14.5 The Fast Fourier Transform

Typically, the time history display of a sound shows you the amplitude of the sound as a function of time but makes no attempt at showing the frequency content. While this works for slicing voice files, we are often more interested in the frequency content of a sound file, for which we need a different presentation—a spectrum display.

14.5.1 Background

In general, a spectrum display shows the amount of sound energy in a given frequency band throughout the duration of the sound analyzed but ignores the time at which the sound at that frequency was generated. Many acoustic amplifiers (see Figure 14.7) include two features that allow you to customize the sound output:

- A spectral display that changes values as the sound is played, indicating the amount of sound energy (vertically) in different frequency bands (horizontally)
- Filter controls to change the relative amplification in different frequency bands

In the following paragraphs, we will consider only the analysis of the sound frequency content. The ability to reshape the sound frequency content as the sound plays is beyond the scope of this text.

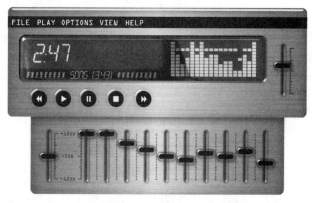

Figure 14.7 *A typical spectrum display*

To achieve the motion of the spectrum display, software to analyze a segment of the sound file runs periodically and updates the spectrum display. Typically, perhaps 20 times a second, 1/20th second of sound file is analyzed and transformed. The software used for this conversion is known as the Fourier transform.

The mathematics of the Fourier transform is beyond the scope of this book. However, we can make use of the tools it offers without concerning ourselves with the mathematics. There are a number of implementations of this transform; perhaps the most commonly used is the Fast Fourier Transform (FFT). The FFT uses clever matrix manipulations to optimize the mathematics needed to generate the forward (time to frequency) and reverse (frequency to time) transforms.

14.5.2 MATLAB Implementation

Figure 14.8 illustrates the overall process of transforming between the time domain and frequency domain. It starts with a simple sound file, a vector of N sound values in the range (−1.0 to 1.0), which, if played back at a sample frequency Fs entries per second, reproduces the sound. Examining the parameters involved, we see the following:

N	the number of samples
Fs	the sampling frequency
Δt	the time between samples, computed as 1/Fs
Tmax	the maximum time is N $\times \Delta t$

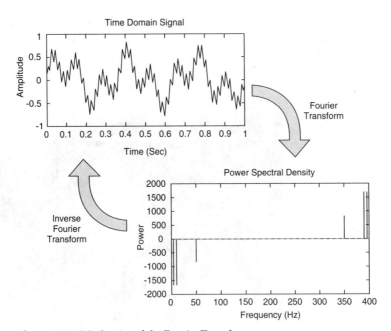

Figure 14.8 *Mechanics of the Fourier Transform*

The FFT consumes a file with these characteristics and produces a frequency spectrum with a corresponding set of characteristics. The frequency spectrum consists of the same number, N, of data points, each of which are complex values with real and imaginary parts. (While many displays actually plot the magnitude of the spectrum values, to accomplish the inverse transform, the complex values must be retained.) The frequency values are "folded" on the plot so that zero frequency occurs at either end of the spectrum, and the maximum frequency occurs in the middle, at spectrum data point N/2.

The equivalent characteristics for the spectrum data are as follows:

N   the number of samples

Δf   the frequency difference between samples, computed as
           1/tmax

fmax   the maximum frequency is $^1/_2 \times$ N $\times$ Δf

In MATLAB, the FFT is mechanized using the function fft(...), which consumes the time history and produces the complex spectrum file. The inverse FFT function, ifft(...), takes a spectrum array with these parameters and reconstructs the time history. This pair of functions provides a powerful set of tools for manipulating sound files.

14.5.3 Simple Spectral Analysis

Listing 14.5 illustrates a script that creates 10 seconds of an 8 Hz sine wave, plots the first second of it, performs the FFT, and plots the real and imaginary parts of the spectrum. Notice the following:

- A sine wave in the time domain transforms to a line in the frequency domain because all its energy is concentrated at that frequency—8 Hz in this example.
- Since the FFT is a linear process, multiple sine or cosine waves added together at different frequencies have additive effects in the spectrum.
- The resulting spectrum is complex (with real and imaginary parts) and symmetrical about its center, the point of maximum frequency. On the MATLAB plot, of course, one cannot make the frequency axis labels reduce from the center to the end.
- The real part of the spectrum is mirrored about the center; the imaginary part is mirrored and inverted.
- The phase of the complex spectrum retains the position of the sine wave in the time domain—it would be totally real for a cosine wave symmetrically placed in time, and totally imaginary for a sine wave in the same relationship.
- The mathematics involved in computing the magnitude of the spectrum value requires integrating sin2ωt in time that results in t/2. Because t is 10,000 samples, the steady state value of the spectral amplitude is 5,000.

The script in Listing 14.5 creates three subplots: the original sine wave, and then the amplitude and phase of the spectrum.

In Listing 14.5:

> Lines 1–5: Set up the time domain signal.
>
> Lines 6–10: Plot the front part of the time trace.
>
> Line 11: Performs the FFT.
>
> Lines 12–14: Set up the frequency plots.
>
> Lines 15–19: Plot the spectrum real part.
>
> Lines 20–24: Plot the spectrum imaginary part.

Figure 14.9 shows the result from running this script. It confirms the earlier statement that the real part of the spectrum is mirrored about the center frequency, and the imaginary part is mirrored and inverted.

Listing 14.5 FFT of a sine wave

```
 1. dt = 1/400              % sampling period (sec)
 2. pts = 10000             % number of points
 3. f = 8                   % frequency
 4. t = (1:pts) * dt;       % time array for plotting
 5. x = sin(2*pi*f*t);
 6. subplot(2, 2, 1)
 7. plot(t(1:end/25), x(1:end/25));
 8. title('time domain sine wave')
 9. ylabel('amplitude')
10. xlabel('time (sec)')
11. Y = fft(x);             % perform the transform
12. df = 1 / t(end)         % the frequency interval
13. fmax = df * pts / 2
14. f = (1:pts) * 2 * fmax / pts;
                            % frequencies for plotting
15. subplot(2,2,3)
16. plot(f, real(Y))
17. title('real part')
18. xlabel('frequency (Hz)')
19. ylabel('energy')
20. subplot(2,2,4)
21. plot(f, imag(Y))
22. title('imaginary part')
23. xlabel('frequency (Hz)')
24. ylabel('energy')
```

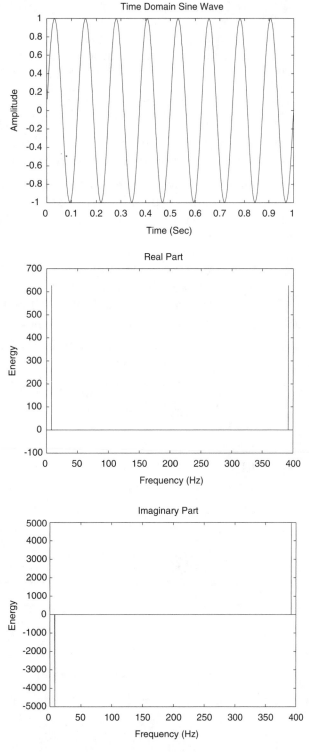

Figure 14.9 *FFT of a sine wave*

14.6 Frequency Domain Operations

We will consider three applications in the frequency domain—analyzing the spectral quality of different musical instruments, inserting a sine wave in the frequency domain, and a simple form of digital filtering.

14.6.1 Analyzing Instrument Sounds

The intent of this section is to develop a plot showing the spectra of a selection of different musical instruments. We will first build a function that plots the spectrum for a single instrument, and then build the script to create all the plots.

Listing 14.6 shows a function that reads the .wav file of an instrument from the music samples in the University of Miami's Audio and Signal Processing Laboratory.[2] All the instruments are carefully playing a note at about 260 Hz.

In Listing 14.6:

> Line 1: Shows a function consuming two strings: the name of the instrument and the title of the plot.
>
> Lines 2–5: Read the file and set up the plot parameters.
>
> Line 6: Performs the FFT and computes the absolute value.
>
> Lines 7 and 8: Scale the plot to be a percentage of the maximum energy at any frequency.
>
> Lines 9–16: Set up and plot the first 10 percent of the spectrum.

The script that uses this function to plot the instrument data is shown in Listing 14.7.

Listing 14.6 Plotting the spectrum of one instrument

```
 1. function inst(name, ttl)
% plot the spectrum of the instrument with
% the given name, with the given plot title
 2. [x, Fs] = wavread(['instr_' name '.wav']);
 3. N = length(x);
 4. dt = 1/Fs;        % sampling period (sec)
 5. t = (1:N) * dt;   % time array for plotting
 6. Y = abs(fft(x));  % perform the transform
 7. mx = max(Y);
 8. Y = Y * 100 / mx;
 9. df = 1 / t(end) ; % the frequency interval
10. fmax = df * N / 2 ;
11. f = (1:N) * 2 * fmax / N;
12. up = floor(N/10);
13. plot(f(1:up), Y(1:up) );
14. title(ttl)
15. xlabel('frequency (Hz)')
16. ylabel('energy')
```

---

[2] http://chronos.ece.miami.edu/~dasp/samples/samples.html.

Listing 14.7 Script to plot eight-instrument spectra

```
 1. rows = 4; cols = 2
 2. subplot(rows, cols, 1)
 3. inst('sax', 'Saxophone');
 4. subplot(rows, cols, 2)
 5. inst('flute', 'Flute');
 6. subplot(rows, cols, 3)
 7. inst('tbone', 'Trombone');
 8. subplot(rows, cols, 4)
 9. inst('piano', 'Piano');
10. subplot(rows, cols, 5)
11. inst('tpt', 'Trumpet');
12. subplot(rows, cols, 6)
13. inst('mutetpt', 'Muted Trumpet');
14. subplot(rows, cols, 7)
15. inst('violin', 'Violin');
16. subplot(rows, cols, 8)
17. inst('cello', 'Cello');
```

In Listing 14.7:

> Line 1: Sets up the subplot configuration.
>
> Lines 2–17: Each pair of lines makes the subplot of one instrument.
>
> The results are shown in Figure 14.10. It is interesting to notice the following:
> - All the instruments have significant amounts of energy at even multiples of the source frequency
> - The flute and piano are perhaps the purest tones with the least harmonics
> - The brass instruments have most of their energy in the second, third, and fourth harmonics rather than the base frequency
> - The strings have very strong third harmonic components
> - Those instruments with noticeable vibrato when played (flute, violin, and cello) show a marked fuzziness in their spectral peaks

Notice the following:

- None of the instruments produces a pure tone. The lowest frequency at which there is energy is usually called the fundamental frequency, and successive peaks to the right at multiples of the fundamental frequency are referred to, for example, as the first, second, and third harmonics.

- Several instruments have much more energy in the harmonics than in the fundamental frequency.

- "Families" of instruments have similar spectral shapes—the strings, for example, have strong fundamental and second harmonic energy. In principle, these characteristic spectral "signatures" can be used to synthesize the sound of instruments, and even to identify individual instruments when played in groups.

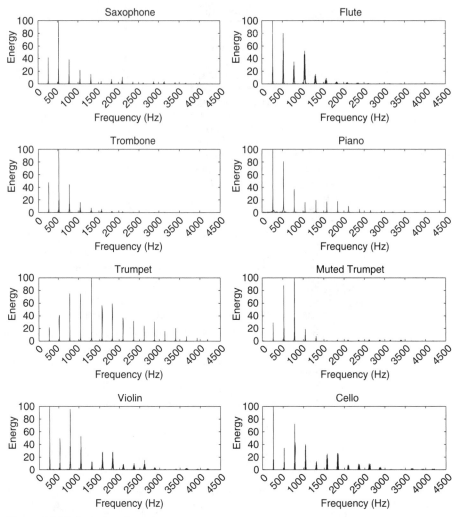

Figure 14.10 *Instrument spectra*

14.6.2 Adding Sounds to the Spectrum

The goal of this section is to understand how to build a signal with two sine waves (3 Hz and 8 Hz) in the time domain, perform the FFT, add a 50Hz wave in the spectrum, and perform the inverse FFT to construct the new time history. The script to accomplish this is shown in Listing 14.8.

Listing 14.8 Adding a signal to the spectrum

```
1. rows = 2; cols = 2;
   % set up two sine waves
2. dt = 1/400; % sampling period (sec)
3. N = 10000;  % number of points
```

continued on next page

```
 4. f1 = 3; f2 = 8; % signal frequencies
 5. t = (1:N) * dt; % time array for plotting
 6. x = sin(2*pi*f1*t) + sin(2*pi*f2*t);
 7. subplot(rows, cols, 1)
 8. plot(t(1:(1/dt)), x(1:(1/dt)))
 9. title('original signal')
10. xlabel('time (sec)')
11. Y = fft(x); % perform the transform
12. df = 1 / t(end); % the frequency interval
13. fmax = df * N / 2;
14. f = (1:N) * 2 * fmax / N; % frequencies
15. subplot(rows, cols, 2) % plot the spectrum
16. plot(f(1:N/3), abs(Y(1:N/3)))
17. title('spectrum')
18. xlabel('frequency (Hz)')
    % find the maximum value and location
19. level1 = max(abs(Y));
20. newF = 50;
21. newBasic = 50 / df;
22. newI1 = newBasic + 1;
23. newI2 = N - newBasic + 1;
24. newV = complex(0, -level1/2);
25. Y(newI1) = newV;
26. Y(newI2) = -newV;        % imaginary part negated
27. subplot(rows, cols, 4) % plot the new spectrum
28. plot(f(1:N/3), abs(Y(1:N/3)))
29. title('spectrum with added signal')
30. xlabel('frequency (Hz)')
31. y = ifft(Y);
32. subplot(rows, cols, 3)
33. plot(t(1:(1/dt)), y(1:(1/dt)))
34. title('reconstructed the new signal')
35. xlabel('time (sec)')
```

In Listing 14.8:

Line 1: Sets up the subplot configuration.

Lines 2–5: Set up the time domain parameters.

Line 6: The time trace consisting of two added frequencies.

Lines 7–10: Plot the original signal.

Line 11: Performs the FFT, preserving the complex values.

Lines 12–18: Set up and plot the absolute values of the spectrum.

Line 19: Finds the peak level on the plot.

Lines 20 and 21: Compute the basic index of the position of a 50 Hz signal.

Lines 22 and 23: The positions of the mirrored spectral spikes at 50 Hz.

Line 24: The complex value (all imaginary) to insert into the spectrum at half the maximum level.

Lines 25 and 26: Insert the spikes—one is negated because they are imaginary.

Lines 27–30: Plot the updated spectrum.

Line 31: Performs the inverse FFT.

Lines 32–35: Plot the new time trace with the 50 Hz signal added.

Figure 14.11 shows the results.

14.6.3 Manipulating the Spectrum

Adding pure sine waves to the spectrum is reasonably straightforward as long as the symmetry of the spectrum components is preserved. It is possible to consider more complex operations on the spectrum as long as these operations are performed in areas of the spectrum where there is no significant sound energy.

Consider, for example, an apparently simple project. If we compare the spectra of the trumpet and the muted trumpet shown on the third row of Figure 14.10, we might consider operating on the spectrum to apply "digital

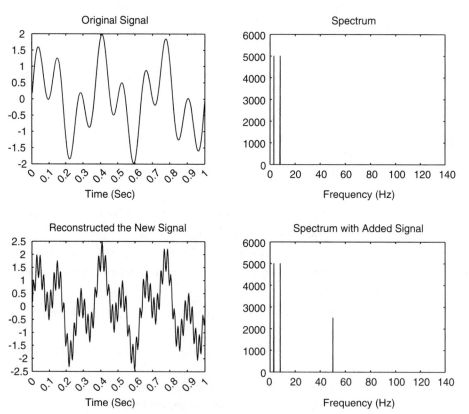

Figure 14.11 *Adding a signal*

muting" to the trumpet spectrum. It seems that this could be achieved by reducing the third harmonic by 80 percent, and eliminating all the energy in the trumpet spectrum above it.

The code shown in Listing 14.9 implements a crude approximation to such an effort, manually defining the location of the third harmonic, reducing that to 20 percent of its original size, and then zero filling the spectrum above that to remove all other harmonics.

In Listing 14.9:

Lines 1–4: Read the trumpet file and set up the parameters.

Lines 5 and 6: Play the sound and wait for it to finish.

Listing 14.9 Synthetic trumpet muting

```
1.  [x, Fs] = wavread('instr_tpt.wav');
2.  N = length(x);
3.  dt = 1/Fs ;        % sampling period (sec)
4.  t = (1:N) * dt; % time array for plotting
5.  sound(x, Fs)
6.  pause(t(N));
7.  Y = fft(x);        % perform the transform
8.  df = 1 / t(end); % the frequency interval
9.  fmax = df * N / 2;
10. f = (1:N) * 2 * fmax / N;
11. subplot(1, 2, 1);
12. frac = floor(N/10);
13. plot(f(1:frac), abs(Y(1:frac)));
14. title('trumpet original')
15. xlabel('frequency (Hz)')
16. ylabel('energy')
17. fcut = 925; %Hz
18. icut = floor(fcut / df);
19. foff = 1100; %Hz
20. ioff = floor(foff / df);
21. Y(icut:end-icut) = Y(icut:end-icut) * 0.2;
22. Y(ioff:end-ioff) = 0;
23. subplot(1, 2, 2);
24. plot(f(1:frac), abs(Y(1:frac)));
25. title('truncated trumpet')
26. xlabel('frequency (Hz)')
27. ylabel('energy')
28. y = abs(ifft(Y));
29. y = y / max(y);
30. disp('synthetic muted');
31. sound(y, Fs);
32. pause(t(N));
33. disp('real muted');
34. [x, Fs] = wavread('instr_mutetpt.wav');
35. sound(x / (max(x)*4), Fs)
```

Lines 7–16: Perform the FFT and plot the first 10 percent of the spectrum.

Lines 17–20: Since the second harmonic lies at 800 Hz, and the third at around 1070 Hz (4 * the fundamental 266 Hz frequency), we estimate the positions where the energy must be cut between the second and third harmonics, and where it must be zero, and compute the corresponding index values.

Line 21: Reduces the energy where it should be cut by 80 percent, not forgetting to leave in place the mirrored portion of the spectrum.

Line 22: Zeros out the remaining energy, again leaving the mirrored portion untouched.

Lines 23–27: Plot the digitally muted spectrum.

Line 28: Performs the inverse FFT and take the absolute value to eliminate any stray complex values introduced by asymmetry in the spectrum.

Line 29: Scales the volume to match the original sound volume.

Lines 30–32: Play the synthetic muted trumpet.

Lines 33–35: Play the real muted trumpet.

Figure 14.12 suggests that the resulting spectrum is superficially similar to a muted trumpet. However, if you run the script and listen, even an untrained ear would observe that the sound is not really the same as a real muted trumpet. The subtleties of level in the harmonics are sufficient to be noticeable even to an untrained ear.

Common Pitfalls

Changes in the spectrum have to be made under circumstances where they do not introduce sudden discontinuities in the spectral levels. These sudden discontinuities cause large, resonant "ringing" patterns in the time domain that can overpower the audio effects being created. The experiments performed in this section succeeded because they were either deliberately introducing spikes to add a single frequency, or changing the spectrum where there was no energy at the edges of the changes.

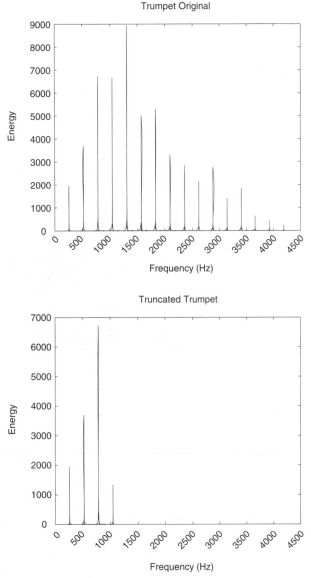

Figure 14.12 *Synthetic muted trumpet*

14.7 Engineering Example—Oil Rig Structural Integrity

Like icebergs, large off-shore oil rigs have an imposing amount of structure visible above the surface of the ocean, but even more structure beneath the surface. The Petronius Platform in the Persian Gulf, operated by Chevron and Marathon Oil, is arguably one of the world's tallest structures at 610 meters (over 2,000 feet) tall. Only 75 meters of its height is above the surface of the sea. It cost half a billion dollars to build and delivers 50,000 barrels of oil and two million cubic meters of gas every day. Figure 14.13 shows a typical oil rig on which several hundred workers are permanently housed. Especially in hostile climate conditions, these structures vibrate significantly, and are susceptible to structural damage due to corrosion and metal fatigue. A number of such rigs have sustained enough structural damage that they physically collapsed, at the cost of lives, loss of oil production, and the resources required to replace the structures.

Figure 14.13 *Oil platform*

The problem we address here is the need to determine whether the structural integrity has been compromised. The size of the structures and the depth of the water make most normal inspection procedures either physically impossible or prohibitively expensive. One technique that has shown promise is the analysis of the modes of vibration of the structure. Figure 14.14 shows the configuration of an experiment performed in 1981 to determine the feasibility of this approach. It shows the configuration of a "small" oil rig model, a shaker to vibrate the structure, a transducer to record the vibration of the structure, and the location of some deliberately induced structural damage.

The premise of this technique is that any flexible structure, like a violin string, has modes of vibration with characteristic frequencies. If the physical characteristics of the structure change—like changing the length of the violin string by placing a finger on the string—we expect the frequency of the modes of vibration to change. We can detect the frequency of these modes of vibration by capturing the vibrations at the transducer for a period of time and then performing an FFT on the data. Figure 14.15 shows the results of one such experiment. It illustrates many of the practical difficulties associated with using this technique:

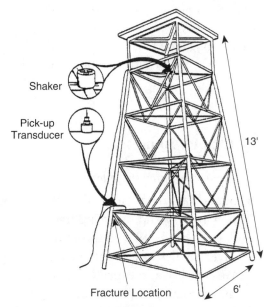

Figure 14.14 *Model diagram*

- The amount of noise generated across the spectrum makes the peaks hard to distinguish
- The noise caused by the instrumentation, such as the 60 Hz peak
- The number and resolution of the peaks

The goal of studies such as this is to determine whether the instrumentation can detect damage to a real oil rig before that damage causes structural failure, and whether the natural impact of the sea and wind can provide enough excitation of the structure to avoid the need to artificially stimulate the structure.

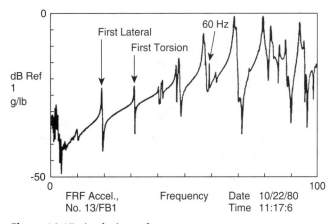

Figure 14.15 *Analysis results*

As a footnote, it was embarrassing to see that one of the oil rigs lost in the North Sea was being analyzed by an early implementation of this capability. It took a long time to resolve the legal liability issues associated with the failure of the monitoring equipment to detect this failure in time.

 Chapter Summary

This chapter presented the following:

- Sounds are read into MATLAB with specific readers that provide a time history and sampling frequency
- Sounds can be played through the computer's sound system and saved to disk as a sound file ready for playing on any digital player
- We can slice and concatenate sounds to edit speeches and change the frequency of the sound to change its pitch
- We can analyze the frequency content of sound using the Fast Fourier Transform (FFT)
- We can modify the spectra by adding, deleting, or changing the sound levels at chosen frequencies under certain controlled conditions

 Special Characters, Reserved Words, and Functions

Special Characters, Reserved Words, and Functions	Description	Discussed in This Section
`[data Fs nb] = auread(file)`	Reads an `.au` sound file in `.wav` format	14.3
`auwrite((data, Fs, nb, file)`	Writes a sound file in `.au` format	14.3
`fft(ftime)`	Performs the Fast Fourier Transform on a sound file	14.5.2
`ifft(ffreq)`	Performs the inverse Fourier transform on a spectrum file	14.5.2
`sound(data, Fs)`	Plays a sound file	14.3
`[data Fs nb] = wavread(file)`	Reads a `.wav` sound file in `.wav` format	14.3
`wavwrite(data, Fs, nb, file)`	Writes a sound file in `.wav` format	14.3

 **Self Test**

Use the following questions to check your understanding of the material in this chapter:

True or False

1. Playing a sound file at double the recorded sample frequency raises its pitch by an octave.

2. Removing every other sample from a sound file lowers the pitch by an octave.

3. The resolution of the recorded data has a significant effect on the quality of the recording.

4. After performing an FFT, the zero frequency occurs at either end of the spectrum and the maximum frequency occurs in the middle.

5. Since the mathematics of the FFT are linear, the spectrum of a sound added in the time domain is also added in the frequency domain.

Fill in the Blanks

1. Sound pressure fluctuations have two attributes: their

   _____ and their _____ characteristics.

2. Each word coming out of the _____ or going into the

   _____ merely represents the _____

   on the microphone at a point in time.

3. The steps from one note to the next higher octave are divided into

   _____ increments: _____ whole note

   steps and _____ half note steps, for a total of

   _____ half note steps.

4. A spectrum display shows the amount of _____ in a

   given _____ throughout the duration of the sound

   analyzed.

Programming Projects

1. Write a script to read in the file `bubble.wav` and perform the following operations on its data.

   a. Store the sampling period in the variable `dt`.

   b. Store the duration of the sound in the variable `t`.

   c. Store the number of samples in the variable `n`.

   d. Store the difference in frequency between the samples (after the FFT) in the variable `df`.

   e. Store the maximum frequency in the variable `f_max`.

   f. Create an array containing the frequency at each sample in the variable `f`.

   g. Create a new sound that has double the frequency of the original sound in the variable `sound_Double`.

   h. Create a new sound that is the same as the original except that the pitch is raised by five half tones. Store your answer in the variable `raised_pitch`.

   i. Plot the original sound, `sound_Double`, and `raised_pitch` all in the same row of a figure using `subplot`. Label each plot accordingly.

   j. Play each of the sounds at a sampling frequency of 22050 Hz in the following order: original sound, `sound_Double`, and `raised_pitch`.

   k. Plot the sound waveform in both the time and frequency domains. Label your plots appropriately. Use `figure` to start a new figure, and `subplot` (one row, two columns).

2. Write and test a script to assemble your own speech from speeches at Addison-Wesley's Instructor Resource Center (www.aw.com/irc).

3. Write a script to play your favorite tune on one of the instruments at www.aw.com/irc.

4. Write a script to construct a 10-second signal with sine waves of unit amplitude and frequencies 5 Hz and 12 Hz at a sampling rate of 1,000 samples per second. Perform the FFT on this signal, and remove the 5,000 elements in the center of the spectrum. Then, perform the inverse transform, and plot and explain your observations.

5. When plotting the results from applying a Fast Fourier Transform to a sampled sound file, what would be appropriate labels for the x-and y-axis?

    a.   x: 'time'   y: 'frequency'
    b.   x: 'frequency'   y: 'time'
    c.   x: 'time'   y: 'power'
    d.   x: 'frequency'   y: 'amplitude'
    e.   x: 'time'   y: 'amplitude'

6. You want to read in a sound `myfile.wav` and perform a Fast Fourier Transform on it. Which of the following lines of code would accomplish this with no errors?

    a.   `[a, b] = wavread('myfile.wav'); r = fft(a, b);`
    b.   `[c, d] = wavread('myfile.wav'); s = fft(d, c);`
    c.   `[e, f] = wavread('myfile.wav'); u = fft(e);`
    d.   `[g, h] = wavread('myfile.wav'); t = fft(h);`

7. Congratulations. Because of your success while working with Acme Clothes over the past few weeks, the company has requested your help again. An agent for Acme Clothes has recorded the average clothes rating for the company in a file, `confused.wav`. However, the file is scrambled. Your job is to read the file in, unscramble it, and play it back.

    Store your modified waveform (the one that has been unscrambled) in the variable `mySound`. Here is how the file was scrambled:

    a. The file was amplified to 10 percent of its original amplitude.
    b. The order of the words in the file was reversed. Each word in the sound file took one second to say. This means what was the first second in the original sound file is now the last second, and the last second in the original sound file is now the first second.
    c. The file was reversed.

Numerical Methods

Chapter Objectives

This chapter discusses the implementations of four common numerical techniques:

- Interpolating data

- Fitting polynomial curves to data

- Numerical integration

- Numerical differentiation

Introduction

Real world data is rarely in such a form that you can use it immediately. Frequently, the data must be manipulated according to the user's actual needs:

- If the data samples have correct values but are not close enough together to be used directly, we can use interpolation to compute data points between the samples provided.

- There are occasions where the data-gathering facilities add some amount of noise to the data. To minimize the effects of the noise, we can compute the coefficients of a polynomial function that best matches the data.

- There are also times when the data must be integrated or differentiated to derive the quantities of interest.

15.1 Interpolation
15.1.1 Linear Interpolation
15.1.2 Cubic Spline Interpolation
15.1.3 Extrapolation
15.2 Curve Fitting
15.2.1 Linear Regression
15.2.2 Polynomial Regression
15.2.3 Practical Application
15.3 Numerical Integration
15.3.1 Determination of the Complete Integral
15.3.2 Continuous Integration Problems
15.4 Numerical Differentiation
15.4.1 Difference Expressions
15.4.2 MATLAB Implementation
15.5 Engineering Example— Analyzing Rocket Data

15.1 Interpolation

If our data samples have correct values but are not close enough to be used directly, we can use either linear or cubic interpolation to compute data points between the samples provided. For example, the MATLAB plotting functions use linear interpolation to draw the lines between data points.

In general, interpolation is a technique by which we estimate a variable's value between known values. In this section we present the two most common types of interpolation: linear interpolation and cubic spline interpolation. In both techniques, we assume that we have a set of data points that represents a set of x-y coordinates for which y is a function of x; that is, $y = f(x)$. We then have a value of x that is not part of the data set for which we want to find the y value. Figure 15.1 illustrates the definition of the interpolation problem.

15.1.1 Linear Interpolation

Linear interpolation is one of the most common techniques for estimating data values between two given data points. With this technique we assume that the function between the points can be represented by a straight line drawn between the points, as shown in Figure 15.2. Since we can find the equation of a straight line defined by the two known points, we can find y for any value of x. The closer the points are to each other, the more accurate our approximation is likely to be. Of course, we could use this equation to extrapolate points past our collected data. This is rarely wise, however, and often leads to significant errors.

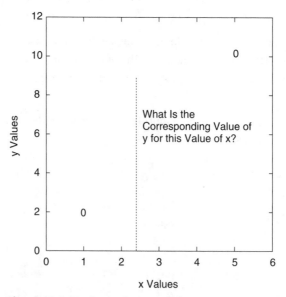

Figure 15.1 *The interpolation problem*

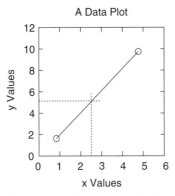

A Data Plot

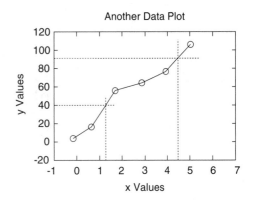

Another Data Plot

Figure 15.2 *Linear interpolation*

The MATLAB function that performs linear interpolation is as follows:

```
new_y = interp1(x, y, new_x)
```

where the vectors x and y contain the original data values and the vector new_x contains the point(s) for which we want to compute interpolated new_y values. The x values should be in ascending order, and the new_x values should be within the range of the x values. Note that the last character in the name interp1 is the numeric 1 (one), not a lowercase L.

These forms are demonstrated in Exercise 15.1.

In Exercise 15.1 we use the data illustrated in Figure 15.2. First we take a single interpolated reading from the data at x = 1.5, and then we plot circles spaced 0.2 units apart on the x-axis, as shown in Figure 15.3. Notice that the circles fall on the straight lines between the given data values. Finally, we attempt to extrapolate to the point x = -0.5, and see that MATLAB returns NaN.

 Exercise 15.1 Linear interpolation

Do It Yourself

Enter the following MATLAB commands:

```
>> x = 0:5;
>> y = [0, 20, 60, 68, 77, 110];
>>  interp1(x, y ,1.5)
    ans =
         40
>> new_x = 0:0.2:5;
>> new_y = interp1(x,y,new_x);
>> plot(x, y, new_x, new_y, 'o')
>> axis([-1,7,-20,120])
>> title('linear Interpolation Plot')
>> xlabel('x values') ; ylabel('y values')
>>  interp1(x, y , -0.5)
    ans =
         NaN
```

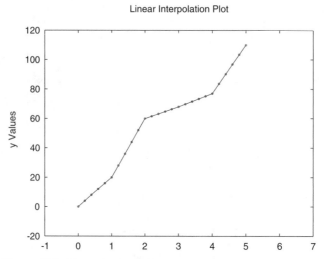

Figure 15.3 *Linear interpolation*

For the advanced student, MATLAB allows us to provide a fourth parameter to the `interp1` function that must be a string that modifies its behavior. The choices are as follows:

`'nearest'`	nearest neighbor interpolation
`'linear'`	linear interpolation—the default
`'spline'`	piecewise cubic spline interpolation (see Section 15.1.2)
`'pchip'`	shape-preserving piecewise cubic interpolation
`'cubic'`	same as `'pchip'`
`'v5cubic'`	the cubic interpolation from MATLAB 5, which does not extrapolate, and uses `'spline'` if x is not equally spaced

MATLAB also provides two-dimensional (`interp2`) and three-dimensional (`interp3`) interpolation functions, which are not discussed here. Refer to the MATLAB help feature for more information.

15.1.2 Cubic Spline Interpolation

A **cubic spline** is a smooth curve constructed to go through a set of points. The curve between each pair of points is a third-degree polynomial that has the general form:

$$x = a_{x0}t^3 + a_{x1}t^2 + a_{x2}t + a_{x3} \text{ and}$$
$$y = a_{y0}t^3 + a_{y1}t^2 + a_{y2}t + a_{y3}$$

where t is a parameter ranging from 0 to 1 between each pair of points. The coefficients are computed so that this provides a smooth curve between the two points and a smooth transition between the adjacent curves. Figure 15.4

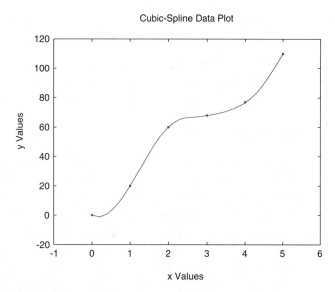

Figure 15.4 *Cubic spline interpolation*

shows a cubic spline smoothly connecting six points using a total of five different cubic equations.

The MATLAB function that performs linear interpolation is as follows:

```
new_y = spline(x, y, new_x);
```

where the vectors x and y contain the original data values, and the vector x_new contains the point(s) for which we want to compute interpolated y_new values. The x values should be in ascending order, and the x_new values should be within the range of the x values.

The curve in Figure 15.4 was created using the code shown in Listing 15.1.

Listing 15.1 Spline interpolation

```
1. x = 0:5;
2. y = [0, 20, 60, 68, 77, 110];
3. new_x = 0:0.2:5;
4. new_y = spline(x, y, new_x);
5. plot(x, y, 'o', new_x, new_y, '-')
6. axis([-1,6,-20,120])
7. title('Cubic-Spline Data Plot')
8. xlabel('x values'); ylabel('y values')
```

In Listing 15.1:

Lines 1 and 2: Show the original x and y values.

Line 3: Shows dense x values to define the curve.

Line 4: Computes the spline function.

Lines 5–8: Plot the original data and the smooth curve.

15.1.3 Extrapolation

A note of caution about extrapolation—attempting to infer the values of data points outside the range of data provided is problematic. Although logically your code may allow you to, you should never do it. The MATLAB interp1 and spline functions behave differently in this respect.

As we saw previously, the interp1 function refuses to supply results outside the range of the original x data. If you try, for every new_x value outside the range of the original x values, it will return NaN—not a number. This is actually quite nice because if you accidentally request interpolated data like this, the plot programs ignore NaN values.

The spline function, however, has no such scruples, and allows you to request any x values you want, using the equation of the closest line segment. So considering Figure 15.4, if you asked for the value at x = -3, it would use the segment between 0 and 1, which has a violent upswing at the lower end (see Exercise 15.2).

This might be what you want, but it looks odd! Chances are the data is not as accurate as you thought, and you probably need to fit a curve to it, as explained in the following section.

 Exercise 15.2 The evils of extrapolation

Do It Yourself

Following Listing 15.1, enter this code:

```
>> spline(x, y, -3)
ans =
  813.3333
```

 15.2 Curve Fitting

There are occasions where the data-gathering facilities add some amount of noise to the data. To minimize the effects of the noise, we can compute the coefficients of a polynomial function that best matches the data. The choice of the order of the polynomial must be made by the user, depending upon our understanding of the underlying physics that generated the data.

Assume that we have a set of data points collected from an experiment. After plotting the data points, we find that they generally fall in a straight line. However, if we were to try to draw a straight line through the points, probably only a couple of the points would fall exactly on the line. A least-squares curve fitting method could be used to find the straight line that is the closest to the points, by minimizing the distance from each point to the straight line. Although this line can be considered a "best fit" to the data points, it is possible that none of the points would actually fall on the line of best fit. (Note that this method is very different from interpolation, because the lines used in interpolation actually fall on all of the original data points.)

In the following section, we will discuss fitting a straight line to a set of data points, and then we will discuss fitting a polynomial of higher order.

15.2.1 Linear Regression

Linear regression is the process that determines the linear equation that is the best fit to a set of data points in terms of minimizing the sum of the squared distances between the line and the data points. To understand this process, first we consider the same set of data values used previously, and attempt to "eyeball" a straight line through the data. Assume, for example, that $y = 20x$ is a good estimate of the curve. Listing 15.2 shows the code to plot the points and this estimate.

In Listing 15.2:

> Lines 1 and 2: Show the original data points.
>
> Line 3: Is our eyeball estimate.
>
> Lines 4–9: Plot the original data and the estimate.

Looking at the results in Figure 15.5, it appears that $y = 20x$ is a reasonable estimate of a line through the points.

We really need the ability to compare the quality of the fit of this line to other possible estimates, so we compute the difference between the actual y value and the value calculated from the estimate:

```
dy = [0, 0, 20, 8, -3, 10]
```

Listing 15.2 Eyeball linear estimation

```
1. x = 0:5;
2. y = [0 20 60 68 77 110];
3. y2 = 20 * x;          estimate
4. plot(x, y, 'o', x, y2);
5. axis([-1 7 -20 120])
6. title('Linear Estimate')
7. xlabel('Time (sec)')
8. ylabel('Temperature (degrees F)')
9. grid
```

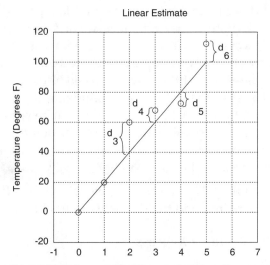

Figure 15.5 *An eyeball estimate of a linear fit*

It turns out that the best way to make this comparison is by the **least squares technique**, whereby the measure of the quality of the fit is the sum of the squared differences between the actual data points and the linear estimates. This sum can be computed with the following command:

```
>> sum_sq = sum(dy^2)
```

For the above set of data, the value of sum_sq is 573. As we will see, MATLAB can automatically produce the best linear fit shown in Figure 15.6 whose sum of squares is 356.82, a significant improvement over our original guess.

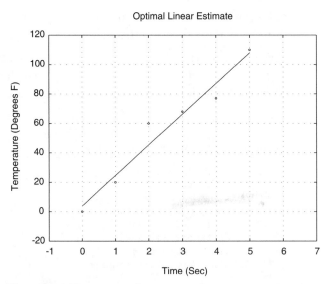

Figure 15.6 *Linear curve fit*

15.2.2 Polynomial Regression

Linear regression is a special case of the polynomial regression technique. Recall that a polynomial with one variable can be written by using the following formula:

$$f(x) = a_0 x^n + a_1 x^{n-1} + a_2 x^{n-2} + a_3 x^{n-3} + \ldots a_{n-1} x + a_n$$

The degree of a polynomial is equal to the largest value used as an exponent.

MATLAB provides a pair of functions to compute the coefficients of the best fit to a set of data, and then interpolate on those coefficients to produce the data to plot:

- `coef = polyfit(x, y, n)` computes the coefficients of the polynomial of degree n that best matches the given x and y values. The function returns the coefficients, `coef`, in descending powers of x. For the least squares calculation to work, the length of x should be greater than n − 1. If this is not the case, the coefficients are still computed, but the curve passes through all the data points.

- `new_y = polyval(coef, new_x)` can then be used to interpolate on these coefficients for the y value(s) corresponding to any x value(s). Note that there is nothing to prevent you from using these coefficients for extrapolation.

Exercise 15.3 illustrates fitting the best straight line to the data used in Section 15.1.1.

So the first-order polynomial that best fits our data is as follows:

$$f(x) = 20.8286x + 3.7169$$

We could interpolate the values of `new_x` with:

```
new_y = coef(10 * new_x + coef(2)
```

or we could use the function `polyval`:

```
new_y = polyfit(coef, new_x)
```

We can use our new understanding of the `polyfit` and `polyval` functions to write a program to study the improvement in the curve fit as n increases, as shown in Listing 15.3.

 Exercise 15.3 Optimal linear fit

Do It Yourself

For example, again using the data from Section 15.1.1:

```
>> x=0:5; y=[0,20,60,68,77,110]
>> polyfit(x, y, 1)
ans =
    20.8286   3.7619
```

Listing 15.3 Higher-order fits

```
1. x = 0:5;
2. fine_x = 0:.1:5;
3. y = [0 20 60 68 77 110];
4. for order = 2:5
5.     y2=polyval(polyfit(x,y,order), fine_x);
6.     subplot(2,2,order-1)
7.     plot(x, y, 'o', fine_x, y2)
8.     axis([-1 7 -20 120])
9.     ttl = sprintf('Degree %d Polynomial Fit', ...
                     order );
10.    title(ttl)
11.    xlabel('Time (sec)')
12.    ylabel('Temperature (degrees F)')
13. end
```

In Listing 15.3:

> Lines 1–3: Set up the data sets.
>
> Line 4: Studies second- through fifth-order fits.
>
> Line 5: Combines `polyfit` and `polyval` calls to compute the new y values.
>
> Lines 6–12: Plot the results. Notice the use of `sprintf(...)` to make a dynamic title for the plots.

The results are shown in Figure 15.7. Notice that with six points, the fifth-order fit goes through all the data points.

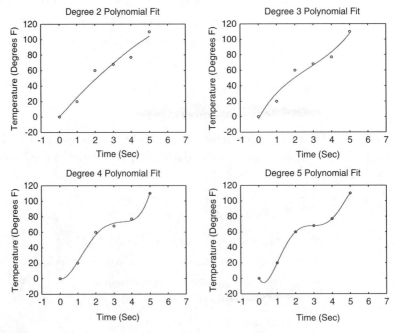

Figure 15.7 *Higher-order polynomial fits*

15.2.3 Practical Application

We return briefly to the problem of replacing the blue sky in Chapter 13. The sky we used to replace the gray skies of Vienna has a power line we need to remove. We can use polynomial curve fitting to create an artificial sky with exactly the same characteristics as the cottage blue sky, but without the wire. We merely need to process each row of the sky, fit a second-order curve to it, interpolate a new sky row from the parameters, and replace the row in the sky. The code to perform this is shown in Listing 15.4.

In Listing 15.4:

> Line 1: Reads the original cottage picture.
>
> Line 2: Obtains its sizes.
>
> Line 3: Shows the x values for the curve fitting.
>
> Line 4: Makes a copy of the original picture.
>
> Line 5: Converts to top 700 rows where the sky is.
>
> Line 6: Treats each color individually.
>
> Line 7: The polynomial approximation needs each row as a double vector.
>
> Lines 8 and 9: Compute a synthetic row.
>
> Line 10: Puts the row into the new sky.
>
> Lines 13 and 14: Show and save the new image.

Figure 15.8 shows the cottage picture updated with a smooth sky. Notice that the chimneys have been smeared off, but this does not affect the part of the sky needed for the Vienna picture. This synthetic sky is ready to be used in the script to replace the original sky (see Listing 13.1). Figure 15.9 shows the Vienna picture with a clear blue synthetic sky.

Listing 15.4 Removing the cable from the sky

```
1. p = imread('Witney.jpg');
2. [rows, cols, clrs] = size(p);
3. x = 1:cols;
4. sky = p;
5. for row = 1:700
6.     for color = 1:3
7.         cv = double(p(row, :, color));
8.         coef = polyfit(x, cv, 2);
9.         ncr = polyval(coef, x);
10.        sky(row,:,color) = uint8(ncr);
11.    end
12. end
13. image(sky)
14. imwrite(sky, 'sky.jpg');
```

Figure 15.8 *Updated sky*

Figure 15.9 *Updated picture*

15.3 Numerical Integration

The integral of a function $f(x)$ over the interval $[a, b]$ is defined to be the area under the curve of $f(x)$ between a and b, as shown in Figure 15.10. If the value of this integral is K, the notation to represent the integral of $f(x)$ between a and b is as follows:

$$K = \int_a^b f(x) \, dx$$

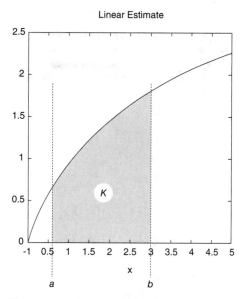

Figure 15.10 *Integration of f(x)*

For many functions, this integral can be computed analytically. However, for a number of functions, this is not possible, and we require a numerical technique to estimate its value. We look at two different scenarios:

- Two different techniques for computing the complete integral with various degrees of accuracy
- A technique for evaluating the continuous integral of $f(x)$

15.3.1 Determination of the Complete Integral

Two of the most common numerical integration techniques estimate $f(x)$ either with a set of piecewise linear functions or with a set of piecewise parabolic functions. If we use piecewise linear functions, we can compute the area of the trapezoids that compose the area under the piecewise linear function. This technique is called the **trapezoidal rule**. If we use piecewise quadratic functions, we can compute and add the areas of these components. This technique is called **Simpson's rule**.

The Trapezoidal Rule If we represent the area under a curve by trapezoids, as illustrated in Figure 15.11, and if the interval [a, b] is divided into n equal sections, then the area can be approximated by the following formula:

$$K_T = \frac{b-a}{2n}(f(x_0) + 2f(x_1) + 2f(x_2) + \ldots + 2f(x_{n-1}) + f(x_n))$$

where the x_i values represent the end points of the trapezoids and where $x_0 = a$ and $x_n = b$. Listing 15.5 shows a MATLAB function that computes this integral.

Listing 15.5 Trapezoidal integration

```
1. function K = trapezoid( v, a, b )
2. %   h = trapezoid(v, a, b )
3. K = (b-a) * (v(1) + v(end) + ...
       2*sum(v(2:end-1))) / (2*(length(v) - 1) );
```

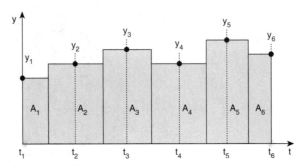

Figure 15.11 *Discrete integration*

Simpson's Rule If the area under a curve is represented by areas under quadratic sections of a curve, and if the interval $[a, b]$ is divided into $2n$ equal sections, then the area can be approximated by the formula (Simpson's rule):

$$K_s = \frac{h}{3}\left(f(x_0) + 4f(x_1) + 2f(x_2) + 4f(x_3) + \ldots + 2f(x_{2n-2}) + 4f(x_{2n-1}) + f(x_{2n})\right)$$

where the x_i values represent the end points of the sections, $x_0 = a$ and $x_{2n} = b$, and $h = (b - a) / (2n)$.

Listing 15.6 shows a MATLAB function to integrate using Simpson's rule.

15.3.2 Continuous Integration Problems

We now consider a slightly different scenario. If $f(t)$ is the rate of change of $F(t)$ defined as $f(t) = dF(t)/dt$, then given $f(t)$, we can find $F(t)$ according to the following formula:

$$F(t) = \int_{t_0}^{t} f(x)\, dt$$

For example, we might be given data that represents the velocity of a sounding rocket, such as is plotted in Figure 15.12. We need to approximate the altitude of the rocket over time by integrating this data.

Listing 15.6 Simpson's rule integration

```
1. function K = simpson( v, a, b )
2. %   h = simpson(v, a, b )
3. K = (b-a) * (v(1) + v(end) + ...
       4*sum(v(2:2:end-1)) + ...
       2*sum(v(3:2:end-2)) ) / (3*(length(v) - 1) );
```

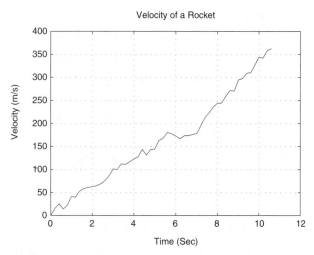

Figure 15.12 *Velocity of a rocket*

To perform this kind of integral, MATLAB provides the function `y = cumsum(v)` that computes the cumulative sum of the vector v. The result, y, is a vector of the same length as v where `y(i)` is the sum of `v(1:i)`. If the data values, v, are regularly sampled, the integral is found by multiplying `cumsum(v)` by the time interval. If they are not regularly sampled, you have to compute the `cumsum(...)` of the scalar product of and the vector of time differences.

Listing 15.7 shows the function that computes this continuous integral, making use of `cumsum(...)`.

Listing 15.7 Integrating rocket velocity

```
 1. v =[ 0.0 15.1 25.1 13.7 22.2 41.7 ...
          39.8 54.8 57.6 62.6 61.6 63.9 69.6 ...
          76.2 86.7 101.2 99.8 112.2 111.0 ...
          116.8 122.6 127.7 143.4 131.3 143.0 ...
          144.0 162.7 167.8 180.3 177.6 172.6 ...
          166.6 173.1 173.3 176.0 178.5 ...
          196.5 213.0 223.6 235.9 244.2 244.5 ...
          259.4 271.4 270.5 294.5 297.6 ...
          308.7 310.5 326.6 344.1 342.0 358.2 362.7 ];
 2. lv = length(v);
 3. dt = 0.2;
 4. t = (0:lv-1) * dt;
 5. h = dt * cumsum(v);
 6. plot(t, v, t, h/5)
 7. legend({'velocity' 'altitude/5' })
 8. title('velocity and altitude of a rocket')
 9. xlabel('time (sec)'); ylabel('v (m/s), h(m/5)')
10. fprintf('cumsum height: %g\n', h(end) );
11. fprintf('trapezoidal height: %g\n', ...
                trapezoid(v, t(1), t(end) ));
12. fprintf('Simpson''s Rule height: %g\n', ...
                simpson(v, t(1), t(end) ));
```

In Listing 15.7:

> Line 1: Shows the original velocity data.
>
> Lines 2–4: Parameters for plotting.
>
> Line 5: Performs the integration.
>
> Lines 6–9: Plot the results.
>
> Lines 10–12: Validate the three integration techniques by checking the results.

Figure 15.13 shows the resulting plot. The MATLAB results in the Command window are:

```
cumsum height: 1848.5
trapezoidal height: 1811.85
Simpson's Rule height: 1811.14
```

The continuous integration produces results within 2 percent of the "accurate" integration techniques.

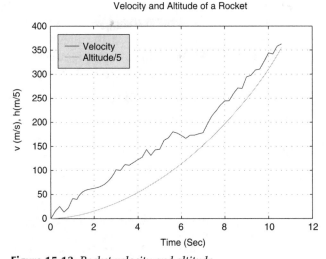

Figure 15.13 *Rocket velocity and altitude*

15.4 Numerical Differentiation

The derivative of a function $f(x)$ is defined to be a function $f'(x)$ that is equal to the rate of change of $f(x)$ with respect to x. The derivative can be expressed as a ratio, with the change in $f(x)$ indicated by $df(x)$ and the change in x indicated by dx, giving us the following:

$$f'(x) = \frac{df(x)}{dx}$$

There are many physical processes for which we want to measure the rate of change of a variable. For example, velocity is the rate of change of position (as in meters per second), and acceleration is the rate of change of velocity (as in meters per second squared).

The derivative $f'(x)$ can be described graphically as the slope of the function $f(x)$, which is defined to be the slope of the tangent line to the function at the specified point. Thus, the value of $f'(x)$ at the point a is $f'(a)$, and it is equal to the slope of the tangent line at the point a, as shown in Figure 15.14.

15.4.1 Difference Expressions

In general, numerical differentiation techniques estimate the derivative of a function at a point x_k by approximating the slope of the tangent line at x_k using values of the function at points near x_k. The approximation of the slope of the tangent line can be done in several ways, as shown in Figure 15.15.

Figure 15.15(a) assumes that the derivative at x_k is estimated by computing the slope of the line between $f(x_{k-1})$ and $f(x_k)$, as in the following:

$$f'(x_k) = \frac{f(x_k) - f(x_{k-1})}{x_k - x_{k-1}}$$

This type of derivative approximation is called a **backward difference approximation**. Figure 15.15(b) assumes that the derivative at x_k is estimated by computing the slope of the line between $f(x_k)$ and $f(x_{k+1})$, as in the following:

$$f'(x_k) = \frac{f(x_{k+1}) - f(x_k)}{x_{k+1} - x_k}$$

This type of derivative approximation is called a **forward difference approximation**. Figure 15.15(c) assumes that the derivative at x_k is estimated by computing the slope of the line between $f(x_{k-1})$ and $f(x_{k+1})$, as in the following:

$$f'(x_k) = \frac{f(x_{k+1}) - f(x_{k-1})}{x_{k+1} - x_{k-1}}$$

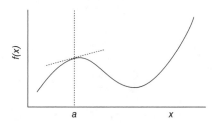

Figure 15.14 *Slope of a curve*

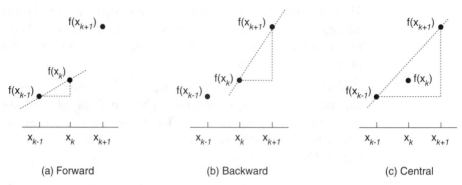

(a) Forward   (b) Backward   (c) Central

Figure 15.15 *Differentiation techniques*

This type of derivative approximation is called a **central difference approximation**, and we usually assume that x_k is halfway between x_{k-1} and x_{k+1}. The quality of all of these types of derivative computations depends on the distance between the points used to estimate the derivative; the estimate of the derivative improves as the distance between the two points decreases.

15.4.2 MATLAB Implementation

To facilitate differentiation, MATLAB provides the `diff(...)` function, which computes differences between adjacent values in a vector, generating a new vector with one less value than the original:

```
dv = diff(V) returns [V(2)-V(1), V(3)-V(2), ..., V(n)-V(n-1)]
```

An approximate derivative dy/dx can be computed by using `diff(y)./diff(x)`. Depending on the application, this can be used to compute the forward, backward, or central difference approximation. The solution to the forward difference is shown in Listing 15.8.

In Listing 15.8:

>   Lines 1–4: Establish and plot $f(x)$.
>
>   Line 5: The difference expression—returns a vector one shorter than the original.

Listing 15.8 Differentiating a function

```
1. x = -7:0.1:9;
2. f = polyval([0.0333,-0.3,-1.3333,16,0,-187.2,0], x);
3. plot(x, f)
4. hold on
5. df = diff(f)./diff(x);
6. plot(x(2:end), df, 'g')
7. grid
8. legend({'f(x)', 'f '' (x)'})
```

Lines 6–8: Plot the differences. By plotting at `x(2:end)`, we accomplish the forward difference version where the slope at `x(i)` is the previous differential value.

The results are shown in Figure 15.16. We could accomplish the backward difference approach by plotting the values at `x(1:end-1)`. The central difference version is left as an exercise for the reader. Suffice it to note that if the samples `x(i)` are close enough, it really doesn't matter which approximation we use.

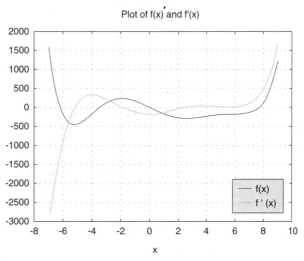

Figure 15.16 *Differentiation*

15.5 Engineering Example—Analyzing Rocket Data

Returning to the sounding rocket example from the previous sections, suppose we are asked to find the acceleration of the rocket as well as its velocity and altitude. As we have seen, when faced with some data of unknown origin, it is wise to perform an initial survey before launching the actual solution. In our initial survey, we make a raw plot of the rocket velocity and attempt to integrate and differentiate to obtain the altitude and acceleration. The complete script (using the velocity values from above) is shown in Listing 15.9.

Listing 15.9 Raw rocket values

```
1. v =[ 0.0 15.1 25.1 13.7 22.2 41.7 ...
        39.8 54.8 57.6 62.6 61.6 63.9 69.6 ...
        76.2 86.7 101.2 99.8 112.2 111.0 ...
        116.8 122.6 127.7 143.4 131.3 143.0 ...
```

continued on next page

```
              144.0 162.7 167.8 180.3 177.6 172.6 ...
              166.6 173.1 173.3 176.0 178.5 ...
              196.5 213.0 223.6 235.9 244.2 244.5 ...
              259.4 271.4 270.5 294.5 297.6 ...
              308.7 310.5 326.6 344.1 342.0 358.2 362.7 ];
2. lv = length(v); dt = 0.2; t = (0:lv-1) * dt;
3. h = dt * cumsum(v);
4. acc = diff(v) ./ diff(t);
5. plot(t, v, t, h/5, t(2:end), acc)
6. legend({'velocity' 'altitude/5' 'acceleration'})
7. title('vel, alt and acc measurements of a rocket')
8. xlabel('time (sec)')
9. ylabel('v (m/s), h(m/5) and acc(m/sec^2)')
```

In Listing 15.9:

> Lines 1–3: As before, compute the velocity and altitude.
>
> Line 4: Differentiates to estimate the acceleration.
>
> Lines 5–9: Plot the three results.

The resulting plot is shown in Figure 15.17.

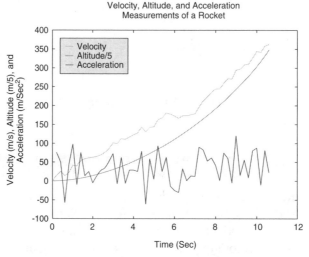

Figure 15.17 *Rocket velocity, altitude, and acceleration*

Having completed the initial survey, we take a look at the data. The results illustrate the problems associated with differentiating inherently noisy signals—whereas integration always smoothes the velocity data, differentiating noisy data amplifies the undesirable effects of the noise.

Our first thought might be to improve the quality of our results by fitting a curve to the velocity data before differentiation. The question must be, however, what order of polynomial to use to fit the data. So we need some further analysis—a short study to assess the right polynomial order. Such a study is shown in Listing 15.10.

Listing 15.10 Curve fitting experiment

```
1. v =[ 0.0 15.1 25.1 13.7 22.2 41.7 ...
        39.8 54.8 57.6 62.6 61.6 63.9 69.6 ...
        76.2 86.7 101.2 99.8 112.2 111.0 ...
        116.8 122.6 127.7 143.4 131.3 143.0 ...
        144.0 162.7 167.8 180.3 177.6 172.6 ...
        166.6 173.1 173.3 176.0 178.5 ...
        196.5 213.0 223.6 235.9 244.2 244.5 ...
        259.4 271.4 270.5 294.5 297.6 ...
        308.7 310.5 326.6 344.1 342.0 358.2 362.7 ];
2. dt = 0.2; t = (0:length(v)-1) * dt;
3. for plt = 1:6
4.     order = plt*3;
5.     y = polyval(polyfit(t, v, order), t);
6.     subplot(2, 3, plt)
7.     plot(t, v, t, y);
8.     str = sprintf('order %d', order);
9.     title(str);
10.    legend({'velocity' 'fitted vel'})
11.    xlabel('time (sec)')
12.    ylabel('vel (m/s)')
13. end
```

In Listing 15.10:

> Lines 1–2: Set up $v(t)$ as before.
>
> Line 3: Makes six subplots.
>
> Line 4: The plots will fit the data from order 3 to order 18.
>
> Line 5: Performs the fit and interpolation.
>
> Lines 6–12: Plot the results.

The results are plotted in Figure 15.18. Clearly, with sufficient data samples, we can push the order of the fit to match the data quite well, including the odd-looking "kink" in the middle.

To reach the obvious (erroneous) conclusion of this experiment, we would write a script to differentiate the smoothed velocity. Listing 15.11 shows this code, together with an extra plot that will reveal the error of our thinking.

Listing 15.11 Differentiating the smoothed data

```
1. v =[ 0.0 15.1 25.1 13.7 22.2 41.7 ...
        39.8 54.8 57.6 62.6 61.6 63.9 69.6 ...
        76.2 86.7 101.2 99.8 112.2 111.0 ...
        116.8 122.6 127.7 143.4 131.3 143.0 ...
        144.0 162.7 167.8 180.3 177.6 172.6 ...
        166.6 173.1 173.3 176.0 178.5 ...
        196.5 213.0 223.6 235.9 244.2 244.5 ...
        259.4 271.4 270.5 294.5 297.6 ...
        308.7 310.5 326.6 344.1 342.0 358.2 362.7 ];
```

continued on next page

```
2.  dt = 0.2; t = (0:length(v)-1) * dt; g = 9.81;
3.  acc = diff(v) ./ diff(t);
4.  vs = polyval(polyfit(t, v, 12), t);
5.  accs = diff(vs) ./ diff(t);
6.  treal = [0 6 6.2 7 7.2 t(end)];
7.  areal = g * [3 3 -1 -1 5 5];
8.  plot(t, v, t(2:end), acc, ...
            t(2:end), accs, treal, areal)
9.  title('attempt to smooth the acceleration')
10. xlabel('time (sec)')
11. ylabel('v (m/s) and acc(m/sec^2)')
```

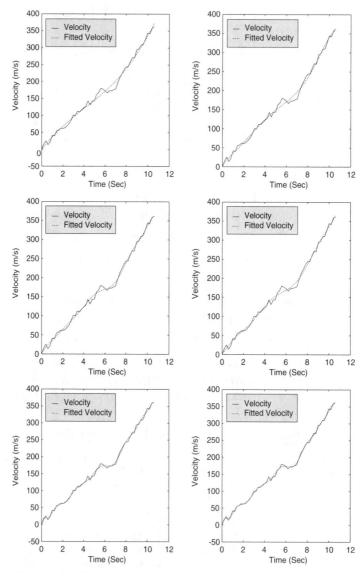

Figure 15.18 *Fit order study*

In Listing 15.11:

>   Lines 1–3: Velocity and acceleration plots as before.
>   Line 4: Computes a twelfth-order smooth velocity.
>   Line 5: Differentiates the smoothed velocity.
>   Lines 6 and 7: The actual acceleration used to generate the data.
>   Lines 8–11: Plot the four lines.

Figure 15.19 shows the resulting plot.

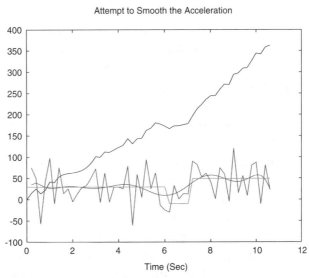

Figure 15.19 *Study conclusion*

This appears to have somewhat improved the situation, but when we take a careful look, guided by the plot that shows the actual acceleration, we see the truth about the actual acceleration used to compute the rocket velocity profile. Being a two-stage rocket, it consisted of six seconds of acceleration at 3g, one second of falling at –g while the first stage motor detached, and the remaining time at 5g. As we can now see, while the curve fitting managed to smooth out the worst of the computed spikiness in the data and it was trying to track the discontinuity in the acceleration profile, it was also beginning to model the shape of the noise on the velocity rather than the underlying truth. Although we could reexamine the choice of order of the polynomial and try a less aggressive fit, we would find that the data would track the noise less carefully, and also not follow the central velocity oddity. We seem to be trapped between fitting to the artifact we want and smoothing out artifacts we do not want.

>   *The Clue*: The fact that we needed to go to a twelfth or higher order to fit the data should have been a strong clue that something else was going on. Ballistic flight is usually a second-order phenomenon—

perhaps third or fourth order if we allow for fuel to burn off and friction—but not twelfth order.

Moral: Curve fitting can sometimes help to clean up nasty looking data. However, there may be some clues in the source of the data (in our case, a sounding rocket that could be multistage) and the character of the data (in our case, the odd discontinuity between burns) that might lead to different and better interpretation of the data. Looking again at the velocity profile in the light of the actual data, it can be seen that the velocity profile is not as noisy as first appeared. Rather, it is two segments of linear acceleration with a discontinuity in the middle. We leave it to the reader to construct piecewise fits to the data to improve the acceleration estimates.

 ## Chapter Summary

In this chapter, we saw the implementations of four common numerical techniques:

- We can estimate data points between given data values using linear (interp1/2/3) or spline interpolation
- We can smooth noisy data by fitting polynomial curves of suitable order to the raw data
- Given, for example, the velocity of an object over time, we can determine its position by integrating using cumsum
- We can differentiate to generate its acceleration

 ## Special Characters, Reserved Words, and Functions

Special Characters, Reserved Words, and Functions	Description	Discussed in This Section
NaN	Not a number	15.1.1
cumsum(v)	Computes the integral of a function, assuming that x is 1	15.3.2
diff(v)	Computes the differences between adjacent values in a vector	15.4.2
interp1(x, y, nx)	Computes linear and cubic interpolation	15.1.1
interp2(x, y, z, nx, ny)	Computes linear and cubic interpolation	15.1.1
interp3(x, y, z, v, nx, ny, nz)	Computes linear and cubic interpolation	15.1.1
polyfit(x, y, n)	Computes a least-squares polynomial	15.2.2
polyval(c, x)	Evaluates a polynomial	15.2.2
spline(x, y)	Spline interpolation	15.1.2

Self Test

Use the following questions to check your understanding of the material in this chapter:

True or False

1. MATLAB functions permit extrapolation beyond the limits of the original independent variable.

2. The cubic spline is a series of parametric curves.

3. You cannot extrapolate the equations generated by curve fitting.

4. You should always match the order of a parametric curve fit to the underlying physics of the data.

5. Simpson's rule is more accurate then the trapezoidal rule for integrating a function.

6. Numerical differentiation produces a vector that is the same length as the original vector.

7. You can only find the solutions to equations that are polynomial in structure.

Fill in the Blanks

1. _____ is the technique by which we estimate a

   variable's value between known values.

2. Nth-order polynomial regression determines the

   _____ of order n that minimize the

   _____ between the line and the data points.

3. The _____ makes the slope at x_k the

   _____ of the line between x_{k-1} and x_{k+1}.

4. To compute the continuous integral of a data set that is not regularly

   sampled, you have to compute the _____ of the

   _____ of _____ and _____.

5. You can find the _____ of a set of data (the points of

   zero slope) by first _____ the data and then

   _____ of the result.

Programming Projects

1. The subject of thermodynamics makes extensive use of tables. Although many properties can be described by fairly simple equations, others are poorly understood, or the equations describing their behavior are very complicated. It is much easier just to tabulate the data. For example, consider the data for steam at 0.1 MPa (approximately 1 atm), given in the following table.

Temperature, C	Internal Energy, kJ/kg[1]
100	2506.7
150	2582.8
200	2658.1
250	2733.7
300	2810.4
400	2967.9
500	3131.6

a. Use linear interpolation to determine the internal energy at 21.5° C.

b. Use linear interpolation to determine the temperature if the internal energy is 2600 kJ/kg.

2. Electric power plants use steam as a "working fluid." The science of thermodynamics makes extensive use of tables when systems such as a power plant are analyzed. Depending on the system of interest you may need only a portion of the table, such as the following:

Temperature	Specific Volume	Internal Energy	Enthalpy
C	m³/kg	kJ/kG	kJ/kg
100	1.6958	2506.7	2676.2
150	1.9364	2582.8	2776.4
200	2.172	2658.1	2875.3
250	2.406	2733.7	2974.3
300	2.639	2810.4	3074.3
400	3.103	2967.9	3278.2
500	3.565	3131.6	3488.1

[1] Data from Steam Tables, SI units by Joseph H. Keenan, Fredrick G. Keyes, Philip G Hill, and Joan G. Moore, New York, John Wiley and Sons, 1918.

Notice that this table is spaced at 50° intervals at first, and then at 100° intervals. Assume that you have a project that requires you to use this table, and you would prefer not to have to perform a linear interpolation every time you use it. Use MATLAB to create a table, applying linear interpolation, with a temperature spacing of 25°.

3. Determining how much water will flow through a culvert is not as easy as it might seem at first. The channel could have a non-uniform shape, obstructions might influence the flow, friction is important, and so forth. A numerical approach allows us to fold all of those concerns into a model of how the water actually behaves.

   Consider the following data collected from an actual culvert:

Height, ft	Flow, ft^3/sec
0	0
1.7	2.6
1.95	3.6
2.60	4.03
2.92	6.45
4.04	11.22
5.24	30.61

   Compute a best-fit linear, quadratic, and cubic fit for the data, and plot the information on the same graph. Which model best represents the data? (Linear is first order, quadratic is second order, and cubic is third order.)

4. The population of Earth is expanding rapidly, as is the population of the United States. MATLAB includes a built-in data file called census that contains U.S. census data since 1790. The data file contains two variables: cdate, which contains the census dates and pop, which lists the population in millions. To load the file into your workspace, type the following:

   ```
   >> load census
   ```

   Use the curve fitting toolbox to find an equation that represents the data.

5. Generate $f(x) = x^2$ for x = [-3 -1 0 2 5 6].
   a. Compute and plot the linear and cubic-spline interpolation of the data points over the range [-3:0.05:6].

b. Compute the value of $f(4)$ using linear interpolation and cubic-spline interpolation. What are the respective errors when the answer is compared with the actual value of $f(4)$?

6. Assume that the following set of temperature measurements is taken from the cylinder head in a new engine that is being tested for possible use in a race car:

Time, sec	Temperature, °F
0	0
1.0	20
2.0	60
3.0	68
4.0	77
5.0	110

a. Compare plots of these data, assuming linear interpolation and assuming cubic-spline interpolation for values between the data points, using time values from 0 to 5 in increments of 0.1 s.
b. Using the data from part (a), find the time value for which there is the largest difference between its linear interpolated temperature and its cubic interpolated temperature.

7. Assume that we measure temperatures at three points around the cylinder head in the engine from Programming Project 6, instead of at just one point. The set of data is then the following:

Time, sec	Temp1	Temp2	Temp3
0	0	0	0
1.0	20	25	52
2.0	60	62	90
3.0	68	67	91
4.0	77	82	93
5.0	110	103	96

a. Assume that these data have been stored in a matrix with six rows and four columns. Determine interpolated values of temperature at the three points in the engine at 2.6 seconds using linear interpolation.

b. Using the information from part (a), determine the time when the temperature reached 75° at each of the three points in the cylinder head.

8. The guidance system for a spacecraft often uses a sensor called an accelerometer, which is an electromechanical device that produces an output voltage proportional to the applied acceleration. Assume that an experiment has yielded the following set of data:

Acceleration	Voltage
4	0.593
2	0.436
0	0.061
2	0.425
4	0.980
6	1.213
8	1.646
10	2.158

a. Determine the linear equation that best fits this set of data. Plot the data points and the linear equation.
b. Determine the sum of the squares of the distances of these points from the line of best fit determined in part (a).
c. Compare the error sum from part (b) with the same error sum computed from the best quadratic fit. What do these sums tell you about the two models for the data?

9. Compute $tan(x)$ for x = [-1:0.05:1].
a. Compute the best-fit polynomial of order four that approximates $tan(x)$. Plot $tan(x)$ and the generated polynomial on the same graph. What is the sum of square error of the polynomial approximation for the data points in x?
b. Compute $tan(x)$ for x = [-2:0.05:2]. Using the polynomial generated in part (a), compute values of y from 2 to 2, corresponding to the x vector just defined. Plot $tan(x)$ and the values generated from the polynomial on the same graph. Why aren't they the same shape?

10. The following data set represents the time and altitude values for a sounding rocket that is performing high-altitude atmospheric research on the ionosphere.

a. Determine the equation that best represents the data, using the interactive curve-fitting tools available in MATLAB 7.
b. Plot the altitude data. The velocity function is the derivative of the altitude function. Using numerical differentiation, compute the velocity values from the data, using a backward difference. Plot the velocity data. (Note that the rocket is a two-stage rocket.)
c. The acceleration function is the derivative of the velocity function. Using the velocity data determined from part (b), compute the acceleration data using backward difference. Plot the acceleration data.

Time, sec	Altitude, m
0	60
10	2,926
20	10,170
30	21,486
40	33,835
50	45,251
60	55,634
70	65,038
80	73,461
90	80,905
100	87,368
110	92,852
120	97,355
130	100,878
140	103,422
150	104,986
160	106,193
170	110,246
180	119,626
190	136,106
200	162,095
210	199,506
220	238,775
230	277,065
240	314,375
250	350,704

11. Although MATLAB makes it easy to find the roots of a function,
     sometimes all that is needed is a quick estimate. This can be done by
     plotting a function and zooming in very close to see where the
     function equals zero. Since MATLAB draws straight lines between
     data points on a plot, it is good to draw circles or stars at each data
     point, in addition to straight lines connecting the points. Plot the
     following function and zoom in to find the roots:

```
>> n = 5;
>> x = linspace(0, 2*pi, n);
>> y = x .* sin(x) + cos(1/2*x).^2 - 1./(x - 7);
>> plot(x, y, '-o')
```

12. Consider the data points in the following vectors:

```
>> x = [0.1 0.3 5 6 23 24];;
>> y = [2.8 2.6 18.1 26.8 486.1 530]
```

   a. Determine the best-fit polynomial of order 2 to the data.
       Calculate the sum of squares for your results. Plot the best-fit
       polynomial for the six data points.
   b. Generate a new x vector containing 250 points evenly spaced
       between 0.1 and 25. Using the coefficients from part (a),
       generate and plot the corresponding y values.
   c. Compute an estimate of dy/dx using the new values in
       part (b).
   d. Compute second- and third-order polynomial fit to the
       derivative data in part (c). Plot each polynomial. Why is the use
       of polynomial fits to derivative data important?

13. The function $f(x)$ is defined by $f(x) = 4\,e^{-x}$. Plot this function over the
     interval [0, 1] with a suitable number of points. Use numerical
     integration techniques to estimate the integral of $f(x)$ over [0, 0.5]
     and [0, 1]. Compare these results to the theoretical answer.

Sorting

Chapter Objectives

This chapter discusses:

■ A technique for comparing the performance of algorithms

■ A range of algorithms for sorting a collection of data

■ Application areas in which these algorithms are most appropriate

First we will digress from the main thread of problem solving using MATLAB to discuss an "engineering algebra" for measuring the cost of an algorithm in terms of the amount of work done. Then we will consider a number of sorting algorithms, using this technique to assess their relative merits.

16.1   Measuring Algorithm Cost
       16.1.1 Specific Big O Examples
       16.1.2 Analyzing Complex Algorithms
16.2   Algorithms for Sorting Data
       16.2.1 Insertion Sort
       16.2.2 Bubble Sort
       16.2.3 Quick Sort
       16.2.4 Quick Sort in Place
       16.2.5 Merge Sort
       16.2.6 Bucket Sort
16.3   Performance Analysis
16.4   Applications of Sorting Algorithms
       16.4.1 Using MATLAB's Internal Sort Algorithm
       16.4.2 Insertion Sort
       16.4.3 Bubble Sort
       16.4.4 Quick Sort
       16.4.5 Merge Sort
       16.4.6 Bucket Sort
16.5   Engineering Example—A Selection of Countries

16.1 Measuring Algorithm Cost

How many times do you ask yourself, "Just how good is my algorithm?" Probably not very often, if ever. After all, we have been creating relatively simple programs that work on a small, finite set of data. Our functions execute and return an answer within a second or two. You may have noticed that some of the image processing scripts take a number of seconds to run.

However, as the problems become more complex and the volume of data increases, we need to consider whether we are solving the problem in the most efficient manner. In extreme cases, processes that manipulate huge amounts of data like the inventory of a large warehouse or a national telephone directory might be possible only with highly efficient algorithms.

Big O is an algebra that permits us to express how the amount of work done in solving a problem relates to the amount of data being processed. It is a gross simplification for software engineering analysis purposes, based on some sound but increasingly complex theory. (Interested readers should look up little-O, Big-Ω, little-ω, and Big-Θ.)

Big O is a means of estimating the worst case performance of a given algorithm when presented with a certain number of data items, usually referred to as N. In fact, the actual process attempts to determine the limit of the relationship between the work done by an algorithm and N as N approaches infinity.

We record the Big O of an algorithm as O (<expression in terms of N>). For example, O(1) describes the situation where the computing cost is independent of the size of the data, O(N) describes the situation where the computing cost is proportional to the size of the data, and O(2N) describes the situation where the computing cost doubles each time one more piece of data is added. At this point, we should also observe some simplifying assumptions:

- We are not concerned with constant multipliers on the Big O of an algorithm. As rapidly as processor performance and languages are improving, multiplicative improvements can be achieved merely by acquiring the latest hardware or software. Big O is a concept that reports qualitative algorithm improvement. Therefore, we choose to ignore constant multipliers on Big O analyses.

- We are concerned with the performance of algorithms as N approaches infinity. Consequently, when the Big O is expressed as the sum of multiple terms, we keep only the term with the highest power of N.

16.1.1 Specific Big O Examples

On the basis of algorithms we have already discussed, we will look at examples of the most common Big O cases.

O(1)—Independent of N O(1) describes the ideal case of an algorithm or logical step whose amount of work is independent of the amount of data. The most obvious example is accessing or modifying an entry in a vector. Since all good languages permit direct access to elements of a vector, the work of these simple operations is independent of the size of the vector.

O(N)—Linear with N O(N) describes an algorithm whose performance is linearly related to N. Copying a vector of size N is an obvious example, as is searching for a specific piece of data in such a vector. One might argue that occasionally one would find the data as the first element. There is an equal chance that we would be unlucky and find the item as the last element. On average, we would claim that the performance of this search is the mean of these numbers: (N + 1) / 2. However, applying the simplification rules above, we first reject the 1 as being N to a lower power, leaving N/2, and then reject the constant multiplier, leaving O(N) for a linear search.

O(logN)—Binary Search Consider searching for a number—say, 89—in a sorted vector such as that shown in Figure 16.1. One could use a linear search without taking advantage of the ordering of the data. However, a better algorithm might be as follows:

1. Go to the middle of the vector (approximately) and compare that element (the 59) to the number being sought.
2. If this is the desired value, exit with the answer.
3. If the number sought is less than that element, and since the data is ordered, we can reject the half of the array to the right of, and including the 59.
4. Similarly, if the number sought is greater than that element, we can reject the half of the array to the left of, and including the 59.
5. Repeat these steps with the remaining half vector until either the number is found or the size of the remaining half is zero.

Now consider how much data can be covered by each test—a measure of the work done as shown in Table 16.1.

In general, we can state that the relationship is expressed as follows:

$$N = 2^{W-1}$$

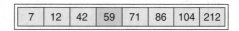

| 7 | 12 | 42 | 59 | 71 | 86 | 104 | 212 |

Figure 16.1 *Binary search*

Table 16.1 Work done in a binary search	
Comparisons	**Coverage, N**
1	1
2	2
3	4
4	8
5	16
.	.
.	.
W	2^{W-1}

However, we need the expression for the work, W, as a function of N. Therefore, we take the log base 2 of each side so that:

$$W = \log_2 N + 1$$

Now we simplify by removing the 1, and then realizing that one can convert $\log_2 N$ to $\log_x N$ merely by multiplying by $\log_2 x$. Consequently, since we reject constant multipliers as irrelevant, we lose interest in representing the specific base of the logarithm, leaving the work for a binary search as O(logN).

$O(N^2)$—Proportional to N2 $O(N^2)$ describes an algorithm whose performance is proportional to the square of N. It is a special case of $O(N \times M)$, which describes any operation on an $N \times M$ array or image.

$O(2^N)$—Exponential Growth or Worse Occasionally we run across very nasty implementations of simple algorithms. For example, consider the recursive implementation of the Fibonacci algorithm we discussed in Section 9.9.2. In this implementation, fib(N) = fib(N − 1) + fib(N − 2). So each time we add another term, the previous two terms have to be calculated again, thereby doubling the amount of work. If we double the work when 1 is added to N, in general the Big O is $O(2^N)$. Of course, in the case of this particular algorithm, there is a simple iterative solution with a much preferable performance of O(N).

16.1.2 Analyzing Complex Algorithms

We can easily calculate the Big O of simple algorithms. For more complex algorithms, we determine the Big O by breaking the complex algorithm into simpler abstractions, as we saw in Chapter 10. We would continue that process until the abstractions can be characterized as simple operations on defined collections for which we can determine their Big Os. The Big O of the overall algorithm is then determined from the individual components by combining them according to the following rules:

- If two components are sequential (do A and then do B), you add their Big O values
- If components are nested (for each A, do B), you multiply their Big O values

For example, we will see the merge sort algorithm in Section 16.2.5. It can be abstracted as follows:

> Perform a binary division of the data (O(logN)) and *then for each* binary step (of which there are O(log(N))), merge all the data items (O(N)).

This has the general form:

> Do A, then for each B, do C

which according to the rules above, should result in $O_A + O_B * O_C$. The overall algorithm therefore costs O(logN) + O(N) * O(logN).

We remove the first term because its growth is slower, leaving O(NlogN) as the overall algorithm cost.

16.2 Algorithms for Sorting Data

Generally, sorting a collection of data will organize the data items in such a way that it is possible to search for a specific item using a binary search rather than a linear search. This concept is nice in principle when dealing with simple collections like an array of numbers. However, it is more difficult in practice with real data. For example, telephone books are always sorted by the person's last name. This facilitates searching by last name, but it does not help if you are looking for the number of a neighbor whose name you do not know. That search would require sorting the data by street name.

There are many methods for sorting data. We present five representative samples selected from many sorting algorithms. First we describe each algorithm, and then we compare their performance and suggest engineering circumstances in which you would apply each algorithm. Note that in all these algorithms the comparisons are done using functions (for example, `gt(...)`, `lt(...)`, or `equals(...)`) rather than mathematical operators. This permits collections containing arbitrarily complex objects to be sorted merely by customizing the comparison functions.

16.2.1 Insertion Sort

Insertion sort is perhaps the most obvious sorting technique. Given the original collection of objects to sort, it begins by initializing an empty collection. For example, if the collection were a vector, you might allocate a new vector of the same size and initialize an "output index" to the start of that vector. Then the algorithm traverses the original vector, inserting each object from that vector in order into the output vector. This usually requires "shuffling" the objects in the new vector to make room for the new object. Figure 16.2 illustrates the situation where the first four numbers of the original vector have been inserted into the new vector; the algorithm finds the place to insert the next number (10) and then moves the 12 across to make space for it.

Listing 16.1 shows the MATLAB code for insertion sort on a vector of numbers. The algorithm works for any data type for which the function lt(A,B) compares two instances.

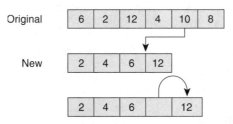

Figure 16.2 *Insertion sort in progress*

Listing 16.1 The insertion sort function

```
1. function b = insertionsort(a)
2. %  This function sorts a column vector,
3. %  using the insertion sort algorithm
4. b = []; i = 1; sz = length(a);
5. while i <= sz
6.    b = insert(b, a(i,1) );
7.    i = i + 1;
8. end

9. function a = insert(a, v)
10. % insert the value v into column vector a
11. i = 1; sz = length(a); done = false;
12. while i <= sz
13. if lt(v, a(i,1))
14.     done = true;
15.     a = [a(1:i-1); v; a(i:end)];
16. break;
17. end
18.    i = i + 1;
19. end
20. if ~done
21.    a(sz+1, 1) = v;
22. end
```

In Listing 16.1:

> Line 4: Initializes the result and the `while` loop parameters.
>
> Line 6: Calls the helper function to insert the latest value into the output vector.
>
> Line 9: Shows the helper function that does the hard work.
>
> Line 11: Initializes the `while` loop
>
> Line 13: The general purpose test to determine whether the inserted variable belongs ahead of the `i`th element.
>
> Line 14: We need the `done` flag set on exit to guard against not finding a place for `v`.
>
> Line 15: Insert `v` into the array.
>
> Line 16: Exit from the `while` loop—nothing left to do.
>
> Line 18: Updates the loop index.
>
> Lines 20–22: If there is no place to put `v` (it is bigger than all the elements), put it at the end.

Later we will refer to the selection sort algorithm that is similar in concept to insertion sort. Rather than sorting as the new data is put into the new vector, however, the selection sort algorithm repeatedly finds and deletes the smallest item in the original vector and puts it directly into the new vector. Both insertion sort and selection sort are $O(N^2)$ if used to sort a whole vector.

16.2.2 Bubble Sort

Where insertion sort is easy to visualize, it is normally implemented by creating a new collection and growing that new collection as the algorithm proceeds. Bubble sort is conceptually the easiest sorting technique to visualize, and is usually accomplished by rearranging the items in a collection in place. Given the original collection of N objects to sort, it makes $(N - 1)$ major passes through the data. The first major pass examines all N objects in a minor pass, and subsequent passes reduce the number of examinations by 1. On each minor pass through the data, beginning with the first data item and moving incrementally through the data, the algorithm checks to see whether the next item is smaller than the current one. If so, the two items are swapped in place in the array.

At the end of the first major pass, the largest item in the collection has been moved to the end of the collection. After each subsequent major pass, the largest remaining item is found at the end of the remaining items. The process repeats until on the last major pass, the first two items are compared and swapped if necessary. Figure 16.3 illustrates a bubble sort of a short vector. On the first pass, the value 98 is moved completely across the vector to the rightmost position. On the next pass, the 45 is moved into position.

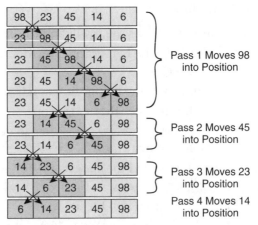

Figure 16.3 *Bubble sort*

On the third pass, the 23 reaches the right position, and the last pass finishes the sort.

Listing 16.2 shows the MATLAB code for bubble sort on a vector of numbers. The algorithm works for any data type for which the function gt(A,B) compares two instances. Since bubble sort performs $(N - 1) * N/2$ comparisons on the data, it is also $O(N^2)$. Some implementations use a flag to determine whether any swaps occurred on the last major pass, and terminate the algorithm if none occurred. However, the efficiency gained by stopping the algorithm early has to be weighed against the cost of setting and testing a flag whenever a swap is accomplished.

Listing 16.2 Bubble sort

```
 1. function bubblesort()
 2. %
 3. %  This function sorts the column array b in place,
 4. %  using the bubble sort algorithm
 5. %
 6. global b
 7. N = length(b);
 8. right = N-1;
 9. for in = 1:(N-1)
10.    for jn = 1:right
11.     if gt(b(jn), b(jn+1))
12.       tmp = b(jn);   % swap b(jn) with b(jn+1)
13.        b(jn) = b(jn+1);
14.        b(jn+1) = tmp;
15.     end
16.    end
17.    right = right - 1;
18. end
```

In Listing 16.2:

> Line 6: In order to be able to access the array in place, we pass it as a global variable instead of as a parameter.

> Lines 7 and 8: Since each pass puts the largest element in place, we can reduce the item count by 1 each time. This initializes the size of the first pass.

> Line 9: Shows the loop for the N − 1 major passes.

> Line 10: Shows the loop for each major pass.

> Line 11: Checks the current item against its neighbor.

> Lines 12–14: Swap the current item with its neighbor. By doing this in place, the largest item is always considered the current item until it reaches the end.

> Line 17: Shortens the row after each major pass because the largest item in the last pass is placed at the right-hand end.

16.2.3 Quick Sort

As its name suggests, the quick sort algorithm is one of the fastest sorting algorithms. It is designed to sort an array "in place." The quick sort algorithm is recursive, and uses an elegant approach to subdividing the original vector. Figure 16.4 illustrates this process. The algorithm proceeds as follows:

- The terminating condition occurs when the vector is of length 1, which is obviously sorted.

- A "pivot point" is then chosen. Some sophisticated versions go to a significant amount of effort to calculate the most effective pivot point. We are content to choose the first item in the vector.

- The vector is then subdivided by moving all of the items less than the pivot to its left, and all those greater than the pivot to its right, thereby placing the pivot in its final location in the resulting vector.

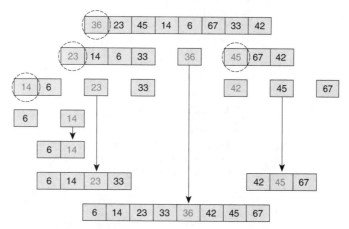

Figure 16.4 *Quick sort*

- The items to the left and right of the pivot are then recursively sorted by the same algorithm.
- The algorithm always converges because these two halves are always shorter than the original vector.

Listing 16.3 shows the MATLAB code for the quick sort algorithm. The partitioning algorithm looks a little messy, but it is just performing the array adjustments. It starts with i and j outside the vector to the left and right. Then it keeps moving each toward the middle as long as the values at i and j are on the proper side of the pivot. When this process stops, i and j are the indices of data items that are out of order. They are swapped, and the process is repeated until i passes j. Quick sort is O(NlogN). As with the previous techniques, this algorithm applies to collections of any data type for which the functions lt(A,B) and gt(A,B) compare two instances.

In Listing 16.3:

Line 1: Each recursive call is provided with the vector to sort and the range of indices to sort. These are initially from = 1 and to = length(a).

Listing 16.3 Quick sort

```
1. function a = quicksort(a, from, to)
2. %  This function sorts a column array,
3. %  using the quick sort algorithm
4.    if (from < to)
5.       [a p] = partition(a, from, to);
6.       a = quicksort(a, from, p);
7.       a = quicksort(a, p + 1, to);
8.    end

9. function [a lower] = partition(a, from, to)
10. %  This function partitions a column array
11.    pivot = a(from); i = from - 1; j = to + 1;
12.    while (i
13.     i = i + 1;
14.    while lt(a(i), pivot)
15.       i = i + 1;
16.    end
17.     j = j - 1;
18.    while gt(a(j), pivot)
19.       j = j - 1;
20.    end
21.    if  (i < j)
22.       temp = a(i); % this section swaps
23.       a(i) = a(j); % a(i) with a(j)
24.       a(j) = temp;
25.    end
26. end
27.    lower = j;
```

Line 4: The terminating condition for the recursion is when the subvector to sort has size 1—that is, when `from == to`.

Line 5: The helper function performs three roles—it places the pivot in the right place, moves the smaller and larger values to the correct sides, and returns the location of the pivot to permit the recursive partitioning.

Lines 6 and 7: Show recursive calls to sort the left and right parts of the vector.

Line 9: Shows the helper function.

Line 11: Initializes the variables.

Line 12: The outer loop continues until `i` passes `j`.

Lines 13–16: Skip `i` forwards over all the items less than the pivot.

Lines 17–20: Skip `j` backwards over all the elements greater than the pivot.

Line 21: If `i` passed `j`, the partitioning is complete.

Lines 22–24: Otherwise, `i` is indexing an item greater than the pivot, and `j` is indexing one less than the pivot. By swapping the contents of `a(i)` and `a(j)`, we rectify both inequities and can continue the inner loop.

Line 27: When the loop exits, both `i` and `j` are indexing the pivot.

There is one performance caution about quick sort. Its speed depends on the randomness of the data. If the data is mostly sorted, its performance reduces to $O(N^2)$.

16.2.4 Quick Sort in Place

A careful study of the performance of the quick sort algorithm indicates that while it performs as O(NlogN) for small collections, this quick sort implementation starts to look like $O(N^2)$ when N gets large. This is because MATLAB requires the arrays to be copied to return them from a function call. An alternative implementation using a global variable b to contain the array being sorted is shown in Listing 16.4. The majority of the comments above apply also to this version of the algorithm.

Listing 16.4 Quick sort in place

```
1. function quicksortip(from, to)
2. %
3. %  This function sorts a column array,
4. %  using the quick sort algorithm in place
5. %
6. if (from
7.    p = partition(from, to);
8.    quicksortip(from, p);
9.    quicksortip(p + 1, to);
10. end
```

continued on next page

```
11. function lower = partition(from, to)
12. global b
13. pivot = b(from); i = from - 1; j = to + 1;
14. while (i < j)
15.    i = i + 1;
16.    while lt(b(i), pivot)
17.        i = i + 1;
18.    end
19.    j = j - 1;
20.    while gt(b(j), pivot)
21.        j = j - 1;
22.    end
23.    if (i
24.        temp = b(i); % this section swaps
25.        b(i) = b(j); % b(i) with b(j)
26.        b(j) = temp;
27.    end
28. end
29. lower = j;
```

In Listing 16.4:

> Lines 1–9: The array is neither passed in nor returned.
>
> Line 12: Global access to the array.

16.2.5 Merge Sort

Merge sort is another O(NlogN) algorithm that achieves speed by dividing the original vector into two "equal" halves. Equality, of course, is not possible when there are an odd number of objects to be sorted, in which case the length of the "halves" will differ by at most 1. The heart of the merge sort algorithm is the technique used to reunite two smaller sorted vectors. This function is called "merge." Its objective is to merge two vectors that have been previously sorted. Since the two vectors are sorted, the smallest object can only be at the front of one of these two vectors. The smallest item is removed from its place and added to the result vector. This merge process continues until one of the two halves is empty, in which case the remaining half (whose values all exceed those in the result vector) is copied into the result.

The merge sort algorithm, like quick sort, is recursive, as shown in Figure 16.5 and as follows:

- The terminating condition is a vector with length less than 2, which is already sorted
- The recursive part invokes the merge function on the recursive call to merge the two halves of the vector
- The process converges because the halves are always smaller than the original vector

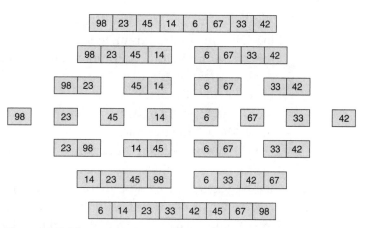

Figure 16.5 *Merge sort*

The code for merge sort is shown in Listing 16.5.

Listing 16.5 Merge sort

```
 1. function b = mergesort(a)
 2. %  This function sorts a column array,
 3. %  using the merge sort algorithm
 4.   b = a; sz = length(a);
 5.   if sz > 1
 6.     szb2 = floor(sz / 2);
 7.     first = mergesort(a(1 : szb2));
 8.     second = mergesort(a(szb2+1 : sz));
 9.     b = merge(first, second);
10.   end

11. function b = merge(first, second)
12. %   Merges two sorted arrays
13.   i1 = 1; i2 = 1;   out = 1;
14.   % as long as neither i1 nor i2 past the end,
15.   % move the smaller element into a
16.   while (i1 <= length(first)) & (i2 <= length(second))
17.   if lt(first(i1), second(i2))
18.     b(out,1) = first(i1); i1 = i1 + 1;
19.   else
20.     b(out,1) = second(i2); i2 = i2 + 1;
21.   end
22.    out = out + 1;
23. end
24. % copy any remaining entries of the first array
25. while i1 <= length(first)
26.   b(out,1) = first(i1); i1 = i1 + 1; out = out + 1;
27. end
28. % copy any remaining entries of the second array
29. while i2 <= length(second)
30.   b(out,1) = second(i2); i2 = i2 + 1; out = out + 1;
31. end
```

In Listing 16.5:

> Line 4: Initializes the parameters.
> Line 5: The terminating condition is an array of length 1, which does not need sorting.
> Line 6: Divides the array in half.
> Lines 7 and 8: Sort the halves of the array.
> Line 9: Merges the two sorted halves.
> Line 11: Shows the helper function to merge sorted arrays.
> Line 13: Initializes the `while` loop.
> Line 16: Stays in this loop until one of the two arrays is used up.
> Lines 17–20: Choose the smaller item to add to the result.
> Lines 25 and 26: Copy the remains of the first array.
> Lines 29 and 30: Copy the remains of the second array.

As discussed for quick sort, this algorithm would greatly benefit from the use of a global variable to contain the collection being sorted. We leave that improvement as an exercise.

16.2.6 Bucket Sort

A discussion of sorting techniques would not be complete without discussing bucket sort. This is also an O(NlogN) algorithm that is frequently used for sorting physical piles of papers, such as students' examination papers. The process begins with a stack of unsorted papers, each with an identifier consisting of a number or a unique name. One pass is made through the stack separating the papers into piles based on the first digit or character of the identifier. Subsequent passes sort each of these piles by subsequent characters or digits until all the piles have a small number of papers that can be sorted by insertion or selection sorts. The piles can then be reassembled in order. Figure 16.6 illustrates the situation at the end of the second sorting pass when piles for the first digit have also been separated by the second digit.

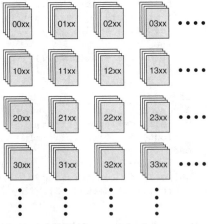

Figure 16.6 *Bucket sort*

There are a number of reasons why this technique is popular for sorting papers, including the following:

- There is a minimal amount of "paper shuffling" or bookkeeping
- The logarithm in the O(NlogN) is either 10 (numerical identifier) or 26 (alphabetic identifier), thereby providing a "constant multiplier" speed advantage
- Once the first sorting pass is complete, one can use multi-processing (in the form of extra people) to perform the remaining passes in parallel, thereby reducing the effective performance to O(N) (given sufficient parallel resources)

16.3 Performance Analysis

In order to perform a comparison of the performance of different algorithms, a script was written to perform each sort on a vector of increasing length containing random numbers. The script started with a length of 4 and continued doubling the length until it reached 32,768. To obtain precise timing measurements, each sort technique was repeated a sufficient number of times to obtain moderately accurate timing measurements with MATLAB's internal millisecond clock. In order to eliminate common computation costs, it was necessary to measure the overhead cost of the loops themselves and subtract that time from the times of each sort algorithm. Note that in order to show the results of the MATLAB internal sort, its execution time was multiplied by 1,000.

Figure 16.7 shows a typical plot of the results of this analysis, illustrating the relative power of O(NlogN) algorithms versus O(N^2) algorithms. The plot on a log-log scale shows the relative time taken by the selection sort,

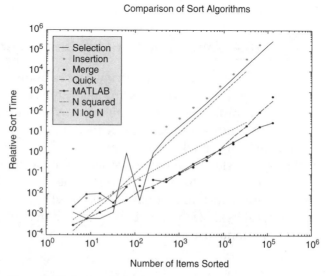

Figure 16.7 *Sort study results*

insertion sort, bubble sort, merge sort, quick sort, and quick sort in place algorithms, together with MATLAB's internal sort method. Also on the chart are plotted trend lines for $O(N^2)$ and $O(NlogN)$ processes. We can make the following observations from this chart:

- Since the scales are each logarithmic, it is tempting to claim that there is "not much difference" between $O(N^2)$ and $O(NlogN)$ algorithms. Looking closer, however, it is clear that for 100,000 items, the $O(N^2)$ sorts are around 1,000 times slower than the $O(NlogN)$ algorithms.

- The performance of most of the algorithms is extremely erratic below 100 items. If you are sorting small amounts of data, the algorithm does not matter.

- The selection sort, bubble sort, and insertion sort algorithms clearly demonstrate $O(N^2)$ behavior.

- The performance of the merge sort and quick sort algorithms is less clear. They appear to have $O(NlogN)$ performance when N is in the modest size range, but are tending toward $O(N^2)$ as N gets above 50,000. This is an artifact of the MATLAB implementation of functions that does not permit a function direct access to an array passed as a parameter, as discussed above. Every recursive call is therefore penalized by having to copy the result array back to the calling function. The quick sort in place algorithm has a well-defined $O(NlogN)$ performance.

- Clearly, the internal MATLAB sort function, in addition to being 1,000 times faster than any of the coded algorithms, is closely tracking the $O(NlogN)$ performance curve, indicating that it is programmed efficiently to take advantage of direct access to the array data.

16.4 Applications of Sorting Algorithms

This section discusses the circumstances under which you might choose to use one or another of the sorting algorithms presented above. We assert here without proof that the theoretical lower bound of sorting is $O(NlogN)$. Consequently, we should not be looking for a generalized sorting algorithm that improves on this performance. However, within those constraints, there are circumstances under which each of the sorting techniques performs best. As we saw in the analysis above, the MATLAB internal sort routine is blindingly fast, and should be used whenever possible. The subsequent paragraphs show the applicability and limitations of the other sort algorithms if you cannot use sort(...).

16.4.1 Using MATLAB's Internal Sort Algorithm

The first and most obvious question is why one would not always use the built-in MATLAB `sort(...)` function. Clearly, whenever that function works, you should use it. Its applicability seems to be limited to sorting numbers in an array, and you will come across circumstances when you need to sort more complex items. You might, for example, have a structure array of addresses and telephone numbers that you wish to sort by last name, first name, or telephone number. In this case, it seems that the internal sort program does not help, and you have to create your own sort.

Extracting and Sorting Vectors and Cell Arrays However, a closer examination of the specification of the sort function allows us to generalize the application of `sort(...)` significantly. When you call `sort(v)`, it actually offers you a second result that contains the indices used to sort v. So in the case where you have a cell array or a structure array and your sort criteria can be extracted into a vector, you can sort that vector, and use the second result, the indexing order, to sort the original array. Furthermore, if you can extract character string data into a cell array, the internal sort function will sort that cell array alphabetically.

For example, consider again the CD collection from Chapter 10. We might want to find the most expensive CD in our collection, and then make a list of artists and titles ordered alphabetically by artist. The script to accomplish this is shown in Listing 16.6.

In Listing 16.6:

> Line 1: Uses the previous script to build the CD collection.
>
> Line 2: Extracts the prices into a vector.
>
> Line 3: Sorts the prices (in ascending order).
>
> Line 4: The most expensive CD will be the last in ascending order.
>
> Line 5: Extracts the artists into a cell array.
>
> Line 6: Sorts the cell array in alphabetical order.
>
> Lines 7–10: Traverse the ordered list, printing the artist and title.

Listing 16.6 Sorting CDs

```
1. buildCDs
2. prices = [cds.price];
3. [np order] = sort(prices);
4. mostExpensive = cds(order(end))

5. artists = {cds.artist};
6. [junk order] = sort(artists);
7. for index = order
8.    cd = cds(index);
9.    fprintf('%30s:%s\n', cd.artist, cd.title)
10. end
```

The resulting output is shown in Table 16.2.

If the sort criteria are more complex, you will have to customize the comparison functions and use one of the following sort algorithms.

Table 16.2 CD display

```
mostExpensive =
    genre: 'Heavy Metal'
    artist: 'Bon Jovi'
    title: '100,000,000 Bon Jovi Fans Can't Be Wrong'
    year: 2004
    stars: 3.8000
    price: 47.1500


                2Pac:Loyal To The Game
                2Pac:Loyal To The Game
                2Pac:Loyal To The Game
Alison Krauss And Union Station:Lonely Runs Both Ways
Alison Krauss And Union Station:Lonely Runs Both Ways
            Anthrax:Greater Of Two Evils
            Ashanti:Concrete Rose
        Bocelli, Andrea:Andrea
            Bon Jovi:100,000,000 Bon Jovi Fans Can't Be Wrong
        Charles, Ray:Genius Loves Company
        Charles, Ray:Spirit Of Christmas
        Charles, Ray:Very Best Of Ray Charles
        Clapton, Eric:Sessions For Robert J
            Cure:Three Imaginary...
        Dream Theater:Live At Budokan
        El Gran Combo:Aqui Estamos y De Verdad
            Eminem:Encore
            Eminem:Encore
                Fey:La Fuerza Del Destino
        Groban, Josh:Closer
          Ivy Queen:Real
            Killers:Hot Fuss
            Ludacris:The Red Light District
            Ludacris:The Red Light District
                Nas:Street's Disciple
                Nas:Street's Disciple
        Phantom Of The Opera:The Phantom Of The Opera: Deluxe
    Edition
            Rammstein:Reise, Reise
        Rogers, Kenny:Gift
            T.I.:Urban Legend
            T.I.:Urban Legend
    Trans-Siberian Orchestra:Beethoven's Last Night
        Trevi, Gloria:Como Nace El Universo
        Twain, Shania:Greatest Hits
            U2:How To Dismantle An Atomic Bomb
        Yankee, Daddy:Barrio Fino
```

16.4.2 Insertion Sort

Insertion sort is the fastest means of performing incremental sorting. If a small number of new items—say, M—are being added to a sorted collection of size N, the process will be O(M * N), which will be fastest as long as M < log N.

16.4.3 Bubble Sort

Bubble sort is the simplest in-place sort to program, and is fine for small amounts of data.

16.4.4 Quick Sort

As its name suggests, this is the quickest of the sorting algorithms, and should normally be used for a full sort. However, it has one significant disadvantage: its performance depends on a fairly high level of randomness in the distribution of the data in the original array. Consequently, if there is a significant probability that your original data might be already sorted, or partially sorted, your quick sort is not going to be quick. You should use merge sort.

16.4.5 Merge Sort

Since its algorithm does not depend on any specific characteristics of the data, merge sort will always turn in a solid O(NlogN) performance. You should use it whenever you suspect that quick sort might get in trouble.

16.4.6 Bucket Sort

It is theoretically possible to write the bucket sort algorithm in MATLAB to attempt to take advantage of its apparent performance improvements over the more conventional algorithms shown previously. However, some practical problems arise:

- In practice, the manipulation of the arrays of arrays necessary to sort by this technique is quite complex
- The performance gained for manual sorts by "parallel processing" stacks using multiple people cannot be realized
- The logic for extracting the character or digit for sorting is going to detract from the overall performance

Therefore we recommend that the use of bucket sort be confined to manually sorting large numbers of physical objects.

16.5 Engineering Example—A Selection of Countries

In the Engineering Application problem in Section 10.5, we attempted to find the best country for a business expansion based on the rate of growth of the GNP for that country versus its population growth. The initial version of the program returned the suggestion that the company should move to Equatorial Guinea. However, when this was presented to the Board of Directors, it was turned down, and you were asked to bring them a list of the best 20 places to give them a good range of selection.

We should make two changes to the algorithm:

- Originally we used a crude approximation to determine the slope of the population and GNP curves. However, now we know that `polyfit` can perform this slope computation accurately, and we will substitute that computation.
- We will use the MATLAB sort function to find the 20 best countries.

The code to accomplish this, a major revision of the code in Chapter 10, is shown in Listing 16.7.

Listing 16.7 Updated world data analysis

```
1. worldData = buildData('World_data.xls');
2. n = 20;
3. bestn = findBestn(worldData, n);
4. fprintf('best %d countries are:\n', n)
5. for best = bestn(end:-1:1)
6.    fprintf('%s\n', worldData(best).name)
7. end

8. function bestn = findBestn(worldData, n)
% find the indices of the n best countries
% according to the criterion in the function
% fold
% we first map world data to add the field
%    growth
 9. for ndx = 1:length(worldData)
10.    cntry = worldData(ndx);
11.    worldData(ndx).growth = fold(cntry);
12. end
% now, sort on this criterion
13. values = [worldData.growth];
14. [junk order] = sort(values);
% filter these to keep the best 10
15. bestn = order(end-n+1:end);

16. function ans = fold(st)
% s1 is the rate of growth of population
17. pop = st.pop(~isnan(st.pop));
18. yr = st.year(~isnan(st.pop));
19. s1 = slope(yr, pop)/mean(pop);
% s2 is the rate of growth of the GDP
```

continued on next page

```
20. gdp = st.gdp(~isnan(st.gdp));
21. yr = st.year(~isnan(st.gdp));
22. s2 = slope(yr, gdp)/mean(gdp);
% Measure of merit is how much faster
%   the gdp grows than the population
23. ans = s2 - s1;

24. function s1 = slope(x, y)
% Estimate the slope of a curve
25. if length(x) == 0 || x(end) == x(1)
26.    error('bad data')
27. else
28.    coef = polyfit(x, y, 1);
29.    s1 = coef(1);
30. end
```

In Listing 16.7:

>Line 1: Reads the spreadsheet of world data.

>Line 2: Selects the number of countries to present.

>Line 3: Calls the function that will return the indices of the n best countries.

>Lines 4–7: Print the list of country names in reverse order (the best first).

>Line 8: Shows an updated version of the original function to return the indices of the n best countries.

>Lines 9–12: Map the worldData structure array, adding to each a field called growth that contains the criterion specified in the fold function.

>Line 13: Extracts the values of growth for each country.

>Line 14: Sorts these, keeping the order.

>Line 15: Returns the last n countries that will have the highest growth values.

>Lines 16–23: The fold function unchanged from Chapter 10.

>Lines 22–27: Unchanged beginning to the slope function.

>Lines 28 and 29: Use polyfit to compute an accurate slope and return it to the calling function.

The results from running this version are shown in Table 16.3. This seems to be an acceptable list of possibilities to take back to the Board of Directors.

Common Pitfalls

A deceptively simple question arises: should you expect the worldData at line 6 of Listing 16.7 to contain the field growth? Actually, it will not. Although it appears that the function findBestn adds this field to worldData, it is working with a copy of the worldData structure array that is not returned to the calling script.

Table 16.3 Updated world data results

Best 20 countries are:

Estonia	Lebanon
St. Kitts & Nevis	Malta
Albania	Cyprus
Vietnam	Tajikistan
Croatia	Taiwan
Kazakhstan	Korea, Republic of
Azerbaijan	Grenada
Uzbekistan	Ireland
Georgia	Portugal
Dominica	Antigua

Chapter Summary

This chapter discussed:

- A technique for comparing the performance of algorithms
- A range of algorithms for sorting a collection of data
- Application areas in which these algorithms are most appropriate

Special Characters, Reserved Words, and Functions

Special Characters, Reserved Words, and Functions	Description	Discussed in This Section
`polyfit(x, y, n)`	Computes a least-squares polynomial	16.5
`[v,in] = sort(v)`	Sort the vector v (a vector or a cell array of strings)	16.4.1

Self Test

Use the following questions to check your understanding of the material in this chapter:

True or False

1. When computing the Big O of sequential operations, you retain only the one that grows fastest with N.

2. All search algorithms have O(N).

3. No sort algorithm can perform better than O(N log N).

4. All sorting algorithms with $O(N^2)$ traverse the complete data collection N times.

5. Quick sort in reality should be listed as $O(N^2)$.

Fill in the Blanks

1. _____ is an algebra that permits us to express how the amount of _____ done in solving a problem relates to the amount of _____ being processed.

2. Any algorithm that traverses, maps, folds, or filters a collection is O(_____).

3. _____ sort and _____ sort perform with O(NlogN).

4. MATLAB's internal sort(...) returns the _____ and a _____ that allow you to sort any collection from whose elements one can derive a _____.

Programming Projects

1. On the following list of attributes, check all that apply to both quick sort and merge sort:
   - Defined recursively
   - $O(N^2)$
   - Linear search
   - Requires an array
   - Second law of thermodynamics
   - O(NlogN)
   - Defined iteratively
   - Binary search
   - Requires a collection with random access

2. Divide and Conquer strategy: Which sorting algorithm makes use of a pivot when sorting?

3. Sort the following array using the algorithms listed below. Show all of the vectors (excluding the empty ones) created at each step.

    [5 4 10 2 9 6 3 7 8 1]

    - Using merge sort
    - Using quick sort
    - Using insertion sort
    - Using bubble sort

4. Write and test an in-place version of merge sort that makes use of the global array, b.

5. Adapt the quick sort in place algorithm to operate on a cell array of strings sorting the strings alphabetically and ignoring case. You will need to adapt the generic comparison functions to include comparing alphabetically.

6. Adapt the bubble sort algorithm to operate on a structure array, one of whose fields is called "name." Sort the structures alphabetically by the name field, ignoring case. You could use the generic comparison functions previously adapted to include comparing alphabetically.

7. Write a script that will take a structure array and sort it using the internal MATLAB sort(...) algorithm. It should request the name of a field in the structure array containing numerical data, and sort the array based on the contents of that field. You could use the CD collection from Chapter 10 and sort it on the value or stars fields, for example.

MATLAB Special Characters, Reserved Words, and Functions

Special Characters	Description	Discussed in This Section
%	Indicates a comment in an m-file	2.4.2
{ }	Defines a cell array	7.2.1
[ ]	The empty vector	3.3.4
[...]	Concatenates data, vectors, and arrays	3.3.1
( )	Used to override operator precedence	3.3.5
( )	Used to identify the formal and actual parameters of a function	5.3.2, 5.3.4
( )	Used to index an array	3.3.3
(variable)	Used to allow a variable to be used as a structure field	7.3.1
'abc'	Encloses a literal character string	2.2.3, 6.2
'	Transposes an array	3.5.1
;	Separates rows in an array definition	3.5.2
;	Suppresses output when used in commands	2.4.5
:	Specifies a vector as `from:incr:to`	3.3.1
:	Used in slicing vectors and arrays	3.3.5
.	Used to access fields of a structure	7.3.1
...	Used to continue a MATLAB command to the next line	4.6.3

Mathematical Operators	Description	Discussed in This Section
=	Assignment operator—assigns a value to a memory location; not the same as an equality test	2.2.2
+	Scalar and array addition	3.3.5, 3.5.5
−	Scalar and array subtraction	3.3.5, 3.5.5
−	Unary negation	3.3.5, 3.5.5
*	Matrix multiplication	12.2.1
.*	Array multiplication	3.3.5, 3.5.5
/	Matrix division	12.2.2
./	Array division	3.3.5, 3.5.5
^	Matrix exponentiation	12.2.3
.^	Array exponentiation	3.3.5, 3.5.5

Logical Operators	Description	Discussed in This Section
<	Less than	3.3.5, 3.5.5
<=	Less than or equal to	3.3.5, 3.5.5
>	Greater than	3.3.5, 3.5.5
>=	Greater than or equal to	3.3.5, 3.5.5
==	Equal to	3.3.5, 3.5.5
~=	Not equal to	3.3.5, 3.5.5
&	Element-wise logical AND (vectors)	3.3.5, 3.5.5
&&	Short-circuit logical AND (scalar)	3.3.5, 3.5.5
|	Element-wise logical OR (vectors)	3.3.5, 3.5.5
||	Short-circuit logical OR (scalar)	3.3.5, 3.5.5
~	Unary not	3.3.5, 3.5.5

Logical Functions	Description	Discussed in This Section
all(a)	True if all the values in a (a logical vector) are true	4.3.3
and(a, b)	True if both a and b are true	4.3.3
any(a)	True if any of the values in a (a logical vector) are true	4.3.3, 17.2.4
not(a)	True if a is false; false if a is true	4.3.3
or(a, b)	True if either a or b is true	4.3.3

File Input and Output	Description	Discussed in This Section
load	Loads the workspace from a file	8.2
save	Saves variables in a file	8.2
csvread(file)	Reads comma-separated text files	8.3
csvwrite (file, data)	Writes comma-separated text files	8.3
dlmread (file, dlm)	Reads text files separated by the given delimiting character(s)	8.3
dlmwrite(file, data, dlm)	Writes text files separated by the given delimiting character(s)	8.3
fclose(fh)	Closes a text file	8.4.1
fgetl(fh)	Reads a line omitting the new-line character	8.4.2
fgets(fh)	Reads a line including the new-line character	8.4.2
fh = fopen(file, fl)	Opens a text file for reading or writing	8.4.1
fprintf(...)	Writes to the console, or to plain text files	8.3, 8.4.2
imread(file)	Reads an image file	13.3
imwrite(data, file, format)	Writes an image file	13.3
[tk rest] = strtok(str, dlm)	Extracts a token from a string and returns the remainder of the string	8.4.2

continued on next page

`ca = textscan(fh, format)`	Acquires and scans a line of text according to a specific format	8.3, 8.4.2
`[data Fs nb] = wavread(file)`	Reads a sound file in `.wav` format	14.3
`wavwrite(data, Fs, nb, file)`	Writes a sound file in `.wav` format	14.3
`[nums, txt, raw] = xlsread(file)`	Reads an Excel spreadsheet	8.3.2
`xlswrite(file, data, sheet, range)`	Writes an Excel spreadsheet in a specific row/column range	8.3.2

Format Control Characters	Description	Discussed in This Section
`%e`	Exponential notation	6.3.1
`%f`	Fixed point or decimal notation	6.3.1
`%g`	Fixed point or exponential notation	6.3.1
`%q`	A quoted string delimited by double quotes	6.3.1
`%s`	Character string	6.3.1
`\n`	Linefeed	6.3.1
`\t`	Tab	6.3.1
`\b`	Backspace	6.3.1

Display Formatting Commands	Description	Discussed in This Section
`format compact`	Sets format to compact form	help format
`format long`	Sets format to 14 decimal places	help format
`format long e`	Sets format to 14 exponential places	help format
`format loose`	Sets format back to default, non-compact form	help format
`format short`	Sets format back to default, 4 decimal places	help format
`format short e`	Sets format to 4 exponential places	help format

Workspace Management	Description	Discussed in This Section
`ans`	Default variable name for results of MATLAB calculations	2.2.2
`clc`	Clears the command screen	2.3.2
`clear`	Clears the workspace	2.4.2
`clf`	Clears the current figure	11.1.1
`close all`	Closes all graphics windows	11.1.1
`exit`	Terminates MATLAB	help exit
`help`	Invokes help utility	3.1
`load`	Loads the workspace from a file	8.2
`quit`	Terminates MATLAB	help quit
`save`	Saves variables in a file	8.2
`who`	Lists variables in the workspace	2.3.3
`whos`	Lists variables and their sizes	2.3.3

Special Constants	Description	Discussed in This Section
eps	Smallest possible difference between two floating point numbers	help eps
false	Logical false	3.2.3, 4.2
inf	Infinity	help inf
NaN	Not a number	8.3.2, 15.1.1
pi	Built-in mathematical constant	2.3.1
true	Logical true	3.2.3, 4.2

Basic Mathematical Functions	Description	Discussed in This Section
This is a partial list of the most commonly used functions. See MATLAB help for the complete list.		
abs(x)	Computes the absolute value	help abs
ceil(x)	Rounds x to the nearest integer toward positive infinity	3.3.5
cross(a, b)	Vector cross product	3.4
exp(x)	Computes the value of e^x	help exp
fix(x)	Rounds x to the nearest integer toward zero	3.3.5
floor(x)	Rounds x to the nearest integer toward minus infinity	3.3.5
log(x)	Computes the natural log of x	help log
log10(x)	Computes the log base 10 of x	help log10
mod(x, a)	Computes the remainder when x is divided by a	help mod
rem(x, a)	Computes the remainder when x is divided by a	help rem
round(x)	Rounds x to the nearest integer	3.3.5
sqrt(x)	Calculates the square root of x	2.4.2

Trigonometry	Description	Discussed in This Section
This is a partial list of the most commonly used functions. See MATLAB help for the complete list.		
acos(x)	Computes the inverse cosine (arcsine) of x	help acos
asin(x)	Computes the inverse sine (arcsine) of x	help asin
atan(x)	Computes the inverse tangent (arctan) of x	help atan
atan2(y, x)	Computes the inverse tangent given the x and y values (4 quadrant resolution)	help atan2
cos(x)	Computes the cosine of x	help cos
sin(x)	Computes the sine of x	help sin
tan(x)	Computes the tangent of x	help tan

Vector, Array, and Matrix Operations	Description	Discussed in This Section
cumsum(v)	Computes a cumulative sum of the values in v	15.3.2
deal(...)	Distributes cell array results among variables	7.2.2

continued on next page

`det(a)`	Computes the determinant of a matrix	help det
`diag(a)`	Extracts the diagonal from a matrix or (if provided with a vector) constructs a matrix with the given diagonal	3.5.2
`eye(n)`	Generates the identity matrix	12.2.1
`find(<logical a>)`	Computes a linear list of the locations of the true values in a logical array	3.2.5, 3.4.5
`fliplr(a)`	Flips a matrix from left to right	help fliplr
`inv(a)`	Computes the inverse of a matrix	12.2.3
`length(a)`	Determines the largest dimension of an array	3.3.2, 3.5.1
`linspace(fr,to,n)`	Defines a linearly spaced vector	3.3.1
`magic(n)`	Generates a magic square	3.5.2
`[v,in] = max(a)`	Finds the maximum value and its position in a	3.3.5
`mean(a)`	Computes the average of the elements in a	3.3.5
`meshgrid(x, y)`	Maps each of two vectors into separate two-dimensional arrays	11.4.1
`[v,in] = min(a)`	Finds the minimum value and its position in a	3.3.5
`ones(r, c)`	Generates an array filled with the value 1	3.3.1, 3.5.1
`prod(x)`	Product of all the items in x	help prod
`rand(r, c)`	Calculates an r × c array of evenly distributed random numbers in the range 0…1	3.3.1
`randn(r, c)`	Calculates an r × c array of normally distributed random numbers in the range 0…1	3.3.1
`size(a)`	Determines the dimensions of an array	3.3.2, 3.5.1
`sparse`	Defines a sparse matrix	17.2.3
`[v,in] = sort(v)`	Sorts the vector v (is a vector or a cell array of strings)	16.4.1, 16.5
`sum(a)`	Finds the sum of an array	3.3.5
`zeros(r, c)`	Builds an array filled with the value 0	3.3.1

2-D Plotting	Description	Discussed in This Section
`bar`	Generates a bar graph	11.2.4
`barh`	Generates a horizontal bar graph	11.2.4
`contour`	Generates a contour plot	11.4.5
`hist`	Generates a histogram	11.2.4
`loglog`	Generates an x-y plot, with both axes scaled logarithmically	11.2.4
`pie`	Generates a pie chart	11.2.4
`plot`	Creates an x-y plot	11.1.2, 11.2.1
`polar`	Creates a polar plot	11.2.4
`semilogx`	Generates an x-y plot, with the x-axis scaled logarithmically	11.2.4
`semilogy`	Generates an x-y plot, with the y-axis scaled logarithmically	11.2.4

3-D Plotting	Description	Discussed in This Section
`bar3`	Generates a three-dimensional bar graph	11.3.3
`barh3`	Generates a horizontal three-dimensional bar graph	11.3.3
`gplot`	Plot a graph	17.2.8
`mesh`	Generates a mesh plot of a surface	11.4.1
`meshc`	Generates a mesh plot of a surface with contours	11.4.5
`meshz`	Generates a mesh plot of a surface with a skirt	11.4.5
`meshgrid(r, c)`	Creates a plaid for 3-D plots	11.4.1
`peaks`	Creates a sample matrix used to demonstrate graphing functions	11.4.2
`pie3`	Generates a three-dimensional pie chart	11.3.3
`plot3`	Generates a three-dimensional line plot	11.3.1
`sphere`	Example function used to demonstrate graphing	11.4.5
`surf`	Generates a surface plot	11.4.1
`surfc`	Generates a combination surface and contour plot	11.4.5
`waterfall`	Generates a mesh plot of a surface with one skirt edge	11.4.1

Plot Appearance Indicator	Line Type	Discussed in This Section
−	Solid	11.2.2
:	Dotted	11.2.2
−.	Dash-dot	11.2.2
—	Dashed	11.2.2
.	Point	11.2.2
o	Circle	11.2.2
x	x-mark	11.2.2
+	Plus	11.2.2
*	Star	11.2.2
s	Square	11.2.2
d	Diamond	11.2.2
v	Triangle down	11.2.2
^	Triangle up	11.2.2
<	Triangle left	11.2.2
>	Triangle right	11.2.2
P	Pentagram	11.2.2
h	Hexagram	11.2.2

Indicator	Color	Discussed in This Section
b	Blue	11.2.2
g	Green	11.2.2

continued on next page

r	Red	11.2.2
c	Cyan	11.2.2
m	Magenta	11.2.2
y	Yellow	11.2.2
k	Black	11.2.2

Figure Control	Description	Discussed in This Section
axis	Freezes the current axis scaling for subsequent plots or specifies the axis dimensions	11.1.2
figure	Opens a new figure window	11.1.1
grid off/on	Turns the grid off or on	11.1.2
hold off/on	Instructs MATLAB to erase figure contents before adding new information or not	11.1.2
legend(ca)	Adds a legend to a graph	11.1.2
shading <value>	Shades a surface plot with one color per grid section	11.1.2
subplot(plts, n)	Divides the graphics window up into sections available for plotting	11.1.3
text(x,y,str)	Adds a textbox to a graph	11.1.2
title(str)	Adds a title to a plot	11.1.2
xlabel(str)	Adds a label to the x-axis	11.1.2
ylabel(str)	Adds a label to the y-axis	11.1.2
zlabel(str)	Adds a label to the z-axis	11.1.2

Color Map Values	Description	Discussed in This Section
autumn	Colormap for surface plots and images	11.1.2
bone	Colormap for surface plots and images	11.1.2
colorcube	Colormap for surface plots and images	11.1.2
cool	Colormap for surface plots and images	11.1.2
copper	Colormap for surface plots and images	11.1.2
flag	Colormap for surface plots and images	11.1.2
hot	Colormap for surface plots and images	11.1.2
hsv	Colormap for surface plots and images	11.1.2
jet	Default Colormap	11.1.2
pink	Colormap for surface plots and images	11.1.2
prism	Colormap for surface plots and images	11.1.2
spring	Colormap for surface plots and images	11.1.2
summer	Colormap for surface plots and images	11.1.2
white	Colormap for surface plots and images	11.1.2
winter	Colormap for surface plots and images	11.1.2

String Operations	Description	Discussed in This Section
disp(...)	Displays matrix or text	3.3.5, 6.4.1
fprintf(...)	Prints formatted information	6.4.2
input(...)	Prompts the user to enter a value	6.3.2
int2str(a)	Converts an integer to its numerical representation	6.3.1
num2str(a,n)	Converts a number to its numerical representation with n decimal places	6.3.1
sprintf(...)	Formats a string result	6.3.1
sscanf(...)	Formatted input conversion	6.3.2
strcmp(s1, s2)	Compares two strings—returns true if equal	6.4.3
strcmpi(s1, s2)	Compares two strings without regard to case—returns true if equal	6.4.3
textscan	Scans a text string	8.3.1, 8.4.2

Time-Related Functions	Description	Discussed in This Section
clock	Determines the current time on the CPU clock	help clock
etime	Finds elapsed time	help etime
pause	Pauses the execution of a program, either until any key is hit or for a specified number of seconds	13.4.5
tic	Starts a timing sequence	help tic
toc	Stops a timing sequence	help toc

Numerical Methods	Description	Discussed in This Section
diff(v)	Computes the differences between adjacent values in a vector	15.4.2
interp1	Computes linear and cubic interpolation	15.1.1
interp2	Computes linear and cubic interpolation	15.1.1
interp3	Computes linear and cubic interpolation	15.1.1
polyfit(x, y, n)	Computes a least-squares polynomial	15.2.2
polyval(c, x)	Evaluates a polynomial	15.2.2
spline(x, y)	Spline interpolation	15.1.2

Program Control	Description	Discussed in This Section
break	A command within a loop module that forces control to the statement following the innermost loop	4.6.4, 4.7.4
case	A specific value within a switch statement	4.1, 4.4.1
catch	End of a suspect code block where the exception is trapped	9.4.3
continue	Skips to the end of the innermost loop, but remains inside it	4.6.4, 4.7.4

continued on next page

else	Within an `if` statement, begins the code block executed when the condition is false	4.2, 4.3.2
elseif	Within an `if` statement, begins a second test when the first condition is false	4.2, 4.3.2
end	Terminates an `if`, `switch`, `for`, `while`, or `catch` block.	4.1, 4.3.2, 4.4.1, 4.6
end	Last element in a vector	3.3.5, 3.5.5
for var = v	A code module repeated as many times as there are elements in the vector `v`	4.1, 4.6
function	Identifies an m-file as a function	5.3.2
error(str)	Announces an error with the string provided	9.4.3
global var	Defines a variable as globally accessible	5.3.8, 9.10
if <exp>	Begins a conditional module—the following code block is executed if the logical expression <exp> is true	4.1, 4.3.2
lasterror	Provides a structure describing the environment from which an exception was thrown	9.4.3
nargin	Determines the number of input parameters actually supplied by a function's caller	5.3.4
nargout	Determines the number of output parameters actually requested by a function's caller	5.3.4
otherwise	Catch-all code block at the end of a `switch` statement	4.1, 4.4.1
switch variable	Begins a code module selecting specific values of the `variable` (must be countable)	4.1, 4.4.1
try	Begins a block of suspect code from which an exception might be thrown	9.4.3
while <exp>	A code module repeated as long as the logical expression <exp> is true	4.1, 4.5

Data Class Operations	Description	Discussed in This Section
char(...)	Casts to a character type	6.2, 6.5
class(obj)	Determines the data type of an object	7.2.4, 17.1.3
double(a)	Casts to type `double`	6.2
int8/16/32/64(a)	Casts to integer type with the specified number of bits	help
uint8/16/32/64(a)	Casts to unsigned integer type with the specified number of bits	help
isa(obj, str)	Tests for a given data type	7.2.4, 17.1.3
ischar(ch)	Determines whether the given object is of type `char`	6.2.3, 7.2.4
iscell(...)	Determines whether the given object is a cell	7.2.4
islogical(...)	Determines whether the given object is of type `logical`	7.2.4
isnumeric(...)	Determines whether the given object is of type `double`	7.2.4

continued on next page

`isstruct(...)`	Determines whether the given object is a structure	7.2.4
`isempty(a)`	Tests for the empty vector []	17.1.2
`isspace(a)`	Tests for the space character	6.2.3

Structure Operations	Description	Discussed in This Section
`fieldnames(str)`	Returns a cell array containing strings that are the names of the fields	7.3.1
`getfield(str,<fld>)`	Extracts the value of the field `<fld>`	7.4.3
`isfield(str, <fld>)`	Returns true if the string is a field in this structure	7.4.3
`str = rmfield(str, <fld>)`	Returns a copy of the given structure with a field removed	7.3.1
`str = setfield (str,<fld>, <value>)`	Constructs a structure in which the value of field `<fld>` has been changed	7.4.3
`struct(...)`	Constructs a structure from `<fieldname>` `<value>` pairs of parameters	7.3.2

The ASCII Character Set

Originally, the American Standard Code for Information Interchange (ASCII) defined a mapping whereby a specific set of characters was assigned the numerical values 0–127. This was sufficient to represent the number symbols, the lowercase and uppercase alphabet, and all the common punctuation marks. However, as the need arose to represent more international characters, this numerical range was inadequate, and the next 128 values were assigned to meet this need. There is no universal agreement on this second mapping. The following table shows the values used by MATLAB.

Then, more international issues arose with other complete alphabets, and the standard international character set now uses a 16-bit representation, of which the original ASCII set are the first 256.

	0	1	2	3	4	5	6	7	8	9
0										
10										
20										
30				!	"	#	$	%	&	'
40	(	)	*	+	,	-	.	/	0	1
50	2	3	4	5	6	7	8	9	:	;
60	<	=	>	?	@	A	B	C	D	E
70	F	G	H	I	J	K	L	M	N	O
80	P	Q	R	S	T	U	V	W	X	Y
90	Z	[	\	]	^	_	`	a	b	c
100	d	e	f	g	h	i	j	k	l	m
110	n	o	p	q	r	s	t	u	v	w
120	x	y	z	{	|	}	~			
130										
140										
150										
160		¡	¢	£	¤	¥	¦	§	¨	©
170	ª	«	¬		®	¯	°	±	²	³
180	´	µ	¶	·	¸	¹	º	»	¼	½
190	¾	¿	À	Á	Â	Ã	Ä	Å	Æ	Ç
200	È	É	Ê	Ë	Ì	Í	Î	Ï	Ð	Ñ
210	Ò	Ó	Ô	Õ	Ö	×	Ø	Ù	Ú	Û
220	Ü	Ý	Þ	ß	à	á	â	ã	ä	å
230	æ	ç	è	é	ê	ë	ì	í	î	ï
240	ð	ñ	ò	ó	ô	õ	ö	÷	ø	ù
250	ú	û	ü	ý	þ	ÿ				

Internal Number Representation

There are two different techniques whereby most computers today store the values of numbers: integer and floating-point. Integer storage has the nice property that it represents the exact value of the number stored; floating-point storage only guarantees a certain number of digits of precision. There is an upper limit to the values that can be stored in both integer and floating-point form. However, significantly larger numbers can be stored in floating-point storage than in integer storage.

By default, MATLAB sets the storage of numbers to double-precision floating-point representation. However, operations like reading images into MATLAB present the large volume of data in the more compact unsigned integer form.

Integers

Integers are represented in computer memory by blocks of data bits of various sizes. Memory is allocated in 8-bit increments, usually referred to as bytes; therefore, it is not surprising that integer storage comes in the same size increments. For a given size, the values of the data bits are represented in two different ways—signed or unsigned. Normally, of course, we expect a number to have both positive and negative values, and when the number of bits is large, this does not seem to have much impact.

However, when a small number of bits is used to store a value, one of those bits must be used to show that the number is positive or negative. The range of numbers that can be stored is therefore reduced by one bit, a factor of 2. The following figure illustrates the internal storage of 8-bit unsigned and signed values.

Unsigned 8-Bit Integer

Power of 2:	2^7	2^6	2^5	2^4	2^3	2^2	2^1	2^0
Value of bit is 1:	128	64	32	16	8	4	2	1

Example:	0	0	1	0	1	1	0	1

$$32 \quad +8 \quad +4 \quad +1 = 45$$

Signed 8-Bit Integer

Power of 2:	sign	2^6	2^5	2^4	2^3	2^2	2^1	2^0
Value of bit is 1:	–128	64	32	16	8	4	2	1

Example:	1	1	1	0	1	1	0	1

$$-128 + 64 + 32 \quad +8 \quad +4 \quad +1 = -9$$

Clearly, for 8 bits, the maximum value is 127 signed, or 255 unsigned. If this is not sufficient storage, numbers can be stored in 16-, 32-, or 64-bit words, with the corresponding increase in the maximum stored size.

Floating-Point Numbers

Floating-point numbers are stored in single precision (32 bits) or double precision (64 bits) using the IEEE 754 standard. As the name suggests, the storage format includes a mantissa and an exponent, each expressed internally in a manner similar to integer storage. The fixed size of the mantissa leads to the fixed amount of precision of each storage type. The `float` data type gives 7 significant decimal digits; the `double` data type gives 15 significant decimal digits.[1]

For details of these storage types, search the Web for "IEEE 754 standard." At the time of writing, there was a good explanation at:

> http://www.geocities.com/SiliconValley/Pines/6639/docs/fp_summary.html

Parameters of Each Storage Type

The following table describes the most commonly used storage types available in MATLAB, their minimum and maximum values, and their equivalent names in C.

MATLAB Name	Size (Bytes)	Minimum Value	Maximum Value	C Name
uint8	1	0	255	unsigned char
int8	1	−128	127	char
uint16	2	0	65,535	unsigned short
int16	2	−32,768	32,767	short
uint32	4	0	4,294,967,295	unsigned int
int32	4	−2,147,483,648	2,147,483,647	int
uint64	8	0	18,446,744,073, 709,551,615	unsigned long int
int64	8	−9,223,372,.036, 854,775,808	9,223,372,036, 854,775,807	long int
float	4	~−3.4E+38	~3.4E+38	float
double	8	~−1.7E+308	~1.7E+308	double

---

[1] Note that although this seems to be a large amount of precision, you must always design your programs to preserve that precision. If, for example, you were to subtract two numbers almost equal in value, the precision of the result would be significantly worse than that of the original numbers.

Index

Symbols

./ (array division operator)   58, 79, 307, 324, A–2

.^ (array exponentiation)   58, 69, 79, A–2

.* (array multiplication operator)   58, 79, 324, A–1

= (assignment operator)   24, 44, A–1

\ (backslash)
controlling formats   140
matrix division and   307, 324

{ } (braces)   90
cell arrays and   158, 177, A–1

: (colon operator)
creating vectors   51, 58, 79, A–1
slicing vectors   60, 79, A–1

<= (comparison operator)   58

>= (comparison operator)   58

> (comparison operator)   58

-= (comparison operator)   58

[...] (concatenates data)   51, A–1

– (dashed line), plotting 2D   266

$ (dollar sign), in variable names   24

. (dot operator)   69
structure fields, accessing   163, 177, A–1

& (element-wise AND)   58, 80, A1

| (element-wise OR)   58, 80, A–2

... (ellipses)   39, 44
commands, continuing   102, A–1
structures and   165

== (equal to)   58, 79, A–2

> (greater than)   58, 79, A–2

>- (greater than or equal to)   58, 79, A–2

< (less than)   58, 79, A–2

<- (less than or equal to)   58, 79, A–2

&& (logical AND)   57, 80, 95, A–2

|| (logical OR)   57, 80, 95, A–2

/ (matrix division)   307, 324, A–2

^ (matrix exponent)   307, 324, A–2

* (matrix multiplication)   304, 307–310, 324, A–1

~= (not equal to)   58, 79, A–2

( ) (parentheses)
access array fields   163, 177, A–1
function definition   119, 127, A–1
overruling precedence   58, A–1
structure fields and   163, A–1

% (percent sign)
formating strings with (sprintf() function)   140
writing comments   37, 44, 56, A–1

+ (plus sign)   55, 58, 79, A–1

.^ (power operator)   58

>> prompt   23
assigning variables and   25

.' (scalar transpose operator)   58

; (semicolons)   44
Array editor and   34
end-of-line characters and   39, 44, A1
separating rows   32, 66, 79, A–1

' (single quotes)   44
character strings and   26, 137, A–1
matrix transpose operator   58, 79, A–1

[ ] (square braces)   54, A–1
[...] (concatenates data)   51, A–1

– (unary minus operator)   55, 79, A–1

_ (underscore), in variable names   24

Numbers

2-D plotting   264–270
parametric   268
2-D rotation   310–314
3-D plotting   270–273
bodies of rotation   284–288
compound surfaces, assembling   289
3-D rotation   314–317
4GLs (fourth generation languages)   12

A

A/D (analog-to-digital)   358

abs() function   A–4

abstraction   11, 118
behavioral   304
data   21, 50

Access (Microsoft)   10

acos() function   A–4

acosd() function   211

activation stack   204

actual parameters   121

Ada   11

ALU (Arithmetic and Logic Unit)   5

AI (artificial intelligence)   13

algorithms   21
sorting   425–435

all() function   95, 109, A–2

alpha() function   288, 296

American National Standard Institute (ANSI)   13

amplitude   358

analog signals   358

analog-to-digital (A/D)   358

AND, element-wise   58

AND, logical (&&)   57, 95

and() function   95, 101, 109, A–2

ans default variable name   25, 29, 44, A–3

ANSI (American National Standard Institute)   13

any() function   95, 109, A–2

arbitrary axis, rotating   288

architectures (computer)   3–4

Arithmetic and Logic Unit (ALU)   5

arithmetic operations   54
   arrays   68
   strings   138

Array editor   34

array exponentiation (.^)   58, 69, 79, A–2

array division operator (./)   58, 79, A–2

array multiplication operator (.*)   50, 79, A–1

arrays   32, 49–88
   cell   158–162
   concatenating   71
   creating   66
   elements, accessing   67
   linearized   72
   matrices   303–328
   operating on   68–79
   problem solving and   234
   properties of   65
   removing elements   68
   reshaping   72
   slicing   71
   strings   145
   structure   166–172
   vectors   50–64
   vs. matrices   65

artificial intelligence (AI)   13

asin() function   A–4

assemblers   15

assembly language   11

assignment operator (=)   24, 44, A–1

atan() function   A–4

atan2() function   A–4

.au (audio) files   188, 359

auread() function   188, 359, 384

auwrite() function   188, 384

AutoCAD   10

auxiliary functions   123

.avi files   188

aviread() function   188

axis() function   260, 295, A–7
   2D plotting and   266

B

\b (backspace)   140, A–3

Babbage, Charles   3

backslash (\)
   controlling formats   140
   matrix division and   307, 324

backward difference approximation   405

bar() function   269, 295, A–5

bar3() function   273, 296, A–5

barh() function   269, 295, A–5

barh3() function   273, 296, A–5

BASIC   11

Basic Input/Output System (BIOS)   7

Big O algebra   422–425

binary encoding   5

binary search O(logN)   423

binary strings   11

BIOS (Basic Input/Output System)   7

bits   5

BMP files   331

bodies of rotation   284

Boolean values   54
   conditional execution   90

braces ({ })   90
   cell arrays and   158, 177

break points   40

break statement   102, 104, A–8

bubble sort   426, 439

bucket sort   434, 439

bugs   14

built-in functions   50

buses (data)   6

bytes   6

C

%c (character conversions)   140

C programming language   11, 13

C++ programming language   13

cache memory   7

CAD (computer-aided design)   10

Cartesian axis system   280
   rotating   311

case statement   90, A–8
   cell arrays and   161

casting (character)   136

catch keyword   A–8
   catching exceptions   209, 227

catching exceptions   209

.cdf (comma data format) files   188

cdfread() function   188

cdfwrite() function   188

ceil() function   59, A–4

cell arrays   158–162
   problem solving and   234

central difference approximation   406

Central Processing Units (CPU)   4, 204

char() function   138, A–9
   arrays of strings and   145

char data type   27

character conversions (%c)   140

character generator   135

character strings   135–156
   arithmetic/logical   138
   arrays of   145
   format conversion functions   139–142
   mapping/casting   136
   operations   142–145
   slicing/concatenating   138

class() function   162, 177, A–9

classes   27

clc (Clear Command) command   29, 44, 75, A–3

clear command   44, 75, A–3

clf command   260, 295, A–3

clock() function   A–8

clones of functions (recursion)   206

close all command   260, 295, A–3

COBOL   11

code blocks   89
   Boolean values and   91

coef() function   397

collections   50, 231
   building   238–241
   filtering   242–244
   mapping   241
   searching   246
   sorting   247
   summarizing   244–246
   traversing   235–238

: (colon operator)
   creating vectors   51, 58, 79, A–1
   slicing vectors   60, 79, A–1

color mapped images   331

color masking 335–346

colormap() function 260, 295

colormap values A–7

Colossus (computing machine) 3

columns, removing from arrays 68

column vectors 66

comma-separated numbers files
(.csv) 188

Command mode 28

command history 28

Command window 27–29
   assigning variables and 25
   Boolean values and 94
   scripts, running 39
   who command and 33

comments 37, 40

common data format (.cdf) files
188

comparison operators 58, A–2

compilers 14

compound conditional statements
91

compound surfaces, assembling
289–291

computers 2–18
   architectures, history of 3–4
   programming languages 10–15

computer-aided design (CAD) 10

concatenation 59
   arrays 71
   sound 360–363
   strings 138

containers (plot) 260

continue statement 104, A–8

contour() function 288, 297, A–5

conditional execution 90

constants, generating parameters
121

constructor functions 165

Control Units (hardware) 5

coordinates, rotating 310–317

cos() function 29, 284, A–4

CPUs (Central Processing Unit) 4,
204

cross() function 64, A–4

.csv (comma-separated numbers)
files 188

csvread() function 188, 198, A–2

csvwrite() function 188, 198, A–2

cubic spline 392–394

cumsum() function 403, 412, A–4

CUR files 331

current directory 33
   scripts, running 38

curve fitting 319–321, 394–400
   practical application of 399

cylinder images, creating 281

cylinder() function 288, 297

Cypher School 3

D

%d (integer conversions) 140, A–3

D/A (digital-to-analog) 359

dashed line (–), plotting 2D 266

data abstraction 21, 50, 304

data buses 6

data collections (see collections)

data manipulation 23–27

data types 25–27, 51

database management 10

deal() function 159, 177, A–4

debugging 14
   scripts 40

default configuration window 27

delimited text files (.dlm) 188, 191

desktop publishing 10

det() function A–4

diag() function 66, A–4

diagonal (arrays) 66

diff() function 406, 412, A–8

difference engines (Babbage) 3

difference expressions 405

digital muting 378

digital-to-analog (D/A) 359

directories, accessing current 33

disks, drawing 289

disp() function 62, 151, A–7
   character string operations and
   142

dissimilar objects, collecting 158

division
   ./ (array) 58, 79, 324, A–2
   / (matrix) 307, 324, A–1

.dlm (general delimited text) files
188

dlmread() function 188, 191, 198,
191, A–2

dlmwrite() function 188, 198, A–2

Document window 34

dollar signs ($), in variable names
24

. (dot operator) 69
   structure fields, accessing 163,
   177, A–1

double() function 138, A–9

double data type 27

drivers 8

E

%e (exponential notation) 140, A–3

Edit mode 28

Editor window 35

EDU>> prompt 23
   assigning variables and 25

element-wise AND (&) 58, 80, A–2

element-wise OR (|) 58, 80, A–2

element-by-element multiplication
56

elements 51, 65
   accessing 67
   removing 68
   structure, accessing 167

ellipses (...) 39, 44
   commands, continuing 102, A–1
   structures and 165

ellipsoid() function 288, 297

else keyword 90, A–8

elseif keyword 90, A–8
   cell arrays and 162

embedded computers 8
   Ada 13

encapsulation 23, 118
   variable scoping 123

end keyword 60, 90, A–8

end-of-command characters 39

Enigma machines 4

eps command A–4

equal (axis) 260

equal to (==) 58, 79, A–2

error() function 210, 227, A–8

errors (compile) 14

etime() function A–8

Excel (Microsoft) 10
   reading/writing spreadsheets
   188–191

exceptions 208–212

execution control 89–116
   conditional 90
   if statements 90–96
   switch statements 96–98

execution of programs 14
  MATLAB 15
`exit` command 23, A–3
`exp()` function A–3
exponential growth or worse O(2N) 424
exponentiation
  `.^` (array) 58, 69, 79, A–2
  `^` (matrix) 307, 324, A–2
eXtended Markup Language (XML) 188
extrapolation 394
`eye()` function 306, 324, A–5

F

`%f` (.fixed point) 140, A–3
`f(x)` function 284
`false` Boolean value 91, A–4
Fast Fourier Transform (FFT) 369–373
`fclose()` function 192, 199, A–2
FFT (Fast Fourier Transform) 369–373
`fft()` function 371, 384, 387
`fgetl()` function 192, 194, 199, A–2
`fgets()` function 192, 194, 199, A–2
Fibonacci series 219
fields (structures), accessing 163
`fieldnames()` function 163, 169, 170, A–9
fifth generation languages 12
`figure()` function 260, 295, A–7
figures (plotting containers) 260
  multiple plots on 261
file extensions 188
files
  I/O (Input/Output)
    high level functions for 187–191
    low level functions for 192–195
  opening and closing 192
  saving information 33
  text files
    reading 193
    writing 195
`fill()` function 269, 295, 314
`find()` function 57, 72, A–5
`.fits` (flexible image transport system data) files 188

`fitsread()` function 188
`fix()` function 59, A–4
flash cards 7
flexible image transport system data (`.fits`) files 188
`fliplr()` function A–5
`floor()` function 59, A–4
flowcharts 91
folding 244
`fopen()` function 192, 199, A–2
`for` loops 90, 98–101
  breaking 101
`for var` 90, 108, A–8
formal parameters 121
`format` command 32
format control strings 139
format conversion functions 139–142
Forth 13
FORTRAN (FORmula TRANslation) 11
  variables and 24
forward difference approximation 405
fourth-generation languages (4GLs) 12
`fprintf()` function 101, 143, 151, 199, A–2, A–7
  plain text files, reading 188
  traversing and 236
`freq()` function 366
frequencies 358
frequency bands 369
frequency domain operations 374–381
functional programming 22
`function` keyword 119, 127, A–8
functions 79, 109, 117–134
  built-in 50
  calling 121
  constructor 165
  definition 119–121
  format conversion 139–142
  library 59
  I/O (Input/Output)
    low-level functions 192–195
    high-level functions 187–191
  multiple results, returning 122
  plots, enhancing 260
  recursive, implementing 206–208
  rotating continuous 284–286

storing/using 121
wrapper 212–215

G

`%g` (general conversions) 140, A–3
general-purpose computers 8
generations (languages) 12
generative recursion 217
`getfield()` function 170, 177, A–9
general delimited text (`.dlm`) 188
GIF files 331
`global var` 124, 227, A–8
global scope 123
Gosling, James 13
`goto` statement 104
Government Code 3
`gplot()` function A–6
graphical user interface (GUI) 20
Graphical User Interface DEvelopment Environment (GUIDE) 20
Graphics window 35
grammar (programming languages) 11
graphs
  creating 35
gray scale images 331
greater than (>) 58, 79, A–2
greater than or equal to (>=) 58, 79, A–2
`grid on/off` 261, 295, A–7
GUI (graphical user interface) 20
GUIDE (Graphical User Interface Development Environment) 20

H

hardware 5
hardwiring (devices) 6
`.hdf` (hierarchical data format) files 188, 331
`hdfread()` function 188
heap 8
`help` command 50, A–3
heterogeneous collections 158
hierarchical data format (`.hdf`) files 188
high-level
  I/O functions 187–191
  languages 11

`hist()` function   269, 296, A–5
`history` (command)   29
`hold on/off`   261, 296, A–7
homogeneous collections   50

I
ICO files   331
identity matrix   306
`if` statements   90–96, A–8
  cell arrays and   162
  strings, comparing and   144
`ifft()` function   371, 384
`image()` function   333, 353
images   329–356
  operating on   333–349
  reading, displaying, and writing   333
  types   331
`imread()` function   188, 333, 353, A–2
`imshow()` function   333, 353
`imwrite()` function   188, 333, 353, A–2
independent of N O(1)   423
indexing vectors   52–55
  for loops and   101
  logical   54
  numerical   53
  slicing   60–64
    cell arrays and   160
`inf`   A–4
inner dimensions   305
`input()` function   93, 151, 212, A–7
  characters and   136
  strings, converting to/from numbers   140–142
  while loops and   104
  writing functions and   124
Input/Output (see I/O)
insertion sort   425, 439
`int2str()` function   141
integer conversions (`%d`)   139
interactive environments   15
`interp1()` function   391, 412, A–8
  extrapolation and   394
`interp2()` function   392, 412, A–8
`interp3()` function   392, 412, A–8
interpolation   390–394
  cubic spline   392–394
intersecting lines   318
`inv()` function   318, 324, A–5

I/O (Input/Output)   4, 185–202
  high level functions for   187–191
`isa()` function   162, 177, A–9
`iscell()` function   162, 177, A–9
`ischar()` function   139, 162, 177, A–9
`isempty()` function   247, A–9
`isfield()` function   170, 177, A–9
`islogical()` function   162, 177, A–9
`isnumeric()` function   162, 177, A–9
`isspace()` function   139, A–9
`isstruct()` function   162, 177, A–9
iteration   98

J
Java programming language   13
JPEG (Joint Photographic Experts Group) files   331
  color masking and   335–346

L
languages (programming)   11–15
`lasterror()` function   211, 227, A–9
Launch Pad window   27
least squares technique   396
`legend()` function   261, 296, A–7
`length()` function   52, 64, A–5
less than (<)   58, 79, A–2
less than or equal to (<=)   58, 79, A–2
library functions   59, 70
`light()` function   347, 353
`lightangle()` function   288, 297, 348
linear
  3-D plotting   270
  arrays/matrices (see vectors)
  equations   317–321
  interpolation   390–392
  regression   395
linear with N O(N)   423
linkers   14
`linspace()` function   51, 80, A–5
  stretching/shrinking images with   334
Lisp (List Processor)   13
`load` command   186, 198, A–3
local functions   123
local scope   124
`log()` function   A–4

`log10()` function   A–4
logic errors   14
logical
  expressions   94
  indexing   54
  operations   56–59
    arrays   69
    strings   138
logical AND (`&&`)   57, 95, 80, A–2
logical OR (`||`)   57, 80, 95, A–2
`loglog()` function   269, 296, A–5
loops
  `for`   98–102
  `while`   98, 102–108
Lotus 1-2-3
  I/O files, reading and writing   188
Lovelace, Ada   13

M
m-files   37
  functions and   121
machine languages   11
`magic()` function   66, 80, A–5
mainframes   8
Maple   11
mapping (character)   136
mass memory (RAM)
`material dull`   347, 353
Mathcad   11
Mathematica   11
matrices   303–328
  coordinates, rotating   310–317
  operations   304–307
  vs. arrays   65
matrix division (/)   307, 324, A–1
matrix exponentiation   307, 324, A–2
matrix multiplication (*)   304, 307–310, 79, A–1
matrix transpose operator (')   58
MATLAB   11
`max()` function   59, 70, A–5
`mean()` function   59, 70, A–5
mechanical memory   6
memory   6–8
Mercator projections   346
merge sort   432–434, 439
`mesh()` function   279, 297, A–6
`meshc()` function   288, 297, A–6

`meshz()` function   288, 297, A–6

`meshgrid()` function   288, 293, 297, A–5, A–6

Microsoft   10

`min()` function   59, 70, A–5

minus operator (–)   56

`mod()` function   A–4

Moore, Charles H.   13

multiplication
  .* (array operator)   50, 79, A–1
  * (matrix operator)   304, 307–310, 324, A–1

mutual recursion   217

MySQL   10

N

`/n` (new line)   140, A–3

`NaN` (Not a Number)   391, 412, A–4
  in empty spreadsheet cells   196, 198

`nargin()` function   122, A–9

`nargout()` function   122, A–9

natural languages   12

`not()` function   95, 109, A–2

not equal (~)

`num2str()` function   139, 151, A–7

numbers
  strings, converting to/from 139–142

numerical methods   389–420
  curve fitting   394–400
  differentiation   404–407
  integration   400–404

numerical values (vectors)   51
  indexing with   53
  of characters   136

`nums` keyword   189, 199

O

O(1) independent of N   423

O(2^N) exponential growth or worse 424

object code   14

object-oriented programming (OPP) 23

objects   27
  dissimilar, collecting   158

off (axis)   260

O(log N) binary search   423, 430
  bucket sort   434

merge sort   432
  vs. O(N^2)   435

O(N) linear with N   423

O(N^2) proportional to N^2 424
  vs. O(log N)   435

`ones()` function   51, 66, 348, A–5
  image collages, creating   343

OOP (object-oriented programming) 23

op code   11

operands   11

operating systems (OS)   9

operators (matrix)   304–307

`OR`, logical (||)   57, 80, 95, A–2

`or()` function   95, 109, A–2

Oracle   10

OS (operating systems)   9

`otherwise` keyword   90, A–9

output (computer data)   6

P

packaging (encapsulation)   23

page buffers   7

paradigms, programming   22

parameters (functions)   119
  calling functions and   121

parametric plots   268
  3-D plotting   272, 280

parentheses (())
  access array fields   163, 177, A–1
  function definition   119, 127, A–1
  overruling precedence   58
  structure fields and   163, A–1

Pascal   11, 13

passing by reference (function parameters)   121

pasting images   346

`pause()` function   348, A–8

PCs (personal computers)   8

PCX files   331

`peaks()` function   280, 297, A–6

percent sign (%), writing comments 37, 44, 56

`pi` constant   29, A–4

picture elements   330

`pie()` function   269, 296, A–5

`pie3()` function   273, 288, 297, A–6

pixels   330

plain text files   188

reading   193
  writing   195

playback/recording sound   358

`plot()` function   260, 296
  2-D plotting   264–270
  3-D plotting   270

`plot3()` function   270, 297, A–6

plots   259–302
  2D   264–270
  editing   262
  functions for   260
  parametric   268
  subplots   261
  surface   273–290

plus sign (+)   55, 58, 79, A–1

PNG files   331

`polar()` function   270, 296, A–5

`polyfit()` function   397, 412, 442

`polyval()` function   397, 412

polynomial regression   397

positions of elements (vectors)   51

power operator (.^)   58

precedence (operator)   58

preferred image format   332

problem solving   231–258
  programs for   15

procedural
  abstraction   21, 118, 304
  programming   22

`prod()` function   A–5

program bugs   14

programming languages   2–18
  background   21–23

`prod()` function   A–5

prompt (>> or EDU>>)   23
  assigning variables and   25

proportional to N^2 O(N^2)   424

`pt()` function   314

punctuating scripts   39

Python   13

Q

`%q` (quoted string)   140, A–3

quick sort   429–432, 439
  in place   432

`quit` command   23, A–3

R

RAM (Random-Access Memory)   7

`rand()` function   51, 66, 146, A–5

`randn()` function   51, 66, A–5

Random-Access Memory (RAM) 7
raw keyword 189, 199
Read-Only Memory (ROM) 72
recording rate 359
recording sound 358
rem() function A–4
resolution 359
RGB (red, green, and blue) 330
    color maps and 332
reserved words 79, 108
recursion 203–230
    generative 217
    implementing functions and
        206–208
    mutual 217
    quick sorts and 431
    tail recursion 215
reshape() function 72
    3-D rotation and 316, 324
rmfield() function 164, 169, 177,
    A–9
ROM (Read-Only Memory) 7
rot90() function 334, 353
rotation
    2-D 310–314
    3-D 314–317
    bodies 284–288
    lines 311
rows, removing from arrays 68
rows() function 71
round() function 59, A–4
    stretching/shrinking images with
        334
row vectors (arrays) 66
runtime errors 14

S

%s (string conversion) 140, A–3
save command 186, 198, A–2,
    A–3
scalar transpose operator (.') 58
scalars 55
scope, using functions and 121, 123
scripts 15, 37–43
    creating 37
    running 39
semicolons (;) 44
    Array editor and 34
    end-of-line characters and 39, 79,
        A–1
    separating rows 32, 66, 44, A–1

semilogx() function 266, 270, 296,
    A–5
semilogy() function 266, 270, 296,
    A–5
serial streams 186
setfield() function 170, 177,
    A–9
shading 261, 296, A–7
simple conditional statements 90
Simpson's rule 401
sin() function 284, A–4
single quotes (') 44
    character strings and 26, 137,
        A–1
    matrix transpose operator 58, 79,
        A–1
size() function 52, 162, A–5
    3-D arrays and 343
slicing 60–64, 138
    cell arrays and 160
    sound 360–363
software 5, 8–14
    tools 10
solid disk, drawing 289
solid state memory 6
sort() function 437, 442, A–5
sorting 421–444
    applications for 436
    algorithms for 425–435
    performance analysis 435
sound 357–388
    frequency domain operations
        374–381
    time domain operations 360–369
sound energy 369
sound() function 359, 384
    changing sound frequency poorly
        364
source code 14
sparse() function A–5
special characters 79, 108
special-purpose processors 8
spectrums
    displays 369–373
    manipulating 378–381
spheres, drawing 283, 297, A–6
sphere() function 288
spline() function 393, 412
spreadsheets 10, 196
    reading/writing spreadsheets
        188–191

sprintf() function 139, 143, 151,
    A–7
square braces ([ ]) 54, A–1
sqrt() function 44, A–4
square (axis) 260
squares (arrays) 66
sscanf() function 141, 151, A–8
stack 8, 204
stack frame 205
star() function 314
Start button 27
starting/stopping 23
state 15
strcmp() function 144, 151, A–8
strcmpi() function 145, 151, A–8
strings 135–156
    arithmetic/logical 138
    arrays of 145
    comparing 143–145
    format conversion functions
        139–142
        sprintf() function and 140
    mapping/casting 136
    numbers, converting to 140–142
    operations 142–145
    slicing/concatenating 138
strong typing 26
Stroustrup, Bjarne 13
strtok() function 193, 199, A–3
struct() function 165, 177, A–9
    structure arrays and 167
structures 163–166
    arrays 166–172
        problem solving and 234
    constructor functions and 165
subplots 261, 296, A–7
sum() function 59, 70, 171, A–5
surf() function 279, 286, 297, 346,
    A–6
surfc() function 288, 297, A–6
surfz() function 288, 297
supercomputers 8
switch statements 90, 96–98, A–9
    cell arrays, using with 161
    strings, comparing and 144
syntax (programming languages)
    11

T

/t (tab) 140, A–3
.tab (tab-separated text) files 188

tail recursion   215
`tan()` function   A–4
`text()` function   261, 296, A–7
text files   37
   file I/O   187
   reading   193
   writing   195
`textscan()` function   188, 193, 199,
   A–3, A–8
   building a collection   240
throwing exceptions   209
`tic()` function   A–8
TIFF files   331
tight (axis)   260
time domain operations   360–369
`title()` function   261, A–7
`toc()` function   A–8
tokens, parsing text files   193
tools (software)   10
`toString()` function   236
trapezoidal rule   401
traversing collections   235–238
`tril()` function   344, 353
`triangle()` function   314
`true` Boolean value   91, A–4
true color images   331
`try` keyword   210, A–9
   catching exceptions   209, 228
twinkling stars   312
two-dimensional arrays   32
   creating   34
`txt` keyword   189, 199
typed languages   26
types (variables)   27

U

`uint8` data type   330, 353, A–9
   gray scale images and   331
`uint8()` function   137

unary minus operator (–)   55, 79,
   A–1
unary not equal operator (~)   57
underscore (_), in variable name   24
untyped languages   25
user friendly computers   9
user interface   27–36
utilities   9

V

value parameters   139
values
   numerical (vectors)   51
   assigning   24
   objects and   27
variables   24
   global   124
   scoping   123
   values, recalling   32
vectors   32, 50–64
   creating   51
   indexing   52–55
   operating on   55–64
   problem solving and   233
   size of   52
   shortening   54
   slicing   60–64
`view()` function   261, 296
virtual memory   7
von Neumann architecture   4

W

`waterfall()` function   289, 297,
   A–6
`.wav` files   188, 359
`wavread()` function   188, 359, 384,
   A–3
`wavwrite()` function   188, 384,
   A–3
weak typing   26

`while` loops   90, 98, 102–108, A–9
   breaking   105
   searching collections   247
   sorting algorithms and   427
`who` command   33, A–3
`whos` command   33, A–3
`.wki` (Lotus 1-2-3 worksheet) files
   188
`wk1read()` function   188
`wk1write()` function   188
word processors   10
Word (Microsoft)   10
words (bits)   6
Workspace window   30–33
workspace (I/O)
wrapper functions   212–215

X

XML (Extended Markup Language)
   188
`xmlread()` function   188
`xmlwrite()` function   188
`xlabel()` function   216, 296, A–7
`.xls` (Excel worksheet) files
   188–191
`xlsread()` function   188–191, 196,
   199, 250, A–3
`xlswrite()` function   188–191, 199
XWD files   331

Y

`ylabel()` function   261, 296, A–7

Z

`zlabel()` function   261, 296, A–7
`zeros()` function   51, 66, A–5